Hamlet Made Simple
and Other Essays

Hamlet Made Simple
and Other Essays

David P. Gontar

Published by New English Review Press
a subsidiary of World Encounter Institute
PO Box 158397
Nashville, Tennessee 37215
&
27 Old Gloucester Street
London, England, WC1N 3AX

Cover Design by Kendra Adams
Cover portrait: Princess Elizabeth (aged 13), c. 1546
formerly attributed to William Scrots

ISBN: 978-0-9854394-9-1

First Edition

NEW ENGLISH REVIEW PRESS
newenglishreview.org

Like or find fault; do as your pleasures are;
Now, good or bad, 'tis but the chance of war.

Contents

Preface

*S*omewhere in the rolling grasslands bordering the Gobi Desert lie the remnants of Xanadu, the fabled summer palace of Kublai Khan. Here and there among half-buried walls still gleam bits of the blue tile that once adorned fantastic chambers of delight. Nothing else survives. Though Coleridge claimed his poem came to him in a dream, Xanadu was in 1263 very much a reality. Not far off, in 2011, this small book on Shakespeare was conceived and written, a work as unlikely but just as real as were those caves of ice, that stately pleasure-dome.

Only the title essay was composed stateside, delivered as a lecture at Concordia University in Portland, Oregon in April of 2008.

As to the prospects of success, it may be sufficient to cite F. H. Bradley's long-forgotten protreptic:

> If the object is not impossible, and the adventure suits us
> -- what then? Others far better than ourselves have wholly
> failed -- so you say. But the man who succeeds is not always
> the man of most merit, and even in philosophy's cold world
> perhaps some fortunes go by favour. One never knows until
> one tries.
> (Bradley, *A&R*, 2)

The writer would like to thank Rebecca Bynum, editor at New English Review Press, for her encouragement and most kind assistance with technical matters. Without her support this project would have remained only a dream. Thanks are also owed to philosopher Christopher D. Gontar, whose searching comments made a better manuscript. The author's debt to his wife is more than words can tell.

David Gontar
Huhhot, Inner Mongolia
March 4, 2012

An Introductory Word to Students

> A book? O rare one,
> Be not, as is our fangled world, a garment
> Nobler than that it covers. Let thy effects
> So follow to be most unlike our courtiers,
> As good as promise.
>
> *-- Posthumous Leonatus*

> And now I will unclasp a secret book,
> And to your quick-conceiving discontents
> I'll read you matter deep and dangerous;
> As full of peril and adventurous spirit
> As to o'erwalk a current roaring loud
> On the unsteadfast footing of a spear.
>
> *-- Earl of Worcester*

The following pages are a collection of thematically related essays on a variety of works by Shakespeare. They lay no claim to being anything more. Those seeking a systematic assessment of Shakespeare (if such a thing were possible) are advised that it is not proffered here. Instead, there are presented a few experiments in the old-fashioned art of reading. Such exercises may be found useful, and it is in this spirit that they may be judged.

If we want to tackle Shakespeare successfully, we could do worse than going directly to him for assistance. He knew about such things, the piquant pleasures of a fine volume, the tart disappointment of a bad one. Will we find just "words, words, words," or the nacreous visions for which we hanker? Much depends not only on the quality of the material, but equally on our assiduity, our willingness to bring our best intellectual equipment to the business. For the richer the text, the more acute must be our skills. In the brilliant comedy, *Love's Labour's Lost*, we meet some eager students whose campaign for knowledge is led astray by polysyllabic proclivities and a penchant for deception and dark meanings. After much tribulation, they begin to learn the merits of simplicity and the meaning of love. Study finds its proper object.

Despite his reputation for difficulty, Shakespeare is never intentionally opaque, nor does he sadistically delight in placing in our path obstacles of obscurity. Yes, his native tongue is Elizabethan English, and his mode of expression metaphor in motion. This is the challenge, the excitement and sheer delight of grappling with early modern drama. While patience and diligence are required, we are often rewarded with far more than might be had from less bountiful, less gifted writers. Our readiness is all that matters, as Prince Hamlet observes. (V, ii, 168)

To engage with Shakespeare productively, four unhelpful tendencies should be eschewed. These are Sentimentality, Convention, Concealment and Technicality. Vices which spoil Shakespeare for many, they are nonetheless easily identified and reformed. Let us put four familiar characters to work, serving as mnemonic exemplars: Ophelia, Polonious, Gertrude and Fortinbras.

I. Ophelia (Sentimentality)

Ophelia is essentially a giddy soubrette, weighed down by sensations and emotions which eventually lead to her demise. Attachments to father, brother, lover, and a seemingly forgotten mother, become so tangled and refractory that there is a complete nervous collapse. In her last hours, all that linger are the pretty baubles, the flowers that delight but betray her. There are those who comb the pages of Shakespeare for edifying or romantic epigrams, sprouting here and there like overripe blackberries, who have no stomach for art as strenuous spiritual adventure, preferring instead to cull fancy souvenirs. These hunters and gatherers are our exegetical Ophelias. The problem is that what appear as textual rosebuds turn out to be symptoms of substantial issues and conflicts of which the neophyte is altogether unaware. This tendency has always made Shakespeare's "sugar'd sonnets" a field of temptation, where camouflaged passions and antagonisms lurk undetected. The emotive approach to Shakespeare is perhaps the least fecund of all, suitable for those who might compose greeting cards or stitch inspirational samplers. Even to pronounce the name "Ophelia" slowly is to wade into a marsh of tears. This does not mean that emotion is negligible in Shakespeare; rather, it is but one dimension of a poetic cosmos, a dimension which lies not ready to hand, but churns in the depths of the anguished heart, or flutters at the pinnacle of exaltation.

II. *Polonious (Convention)*

Ophelia's teary-eyed bewilderment is opposed by her father's stern and stale wisdom. As his famous counsel to the departing Laertes shows, Polonious finds the badge of truth in sayings whose edges are worn smooth by iteration. He is the duke of dull, the king of cliché. In Polonious, as in Solomon, nothing is new under the sun, for all is but tiresome repetition of what has been already. He is thus the perfect foil for Prince Hamlet's mocking self-consciousness and derisive repartee. As his high-strung daughter embodies the affective approach to life and art, so Polonious represents the dead hand of the past, the sheer inertia bequeathed by our ancestors. Beware the "Polonious complex." Once infected, we are never quite free of it.

His own status may be used to illustrate. Consider the view of him most common in literature classes. We are told he is a caricature of William Cecil, Lord Burghley, chief advisor to Queen Elizabeth I of England. In itself this is a vaguely interesting and innocuous proposition, and probably correct. But it is almost never supported or amplified by related facts, argument or evidence. The banner of Polonious as Cecil is hoisted according to mere custom, without connecting it with larger themes and meanings. No one is prompted to ask whether other characters might have historical correlatives too, including Prince Hamlet. Who might he be? Nor is it ever explained how William of Stratford-Upon-Avon might have had the temerity to satire such an omniscient and deadly individual. How did he get away with that? Instead of seizing upon such a conundrum as a springboard to investigation, the idea of Cecil-as-caricature is offered as inert filler whose only apparent purpose is to pop up unexpectedly on quizzes and tests.

Instructors hobbled by convention must inevitably parade in shreds and patches of creeds outworn. Thus, *e.g.*, Romeo and Juliet are viewed as twinned angels whose sad and hyperbolical romance demonstrates the folly of their bickering elders. This is as shallow and jejune as *West Side Story*. Are we going to fob off on unsuspecting children such a sorry substitute for thought? What would Shakespeare say? Is the play not equally a comedy, a satire on the downright silliness and narcissism of adolescence? Who is Romeo after all, if not "a lover, that kills himself most gallant for love"? Do we not laugh at such stuff? Are we to weep crocodile tears at *R&J* and burst our risible seams at "*A tedious brief scene of young Pyramus and his love Thisbe: Very Tragical Mirth*"? It is the same jest. How is it that Thisbe is received as "mirthful," while Juliet is lamented as "tragic"? If she *is* tragic, in what does that tragedy consist?

And what of the authorship issue? While to a rarefied elite this is a burning topic of contention, in the hornbook routine of class the question hardly ever surfaces, and if it does, it is instinctively put down as nonsense by hidebound teachers in panicky flight from conjectured anarchy. What does this impart to students of intelligence and curiosity?

Convention is a species of habit, a natural behavioral trait, as philosophers from Aristotle (*Nicomachean Ethics*) down to William James (*Principles of Psychology*) have explained. But habit unchecked by experiment and novelty conduces to mental atrophy, to the ossification of the brain and utter mindlessness.

What is a student's job in an arid academic wasteland in which the teacher cannot promote independent analysis? It is up to the student to lead the way with his own questions designed to spark debate. It is *the student* who must so master the lesson that lines of inquiry overlooked by the instructor are introduced in class. Less enslaved to Pleistocene platitudes, the student is often in a better position to spot anomalies and aporias, the keys to learning's treasury. It should be kept in mind that study is a prolegomenon to teaching. Practice can and should occur now. We are exposed to intellectual fables not to swallow them whole but to test their sufficiency. That was the method of Socrates. It is *Paedeia*, the royal road to erudition. As students, we can help our teachers to emulate the famous philosopher by our own probing. And nowhere is this more appropriate than in the case of Shakespeare. Was Macbeth really ambitious? What about Brutus? Don't be like old Polonious. Raise your hand and ask. The challenge of learning is to challenge others.

III. Gertrude (Concealment)

At the outset of *Pericles, Prince of Tyre*, when the hero has solved the riddle and discovered the forbidden relationship between Antiochus and his own daughter, Pericles wisely signals that he knows the public announcement of the truth will result, not in the prize advertised, but in his decapitation.

> Great King,
> Few love to hear the sins they love to act.
> 'Twould braid yourself too near for me to tell it.
> Who has a book of all that monarchs do,
> He's more secure to keep it shut than shown . . . .
> (I, i, 134-138)

In a real sense, the book to which young Pericles alludes is the *Works of Shakespeare*, the poet who made it his mission to chronicle many of the royal indiscretions and peccancies of Tudor England. Opening it, even four centuries later, requires nerve.

Perhaps the most generous comment we can offer about Queen Gertrude is that she has a rather casual connection with reality. It can hardly be otherwise, considering the nasty things she's done, things she'd rather not think about. Compared to Gertrude, Blanche DuBois is a gritty Sherlock Holmes. Does anyone suppose that Gertrude waited patiently until her lawful spouse, King Hamlet the Dane, was safely slumbering in his grave before she started her lascivious affair with Claudius? Does anyone truly believe she wasn't an accomplice in his murder? To pose such a question is already to possess the answer. A fearful mind forgets. It blinks. It runs for cover, like nocturnal vermin. In other words, it censors. Cover-up is the mark of the guilty mind. Just listen.

> O, Hamlet, speak no more!
> Thou turn'st mine eyes into my very soul,
> And there I see such black and grainèd spots
> As will not leave their tinct.
> (III, iv, 78-81)

Dare we translate? "O, Hamlet! Don't make me look at myself and make me see what I've become, what I am. Leave me alone with my self-deceptions. You are my son. If you care for me, you'll flatter me, conspire with me in my mendacity."

Prince Hamlet, of course, is revolted by this spectacle. He is a truth teller by instinct, like Shakespeare. But his difficulty, as we will see, is that he does not quite know the truth. He only senses it. He is a would-be soothsayer surrounded by fools, cheats, charlatans and self-deceivers. And that is precisely the position of Shakespeare. Indeed, "Hamlet" and "Shakespeare" are ultimately two names for the same person.

In all of literature there has never been a more suppressed and blotted writer. From day one, his poetry has been smothered, butchered, traduced, gouged, vivisected, erroneously edited, neglected, ignored, re-written, "translated," and incinerated, as a few hours spent in any competent library will demonstrate. Even though he wrote discreetly of history and the human condition, showing us "sparingly and far off" his meaning (*Henry V*, I, ii, 237-240), it was all too much for the delicate English-speaking people, who, like Gertrude, did everything in their power to muzzle his voice and destroy his message. As Falstaff sagely cautions, "it was alway yet the trick of our English nation, if they have a good thing, to make it too common," (*King Henry IV*, Part Two, I, ii, 215) and so lose its precious vitality.

In the middle of the nineteenth century there were two books in every American household: the *Holy Bible*, and *The Family Shakespeare* (1807, 1818). The latter was a highly selective edition put together by Thomas and Harriet Bowdler, from whose surname we get the verb "bowdlerize," meaning to expurgate a text. The Bowdlers made a fortune by ripping out of Shakespeare anything they judged distasteful, obscene or politically offensive, and they, like many other third-rate minds, offered re-composed plays with the "happy endings" they believed that readers craved.

Why should anything change? There are still plenty of Gertrudes among us, cringing at themselves and the less flattering facts of life. Censorship of Shakespeare is alive and well. His plays teem with scurrility, bawdry, double entendres, puns, imprecations, malevolence, rebellion, insult and a thousand proscribed locutions which, it is feared, would somehow set a bad example. But they belong in the plays and poems for important aesthetic, literary and educational reasons, and cannot, without crippling our interpretive efforts, be eliminated. Think of the witches' foaming obscenities in *Macbeth* (I, iii, 3-27; IV, i, 1-65), or the porter's ribald divagation on "nose-painting," "sleep," "urine," and "lechery." (II, iii, 23-40) Such vexing passages adumbrate the sexual stratagems of Lady Macbeth and her emasculated spouse, whose murder of Duncan is as much a function of uxorial intimidation and extortion as it is of her husband's supposed "ambition." Imagine a version of *Macbeth* edited by Queen Gertrude! What, if anything, would have been left of its promethean stanzas?

Students should be encouraged to assimilate Shakespeare not in saccharine fragments, but in its entirety, supported by editions with copious footnotes that adequately address all evocative terms and phrases, including those fastidious editors would rather omit. Shakespeare studies are not for dissemblers or the faint of heart, nor are our scholarly endeavors of much value when, instead of presenting the actual works, they give readers a false confidence based on abridgement, redaction and other forms of textual tampering. Certainly quartos and folios need to be harmonized, but not dismembered. Directors, too, have a responsibility to put upon the stage or screen renditions of Shakespeare faithful to the originals. One wonders how often "limitations of time" have been used to rationalize the disembowelment of the world's finest dramas.

The insistence on putting before audiences the overworked confections of *Romeo and Juliet* and *The Merry Wives of Windsor* rather than face, for example, the challenges of the fresher and more nourishing *Timon of Athens* becomes over many years a form of *de facto* censorship, all the more insidious on account of its imperceptibility. Such thoughtless omissions have led to a general misapprehension as to the actual breadth and significance of Shakespeare's artistic triumph.

Those who would seek to eliminate all discussion as to the identity of the author of the works of Shakespeare must rank among the most reprehensible of today's censors. The sentimental legend of the man from Stratford who rises from humble glover's son to become the cynosure of the literary world is a rags-to-riches saga of which many are enamored. But legends have a way of disappointing. One traditionalist, A. N. Nuttall, informs his readers that the author's reputed father, John Shakespeare, committed suicide in 1579. (Nuttall, 4) Yet another, Ian Wilson, confidently dates John's death at 1601 and infers John's Catholic faith on the basis of a will made out in 1580. (Wilson, 286, 468) Can both be correct? If wrong about John, might they be so about William? That is one reason we have the study of history and science, to subject tall tales to scrutiny. This can only be done, however, in a society in which the free exchange of ideas, so well defended by J.S. Mill in *On Liberty*, prevails. Traditionalists, who promote the miracle of Stratford-Upon-Avon, go so far as to aver that there is "no question" that the author was its poetic swan. If so, there is nothing to discuss, and no reason to listen to those who would make themselves heard on the issue. And that is censorship. Of course, these same censors revel in the subject when they fret about whether Kyd or Marlowe or Fletcher had a hand in the composition of the plays. That's OK. It is only when the sacred cow of William of Stratford is challenged directly as The Author that the authorship debate would be stricken.

In 1815, a young American named Washington Irving, having failed in the practice of law and various other enterprises, travelled to England to join his brothers' business, which also soon failed. While in England, Irving sojourned at Stratford-Upon-Avon to soak up its seedy atmosphere to use as material for his *The Sketch Book of Geoffrey Crayon, Esq. (1819-1820)*. Irving was deliberately following in the footsteps of impresario and mountebank David Garrick, whose Shakespeare Jubilee had put Stratford on the map as a shady tourist trap in 1769. Irving delighted hugely in the amusement park props offered as authentic relics of "the Bard," including the "shattered stock of Shakespeare's matchlock" with which he poached deer as a youth, his tobacco box, the very sword he held when he played Prince Hamlet, and the actual lantern Friar Lawrence held in the tomb of the Capulets. The original mulberry tree said to have been hacked down by the lad Shakespeare had been fashioned into so much tchotchke that the wood needed to do so would have been sufficient "to build a ship of the line." An ancient sexton who had guarded the poet's grave confided that during renovations he had peeked inside and found nothing at all, no coffin or earthly remains of any kind. Confronted with a monstrous, self-proclaiming fraud, Irving was unfazed. Taking up the pen of "Geoffrey Crayon," he affably provided one of the most candid glimpses ever into the crevices of the human soul:

> I am always of easy faith in such matters, and am ever willing to be deceived, where the deceit is pleasant and costs nothing. I am therefore a ready believer in relics, legends, and local anecdotes of goblins and great men; and would advise all travellers who travel for their gratification to be the same. What is it to us, whether these stories be true or false, so long as we can persuade ourselves into the belief of them, and enjoy all the charm of the reality? There is nothing like resolute good-humored credulity in these matters; and on this occasion I went even so far as willingly to believe the claims of mine hostess to be a lineal descendant from the poet . . . . (Irving)

Indeed, few things are quite as pleasant as our little excursions in bad faith. One would think that such a bold confession would give us pause.

Yet Mr. Stephen Greenblatt of Harvard is so confident in his version of The Legend that he will brook no dissent, comparing any academic discussion of the authorship question to entertaining the claims of Holocaust deniers. (Greenblatt, 2005) So great is the Stratfordian consensus, implies Mr. Greenblatt, that it has ascended the brightest heaven of invention and morphed into Incontrovertible Fact, whose slightest challenge would be tantamount to mental instability or - worse - some sort of hate crime. There shall be no questioning of *Established Facts* in Mr. Greenblatt's tidy world, especially those he finds congenial. The flaw here is that self-evidence was long ago discarded as a test of truth, and the virtue of good ideas lies not in their transcendence of the fray but in their capacity to withstand criticism, which, according to J.S. Mill, is their very *raison d'être.*

In the sixteenth century "everyone knew" that the sun, moon and stars went about the earth. Only a few crackpots like Copernicus thought otherwise. Had Mr. Greenblatt been in charge of things back then he would have exerted all his vast energies and eloquence to keeping the crazy notion of heliocentricity out of the cosmology classroom. And historically that's what many sought to do. Problem is, they were wrong. Heliocentricity deserved a hearing and eventually got it. It did not merit a hearing because it was correct; it was found to be correct because it got a hearing.

Thomas Kuhn, the famous philosopher of science, teaches that every so often there is a fundamental or paradigm shift in our models of knowing which sweeps away current doctrines or preconceived ideas. The theory advanced in these pages represents an attempt at just that, a paradigm shift in our understanding of Shakespeare's texts based on a radical alteration in our perception of his identity. Such a drastic alteration is precisely the sort of thing that belongs in the forum of ideas, because any such theory is nothing but a creature of intellectual exchange. Even if what is here proposed were nothing more than an ordinary suggestion to consider a different candidate as the author, such an inquiry could not be blockaded by prevailing concepts, since those old ideas won their place in the same theatre of contention, and can be effective now only to the extent that they continue to prove themselves. But what is here advanced is not the ordinary so much as the ornery, a miniature revolution as potent as it is diminutive. For like King Harry in his wrath, we can be wranglers too. (*King Henry V*, I, ii, 264)

Seeking to prohibit its very consideration is a bootless exercise, a quixotic attempt to retard time itself. And what strong hand could hold *that* swift foot back?

That Mr. Greenblatt would seek to inject *obscuram per obscuris* the issue of the suffering of the Jewish people in the 1940's into the controversy surrounding the Shakespeare authorship debate suggests that even staid traditionalists can slip off the deep end. All we can suppose is that those who work so diligently at concealment must have something to hide. There will be no authorship talk in Cambridge, Massachusetts by Order of His Majesty, Stephen Greenblatt. Therefore, let all noble youth, starved for the freedom of thought and discourse, and finding themselves banished from King Greenblatt's frosty classroom, take refuge in mine.

IV. Fortinbras (Technicality)

Compare two soldiers, Hotspur and Fortinbras. Hotspur, whatever his impetuousness, fights for honor and justice. So do Talbot, Coriolanus, Antony, Titus, Margaret, Queen Elinor, and, in fact, most of the warriors in Shakespeare. But others, like Fortinbras in *Hamlet* and Octavius in *Julius Caesar* and *Antony and Cleopatra*, make it their business to fight. That is their vocation, their livelihood, and they perform it methodically, professionally, impersonally. In their hands, a glorious enterprise giving protection to one's people and scope to one's bravery is reduced to the grim task of exterminating an enemy. Such fighters are military automata for whom battle is a dry affair, a set of tasks to be undertaken irrespective of the niceties of principle. They live not by ideals but by the sword and strength of arms.

Contemporary Shakespeare scholarship is in the hands of technocrats and technicians. Where an Ophelia might swoon at the passion of a Juliet or Imogen, a cold-blooded literary Fortinbras peers down his microscope at minute details, facts, definitions and notes, organizing, enumerating, assembling and comparing the data, often in a pseudo-historical context. The technocrat is, after all, an expert. And what is an expert but someone who knows where he went wrong?

Unfortunately, since the particular object of this expertise is a "fine frenzy rolling," a spontaneous realm of imagination, creativity and symbolic expression, the mode of quantification is a tad inapposite. It yields a reading which stands at the opposite extreme of the sentimental: instead of being overwhelmed by impulse and feeling, the technician puts such gushy and ungovernable reflexes away in favor of what is known as "criticism." The purpose is no longer the deeper appreciation of the poet's song, or the rueful contemplation of the travails of tragic character, but the investigation of the dramatist's "*technique.*" Focus is on the implements of the poet's craft and the manner in which these are marshaled and "deployed," (a favorite term nowadays) as in a military expedition, to achieve a certain objective. Shakespeare is elevated to the rank of general, the Napoleon of words. To perform his critical mission, the technocrat must perforce withhold himself, rise above the skirmish, stay vigilant and aloof, allowing no seduction by a skein of smarmy syllables. Instead of developing a more impassioned attunement, criticism is suspicious of any personal or intimate involvement with art and, in this case, with Shakespeare. Sensibility thus becomes demoted to a species of pathology. In the glittering laboratory, the critic dons his fetishistic gloves of white latex and holds the antique tome between his fingers, as Calvin says the Deity grasps the sinful soul, "like a pestiferous spider over the flames." As the pitiless dissection commences, the unruly text expires, and the hapless verses, pinned and wriggling, finally breathe their last on the doctor's desk. The learned journal article is the autopsy report. Clinical titles like "Animal Imagery in *Othello*" proliferate. Students are discouraged from any response to Shakespeare's dramas redolent of a quest for meaning and significance. They are taught that our impressions and natural responses are naïve, to be snuffed out and supplanted as quickly as possible by a pose of arch sophistication.   When the text dies, then, it does so in the soul of the professional exegete, who outdoes the sacrificial Aztec priests by the chilling excision of his own heart.

Well-endowed libraries and institutions artifactualize Shakespeare, exhibit his textual remains, interring them in caskets of thick plexiglass under track lighting, where they can do us no harm. Chummy euphemisms such as "the Bard" and "Willie," which purport to draw us closer to him, in fact move us to take him tongue-in-cheek, neatly obscuring his significance *als Mensch, Dichter und Denker*. Shakespeare is dead and we aim to keep him so.

Human nature being what it is, however, the technician can only with some difficulty remain a mere jack. Aggrandizement of self inevitably intrudes, particularly as the critic is handling items of cultural prestige, *i.e.*, the splendors of "Shakespeare." Such a Zeus-like role is far above the puttering and muttering of the common herd, and soon enough the literary journeyman becomes a patrician by degrees, a demigod, in short, a snob. Fortinbras becometh Octavian. What is significant about the snob is not his sense of superiority over the tribe of average readers, but his presumption that he is better than his object. After all, do we not detect regrettable solecisms and infelicities in the "Bard"? Were there not a thousand lines he might have blotted? Here Octavian the Technocrat makes alliance with Gertrude the Censor. As such savants turn the mottled pages of Shakespeare they seem to hold their noses. Thus, "Richard III," titters *The New Yorker's* John Lahr, "has all the earmarks of the work of a young playwright: too long, too plotty, too repetitive." (January 30, 2012) There's a snarky bit you can toss off at your next Park Avenue wine-and-cheese bash. Any idea why such an immature potboiler's still being performed after 400 years, John? Others of this ilk complain that *Titus Andronicus* is a "crude and coarse spectacle," unworthy of the delicate hand that wrought *King Lear*. It must be a "send up of Seneca," a vulgar experiment, a horror flick for the groundlings, of little account and far beneath the lofty creations we find in the "Jacobean" Shakespeare. In *Titus* we may suppose the wily showman was simply exploiting sensationalism to increase ticket sales and so singlehandedly rescue the English stage from Puritan oblivion. *Titus* is certainly a distressing, yea, a dreadful interloper in the canon, and most unsuitable for the innocent youngsters who batten on the tender shoots of video game carnage. Let it be anathema. Of course, when professors react this way what they are really doing is insulating themselves from emotional risk and involvement in the drama under the guise of scholarship. A trivialized Shakespeare represents no threat. His fangs are plucked. And this is the defense mechanism which is taught to generations of graduate students. The agonies of *Titus* move us no more than the writhing of a loathsome insect in our terrarium. If *Titus* is our text, its traducers are the critical equivalents of Tamora, Saturninus and Aaron. The hand they would amputate is Shakespeare's own.

The style of choice of the mature critic is a genteel patronizing which stoops to grade the works of Shakespeare as though they were student term papers. Thus, a literary juggernaut like *King Henry VI*, Shakespeare's massive triptych of the Wars of the Roses and the rise of the House of Tudor, the envy of Tolstoy, wilts to a juvenile and amateurish effort on the part of a struggling actor just figuring out how to put one word beside another. Peering down through pinched monocle from Olympian heights, the brilliant doctoral candidate observes the inexcusable excesses of this "early history play," a hoary relic of interest to none but "specialists," whose only true significance lies, if anywhere, in its promise of better things to come. No matter that its three parts constitute Shakespeare's longest opus, that it renders the history of England in riveting verse, and that it features the most electrifying human confrontations in all literature. No matter that, far ahead of its time, it features strong-willed martial women, Joan and Margaret, anticipating a feminism which would only see the light of day 350 years later. Almost never mounted on stage or visited in the classroom, we owe the neglect of this soaring masterpiece to the animadversions of Lilliputian critics for whom it appears a pitiful dinosaur, more suited for the dusty storerooms of a museum than the enjoyment of a public starved for illumination and aesthetic substance.

To complicate matters further, the world of technical criticism is now afflicted by the Great Authorial Schism. Conventionalists, Censors, Sentimentalists and Technicians, in the manner of Custer's band of brothers at Little Big Horn, cleave to their champion, the illustrious William of Stratford. Many of these folks feel no need to trouble with facts and argument. For those who wish to do so, there are many excellent sources. Students are encouraged to start with: *The Man Who Never Was Shakespeare: The Theft of William Shakespeare's Identity* by Professor A. J. Pointon, Parapress, 2011. On the other hand, faced with an insupportable discrepancy between the content of the poems and plays and the few scraps left behind by William, the more logical and satisfactory candidacy of Edward de Vere, 17th Earl of Oxford, is advanced by multitudinous renegades of the intelligentsia. Tragically, with all its faults, the finest studies of Shakespeare continue to come from the Stratford camp. In a cruel paradox, those who know "Shakespeare" the man least write most rewardingly about his poetry, while those who know him best, the Oxfordians, anxious at every turn to reduce meaning to biography, reveal themselves as the most lackluster of expounders. Until these two warring factions can be reconciled and united, like the feuding houses of York and Lancaster, Shakespeare studies will remain hobbled by dissension and confusion. The most expedient device now appears to be the wholesale doing away with the authorship controversy by throwing out the author altogether. Criticism afflicted by the *bacilli* of post-structuralism and deconstruction manifests this syndrome. There remains nothing outside the text, nothing that is, except poor William, who, like Master Froth, can be drawn back in whenever a busy technician feels like doing so. (*Measure for Measure*, II, i, 201-202)

The cardinal failing of the technician is the fallacy of misplaced object. A Neanderthal literalism persuades him via tautology that *Julius*

Caesar is about Julius Caesar, and *Hamlet* is about Prince Hamlet. As such they are scientifically scrutinized. But we all know that the only reason these works have any importance is because, in the final analysis, they are about the audience. Shakespeare holds up his glass not to nature, but to each of us. (Kirsch, 154; Howe, 144) And like Gertrude, we modestly avert our gaze.

Faced with all this, whither our young charge, our faithful student?

O, how shall summer's honey breath hold out
Against the wrackful siege of battering days,
When rocks impregnable are not so stout,
Nor gates of steel so strong, but Time decays?
O, fearful meditation!

Now, as then, the answer is the same. Be not afraid. The isle is full of noises. But Shakespeare remains with us, in the immortal works he quarried. Though we lose our way, we have the text. The Rock Impregnable is cleft for us. There must we abide, that in bright ink his love - and ours - may still shine bright.

WORKS CITED

James Howe, *A Buddhist's Shakespeare*, Associated University Presses, 1994

Arthur C. Kirsch, "The Emotional Landscape of King Lear," *Shakespeare Quarterly*, Vol. 39, No. 2, 1988

Thomas S. Kuhn, *The Structure of Scientific Revolutions*, University of Chicago Press, 1996

A.N. Nuttall, *Shakespeare the Thinker*, Yale University Press, 2007

A. J. Pointon, *The Man Who Never Was Shakespeare: The Theft of William Shakespeare's Identity*, Parapress, 2011

Ian Wilson, *Shakespeare: The Evidence, Unlocking the Mysteries of the Man and His Work*, St. Martin's Press, 1993

Online Sources

Washington Irving, *The Sketchbooks of Geoffrey Crayon, Esq. (1819-1820)*

Stephen Greenblatt, Letter to *New York Times* Op Ed Page, August 3, 2005

1
An Unquiet House:
Deferral of Discord in Shakespeare's Comedies

I. Deferral of Discord in "The Merchant of Venice"

*S*hakespearean comedy usually concludes with marriage. This is true of *The Merchant of Venice*, but with one small difference. Here, unlike so many of the other comedies, we are granted a glimpse into the lives of the principal characters subsequent to the ceremony that unites them. And what we see is a harsh note of discord inconsonant with the traditional happy ending. That unharmonious moment is presaged in Act V, sc. i., by a bit of badinage between Jessica and Lorenzo. He punningly teases her by accusing her of spending too much of the money she has removed from her father's house ["In such a night did Jessica steal from the wealthy Jew, And with an unthrift love did run from Venice as far as Belmont"]. She answers with a little dig of her own, charging him with playing her false in love ["In such a night Did young Lorenzo swear he loved her well, Stealing her soul with many vows of faith, And ne'er a true one"]. Such banter feels out of place at this advanced narrative juncture because the villain Shylock has been discomfited, and apparently all that remains is for the couples to recite their vows and then celebrate.

In Act V, another spat erupts, this time between Nerissa and Gratiano, during the welcoming of Bassanio and Gratiano by Portia as they return triumphantly to Belmont from the Venetian Court of Justice.

GRATIANO

By yonder moon I swear you do me wrong;
In faith, I gave it to the judge's clerk:
Would he were gelt that had it, for my part,
Since you do take it, love, so much to heart.
(V, i, 143-145)

Portia immediately remarks that something is amiss, and all too soon:

A quarrel, ho, already! what's the matter?
(V, i, 146)

Of course, Portia is disingenuous. She knows well enough what is
the matter, as she and Nerissa have plotted this contretemps in advance.
At the trial in Venice, Portia, disguised as legal scholar Balthasar, contrived to demand and receive of Bassanio as a reward the ring given him
by her as a symbol of trust. Nerissa, also in male guise, similarly obtains
her ring of fidelity from Gratiano. Both ladies are somewhat piqued by
having heard their husband's inflated professions of love for one another
and now intend to make some mischief to teach them a lesson.

The words of Bassanio which rankle the heart of Portia are:

Antonio, I am married to a wife
Which is as dear to me as life itself,
But life itself, my wife, and all the world
Are not with me esteemed above thy life.
I would lose all, ay, sacrifice them all
Here to this devil, to deliver you.
(IV, i, 279-284)

Gratiano's words are equally inflammatory:

I have a wife who, I protest, I love.
I would she were in heaven so she could
Entreat some power to change this currish Jew.
(IV, i, 287-289)

To this Nerissa comments *sotto voce*:

Tis well you offer it behind her back;
The wish would else make an unquiet house.
(IV, i, 290-291)

This resentment soon issues in a plot to embarrass their husbands:

PORTIA

. . . I warrant we shall have old swearing
That they did give the rings away to men.
But we'll outface them, and outswear them too.
(IV, ii, 15-18)

That is, the ladies conspire to raise an issue, planning to insist their rings are missing, not because they were given to male legal agents, but rather because they were actually favors bestowed on Venetian women. And sure enough, that is exactly what happens. In the course of the bickering which follows, Portia and Nerissa announce that they will not sleep with their husbands until they see the rings. (V, i, 189-194) Then Portia threatens to give herself to the man who took her ring from Bassanio, and soon thereafter goes so far as to state that "by this ring, the doctor lay with me." (V, i, 259) The corollary is provided by Nerissa: "And pardon me, my gentle Gratiano, For that same scrubbed boy, the doctor's clerk, In lieu of this last night did lie with me." (V, i, 260-262)

Having exploited the misunderstanding as far as possible, Portia relents and confesses the disguises and the ladies' participation in the trial. And it is on this merry note that the play concludes. Yet doubts linger. Taking the events of the play in a spirit of realism, the audience must realize such hurtful utterances cannot be unsaid. Portia and Nerissa have listened to Bassiano and Gratiano declare in open court that their male bonds and love for Antonio are the very centerpieces of their lives, trumping even their resplendent marriages. In response, they vengefully threaten to bar these husbands from their beds, and go on to aver that they have lain with the very gentlemen whom they have actually impersonated at the trial.

While we perceive the jest, Bassanio and Gratiano do not. Such cross purposing makes for entertaining stagecraft, but tends to either subvert the comic moment, or alter its meaning. Abrasive exchanges can have long shelf lives, and during stressful moments may revive. Accusations and angry words are often replayed. In fact, the squabbling in

Act V between these newlyweds is a repetition of the first verbal injury inadvertently suffered by the wives during the trial. The specter of future dissension over these issues looms as a shadow upon the principal characters, and the comic significance shifts from conflicts resolved to latent conflicts presaging further disruptions. Nerissa's "unquiet house" has simply been deferred, moved down the road. To the comedic relief of tension represented by marriage is now added a new comic dimension which expresses the ironic tension between the happiness of the moment and those latent frictions which must at some point emerge.

The Merchant of Venice, distinguished by being the only Shakespearean comedy in which we actually witness *a posteriori* the eruption of marital discord growing out of pre-marital or honeymoon-stage imbroglios, suggests the appropriateness of re-examining others, in which the marital consequence is not given but implied. Let us turn to *Twelfth Night* for further illumination.

II. Alienation of Affection in Twelfth Night

It will be recalled that in *Twelfth Night*, in far off Ilyria, Duke Orsino adores Olivia, the lonely noblewoman of the neighboring estate who mourns a brother's death. He employs his new female page, Viola, disguised as the lad Cesario, to plead his love to this lofty dame on his behalf. What Orsino does not know is that Cesario is actually the recently shipwrecked Viola, who is as much in love with him as he is with Olivia. With great pluck and determination, and in desperate fidelity to her lord and his happiness, Viola makes a series of embassages to haughty Olivia, appealing Orsino's lost case of love. In one of those contrived coincidences which nevertheless function so magnificently for Shakespeare, Viola supposes her twin brother Sebastian has drowned in the same wreck which cast her up on these strange shores, thus placing her also in mourning for her own departed sibling.

Olivia grudgingly receives Cesario (Viola), and once again indicates that she does not and cannot love Orsino, but instead of sending the messenger off, a conversation ensues. Viola suggests that Orsino's prior attempts to win Olivia's hand have been faint hearted, and that had she been the lover, she would have never taken 'no' for an answer. Olivia is curious. "Why," she ventures, "what would you?" (I, v, 257) Cesario leaps at this opportunity:

Make me a willow cabin at your gate
And call upon my soul within the house,
Write loyal cantons of contemnèd love,
And sing them loud even in the dead of night;
Halloo your name to the reverberate hills,
And make the babbling gossip of the air
Cry out 'Olivia!' O, you should not rest
Between the elements of air and earth
But you should pity me.
(I, v, 258-265)

"You might do much," gushes Olivia, clearly smitten by the youth's passionate oratory. She has in this very instant fallen in love. It happens right before our eyes. But then, exactly whom does she love? Not, to be sure, the remote Orsino, nor can we say in good faith that she fancies "Cesario," since "he" is but a mask concealing Orsino's true ambassador. No, the speech so trippingly on the tongue told is Viola's alone, and, quite unwittingly, Olivia has fallen in love with one of her own sex. She and Viola are kindred spirits. They both turn in Orsino's dark sphere, and we sense that somehow the loss of Olivia's brother, a loss which still "reverberates" in her soul (using Viola's own word), makes her psyche and that of the wounded Viola sweetly resonate. When this misplaced desire dawns on Viola, she can only shake her head in dismay. "Poor lady," laments Viola, "she were better love a dream!" (II,ii, 26)

Unable to return the affections of Olivia, Viola focuses on her longing for Orsino, who, continuing in his belief that she is a lad, confides in her, deepening her love for him. Meanwhile, Viola's handsome twin Sebastian, who survived the storm at sea, stumbles into the presence of poor Olivia. He is instantly entranced, and when she raises the prospect of his being "ruled by" her -- that is, married -- he readily agrees. They are promptly made one in matrimony.

Comes the crisis. In the presence of Orsino and Olivia, Viola and Sebastian, brother and sister, dressed alike, discover each other. Everyone realizes the confusion which has happened. Olivia remains content with the amorous Sebastian, and Orsino, struck at the heart by Viola's love for him and her relentless promotion of his cause, decides to marry her, once he can see her "in [her] woman's weeds," that is, a dress.

And so once more to the altar, and all is well. Or is it? What is the prognosis? Take Olivia and Sebastian. She was eager to marry him because she thought he was Cesario. But he is not. From a strictly legal perspective, there has actually not been a marriage of these two at all, because, on account of mistaken identity, the essential element of consent is absent. Olivia willed to marry Cesario (Viola), and at the nuptial moment was deceived as to whom she was being joined to make one flesh. Such a false union is easily nullified at law. Further, on an emotional level, Sebastian is no match for his brilliant sister. In truth, he is a good but simple fellow. But Olivia fell in love with quite a different person, with the one who would build a willow cabin at her gate, and cry "Olivia" to the reverberate hills. It must be thought unlikely that Olivia will be content with the dullard she is marrying, even though in a sense he is an unconscious substitute for the brother she still misses. Put simply, she cannot be in love with the man to whom she is now united, but is quite oblivious of this fact. Is not this amusing? Though the match is doomed, no one notices.

What about Viola and the Duke? There is no doubting her love for him. But up until a short moment ago, her fiancé remained hopelessly enamored of Olivia, a love that seemed to abate only when it was discovered that she is now taken by Sebastian. It is at this catalytic moment that he extends his hand to Viola, still clad in the vestments of a boy.

Actually, neither Olivia nor Orsino knows whom they are marrying. Sebastian is not the "man" Olivia fell in love with, and Viola will need to absorb the ineluctable fact that her new husband was so in love with another woman that he remained so until he realized she belonged to another. Again, in the spirit of dramatic realism, when the "marriage" of Olivia and Sebastian fizzles, to whom could Olivia turn, if not to the man who pursued her so ardently?

Tellingly, it is just here at the finale that wretched Malvolio is brought on again, now released from the "dark house," where the machinations of Maria, Feste and Sir Toby put him. All recognize his pain, and see that he was treated too harshly. But the exulting couples easily shrug off the distress of a mere domestic. Malvolio's misery seems dangerously prophetic, as he rails at them: "I'll be revenged on the whole pack of you." The symbolism is plain: these couples, for all their conjugal zeal, are now caught in fundamentally incommensurable relations with one another, and, once the echo of the wedding bells fades away, they will be left to confront each other in the unsparing light of day.

Just as Portia and Bassanio must tread gingerly into the future haunted by the spectacle of the ruined Shylock, in much the same way the couples in *Twelfth Night*, expressly cursed by Malvolio, will have to work hard if they are to avoid the dark, unquiet houses that seem to lie ahead.

III. Comedies of Eros, Comedies of Eris: A Connubial Potpourri

Once the pattern is grasped, most of the other comedies follow suit.

The Two Gentlemen of Verona, which ends triumphantly with Valentine's boast of "one feast, one house, one mutual happiness," makes a claim unsupported by the text. For only with preternatural heroism can Julia forget Proteus's infidelity, breaches, perjury and perfidious deeds. Nor can Silvia easily overlook that Valentine ceded his right in her to Proteus, as Valentine can surely not dismiss what Proteus has done to him. And therein lies the subtle virtue of the jest: the comedy resides not so much in simple hymeneal happiness as it does by contrast in the dimly perceived seeds of wedded agony, fated to blossom in due course.

Consider that touching masterpiece, *The Winter's Tale*. When the statue of Hermione becomes alive, steps down from her icy pedestal and returns after sixteen years to the arms of her penitent and grieving spouse, Leontes, there is not a dry eye in the house. As the curtain falls, the connubial union is restored, Polixenes and Leontes are again friends, and mother and daughter Perdita are brought together at last. That is what our will-to-believe would have us embrace in our eagerness for restoration and amity. But is it so? Mamillius is dead. Hermione's sufferings, her losses of son, of husband and daughter, her public humiliation at the hands of a jealous tyrant, none of this can altogether vanish. The marriage hereafter can be but a gloss upon unspeakable tragedy, and the characters who had been in the prime of life are now old, held fast in a world of memories too painful to be recalled and too great to be dismissed. There will be a home again, the text insists on it. But what will pass within that home may well be wondered at. In Homer's *Odyssey*, when Odysseus comes back to Penelope and his kingdom in Ithaka, they sleep once more in the bed he made for them, fashioned out of the trunk of an immense tree, its roots still clutching the soil of their island. Their home is built around that bed. And, in the rhetoric of Albert Camus, we must imagine Odysseus happy. Penelope is distanced from the dalliances of her mate with Circe and others during the long voyage back. The focus, therefore, is on a wholly positive future in which a beautiful family is reconstituted through patience and bravery. But Leontes has made a different bed, and must lie in that. Whether it will be shared by Hermione is not for us to know.

Consider Helena and Bertram in *All's Well That Ends Well*. The ironic title says it all. Isn't Bertram a cad who has spent the entire play avoiding the virtuous and alluring young Helena? She is willing to follow him anywhere, and even stoop to trickery to capture him, yet we admire her still. In Viola's plaintive words, how will this fadge? Bertram learns that through a curious deception he has slept not with the female he was trying to seduce, but with the wife he was trying to escape. That stubborn wife, enforced upon him by the King of France, is carrying his child. Now he stands in the spotlight. In a sudden *volte-face*, he agrees to honor his perfunctory pledge and marry her. But would such a callow fellow in our "real world" love such a woman with sufficient sincerity and ardor to sustain a marriage? Probably not. He simply hasn't the backbone or the character to do so. Though the play "ends well," it must be a nominal ending in the end, for in truth all is not well. Shakespeare knew that, and so do we. Our doubts outweigh our hopes.

Interestingly, the future looks more promising for Petruchio and his Kate than it does for Beatrice and Benedick (and Claudio and Hero). By the conclusion of *The Taming of the Shrew*, with its notorious paean to patriarchy proclaimed by Kate, the audience has a feeling that this couple just might survive. Her love for this obstreperous man savors of authenticity, and the eponymous rages she exhibited may be explained as symptoms of a felt lack of love and affection, and simple envy over her pretty sister's popularity. Partnership with Petruchio has cured these issues. For with all her bluster, Kate was never really alienated from him. His absolute dedication to her was too genuine and too flattering to permit such a development. And thus surprisingly we have a more conventional resolution in *The Taming of the Shrew* than we might have expected. This is a play for all audiences.

With sniping Beatrice and Benedick in *Much Ado About Nothing*, however, we once more face permanent problems. Long ago these two were lovers, but Beatrice was jilted. "You always end with a jade's trick. I know you of old," she admits at the outset. (I, i, 138-9) "Signor Mountanto" (the sexual allusion is plain) "wears his faith but as the fashion of his hat," and the anguish in this characterization gives away Beatrice's wounded psyche. Benedick is in her caustic estimation a "valiant trencherman" whose romantic diet has carried him too far afield for her taste. Yet she remains almost against her will steadfastly attached to him. In the masked dance, her abiding desire and hope are briefly visible, as she accidentally confides to him:

> Why, he [Benedick] is the Prince's jester, a very dull fool.
> Only his gift is in devising impossible slanders. None
> but libertines delight in him, and the commendation is
> not in his wit but in his villainy, for he pleases
> men and angers them, and they laugh at him,
> and beat him. I am sure he is in the fleet. I would he
> had boarded me.
> (II, i, 127-133)

Benedick for his part will not admit his love for Beatrice, and prefers instead the role of a committed bachelor who politely declines to "hang [his] bugle in an invisible baldric." (I, i, 226) To overcome these impediments, their companions plot to bring these two squabblers together by allowing them to overhear the news that each is in love with the other. This device succeeds so well that by the last act they are writing love sonnets to one another. But verses are not vows fulfilled. The flaw here is that to be tricked into love may not be the best way to forge a lasting linkage between man and woman. Under the pressures and adversities of daily life, such a meager bridge may collapse, leaving the parties separate and alone. Second, Beatrice has plainly been hurt by Benedick's philandering, and to trust him again is her biggest challenge. In this regard it is useful to look at the Balthasar's song, which features the faithlessness of men:

> Sigh no more, ladies, sigh no more
> Men were deceivers ever;
> One foot in sea, and one on shore;
> To one thing constant never:
> Then sigh not so,
> But let them go,
> And be you blithe and bonny;
> Converting all your sounds of woe
> Into hey nonny, nonny.
> (II, iii, 61-68)

In other words, mankind is essentially faithless. That is the mocking lesson of the play. Since Beatrice has already been the victim of Benedick's roving, what are the odds that they might enjoy success as a married couple? Every reliable indicator in the play hints not at mutual fulfillment but at conflict. Asked about the couple's prospects, Leonato, Beatrice's uncle, sums them up with gentle cynicism: "O, Lord, my lord, if they were but a week married, they would talk themselves mad." (II, i, 330-331)

And just as the problems of Portia and Bassiano are reflected in their understudies, Gratiano and Nerissa, so the dysfunctional connection of Beatrice and Benedick is mirrored in the terrible dilemma of Claudio and Hero. Claudio has brought slanderous accusations against his fiancée, and publicly cast her away at the wedding. Though she is resurrected from a supposed death for the purpose of rejoining him, one can hardly have sanguine expectations in their case. Claudio has poisoned the well, and revealed himself to be immature, self-centered and rash. Though such a couple might be able to preserve a marriage, the odds are against it. More to be expected would be, in Beatrice's monitory words to Hero, "wooing, wedding and repenting." (II, i, 65-66)

Finally, we would be remiss if we neglected our friends in *A Midsummer Night's Dream*. For however brief a duration, Lysander deserted Hermia for Helena. Demetrius forsakes Helena for Hermia. Will these courtship infidelities slip away and disappear after their nuptials are solemnized? What grounds are there to think so? Note that throughout this comedy runs the bright thread of romantic tragedy in the form of the myth of *Pyramus and Thisbe*, the story at the foundation of *Romeo and Juliet*. Why is a tragedy lodged in the heart of what seems a light-hearted comic farce? As a signifier, in which direction does it point? As one may treat a tragedy as a comedy, we may also find in comedy a covert tragedy. That is why Plato concludes the *Symposium* with the observation that the best writer of tragedy will be the best for its supposed opposite.

Of course, these star-crossed lovers have their quarrels because of the cosmic schism of Titania and Oberon; all mortal enmities come "from our debate, from our dissension," Titania tells her Oberon. (II, i, 115-116) Their latest dissension concerns a child custody dispute over a little Indian boy, whose mother was a devotee of Titania. Oberon covets the child, and there is no room for bargaining over this. Only when the lovers and the rude mechanicals arrive in the woodland, where gross confusion and erotic magic reigns, is Oberon able to persuade Titania, now helplessly swooning over a jackass, to surrender the babe to him. When he releases the fairy queen from the spell which made her topple into bed with such a beast, the two demi-gods reconcile.

But . . . what of the child? After Oberon snatches him, no more of him is heard. We are left to infer that perhaps a joint custody arrangement is accepted, in which Titania and Oberon raise the boy together. But this is fantasy, after all, and cannot be pressed too hard for facts. The issue seems to dissipate. But conflict could arise again on just this score. We might wish too to bear in mind that at some point Titania is bound to learn that the reason she had a romantic fling with a brute is because of a scheme on Oberon's part to steal the child from her. It's bad enough that she was lured into sleeping with a crude mortal, but the tinge of bestiality is distinctly offensive, or might be when recollected in tranquility. One suspects, then, given their respective vanities and poor track record, that the fight over the little changeling boy is only the latest in a series of battles to be staged by this pair of clumsy narcissists.

IV. Conclusion

All of Shakespeare is poetry, not literal history or biography, and it is a notorious exercise in futility to raise idle questions in the form of, "How many children had Lady Macbeth?" (an issue to which we will return in due course). Such inquiries are indeed artificial and impossible. On the other hand, it is equally impossible to form a conception of characters without reference to their future. The very meaning of character lies in its temporality. As each story closes, character and audience are left facing tomorrow. The comedies point through their weddings and celebrations to anticipated joys, and that is inevitably how all such tales are received and digested by the human mind. It is an essential component of dramatic significance. We are never confined to the last instant onstage, but naturally apprehend likely consequences for each major character. Yet, where the comic foundation is sufficiently riddled with defects and trauma, we may find ourselves inferring sorrow as well as joy. Characters are not assimilated and appreciated in their fullness when they are confined to snapshots of a wedding, their ignoble moments swept tidily under the carpet. Comedy in its depth and richness is an opportunity, not only for mirth, but equally for compassion.

Read superficially, festive comedies capped with marital bliss can be legitimately labeled "happy." But on further reflection, as we consider what we have read or beheld onstage, including the plainly pathological components in each play, in relation to our own experience and the complexities of life, we come to appreciate the ironic dimension of the poet's art. The moment of wedded triumph with which each comedy finishes may then appear sandwiched flatteringly between the earlier time of troubles and troubles yet to come. From what we know of Portia, she would eventually seek to provoke Bassanio in some domestic vendetta. When Orsino falls into his next fit of self-absorption, will not Viola have occasion to remember his obsession with Olivia and Viola's own foolish willingness to serve as an accomplice to the campaign of wooing her? At that point in our deliberations, we can discern the outlines of the unquiet house beyond. It is just here that the meaning of comedy suffers a sea change. It is no longer a mere function of the release of tension brought about by reconciliation, but grows in the direction of a rueful contrast between momentary glee and long-run challenges, tribulations and losses. Thus we put away our childish reckonings, and read as chastened adults, with Shakespeare.

WORKS CITED

William Shakespeare: The Complete Works, second edition, G. Taylor & S. Wells, eds., Clarendon Press, 2005.

2
Let Us Not To The Understanding of Sonnet 116 Admit Impediments

If we want to know what a sonnet was for Shakespeare, how it was used and what it meant, one logical place to look is the plays. There we learn that in Elizabethan England, the sonnet emerged as a private written communication, usually a token of love. Not originally an idle amusement or vainglorious display of skill, it was rather a mode of *envoi*, an epistolary exercise which expressed devotion directly to a chosen other. Such poetic declamations descended from the troubadors, (de Rougement, 75 ff.) who had sought every discreet means of conveying amorous sentiments to high-born ladies, a legacy echoed in Falstaff's *envois* to the spouses of Page and Ford in *The Merry Wives of Windsor*. Later, as the sonnet form became popular and examples flourished, some were eventually gathered in books, as was the case with Shakespeare's own sonnets in 1609. In this way, adept practitioners of the art earned renown. Yet, it is well to bear in mind that the early sonneteers were not professionals, but rather those who employed this form of *envoi* with a distinctly practical aim in view. When Shakespeare shows us sonnets in his plays, then, we never find them to be creations of a genius intent on promoting his craft, but rather to be rhetorical engines of conquest marshaled by plighted souls in the service of Eros.

Three examples will suffice.

i. In *Love's Labour's Lost*, a "refined traveler of Spain" and sententious boob, Don Adriano de Armado, finds himself infatuated with country wench Jaquenetta. The sonnet is instantly chosen as the vehicle to capture her affections. Notice that Armado does not dash to the king's well-stocked library to soak up the sonnets of yesteryear, but proposes to make his own to impress the lady.

> Adieu, valour! rust, rapier! be still, drum! for your
> manager is in love; yea, he loveth. Assist me some
> extemporal god of rhyme, for I am sure I shall turn
> sonnet. Devise, wit, ----write, pen; for I am for
> whole volumes in folio.
> (I, ii, 172-176)

Though the sonnet project proves far beyond his meager capacities, a bombastic *envoi* is sent by Adriano via bungling courier to Jaquenetta. Through misdirections it arrives in the hands of the elegant Princess of France, who, with her ladies-in-waiting, have much merriment reading it together at Adriano's expense.

Later, the male protagonists, all of whom have sworn to steer clear of women and pursue a monastic regimen of scholarship, discover to their chagrin that they are madly in love with the aforesaid ladies. Not surprisingly, these four pretentious gentlemen, including the esteemed King of Navarre, traduce their oaths and pen florid sonnets, each to his own magnificent mademoiselle. This quartet of verses is of interest, not only because it illustrates the thoroughly applied nature of the sonnet in 16th century Albion, but also because the quality of the verses degenerates seriatim, providing evidence of the sonnet's use by ordinary courtiers to signal their love. The best of these, to Rosaline, is by the merry madcap lord, Biron, surely a stand-in for Shakespeare himself.

> If love make me forsworn, how shall I swear to love?
> Ah, never faith could hold, if not to beauty vowed.
> Though to myself forsworn, to thee I'll faithful prove.
> Those thoughts to me were oaks, to thee like osiers bowed.
> Study his bias leaves, and makes his book thine eyes,
> Where all those pleasures live that art would comprehend.
> If knowledge be the mark, to know thee shall suffice.
> Well learnèd is that tongue that well can thee commend;
> All ignorant that soul that sees thee without wonder;
> Which is to me some praise that I thy parts admire.

Thy eye Jove's lightning bears, thy voice his dreadful thunder,
Which, not to anger bent, is music and sweet fire.
Celestial as thou art, O pardon, love, this wrong,
That singeth heaven's praise with such an earthly tongue.
(IV, ii, 106-120)

Featured here is the conceit of lover's doubtful credibility in light of having been forsworn in relation to his oath of chastity. The flattering solution is to claim that Rosaline's charms are so overwhelming that she has supplanted bookish learning as a desideratum, and now is herself all his study, a theme reflected in his stirring speech to his colleagues about ladies' eyes bearing the "right Promethean fire." Although the sudden death of the King of France calls the ladies home, and Rosaline imposes a penalty on poet Biron to pass a year as an entertainer in a hospital before she will take his vows seriously, one senses that his sonnet has found its mark. As the scholar abandons the library for the bedchamber, he enlists the sonnet to serve as a seductive talisman on his behalf. This is not poetry for aesthetes, but for wooers. All four of the forlorn gentlemen's sonnets/*envois* are in this rhetorical vein.

ii. The situation of Benedick in *Much Ado About Nothing* is congruent, in that he has sworn to live a bachelor, but as a result of the machinations of his friends, he finds himself awkwardly in love with his verbal adversary, Beatrice. The solution? Present her with a sonnet, naturally. The problem is not merely the reversal of his will, but, as a soldier, his complete lack of talent. He begins fitfully.

The god of love,
That sits above,
And knows me, and knows me,
How pitiful I deserve, --

And here his truant muse, like a capricious lover, deserts him.

I mean in singing; but in loving, Leander the
good swimmer, Troilus the first employer of pandars,
and a whole book full of these quondam carpet-
mongers, whose names yet run smoothly in
the even road of a blank verse, why they were
never so truly turn'd over and over as my poor

self in love. Marry, I cannot show it in rhyme. I
have tried. I can find out no rhyme to 'lady' but
'baby', an innocent rhyme; for 'scorn' 'horn', a
hard rhyme; for 'school' 'fool', a babbling rhyme.
Very ominous endings. No, I was not born under
a rhyming planet, nor I cannot woo in festival terms.
(V, ii, 29-39)

Yet, by the last scene of the play, reluctant Benedick, the wouldn't-
be married man, has fashioned a would-be sonnet for his intended. It is
discovered clutched in his hand by Claudio.

And I'll be sworn upon't that he loves her,
For here's a paper written in his hand,
A halting sonnet of his own pure brain,
Fashioned to Beatrice.
(V, iv, 85-88)

And coincidentally the lady has turned sonneteer herself!

And here's another, [exclaims Hero]
Writ in my cousin's hand, stol'n from her pocket,
Containing her affection unto Benedick.
(V, iv, 89-91)

These sonnets attest to the mutual loves of this mistrustful pair,
and demonstrate that despite herself, woman can woo as well as man.
We are not shown their verses, but no matter, love's labors are plainly triumphant, at least for now. Years later, in the coils of matrimony, perhaps
these letters will be anxiously exhumed, to verify feelings once cherished for one another.

    iii. The reader will also recall that the first words spoken to each
other by Romeo and Juliet form a sonnet *a duetto*. This incandescent
collaboration is unique in the history of sonnet composition. In the instant of first touch, there is no space in which *envois* can fly. None is
needed. Their speech makes them one spirit.
    It is with these samples in mind that we turn to Sonnet 116. Based
on what we have just seen in the plays, there would appear to be a rebuttable presumption that many if not all of Shakespeare's sonnets were

envois appealing to one or more significant personages in the sphere of their author. Indeed, nothing is positively known which would disconfirm that hypothesis. The characterization as *envois* is significant on account of the tendency to view Sonnet 116 and certain others as literary editorials or cerebral disquisitions on the nature of love and other aspects of human nature. This tendency gains support from sequestration of the poem from its brethren, and the absence of any salutation or direct address in 116 to the intended recipient.

Let me not to the marriage of true minds
Admit impediments. Love is not love
Which alters when it alteration finds,
Or bends with the remover to remove:
O no, it is an ever-fixèd mark,
That looks on tempests, and is never shaken;
It is the star to every wand'ring barque,
Whose worth's unknown although his height be taken.
Love's not Time's fool, though rosy lips and cheeks
Within his bending sickle's compass come;
Love alters not with his brief hours and weeks,
But bears it out even to the edge of doom.
If this be error and upon me proved,
I never writ, nor no man ever loved.
(Taylor and Wells, p. 793)

Is this to be construed as a sociological abstract, or are the feelings of the writer engaged? The project of deciphering these words, now over four centuries old, may benefit from a perspective which views them as directed to actual individuals. Though we do not find "thou" and "you" in this particular poem, Shakespeare's sonnets do contain those terms, making it impossible to render them without considering what personal purposes they may have served. Only patient scrutiny and deliberation will determine whether Sonnet 116 was part of the author's correspondence or dialogue with others of his era.

Also to be avoided is the shallow temptation to receive these lines as though the poet were teaching the dubious moral that genuine love should focus on internal qualities only, and pay no worship to garish outer beauty. Try telling that to Biron, Benedick and Romeo! No writer was ever at greater pains to celebrate youth and physical comeliness than was Shakespeare, and we do a disservice to readers when we lure them into an acceptation of Sonnet 116 which pretends that physical attractiveness plays no legitimate part in our lives. That way lie only confusion, myopia and bad faith. Likewise, to assume the poet is recommending as a conjugal prescription that emotional trauma ("tempests") be ignored, leaving us "never shaken," is simply unrealistic. Can we just close our eyes to physical and affective losses? What counsel would that be?

The better strategy is to seize on the poem's mission as an *envoi* to help us to get past (1) the sort of adolescent analysis which sees Sonnet 116 as little more than a cosmetic anodyne, or (2) the avuncular suggestion that maturing couples ignore the ravages of time or the emotional ruptures that inevitably afflict relationships.

Another obstacle to understanding is the assumption that the relationships attendant to Sonnet 116 are exclusively binary. That is, some seem to suppose that the poem concerns either the connection between the writer and his wider audience, or the intended recipient and the object of his love, ignoring the possibility of a three-cornered hat. In fact, Shakespeare's sonnets teem with reflections on the foibles of *ménage à trois*, amorous intrigue, disappointments, frustrations, betrayals, and -- in some instances -- if not reconciliations, at least forgiveness. Once we move past the procreative sonnets, we step into a maze of triangulation which cannot be escaped, and should always be reflected in our hermeneutical undertakings. Though many critics understandably wish to read the Sonnets without reference to biographical investigations, that does not relieve us of the obligation to determine whether Sonnet 116 is best set in the context of pairing or triangulation.

Consider, for example, Sonnet 42, which addresses the "loving offenders."

> That thou hast her, it is not all my grief,
> And yet it may be said I loved her dearly;
> That she hath thee is of my wailing chief,
> A loss in love that touches me more nearly.
> Loving offenders, thus I will excuse ye:
> Thou dost love her, because thou know'st I love her,
> And for my sake even so doth she abuse me,
> Suff'ring my friend for my sake to approve her.
> If I lose thee, my loss is my love's gain,
> And losing her, my friend hath found that loss:
> Both find each other, and I lose both twain,

And both for my sake lay on me this cross.
But here's the joy: my friend and I are one.
Sweet flattery! Then she loves but me alone.
(Taylor and Wells, p. 784)

Read forthrightly, these lines comment on a complex of liaisons in which the poet's male love object has formed an intimate alliance with a woman who has loved the narrator. In attempting to accept what appears to be a joint betrayal, the poet employs a rhetorical stratagem reminiscent of the sonnet of Biron, above. Biron's dilemma, that in swearing fidelity to a woman he is breaking his oath of chaste scholarship, forces him to fuse the female love object with that forsaken study. Thus, in loving Rosaline, now viewed as the source of knowledge and wisdom, Biron can fancy that he remains true to his pledge of learning. Rosaline and Knowledge are henceforth one. In Sonnet 42, despite the profound bond with his male friend, that friend has stolen a treasured female from the narrator. Here the poet is caught between perfidious desertion on the one hand, and his abiding love for both these "loving offenders" on the other. Again, the solution lies in a metaphysical identification: on account of the narrator's limitless love for him, he and his friend are indistinguishable. Thus, the woman's attraction to his friend becomes desire for the poet *via* categorical syllogism.

Interpreting Sonnet 116 by itself carries a risk of abstraction and misunderstanding. It is this sad alteration we now must bend with our removers to remove. To be assimilated and appreciated this poem needs to be noted in relation to other key sonnets, particularly Sonnet 42. Modern scholarship has failed in coming to terms with the sonnets, first because they were allowed to be divorced from the substance of the poet's personal experience, and secondly, because they were isolated from one another. This leaves an intellectual vacuum to be filled in by subjective speculation cast in a barely intelligible technical jargon.

Credit must be given to Mr. Hilton Landry, who 44 years ago drew attention to the miscomprehension of Sonnet 116 caused by not digesting it in its setting in the whole collection. Much of the praise heaped on this poem is thus improperly founded.

It now seems clear that for modern readers of Sonnet 116 must be among the least understood of Shakespeare's poems even though it is a hallowed anthology piece, is frequently quoted, and just as frequently praised. This Sonnet is usually

taken to be an exalted celebration of love, or "perfect friendship," or the "unfailing constancy of true love," when in fact
it *celebrates* nothing at all. If we are to discover what Sonnet
116 does signify, to define its sense, feeling, and tone, we must
consider it in its context. (Landry, 98, emphasis Landry's)

This is admirable. Regrettably, Mr. Landry did not find that context. It might have been easily done, had the "groupings" of the sonnets
been taken a bit less literally.

One cuts the Gordian knot of Sonnet 116 when one recognizes
in its "true minds" the "loving offenders" of Sonnet 42. The underlying
circumstances are the same, as is the poet's complaint. Sonnet 116 is
supplemental *envoi* to these two reminding them of the hurt they have
caused. The unmistakable tone of injury sounded in Sonnet 42 carries
through loud and clear in 116. Thus, the marriage trope and reference to
"truth" are robustly ironic, as these offenders have been grossly false to
the speaker. Behind the brave metaphysical rationalization of Sonnet 42
one can still detect the accusatory voice. "Yes," the poet seems to boast,
"I can celebrate your love with you, because I love my friend so much
that he and I constitute but a single self. So this lady's desire for him is
in reality love of me." Of course this sophism is a patent failure, but precisely in virtue of that failure it succeeds dramatically in putting these
offenders in a bad light, the emotive mission of the message. We can
see that the poet intends that these two offenders feel a twinge of guilt.
And the over-generous accommodation of Sonnet 116, theatrically ap-
proving of the union of these two loving offenders (true minds), is easily
seen through. The "alterations" which love accepts and tolerates are not,
then, mere wrinkles of age and fading of "rosy lips and cheeks." Those
are merely illustrative images. What has befallen the poet is *Sturm und
Drang*, a veritable emotional maelstrom ("tempests") and impending
"doom." Language of this gravity is inconsistent with mere dimming of
youthful luster, and can refer only to loss of the beloved partner. "Even
though you have cruelly betrayed me," the poet expostulates, "I shall
continue to love you and wish you happiness." This posture is consonant
with the careful housewife of Sonnet 143, who is permitted to set down
"her babe" to run after some "feathered creature," so long as she returns
to give that babe a kiss. To bring the "true minds" of these "loving offenders" to their senses, the poet is willing to twist the blade in his own
wound, the one they have given him. We would even be inclined to view
Shakespeare's embrace of his friends' affair as a Nietzschean moment

of *amor fati*, were it not for the suspicion that Nietzsche's thought is *au fond* Shakespearean.

All of this is far too simple and naïve for our academic guardians of the written word. Professor Helen Vendler of Harvard rightly finds that Sonnet 116 is not essentially "a definition of true love." (Indeed, how could it be, when it is a cry of anguish and despair in iambic pentameter? Since when is a love sonnet a philosophical argument?) But instead of acknowledging the most accessible meaning and purpose of this famous communiqué as *envoi*, we learn from Professor Vendler that this poem is "an example . . . of dramatic refutation or rebuttal." Out of whole cloth an entire nuanced conversation is fabricated, of which Sonnet 116 is thought to be a moment. No matter that there is no discernible "anterior utterance" to "refute." Without the ballast of Sonnet 42 (or any other contextualizing instrument) to tether the discussion to earth, the explication swells and floats into the blue, where the "true minds" are willy-nilly misidentified as those of the young friend and the narrator. "I did love you once," Vendler has the young man say, "but you have altered, and so there is a natural alteration in me." (Vendler, 488) This gratuitous inference becomes a "law" which it is the business of Sonnet 116 to "rebut" or "refute." The inconvenient fact that we have no writings from the "young man" but only from Shakespeare need not detain us. Sonnets here are viewed as conceptual contortions, not symptoms of the rigors of living. It is all smoke and mirrors, riddles designed to baffle generations to come, like Babylonian acrostics buried in a time capsule. The mundane possibility that the author had an actual and eventful human existence, was jilted simultaneously by erstwhile lovers, and protested in his wonted medium of poetry, is too easy, not deemed worthy of notice. The mythical "interlocutor" remains unidentified and undefined, and is not assigned clear ontological status, as either (1) an historical person, (2) a dramatic character, or (3) some sort of literary hybrid. The same problem attends Vendler's speaker. What is this ghost to Shakespeare, or he to it? We cannot know. What we are given by Vendler is a smarmy, fictive dialogue, not so much resurrected as cobbled together by a literary expert, who then wields the glittering instruments of modern criticism to unravel super-subtle intricacies she has herself spun out.

The plain problem with this kind of treatment is that it violates Occam's razor, the principle of economy of explanation. Shakespeare's plays demonstrate that Elizabethan sonnets were used by romantically-inclined persons to convey their sentiments. That is what we sidestep at our peril. Instead of taking them forthrightly for what they appear to be, the sonnets are utilized as a scaffold on which a facade is erected to display the scholar's recondite musings. But we can far more easily discover a reasonable account of the sonnets in the manner of literary naturalism; there is no warrant for the leap into speculative gamesmanship.

The error is not without consequences. A major theme of Shakespeare's artistic vision is the problematic character who allows alienation and resentment to fester, leading to plots, villainies and catastrophes. In some cases, it is possible to restore such a one to a sympathetic relation with others and thereby with his own soul. In other cases it is too late, and only the audience learns the lesson. Thus, when contemporary teachers depart from the realm of authentic feelings, when they cultivate and offer to students an armamentarium of congested theory, allowing and actually encouraging learners to keep real poetry and its emotional catharsis at bay, to ward off tears and laughter, they promote a pathological sophistication, and take up *against* Shakespeare the very attitudes of Brutus, Don John, Aaron, Edmund, Goneril, and a host of other cold-blooded organisms only too willing to share their ennui and anomie with others. The follies and frustrations of the young cavaliers in *Love's Labour's Lost* show that the drawback of the euphuistic style lies not in a mere excess of syllables, but in its rejection of affective immediacy in favor of subterfuge, deception and self-ignorance. In the end, our four philosophical musketeers are persuaded by their wiser ladies to put away their masks, and Biron and his friends trade their arch, superheated vocabularies and needless artifices for "russet yeas and honest kersey noes." (V, ii, 414) That is the very touchstone of Shakespeare's art.

After all, what distinguishes Brutus from Marc Antony? Brutus casuistically argues that he "loved" Caesar but "loved Rome more," implying that love of Rome carried with it the right of bloody assassination. But Antony proclaims the simple truth that, "He was my friend, faithful and just to me." Can there be any doubt which leader Shakespeare preferred? We suffer our friend's faults, we do not slaughter him for them. Brutus was foiled by his own ambition, an ambition he was too estranged from his own psyche to apprehend.

In a less compromised, more straightforward day, Professor Edward Hubler put his finger on the central issue in his 1952 classic, *The Sense of Shakespeare's Sonnets*, which contains his unsurpassed essay, "The Economy of the Closed Heart": Shakespeare is the spokesperson of vulnerability. Hubler observed:

In Shakespeare's view the open heart must give itself away in

order to maintain its existence. It is confronted with a perpetual dilemma: it can know of its being only through self-
loss. The alternative is to conserve itself until it has withered
away.

Both courses of action are illustrated in the plays; both are
observed in the sonnets with an acuteness Shakespeare was
never to exceed. (Hubler, 419)

We can perceive this in the brace of sonnets we've been examining, numbers 42 and 116. The loving offenders are excused, and no impediment is raised to the annexation of these "true minds." Though the
pardon granted is filled with tension, it is gracefully performed by the
narrator as a sincere self-effacing for the sake of love

When the Sonnets are aware that the friend's faults constitute
a threat to the friendship, there is a recurrent accompani-
ment of ironic self-consciousness, arising, it appears, from a
knowledge of the waywardness with which affection, in order to maintain its being in an imperfect world, bestows itself
with imperfect cause. It must, at times, debase its currency in
order to exist. The alternative to this dilemma is the economy
of the closed heart. (Hubler, 419-420)

This ironic self-consciousness, so painfully apparent in the locution "true minds" that it is nearly embarrassing, points to a critical blind
spot or parapraxis in the contemporary reading of Shakespeare. Our finest and most acute analysts are so intent on ferreting out his esoteric
meaning that they miss his heart. And in so doing, tragically, they miss
their own.

Postscript

The foregoing analysis was never intended as anything like a
complete exposition or exegesis of Sonnet 116. Rather, it constitutes a
mere dialectical step aimed at clearing away some popular rubbish left
by literary tourism. Such an enterprise cannot illuminate in any positive sense. It must be provisional only, as a voice crying in the wilderness. Without additional information, it is impossible to make genuine

progress. St. Thomas Aquinas makes a useful distinction between reason and revelation. On the basis of reason alone, our appreciation can only advance so far. Miraculously, in the case of the Sonnets that revelation is at hand. We now have Mr. Hank Whittemore's historical study, *The Monument* (Meadow Geese Press, 2005), which painstakingly sets out the long sought-after autobiographical significance of the Sonnets. To be adequately assimilated, Sonnet 116 must be set in the context of English history, with special attention paid to the careers and conflicts of Edward de Vere, 17th Earl of Oxford, Henry Wriothesley, 3rd Earl of Southampton, and Queen Elizabeth I. Against all odds, Mr. Whittemore accomplishes that end. As a result, the "tempests" mentioned in line six are successfully identified. To attempt in this place a summary of his magisterial argument would be impractical and inappropriate. Some related ideas are taken up in the chapter on *Lucrece*, "Wanton Modesty." But it is best to let Mr. Whittemore speak for himself, and then re-visit some of these issues. One simple caveat must suffice: any attempt to come to terms with the Sonnets of Shakespeare (or the present essays) which neglects *The Monument* cannot be taken seriously, and is doomed to failure. Readers are encouraged to seek out this indispensable resource. They will be amply rewarded.

The challenge after studying Mr. Whittemore's book will be, of course, not what the sonnets meant immediately to their author, but what they may be for us today. Secret messages serving a practical design could always have been conveyed by the use of ciphers rather than poetry. The choice of the latter is thus significant. It is the business of the cryptogram to transmit information, not to illuminate or inspire. By electing to employ the medium of poetry, which well the poet knew would be perused by later generations, strata of broader significance were entailed. Acquiring a firmer impression of the historical utility and import of the sonnets, then, wipes away some but not all of the readings that have been given over the past four centuries. The art of fathoming the sonnets will remain what it has been always, a navigation between the shores of literalism and transcendence.

WORKS CITED

Denis de Rougement, *Love in the Western World*, Princeton University Press, 1983.

Ernest Hubler, "The Economy of the Closed Heart," in *The Sense of Shakespeare's Sonnets*, Princeton University Press, 1952, Reprinted in *Shakespeare: Modern Essays in Criticism*, Leonard F. Dean, ed., Oxford University Press, 1961.

Hilton Landry, "The Marriage of True Minds: Truth and Error in Sonnet 116," *Shakespeare Studies* 3, 1967.

William Shakespeare: The Complete Works, 2d Edition, S. Wells and G. Taylor, eds., Clarendon Press, 2005.

Helen Vendler, *The Art of Shakespeare's Sonnets*, Harvard University Press, 1998.

Hank Whittemore, *The Monument*, Meadow Geese Press, 2005

3

Is Juliet Tragic?

Patience, good lady -- wizards know their times.
Deep night, dark night, the silent of the night,
The time of night when Troy was set on fire,
The time when screech-owls cry and bandogs howl,
And spirits walk, and ghosts break up their graves --
That time best fits the work we have in hand.
Madam, sit you, and fear not.

-- Roger Bolingbroke, *Henry VI Part Two*

*T*he question must be faced, especially as, sooner or later, we discover that it is she, not lightweight Romeo, who is the play's prime mover. Any serious discussion of the tragic dimension must come to focus on her. The text advertises itself as: "The Most Excellent and Lamentable Tragedy of Romeo and Juliet," but where shall we gather its substance? Isn't the principal protagonist little more than a misfortunate ingénue at whom Eros has unleashed an injudicious dart? If the terrible hubris that bedevils such wounded giants as Othello, Lear, Brutus, Hamlet and Coriolanus, to name a few, is in her absent, how then can the adjective "tragic" possess any sense beyond the merely equivocal or demotic?

For Shakespeare, the fault almost never lies in outward circumstances but in ourselves. Remove the aspects of voluntary over-reaching and self-alienation and Juliet becomes a mere victim of traditional patriarchy and social disorder, a love-bound creature helplessly caught in the pitiless pincers of war. Her unhappy death would then be more consistent with sentiment and melodrama than tragedy. Once it is recognized that it is Juliet, not Romeo, who is the star illuminating the action, we seek at once for signs in her of moral meltdown. But a chorus of readers and scholars exclaims that she is without fault. For conventional theatre goers, she is essentially a sensitive and stubborn girl who foolishly chooses the poetical son of a rival clan. Period. No more spiritual depth is allotted her than is exhibited by Cinderella, Snow White, or, more tellingly, Maria Nunez in *West Side Story*. Again, this view of her pedestrian perfection leads logically to the idea that the "tragedy" which befalls her and Romeo, because it is not a function of character, is one of mere happenstance.

If we glance briefly at representative scholars, we find that they are united in placing her on a par with the proverbial well-scrubbed girl who wins blue ribbon for apple pie at the county fair. Modern thought finds in *Romeo and Juliet* little but coincidence, *de casibus* and carnage, decked out in old fashioned verse. Harold Goddard, for example, apprehending the female lead as beyond reproach, can only blame Romeo by default for the bad outcome. A headstrong and passionate hoodlum, he spurns the charity and pacifism of Juliet by brawling in the street.

> Romeo was free to act under the compulsion of force or under the compulsion of love . . . . Granted that the temptation to surrender to the former was at the moment immeasurably great, the power of the latter, if Juliet spoke true, was greater yet: "My bounty is as boundless as the sea,/ My love as deep;/ the more I give to thee,/ The more I have, for both are infinite." Everything that has just preceded shows that the real Romeo wanted to have faith in Juliet's faith . . . . But Romeo . . . descends from the level of love to the level of violence and attempts to part the fighters with his sword. (Goddard, I, 129)

What is Goddard talking about? There is nothing in our text suggesting that 13-year-old Juliet ever preached a lofty Satyagraha when she returned Romeo's affections. And Goddard himself acknowledges that the lad was not fighting but seeking to restore peace when he becomes embroiled. It is hard to avoid the conclusion that Professor Goddard attributes to Juliet a creed to which he himself is partial, without actually showing that this is a doctrine she held and sought to impart. Further, he attempts to persuade us that, unlike the ribald Mercutio and bawdy Nurse, Juliet is swept up in a romantic delirium which is somehow "pure," untainted by inordinate or consuming physical demands. Yet these precocious youngsters engage in intimacies in their very first encounter, albeit decorously camouflaged by high-flown verbiage. While it is undeniable that Juliet defers intercourse until a hasty exchange of vows, the stunning brevity of the engagement hints that matrimony may be scarcely more than a nod to propriety, and not what the country and western ballad bluntly calls "the main attraction." There is no talk of family or raising children, for they are themselves children. Both lunge towards *l'amour* as a salve for adolescent crises: Juliet wants to escape a stifling domicile and imposed spouse, while Romeo is on the rebound from icy Rosaline. In Juliet he discovers someone equally beyond reach, and appoints her to rescue him. Any sensible female so approached would perceive this and send him packing. But Juliet, in flight herself from an unhappy home, and susceptible to the attentions of a (we may suppose) handsome youth of fanciful expression, whose whole demeanor is supercharged with libido, makes no resistance. His words ignite the dry fibers of her soul, and the flames leap up to engulf them. This is a woman, not an icon. Of course, to read thus is to dwell on the level of mere psychology, a stratum which the play soon transcends.

Goddard's disciple, Harold Bloom of Yale, struggles with the tragic nodus, but cannot free himself from his mentor's hagiographical *mise en scène*. Sensing that Juliet is genuinely tragic, he has nowhere to turn to situate that note of tragedy but love. How is love tragic? Bloom, in step with the majority, dogmatically rejects the idea that Juliet craves death. What's left? Well, she is plainly sublime, and "her sublimity is the play, and guarantees the tragedy of this tragedy." (Bloom, 89) That might be so. Still we may want to ask, How is she sublime? Critical superlatives and hyperbole won't help. Kant and Shaftesbury observe that sublimity in nature and art is essentially linked to risk and the threat of great harm or extinction. Does Juliet look in that direction? Return to the same lines cited above, now etched in western consciousness: "My bounty is as boundless as the sea, My love as deep: The more I give to thee,/ The more I have, for both are infinite." Bloom here errs in seizing on what Hegel called "bad infinity," an endless quantity formed by incessant addition. Far from being sublime, this mechanical series is a crashing bore. In this context, it reduces Juliet's utterance to the tame proposition, "I shall continue to love you." Tomorrow and tomorrow and tomorrow... And yet, the sublime abides in Juliet nonetheless, for a boundless sea may rage in storm, sweeping all below. Sailor take warning! Faced with Juliet's "infinite" torrent of love, Romeo (*and* Juliet) may drown. There's the rub. But Bloom, contracted to a two-dimensional *personam*, misses the possibility of a tumultuous yearning in Juliet for an unconditioned, complete and total absolution, the ultima Thule of the heart, a conclusion incongruent with every form of bourgeois qualification. Only death can temper an edge of passion that keen. Here is the stuff of tragedy. It lies in the soul, not in the cobbled streets.

Like Goddard, Professor Ruth Nevo detects the tragic impetus exclusively in the reckless male lead. Juliet seems to have a supporting role only, lacking even the preternatural sanctity lauded by Goddard. While Nevo grants that Shakespeare's play is perched on the fringes of moral chaos, the action is never infected by depravity. "Evil in Romeo and Juliet," she writes,

> is not accorded the diabolic station it has in the great tragedies, *never invades experience*, nor undermines the possibilities of existence to the same degree. It is nevertheless present in the very fabric of events, in the interplay of the *bad luck* which dogs the lovers with the bad habits of ingrown pride in the Capulets and Montagues. (Nevo, 246, emphases mine)

Though Romeo is cast as the pseudo-tragic heavy, boy and girl nonetheless share a prelapsarian lack of guile. While "random events press towards evil," we learn that "the willed actions of the protagonists are *radically innocent*." [emphasis mine] Nevo concurs with Goddard in locating the *peripeteia* or reversal in Romeo's intervention in a *mêlée*, ironically a function of his love and virtue. Inasmuch as Juliet is drained of tragic significance by Prof. Nevo, she barely figures in the discussion. Of the play's major soliloquy, not quoted in her article, she comments politely: "Juliet's 'Gallop apace' is remarkable because it . . . is purely erotic, without a trace of the mysticism in which sex is mere symbol." Prof. Nevo is quite certain that Juliet is not enamored of death. "There is no naked sword between these two lovers. Theirs is not a desire to die to the world, but a most energetic desire to live in it." (Nevo, 255) That's nice, but what in the text supports this claim? Notice that all Nevo can muster of the play's central figure is: "Essentially Juliet's suffering is the realization of loneliness and isolation." (Nevo, 256) With all due respect, is this an insight? With the orthodox position before us, we can now take its measure as we go in search of "radical innocence."

II.

From the moment Romeo vaults over the orchard wall, this play morphs into one of the most death-saturated in the canon. Every other line is redolent of the grave. Obsessive reflections of mortality proliferate, but Juliet's are, if anything, more toxic than his, evincing a bizarre preoccupation with his annihilation. Granted there is a feud between the two families, and this particular purlieu is a perilous place to woo. It is also undeniable that Juliet has fallen heels over head in love with a member of a hated kinship group. Yet these facts fail to account for her chronic reversion to death, a psychic undertow which more than once takes the form of a wish to put an end to her own suitor.

JULIET

Tis almost morning. I would have thee gone--
And yet no farther than a wanton's bird,
That lets it hop a little from his hand,
Like a poor prisoner in his twisted gyves,
And with a silk thread plucks it back again,
So loving-jealous of his liberty.

ROMEO

I would I were your bird.

JULIET

Sweet, so would I.
Yet I should kill thee with much cherishing.
(II, i, 221-229)

"Kill thee"? Here's a curious model of affection, a sadistic teasing of a helpless pet which contemplates extinguishing its life. If this be "radical innocence," it is a mutant variety. Later the same trope is echoed by the Nurse, who in planning the conjugal assignation says, "I must another way, to fetch a ladder, by which your love must climb a bird's nest soon when it is dark." Sad bird to labor thus for such a cruel fate! Ladder climbing is dangerous business, and a weak prop to support so weighty an enterprise. Notice, too, that Juliet pictures herself in the role of a "wanton," a term by which she distances herself from staid notions of seemliness. One might object that her only meaning is that if she detains Romeo, or keeps bringing him to her father's house for trysts, he will be detected and slain. But that isn't what she says, and her strange fascination with Romeo's mortality is suspect and disturbing. Or, consider what she later tells her mother:

> Indeed, I never shall be satisfied
> With Romeo till I behold him, dead . . .
> (III, v, 93-94)

To be sure, the audience understands the ironical aspect of these words, but there it is again, the same gratuitous theme. And as the iterations pile up a pattern is formed that affects our reception of her character.

Now arrives *la pièce de résistance*. We are in Juliet's boudoir, overhearing a young bride's poignant musings. Romeo has slain Juliet's cousin Tybalt and been banished by Prince Escalus, but of these recent (or simultaneous) events she knows nothing. They are now husband and wife, thanks to the good offices of that incompetent meddler and rogue pharmacist, Friar Laurence. Romeo will soon ascend the aery to consummate their nuptials. This is how our radically innocent one expresses her anticipation:

> Gallop apace, you fiery-footed steeds,
> Towards Phoebus' lodging. Such a waggoner
> As Phaeton would whip you to the west
> And bring in cloudy night immediately.
> Spread thy close curtain, love-performing night,
> That runaways' eyes may wink, and Romeo
> Leap to these arms untalked of and unseen.
> Lovers can see to do their amorous rites
> By their own beauties; or, if love be blind,
> It best agrees with night. Come, civil night,
> Thou sober-suited matron all in black,
> And learn me how to lose a winning match
> Played for a pair of stainless maidenhoods.

Hood my unmanned blood, bating in my cheeks,
With thy black mantle till strange love grown bold
Think true love acted simple modesty.
Come night, come Romeo; come, thou day in night,
For thou wilt lie upon the wings of night
Whiter than new snow on a raven's back.
Come, gentle night; come, loving, black-browed night,
Give me my Romeo, and when I [he] shall die
Take him and cut him out in little stars,
And he will make the face of heaven so fine
That all the world will be in love with night
And pay no worship to the garish sun.
O, I have bought the mansion of a love
But not possessed it, and though I am sold,
Not yet enjoyed. So tedious is this day
As is the night before some festival
To an impatient child that hath new robes
And may not wear them.
(III, ii, 1-31)

Note that in this necrophilic fantasy Romeo enters not as a Satyr Rampant or Priapus, but as something more resembling "a patient etherized upon a table." The text leading up to and following this monologue establishes him as a Prince of Darkness whose apotheosis this speech is. Night, customarily a vessel of malevolence, death and all things to be feared, is personified as an agent of some utility and value, yet it retains an ominous ambience. It envelops the spirits of the dead and malicious potencies. In formal terms, these lines adumbrate Juliet's experience of horror and dread in the family crypt near the play's conclusion. While there is a tendency to portray this soliloquy as merely an impatient young wife's exuberant wish that her honeymoon commence, it becomes apparent, does it not, that there is more going on here than drumming of maidenly fingers?

Recall that their first dialogue at Capulet's feast reflected the couple's sense of the venal aspect of their eruptive desire. Now the gloom of night serves to screen from prying eyes the "amorous rites" of love. Night does not absolve sin, but merely obscures it. Narcissistic lovers need no "garish" daylight to see what they are doing; their own physical comeliness provides sufficient illumination. Does not this idea trench closely on the view that youthful sensuality is a divinity in its own right, an invention rendering sunshine obsolete? Copulation, which, moments before, was a peccancy needing concealment, has now become a god. Night's curtain will descend to veil maidenly blushes, as "strange love, grown bold" becomes at last benign by dint of sheer repetition. Juliet speaks of modesty while betraying a latent exhibitionism. Exactly what activities does this young lady have in mind? Did innocence ever speak thus?

Not content with this, she would have a new constellation installed above comprised of the remnants of Romeo's body. In some dubious textual versions (*e.g.*, Taylor and Wells) he is to be dismembered even before he dies ["and when I shall die,/ take him and cut him out in little stars . . ."] and tacked up painfully in the firmament. This new constellation, featuring the remains of the young gentleman she has just met, is guaranteed to be sufficiently awe-inspiring to cause the human race to leave off lollygagging at the sun, and fall in with the league of Darkness. But, promotion of dungy mortals to the celestial sphere is notoriously anathema to the gods. Might the plan to install Romeo in the Empyrean realm just possibly lead to a spot of Jovian apprehension? In this very speech, Shakespeare deliberately mentions Phaeton, and it may be useful to read this soliloquy in the context of the Phaeton myth, and its brethren, Prometheus and Bellerophon, for all these heroes pay a price for the aggressive *hubris* which challenges heaven. While the gods relish our attentions, they resent our encroachments.

Later we find Romeo infected by Juliet's death wish for him as by a psychic contagion. "Let me be ta'en," he says, "let me be put to death. I am content, so thou wilt have it so." He then adds, "I have more care to stay than will to go. Come, death, and welcome; Juliet wills it so." (III, V, 17-24)

Though contemporary Shakespeare scholars are chary of suggesting it, the "Gallop apace" soliloquy may strike us as eerily familiar. The following passage may explain why.

> The raven himself is hoarse
> That croaks the fatal entrance of Duncan
> Under my battlements. Come, you spirits
> That tend on mortal thoughts, unsex me here,
> And fill me from the crown to the toe top-full
> Of direst cruelty. Make thick my blood,
> Stop up th' access and passage to remorse,
> That no compunctious visitings of nature

Shake my fell purpose, nor keep peace between
Th' effect and it. Come to my woman's breasts,
And take my milk for gall, you murd'ring ministers,
Wherever in your sightless substances
you wait on nature's mischief. Come, thick night,
And pall thee in the dunnest smoke of hell,
That my keen knife see not the wound it makes,
Nor heaven peep through the blanket of the dark
To cry 'Hold, hold!'
(*Macbeth*, I, v, 38-54)

To screw her courage to the sticking place and achieve the will to murder her royal houseguest, Lady Macbeth hails the denizens of darkness, just as Juliet summons them to present her with the lugubrious and quasi-moribund Romeo. Not to be outdone, in their later colloquy in Act III, sc. ii, in answer to Lady Macbeth's frantic post-homicidal question, "What's to be done?", the Thane of Cawdor himself speaks these words of comfort. (Note the emphasis on Lady Macbeth's "innocence.")

Be innocent of the knowledge, dearest chuck,
Till thou applaud the deed. -- Come, seeling night,
Scarf up the tender eye of pitiful day,
And with thy bloody and invisible hand
Cancel and tear to pieces that great bond
Which keeps me pale. Light thickens, and the crow
Makes wing to th' rooky wood.
Good things of day begin to droop and drowse,
While night's black agents to their preys do rouse.
Thou marvell'st at my words; but hold thee still.
Things bad begun make strong themselves by ill.
So prithee go with me.
(III, ii, 46-57)

Lady Macbeth enjoins the agents of night to aid her in dispatching Duncan. Macbeth, too, entreats the night to let its soft curtain smother what's been done, that there be surcease of guilt. In so doing, they forge a stygian conspiracy which sets in motion the bloody progress leading to their own deaths. Similarly, by bonding with the chthonic agency of night, Juliet ignites the petard that must do away with herself and Romeo. Lady Macbeth and Juliet, umbrageous confederates, both take their own lives. Both talk of weapons. Just as Lady Macbeth dreams of Duncan's doom, so does Juliet salivate over the end of Romeo.

We may reflect at last on the self-destruction of another femme fatale, Cleopatra. Like her and her paramour, the debilitated Antony, Juliet and Romeo retreat from the larger world to create their own hermetically sealed society. Here are their valedictions side by side. First Juliet, discovering the deceased Romeo and the poisoned chalice in his limp hand:

> O, churl! -- drunk all, and left no friendly drop
> To help to help me after? I will kiss thy lips.
> Haply some poison yet doth hang on them,
> To make me die with a restorative.
> Thy lips are warm.
> (V, iii, 165-167)

Now observe Cleopatra, reveling in an exalted mood with her handmaids, Charmian and Iras, and a basket of venomous vipers. Iras heralds the catastrophe.

> Finish, good lady. The bright day is done,
> And we are for the dark.
> (*Antony and Cleopatra*, V, ii, 188-190)

Clad in her regal robes and tiara, the Queen embraces them.

> Come then, and take the last warmth of my lips.
> Farewell, kind Charmian. Iras, long farewell.
> [Iras falls and dies]
> Have I aspic in my lips? Dost fall?
> If thou and nature can so gently part,
> The stroke of death is as a lover's pinch,
> Which hurts and is desired.
> (V, iii, 286-291)

How are these characters alike? Let us count the ways.

1. Both Juliet and Cleopatra celebrate the advent of death;
2. Each has just lost her beloved husband to suicide;
3. Romeo and Cleopatra die by poisonous substance;

4. Antony and Juliet die by blades;
5. Juliet, devotee of the dark, dies in a somber vault;
6. Cleopatra, too, is "for the dark";
7. Juliet in a kiss finds Romeo's lips still warm;
8. Cleopatra gives the "last warmth" of her lips in kissing her maids;
9. Juliet teasingly jests that Romeo has selfishly drained off the poison, leaving no drop on his lips for her;
10. Cleopatra teasingly jests that Iras has been killed by poison on her lips.

Conclusion

Let us answer our question. Is Juliet a tragic hero? Yes. Once the flawed notion of her "innocence" is set aside, and closer attention is paid to her thanatological personality, the way is cleared to consider her as an authentic individual who undoes herself for love, rather than a plastic kewpie doll accidentally trampled. An embryonic or juvenile *hubris* is noted to be present adequate to support the diagnosis of tragic character. There is therefore no need to re-inscribe the tragedy within the circumstantial framework of her interactive life in Verona, with all its well-known patriarchal interference and civil squabbles. That were to reduce genuine tragedy to soap opera. For Juliet, those external and adventitious forces are but the trappings and the suits of woe. But she manifests within precisely that awful self-diremption and self-transcendence which are so often the undoing of Shakespeare's larger-than-life heroes. Reacting to her parents' conventional plans for marriage, she can neither cooperate nor, on account of her age, react with frank opposition, as do Katherine, Bertram, Imogen, *et al.* No sooner is she struck by Eros's arrow, than she returns fire, liberating supernal impulses which gain in intensity and eventually annihilate both lovers.

Evocation of Night is the tragic apogee. Juliet calls out to what is known in popular culture as "the dark side of the force." Like Cassius in *Julius Caesar*, she has bared "[her] bosom to the thunderstone." This is the still point where good and evil shed their mortal wings.

The functional setting of such a play thus can no more be "Verona" than the functional setting of *A Midsummer Night's Dream* is Athens, Greece. Despite a measure of verisimilitude, we are dealing with a symbolic Verona; the real venue of the action is the English memory and imagination. Behind the houses of Montague and Capulet loom the towering mansions of York and Lancaster. Through this rich and verdant psychic landscape courses the collective unconscious of a proud but embattled people. And - in the background - behind and beneath the internecine skirmishes of Rome and its reformers, smolder the ancient and suppressed "pagan" rituals. Shakespeare gives us a sharply etched portrait of these rites in *King Henry VI*, Part II, Act I, sc. iv.

In indigenous Anglo-Saxon culture an invocation of Night was not a game. There she was known as "Niht," while in Norse legends she was called "Nott." As the dialectical goddess of fate, she was referred to as "Wyrd," etymologically related to "weird" (as in the "weird sisters"). Throughout the play, and despite her straitened circumstances, Juliet offers no prayers to the Christian deity. Instead, a primal nature goddess is importuned. Going back in time, we know that the historical antecedent of Niht and Nott was the Egyptian sky-goddess, Nut. One of her daughters was Isis, who later marries her brother, Osiris. When another son of Isis attempts to destroy him, he climbs a ladder to take refuge in the body of Nut, probably as a grouping of stars. Do the following words call anything to mind?

> Because of her role in saving Osiris, Nut was seen as a friend and protector of the dead, who appealed to her as a child appeals to its mother: "O my mother Nut, stretch yourself over me, that I may be placed among the imperishable stars which are in you, and that I may not die. (Lesko; Budge)

Shakespeare's poetic drama in its robust vitality refuses to countenance its protagonist as a helpless victim. Instead, we are given a true tragic hero. Like Joan of Arc, this maid is far and away the most potent character in the whole company. Seeking to suppress her is like stepping on a live cable bearing the energy of the universe. To achieve this effect, a three-dimensional character with destructive as well as amiable features must be brought to life. This is the magical *trompe l'oeil* of Shakespeare's art. Were she as primly immaculate as some suppose, she would be insufferable. It is precisely her mix of vulnerability and uncanny determination which makes her vivid, real, and kin to us. In one stroke, she breaks through the husks of convention and stale mediocrity, to touch a transformational realm so alien to our everyday consciousness that most of us fail to recognize it. A troubled Renaissance girl in crisis reaches out to Wyrd, *abyssus abyssum invocat*, and is heard. It is Juliet the wizard, not poor dithering Romeo, who merits a personal constellation. In the words of Goethe: "*Das Ewig-Weibliche zieht uns hinan.*"

WORKS CITED

Harold Bloom, *Shakespeare and the Invention of the Human*, Penguin-Putnam, 1998

Wallis Budge, *The Egyptian Book of the Dead, the Papyrus of Ani in the British Museum*, the Original 1895 edition. Cosimo Books, 2010

Harold C. Goddard, *The Meaning of Shakespeare*, The University of Chicago Press, 1960

Barbara Lesko, *The Great Goddesses of Egypt*, University of Oklahoma Press, 1999

Ruth Nevo, "Tragic Form in Romeo and Juliet," *Studies in English Literature 1500-1900*, No. 2 (Spring, 1969)

William Shakespeare: The Complete Works, Second edition, G. Taylor and S. Wells, eds., Oxford University Press (Clarendon), 2005

4
Extra Pointz

"I am your shadow, my lord; I'll follow you." - E. Pointz

I. A Person of Interest

We all know him. He's a charter member of the Eastcheap crowd, a rogue's gallery which famously includes Bardolph, Pistol, Nym, Peto, Gadshill, as well as strumpet Doll Tearsheet and Mistress Quickly, the bawd. Picaresque denizens of the London demimonde, they are all glorified extras, sufficient to swell a scene or two, corrupt the prince, and then discreetly vanish. Like them, Pointz is lowborn. In stage productions of *King Henry IV* he is even equipped with an Alfred P. Doolittle accent to make things official. Almost invisible in the glare of Falstaff's brilliance, he is largely overlooked. Is he really what he seems?

The issue is significant because this two-part play (three-part if you add *King Henry the Fifth*) is at once an historical narrative and a work of creative art. We rely on it for much of our *Verstehen* of the English past. Yet many have objected that the sparkling Boar's Head scenes featuring these characters, including Sir John Falstaff, are unchecked fantasy, that the "riotous youth" ascribed to Prince Hal, which these acts display, never occurred. Hal, even in his minority, was a grim soldier, too wrapped up in incessant military exigencies to squander his time in pubs and brothels. We are also told that Sir John Oldcastle (re-dubbed Falstaff) bore no resemblance to the Dionysian giant whose bombast still delights theatre-goers around the world. The result is an uncomfortable schism between the deliverances of historical drama and the theses of historiography. We are asked, in effect, to suspend, temper or qualify our reception of the plays, to set down their comic cavalcade as an insubstantial pageant faded, leaving not a fact behind. But can one actually prove the negative proposition that these scenes are just make-believe? No one has done so. Shakespeare's version of Prince Hal's biography is founded on traditional accounts of what transpired. (Saccio, 58) Those traditions may not be easily scanted. Our version of the Trojan war began as an assemblage of songs and anecdotes which long predated Homer. Cynics, disdainful of mythological content, doubted that Troy had ever existed until Heinrich Schliemann found its remains in 1871. If Hal never had a stormy adolescence and louche lifestyle as thought, why does Shakespeare return to reinforce that impression in *King Henry the Fifth*? There, no less a person than the Archbishop of Canterbury affirms confidentially to another cleric that the Prince's

> addiction was to courses vain,
> His companies unlettered, rude, and shallow,
> His hours filled up with riots, banquets, sports,
> And never noted in him any study,
> Any retirement, any sequestration
> From open haunts and popularity.
> (*King Henry the Fifth*, I, i, 55-60)

And let us not forget that Shakespeare has King Henry V, seated in the very chair of state, utter *ex cathedra* confirmation of his misspent youth.

> And we understand [the Dauphin] well,
> How he comes o'er us with our wilder days,
> Not measuring what use we made of them.
> We never valued this poor seat of England,
> And therefore, living hence, did give ourself
> To barbarous licence -- as 'tis ever common
> That men are merriest when they are *from home*.
> (I, ii, 265-272) (emphasis mine)

There are substantial emotive reasons why Prince Hal *would* have turned to dissolution. He was not happy at home. In *King Henry*

IV Part Two, as he lies dying, in private conference with Prince Hal, Henry the Fourth groans: "God knows, my son, by what bypaths and indirect crook'd ways I met this crown." (IV, iii, 313-315) Those "crook'd ways" by which his father seized supreme power were painfully felt by his heir, including the brutal assassination by Bolingbroke's henchmen of his guardian, King Richard the Second, the monarch who cared for 12-year-old Hal during his father's banishment. As late as the Battle of Agincourt, we can still detect the anguish in Hal's voice:

> O, not today, [Lord], think not upon the fault
> My father made in compassing the crown.
> I Richard's body have interrèd new,
> And on it have bestowed more contrite tears
> Than from it issued forcèd drops of blood.
> Five hundred poor have I in yearly pay,
> Who twice a day their withered hands hold up
> Toward heaven to pardon blood. And I have built
> Two chantries, where the sad and solemn priests
> Sing still for Richard's soul. More will I do,
> Though all that I can do is nothing worth,
> Since that my penitence comes after ill,
> Imploring pardon.
> (*King Henry the Fifth*, IV, i, 290-302)

A tacit corollary of the hypothesis that the Boar's Head scenes do not arise from historical elements seems to be that their characters are invented as well. Yet it is established Prince Hal was definitely associated with Sir John Oldcastle, later to be re-presented by Shakespeare in the more festal "Falstaff." What about Pointz? Suppose he is another with one real foot planted squarely in the past. If so, it becomes a bit more difficult to contend that Hal's antics are nothing more than amusing mirages. When the dream is rooted in reality we should tread with care. Before surrendering to the skeptical undertow, let us pause for a closer look at Monsieur Pointz.

1. What's in a Name?

Unlike his scruffy cohorts, Shakespeare's *Pointz has a full name*: Edward Pointz. He is affectionately dubbed "Ned" or "Yedward" by Prince Hal and Falstaff. Such nominal variations occur only in his case, not with the other bohemians. Further, the surname "Pointz" (spelled variously as Poyntz, Poynts, Poins, Poines, Poynes, etc.) is a celebrated one. As for "Ned," the only persons enjoying this diminutive are all princes: Queen Margaret's son in *King Henry VI*, the son of Clarence in *King Richard III*, and the Black Prince as he's referred to by King Edward III in the play of that name.

2. His Relationship with Prince Hal

While the partnership of Prince Hal and Sir John Falstaff is fraught with palpable tension, Hal's bond with Pointz is more intimate and less problematic, as though they shared a common background. In Part Two of *King Henry IV*, it is even suggested that Pointz contemplates the marriage of Hal to his own sister, (II, ii, 118-120) something Falstaff protests in writing. Marriage of the future King of England to a common thief's sister would be unthinkable.

3. His Wit

While the other Eastcheapers are laughable, Pointz is witty. Doll says so expressly in *Part Two* (II, iv, 241). His attitude towards Falstaff is one of benign mockery; Pointz uses practical jokes to deflate Sir John's vast ego. Wit is refined and subtle humor typical of courtiers and their ladies, not slovenly alehouse patrons like Christopher Sly (featured in the introit to *The Taming of the Shrew*).

4. His Wisdom

Pointz is a thinker with a flair for piquant observation. Remarking on the spectacle of Falstaff dandling Doll on his knee, he queries: "Is it not strange that desire should so many years outlive performance?" *Part Two* (II, iv, 261-262) This rhetorical interrogatory forges a direct link to *Troilus and Cressida* (III,ii, 81-86), arguably the most directly philosophical of all Shakespeare's plays.

The close reader will also notice that Pointz's quips reflect a choice stock of metaphor. When he and Hal crash the party at the Boar's Head Tavern disguised as drawers, they mock not only Falstaff, Doll and Mistress Quickly, but Bardolph (the red nosed toper) as well.

Hal draws sarcastic attention to Falstaff's and Doll's playful intimacies.

PRINCE HARRY

Saturn and Venus this year in conjunction! What says th' al-
manac to that?

Without missing a beat, Pointz follows suit respecting Mistress Quickly
and Bardolph:

POINTZ

And look whether the fiery Trigon his man be not lisping
to his master's old tables, his note-book, his counsel-keeper.
(II, iv, 265-269)

Charles Wisner Barrell commented astutely on this passage back
in 1943. "The fiery Trigon refers to Falstaff's servant Bardolph, who is
making the most of his time with Falstaff's old love, the hostess of the
Boar's Head. In the language of astrology, the Trigon represents the triangle." It is then added, "A 'fiery Trigon' develops when the three upper
planets meet in a fiery signifying rage and contention to follow." (Barrell,
1943, online)

For Pointz as for Prince Hal, the denizens of Eastcheap are a bunch
of lovable clowns whose company always entails a social descent. The
gulf between these aristocratic wits and the Boar's Head crew is height-
ened by Pointz's familiarity with and adroit use of an arcane astrological
term, which alludes at once to a lovers' triangle and also to Bardolph's
ruddy and bulbous proboscis.

5. *His Reputation in Court*

Though Falstaff has the rank of knight, there is no indication that
Pointz is his inferior. And though Prince Hal is heir to the crown, he
tends to treat Pointz fraternally, while retaining his position as *primus
inter pares*. Even when seeming to disdain him, Hal talks with Pointz
as a confidante who is allowed to keep the secrets of the heart, much as
Horatio attends on Prince Hamlet.

When King Henry IV inquires of Prince Hal's whereabouts, Clarence responds that Hal is: *"With Pointz and other his continual followers."* (*Part Two*, IV, iii, 53)

This is a vital clue. It shows that Pointz is a leader, not a mere hanger-on. Clarence might have said, "With *Falstaff* and other his continual followers." But instead he mentions Pointz. Falstaff is one of the "continual followers" of Pointz, not the other way round. Further, King Henry is familiar with him. That's odd. How should the lofty Sovereign, wholly preoccupied with stamping out pesky mutinies, be personally acquainted with anonymous ruffians scambling in the lanes of Eastcheap? Sir John is a better candidate to be recognized on account of his role in the Battle of Shrewsbury. But it is Pointz to whom reference is made. King Henry is quite aware of him. How can this be? If such acquaintance came from an intelligence, Henry would already possess the information about his son's activities which he is seeking.

6. His Voice

There is a textual foundation for the brogues put on by actors who impersonate Bardolph, Peto, Nym, Pistol, Doll and Quickly. A working class enunciation is even imposed occasionally on Falstaff. But the speech of Pointz is linguistically indistinguishable from Hal's own language.

To get a better idea of the difference between Pointz and his colleagues, let's eavesdrop on Hostess Quickly's colorful discourse in *King Henry V* as she laments the death of Falstaff.

> Nay, sure, he's not in hell. He's in Arthur's
> bosom, if ever man went to Arthur's bosom. A made
> a finer end, and went away, an it had been any christom
> child. A parted ev'n just between twelve and one, ev'n
> at the turning o' th' tide -- for after I saw him fumble
> with the sheets, and play with flowers, and smile upon
> his fingers' end, I knew there was but one way. For
> his nose was as sharp as a pen, and a babbled of green
> fields. 'How now, Sir John?' quoth I. 'What, man! Be
> o' good cheer.' So a cried out, 'God, God, God', three
> or four times. Now I, to comfort him, bid him a should
> not think of God; I hoped there was no need to trouble
> himself with any such thoughts yet. So a bade me lay
> more clothes on his feet. I put my hand into the bed
> and felt them, and they were as cold as any stone.
> Then I felt to his knees, and so up'ard and up'ard and
> all was as cold as any stone.

(II, iii, 9-25)

In this unpremeditated eulogy, the Hostess expresses herself in her native patois. Professor Henry Higgins would cringe. The pronoun "he" shrivels to "a" and "Christian" is slurred as "christom." "As if" is crushed to "An." The part of the Hostess should be played by a limey who can utter these lines convincingly. Now let's give an ear to Pointz in Act I of *King Henry the Fourth, Part One*.

> Good morrow, sweet Hal. -- What says
> Monsieur Remorse? What says Sir John, sack-and-
> sugar Jack? How agrees the devil and thee about thy
> soul, that thou soldest him on Good Friday last, for a
> cup of Madeira and a cold capon's leg?
> (I, ii, 111-115)

This is elegant and faultless, including the proper use of "thee" and "thou." French is casually adopted in mocking rue. Unlike the Hostess, who refers to Falstaff politely as "Sir John," Pointz relies on the nickname "Jack." He insinuates that the fat knight is a hopeless boozer, willing to sell his soul to the devil on a religious holy day for a glass of wine. No grammatical errors, coarse conflations or contractions are visible.

Consider the Hostess complaining of Falstaff in *King Henry the Fourth, Part Two*:

> I am undone by his going, I warrant
> you; he's an infinitive thing upon my score. Good
> Master Fang, hold him sure. Good Master Snare, let
> him not scape. A comes continuantly to Pie Corner --
> saving your manhoods -- to buy a saddle, and he is
> indited to dinner to the Lubber's Head in Lombard
> Street, to Master Smooth's the silkman. I pray you,
> since my exion is entered, and my case so openly
> known to the world, let him be brought to his
> answer. A hundred mark is a long one for a poor
> lone woman to bear; and I have borne, and borne, and
> borne, and have been fobbed off, and fobbed off, and
> fobbed off, from this day to that day, that it is a shame
> to be thought on.
> (II, i, 22-35)

Notice amongst the many solecisms in this delightful passage, the lawsuit is not "my action," but, charmingly, "my exion." By contrast, Pointz makes rejoinder to Hal this way:

> How ill it follows, after you have laboured so hard,
> you should talk so idly! Tell me, how many good young
> princes would do so, their fathers being so sick as yours
> is?
> (*King Henry IV, Part Two*, II, ii, 23-26)

The locution "how ill it follows" is the tip off; it is drawn from the study of logic, which treats the principles by which one proposition or act intelligibly yields another. There is no slang. This man has been to school. Pointz's vocabulary and diction mirror Hal's own.

II. Pointz as Shakespearean Character

Having seen what distinguishes him, let us proceed to a brief review of Pointz's function in the two plays. When he is introduced, he proposes that the Gadshill group rob some passing travelers. He aims to persuade Falstaff and Hal to take part in this escapade. Prince Hal, heir apparent to the English crown, is tempted ("Well then, once in my days I'll be a madcap") but unsure. (I, ii, 140-141) After Falstaff's exit, Pointz admits the actual purpose of the plot is to embarrass Falstaff by taking the goods from him and his associate in a second robbery; "and when they have the booty, if you and I do not rob them, cut this head off from my shoulders." (I, ii, 162-164) Two things are noteworthy here. First, Pointz's offer to accept decapitation if the deed is not accomplished is a courtier's stock gesture to a lord. Polonious in *Hamlet, Prince of Denmark*, makes use of the same deferential trope in speaking to King Claudius ("Take this from this"), (II, ii, 159) as does Helicanus in *Pericles, Prince of Tyre* in showing his fidelity to King ("I have ground the axe myself; do you but strike the blow"). (ii, 63) Pointz's communicative style in relation to Hal is that of a sophisticated courtier, not a street thug. He frequently responds to Hal as "my lord." In Act II, sc. v, he takes his leave, saying to Hal: "Good morrow, *good my lord*," employing polished courtier's language. (*Part One*, II, v, 553) Though Taylor and Wells bizarrely assign this line to someone named "Harvey," such use of "lord" implies the temporal peerage of the Prince of Wales, making unknown and presumably unlettered "Harvey" an inapposite choice as interlocutor.[1] Second, the aspect of necessity as an inducement to thievery is nowhere apparent in Pointz. His primary interest is not in financial gain, but in:

> the incomprehensible lies that this same fat rogue will
> tell us when we meet at supper: how thirty, at least,
> he fought with; what wards, what blows, what extremities
> he endured; and in the reproof of this lies the jest.
> (*Part One*, I, ii, 183-187)

Pointz is not engaging in felonies through poverty or desperation, as do Saunder Simpcox and his wife, who practice fraud in *King Henry VI, Part Two* (II, i, 70-155). Rather, he takes purses for sport, looking to Hal for fellowship. How different things are in *King Henry V*, when Hal, as the reigning monarch, approves the execution of his old chum Bardolph for pilfering during the campaign in France! Bardolph steals for "pure need"; Pointz for entertainment. No hanging for him.

Later, as the Battle of Shrewsbury looms over the land, Hal calls out to Pointz for urgent assistance: "Go, Pointz, to horse, to horse: for thou and I have thirty miles to ride yet ere dinner-time." (III, iii, 199-200) None of the other desperadoes of Eastcheap is selected to accompany Hal to the war. Pointz is indeed his lord's "shadow." (Some editions again substitute "Harvey" or "Peto" here, but Pointz is plainly warranted.)

More may be gleaned from *King Henry IV, Part Two*. Hal is grouchy and wants to go on a bender. Pointz serves as whipping boy for the royal wrath, in a passage that deserves scrutiny.

PRINCE HENRY

Doth it not show vilely in me to desire small beer?

POINTZ

---

1 On page 481, Taylor & Wells assert that the names "Russell and Harvey" are restored to the text, names "Shakespeare was probably obliged to alter to Bardolph and Peto." Thus, in *Part One* appear characters Harvey and Russell, not Bardolph and Peto; but in *Part Two* of Taylor and Wells, we find Bardolph and Peto, not Harvey and Russell. This is not satisfactory. Further the rationalization provided by Taylor & Wells was considered and rejected in 1969. (Scoufos, 1969) Certain lines ascribed to "Harvey" belong properly to Pointz.

Why, a prince should not be so loosely studied as to
remember so weak a composition.

PRINCE HENRY

Belike then my appetite was not princely
got; for, by my troth, I do now remember the poor
creature small beer. But, indeed, these humble
considerations make me out of love with my greatness.
What a disgrace is it to me to remember thy name! Or
to know thy face tomorrow! Or to take note how many
pair of silk stockings thou hast -- videlicet these, and
those that were thy peach-coloured ones! Or to bear
the inventory of thy shirts -- as one for superfluity, and
another for use. But that the tennis-court keeper knows
better than I, for it is a low ebb of linen with thee
when thou keepest not racket there . . . .
(II, ii, 9-20)

Pointz is sufficiently vain and affluent to sport silk stockings and
a variety of colorful shirts. Is such attire de rigueur in Eastcheap? For
a hedge-born swain to prance about in silks and satins in Merrie Olde
England would risk prosecution under applicable sumptuary laws. As
for tennis, it is hard to imagine Pistol and Bardolph keeping rackets at
Wimbledon. Are Pointz's Ascot tastes adequately maintained by a career
of impromptu pocket picking?

Hal is plainly embarrassed by Pointz. Yet he isn't troubled by Nym
or Peto. There is something between them then. What? With respect to
his father's illness, Hal has the effrontery to blame Pointz for his own
lack of concern: "keeping such vile company as thou art hath in reason
taken from me all ostentation of sorrow." Pointz's answer tantalizes:

By this light, I am well spoke on; I can hear it
with mine own ears. The worst that they can say of
me is, that *I am a second brother*, and that I am a
proper fellow of my hands; and those two
things I confess I cannot help.
(II, ii, 57-61)

What does it mean when he expostulates that he is "*a second broth-*

er?" Could this be a reference to blood kinship with Hal? To illegitimacy? Suppose one or both his parents were of the nobility. Wouldn't that go a long way toward explaining the anomalies, the patricianly evidences, we have disclosed? Are there other traces? Later in scene iv, we encounter this revealing exclamation from Falstaff at the approach of Hal and Pointz dressed as waiters:

> Ha! a bastard son of the king's? -- And art not thou
> Pointz his brother?
> (II, iv, 286-287)

This is telling. Though Hal and Pointz are disguised as drawers, Falstaff is not deceived. Quickly he seizes the chance to poke fun. Since Hal-the-drawer looks like the Prince but is presented as someone else, Falstaff jokingly infers it must be one of Hal's brethren, most likely illegitimate. On another level, it allows Falstaff to get away with calling Hal a bastard. And at the same time, the idea of bastardy is allowed to cloud Pointz as well. Then, to demand of Pointz, "art thou not Pointz his brother?" entails either that Pointz is (1) Hal's brother, or (2) Hal's brother's brother (which amounts to the same thing), or (3) Hal's illegitimate brother. This clever gambit gains force when it's observed that Pointz and Hal resemble one another, as Falstaff explains to Doll in trying to account for Hal's love of this "brother."

> Because their legs are both of a bigness; and a'
> plays at quoits well, and eats conger and fennel,
> and drinks off candles' ends for flap-dragons, and
> rides the wild mare with the boys, and jumps
> upon joint stools, and swears with a good grace,
> and wears his boots very smooth, like unto the
> sign of the leg, and breeds no bate with telling of
> discreet stories; and such other gambol faculties
> a' has, that show a weak mind and an able body;
> for the which the prince admits him; for the prince
> himself is such another - the weight of a
> hair will turn the scales between their avoirdupois.
> (II, iv, 246-256)

They are nearly twins.

Little else of biographical import emerges after this. In *King Henry*

V, which looks back to Falstaff, Pointz is replaced by poor Nym, who can barely put one word next to another. Only in *The Merry Wives of Windsor* is there a final salute to Pointz:

PAGE

Not by my consent, I promise you. The gentleman
[Master Fenton] is of no having: he kept company
with the wild prince and Pointz; he is of too high a region;
he knows too much.
(*The Merry Wives of Windsor*, III, ii, 65-68)

Nothing in this entails a low condition for Pointz. On the contrary, Fenton's high-born breeding and manner are consistent with having rubbed elbows with Pointz and Prince Hal. Had Pointz betrayed only vulgarity there would be no reason for Page to cite him for this purpose.

III. Lancaster

Could Hal and Pointz then have been actual brothers, as these passages imply? Nothing bars that prospect. Of course, there isn't any non-literary documentation that prior to his accession to the throne Henry the Fifth socialized with a fellow named "Pointz." Yet Shakespeare's dramatization insists on this systematically, bringing it to life in three successive plays. And, as we shall see, there were individuals bearing that surname with whom Hal might have shared a pint or two. Keep in mind Clarence's statement that Hal is with "Pointz and other his continual followers." Certainly, one way Bolingbroke might recognize that name is if Pointz were his biological son, supported by the royal fisc to permit the luxury of fine blouses, silk stockings and a tennis racket at the club. Does the historical record absolutely rule this out? Not really.

Bolingbroke (later King Henry IV) and Mary de Bohun were married when the bride was just twelve years old. Together, they had seven children, including Hal, (later King Henry V), Prince John and Humphrey, Duke of Gloucester. Their first child, "Edward," arrived when Mary was just 14 or 15, in 1383. He was born at Monmouth Castle and supposedly lived only a few days. Had he not perished, this Edward would have been Hal's eldest brother. John of Gaunt, Bolingbroke's father, who arranged the marriage, had planned that it be consummated when Mary attained the age of 16, but the young couple was disobedient. Hence the child "Edward" was an affront to powerful John of Gaunt. The most humane and discreet solution, if the babe survived, would be to send it away, and let on that it had "died." This was standard practice.

Prince Hal was born four years after his brother Edward, in 1387. At the time of the banishment of his father, he was sent at age 12 in 1398 to reside with King Richard the Second. When Hal turned 16, his "late" brother Edward would have been 20.

Grant for discussion that "Edward" thrived and was sent away, as many unacceptable children of eminent families were. Such unacknowledged progeny would ordinarily be placed in another household under a quid pro quo. They would then be given the surname of that foster family. Were there any families available with the name Pointz, Poyntz, Poins or Poines? Indeed. Thus, if "Edward Pointz" the son of Bolingbroke, completed his breeding and education in France at age 20 and returned to England, he would eventually hook up with Prince Hal and form a bond. Stranger things have happened. Is this speculation? You bet. But it rests on a firmer foundation than the gratuitous doctrine that Pointz is an uncouth plebeian whose entire existence is confined to script and stage. Against that complacency, three uncooperative facts stand in the way: (1) the text itself refutes Pointz's "lowborn" status; (2) there was a plethora of Pointzes in England, including some with the name "Edward," and (3) so far as we can determine, every single one of them belonged to the nobility.

IV. The House of Poyntz

During the epoch under consideration, for example, one Robert Poyntz was the Sheriff of Gloucestershire in 1397. He died June 15, 1459. With Katherine FitzNichol he had six children: Sir Nicholas Poyntz, Thomas Poyntz, Maurice Poyntz, Blanche Poyntz, Isabel Poyntz and Joan Poyntz. According to information readily available online via "the-peerage.com," which cites *Burke's Genealogical and Heraldic History of the Landed Gentry*, 18th Edition, this was a large, ancient and honored clan, both in the Hal's era and in Elizabethan England. We can use the peerage website to trace the lineage back to 1066.

Please note that when Shakespeare wrote the history plays featuring a comrade of Hal's having the name "Edward Pointz," he was employing a famous Norman moniker, instantly recognizable to English readers and audiences. These contemporaries would automatically understand that "Ned Pointz" of Eastcheap bore some connection to the

Poyntz dynasty. To suggest that Shakespeare's audiences would regard Pointz as of "lowborn" provenance is to wallow in anachronism.

According to a splendid little website, "Acton Court," in 1535, Nicholas Poyntz, a wealthy and powerful lord, entertained His Majesty King Henry VIII and his second wife, Anne Boleyn, at his estate in Acton Court during the King's summer progress. Poyntz went so far as to have constructed a stunning annex especially for the happy couple. So impressed was the Regent with the hospitality of Nicholas Poyntz that he knighted him for his services during the course of the visit. Today this wing is all that remains of the Poyntz residence. It has been lovingly restored and refurbished, and is open to the public. The direct line of succession of Sir Nicholas Poyntz continued unabated until 1680, according to records of the Acton Court trust.

Importantly, the records of "thepeerage.com" also show that there was an "Edward Poyntz" in England, born in 1575, who died October 5, 1613. These are dates which overlap with the career of William Shakespeare. Edward Poyntz was the son of the aforementioned Sir Nicholas Poyntz, and was educated at Magdalen College, Oxford University. For all we know, this gentleman may have occupied one of the best seats at The Globe in performances of *King Henry the Fourth* to watch his namesake Edward Pointz strut the boards.

V. *Poyntz in Poetry and Painting*

A superlative portrait of "N. Poines, Knight" was done by Hans Holbein the Younger in England around 1530. This icon of privilege and sophistication, after a print by "J. Chamberlain, January 1, 1812," is shown online at "Shakespeare's Sonnets, Thomas Wyatt." Readers may wish to compare this portrait with the handsome painting of Sir Nicholas Poyntz reproduced in the Acton Court website, *supra*. Both figures are in full profile facing left, and exhibit consanguineous features.

There is a long satirical poem, "Mine Own John Poynz," by Thomas Wyatt, a courtier who had been imprisoned in 1536 on charges of having had adulterous relations with Anne Boleyn. It is thought Wyatt was able to witness Boleyn's execution from his window in the Tower of London. It is probably there that he composed "John Poynz." The poem is an elegant condemnation of court life with its insincerities, fawning and corruption. It is believed to be an adaptation of an earlier work by the Italian Luigi Alamanni, *Tenth Satire* (1532). Wyatt's "Mine Own John Poynz" contains references to Venus, Julius Caesar, and Chaucer's

"Knight's Tale," on which Shakespeare's play "The Two Noble Kinsmen" is based. According to the website "Representative Poetry Online," the "John Poynz" addressee of the poem was a courtier and scholarly correspondent of Wyatt. There is also a second poem by Wyatt entitled "Addressed to John Poynz," which can be read in the website "Shakespeare's Sonnets (Poems, Satires)."

N. Poines, Knight by Hans Holbein the Younger

VI. Argument

Professor Peter Saccio, in *Shakespeare's English Kings*, writes:

Obviously Hal, being human, must occasionally have sought diversion. There may be some truth behind the mid-fifteenth-century tales of highway robbery and riotous activity in East-cheap. On the other hand, these stories may be mere gossip . . . Above all, the character of his chief crony in Shakespeare, Falstaff, is a dramatic invention. (Saccio, 61-62)

One difficulty with this argument is that it is outdated. More recent scholarship finds in Falstaff an actual extension of Oldcastle's Puritan-ism, which satirizes the pretensions and theatricality of English mon-archism. Falstaff is not so much an "invention," but rather a Puritan Sir John Oldcastle in festive guise. (Tiffany, 1998)

Another problem with this somewhat equivocal concession is that it is not Falstaff who is the "chief crony" of Hal in the plays. That is dangerously misleading. Marjorie Garber gets it right when she declares that Hal's closest friends "appear to be Poins and Falstaff," in that or-der. (Garber, 329) Instigator of the libertine excesses of Hal according to *Shakespeare* is *Pointz*, not Falstaff. Pointz is never even mentioned in Saccio's book. Poetic liberties taken with the hybrid figure of Oldcastle/Falstaff do not warrant cavalier dismissal of Eastcheap and what it shows us of Hal's personality. Accepting the historicity of Pointz moves us in precisely the opposite direction under Saccio's own reasoning: Pointz stands for the authenticity of Eastcheap.

But if Hal caroused there, it wasn't videotaped to "go viral" on Youtube. It required dramatization by the artist. Such dramatization doesn't show such events didn't happen. *Ceteris paribus*, it shows they did. Based on the foregoing analysis, there is a rebuttable presumption that the vignettes which circulated in England of Hal's wilder days are veridical. Aspects of oral history (and written accounts) were brought together and reinforced dramatically by Shakespeare, who plainly ac-cepted them. Moreover, Prince Hal's meretricious behavior is conceptu-ally congruent with other elements of the narrative, and is a specimen of his alienation. In seeking to understand this significant theatrical character and his historical *doppelgänger*, consulting the totality of the evidence, including the dramatic texts, is mandatory. The theme of Hal's dissolution is one of the most insistent and perdurable in Shakespeare, coursing through three plays, including *King Henry the Fifth*. "Shakespeare nowhere says so . . . ," observes Isaac Asimov,

> but we might fairly argue that Prince Hal has never really reconciled himself to the manner in which his father attained the throne. Secretly, he may consider his father a usurper and himself merely the heir to a usurped crown. He can scarcely value either his own title or his own position, and it is just this, perhaps, that causes him to pass his time in wasting and roistering. Why behave like a Prince of Wales when, in his heart, he doesn't really feel like one? (Asimov, II, 350)

In this respect the notorious "I know you all" speech of Hal (*Part One*, I, ii, 192-215) must be set down as more *ad hoc* rationalization than key to Hal's psyche. Hal's revels are not indulged in deliberately to serve as a foil to enhance his projected greatness. Rather, having immersed himself in a steamy environment to avoid the monstrosities of *realpolitik*, he learns that, despite the hi-jinks, he is now even more alienated than he was back in the House of Lancaster. These clowns are not his people. Sadly, Hal can only exorcise the dybbuk of Bolingbroke by becoming Bolingbroke himself. And it is that tragic nisus that spells the doom of Falstaff . . . *and* Harry Monmouth.

Thus, there is ample motive to account for the princely misbehavior Shakespeare so generously sets forth. We have the mode of misconduct before us. All that is wanting is the mechanism. How could the Prince of Wales have found his way to Eastcheap, of all places? Enter Pointz. Historically the first encounter with Oldcastle occurred in the wars, where he and the Prince became buddies. But Oldcastle was a religious Lollard, not a frequenter of taverns and brothels. Who then might have carried out such a retrograde adventure, if not elder brother and merry prankster, Pointz, leader of the Plantagenet Rat Pack? Obviously, we cannot step into a Time Machine to check. We don't even know with apodictic confidence whether "Ned Pointz" was a factor in the real Prince Hal's life. But literary characters Hal and Pointz certainly give every indication of being conspiratorial rebels without a cause. And it is in that context that it may be helpful to see in Pointz the outcast son of King Henry IV and/or possibly an illegitimate son of the House of Pointz, rather than an irrelevant vagrant. Subtract the background we have exhumed and questions assail us, *e.g.*, What on earth was the

Prince of Wales doing in Eastcheap? Why is Pointz so different from the rest? As far as the drama itself is concerned, the most coherent and commendable view is that, prior to the curtain's rise, Pointz is already an Eastcheap Baedeker. Encountering the troubled Hal, he guides him to the haunts of the usual suspects. Literature is not scientific history, to be sure, but may at times serve as part of the documentary record.

The above findings and argument dovetail nicely with recent scholarship, which finds in the Henriad a sustained effort to employ Falstaff/Oldcastle as a quasi-Puritan hero whose loose morals and sophistic argumentation ultimately cast monarchy in a bad light. Professor Grace Tiffany contends that through the Boar's Head chaos and Falstaff's comic nihilism, these plays achieve "an overall destabilization of monarchy's claims to intrinsic authority," as Falstaff's sophisms come to be symbols of the sophisms of King Henry IV himself. (Tiffany, 1998) Falstaff's role playing of the king thus is a sign of the king's own role playing, a poor substitute for intrinsic right. The inscription of Edward Pointz, a recognizable refugee from the teetering house that Bolingbroke built, within the Falstaffian realm, is consistent with the "exposure of royalty" which modern scholarship identifies. The evidences of illegitimacy in Pointz can be seen to reflect the more fundamental illegitimacies of Bolingbroke's reign - and Hal's.

WORKS CITED

Isaac Asimov, *Asimov's Guide to Shakespeare*, Random House, 1970.

Charles Wisner Barrell, "Who Was John Soothern?" in *The Shakespeare Fellowship*, October, 1943, Online. And see also, Benjamin Wooley, *The Queen's Conjurer*, Part Five, "The Fiery Trigon," Henry Holt and Company, 2001

Burke's Genealogical and Heraldic History of the Landed Gentry, 18th Edition.

Marjorie Garber, *Shakespeare After All*, Anchor Books, 2004.

Peter Saccio, *Shakespeare's English Kings: History, Chronicle and Drama*, Second Edition, Oxford University Press, 2000.

Alice Lyle Scoufos, "A Name Change in Henry IV," *ELH*, Vol. 36, No. 2 (June, 1969), 297-318.

William Shakespeare: The Complete Works, G. Taylor and S. Wells, eds., Clarendon Press, 2005. (Note: Spelling of "Poins" employed by this Taylor & Wells is changed to "Pointz" to conform to the Stratford Town Edition, 1904.)

Grace Tiffany, "Puritanism in Comic History: Exposing Royalty in the Henry Plays," *Shakespeare Studies* (January, 1998).

Online Sources

1. "Acton Court"
2. "Representative Poetry Online"
3. "Shakespeare's Sonnets: Thomas Wyatt"
4. "Shakespeare's Sonnets, Poems, Satires"
5. "thepeerage.com"

5

This Thing of Darkness

. . . the whoreson must be acknowledged. - Gloucester

I. Prospero's Secret

*A*s *The Tempest* is a "romance" and largely fantasy, featuring goddesses, witches, goblins and sprites, there is a tendency to receive it almost as one might a fairy tale. (Collington, 84) That would be to short-circuit critical faculties when they are most needed. To give this problematic text such benefit of the doubt is surely to confer a doubtful benefit. As we deal with issues of growth and maturity, these cannot be responsibly addressed if we allow ourselves to encounter them in the manner of "once upon a time." On the other hand, to give theory free rein, leaping, *e.g.*, to the anachronistic view that *The Tempest* was designed to set off proto-Marxist preoccupation with the exploitation of indigenous populations, may represent its own form of naïveté. Well before we take up sociological speculations or theological allegory, we need to see if the text can make sense as a quotidian narrative. For every tub must stand on its own bottom. Any more recondite approaches are for us premature. We remain with preliminaries, testing the seemingly obvious.

Does Prospero's story add up? That is the threshold question. As the "prince of power" on the island, he conducts the very elements, the seen and the unseen. He can make the sea to rage, convey the gods to ceremony, and can manipulate ordinary mortals as if they crept in his palm. Prospero proffers a modest resume:

> I have bedimmed
> The noontide sun, called forth the mutinous winds,
> And 'twixt the green sea and the azured vault
> Set roaring war -- to the dread rattling thunder
> Have I given fire, and rifted Jove's stout oak
> With his own bolt; the strong-based promontory
> Have I made shake, and by the spurs plucked up
> The pine and cedar; graves at my command
> Have waked their sleepers, oped, and let 'em forth
> By my so potent art.
> (V, i, 40-50)

When did he acquire those redoubtable skills? Evidently he was already a seasoned *Übermensch* when he first trekked the island. That's how he was able to free Ariel from the cloven pine and seize control of Caliban and his environment. Or did he perhaps become a wizard as he and his infant languished in that "rotten carcass of a butt"? (I, ii, 146) We can safely rule that out. Very well then, at the time of his overthrow and exile from Milan, where he was Duke, he should have already possessed those vast and fabulous potencies employed so liberally in the course of the play. For it was there he pursued his necromantic curriculum, pursued it so assiduously that he had no time for matters of state. We should then confront Prospero with some stubborn questions: (1) How was he, the "prince of power," unable to previse and prevent the plot that toppled him from the throne in Milan? (2) Why was he not able to direct the small craft in which he and Miranda drifted to a more accommodating port of call than a glorified sandbar in the middle of the chartless main? (3) If he raised the dead, it wasn't on a deserted island. It would have been back in Italy. But there, says he, he was helpless and defeated. When did his resurrecting enterprise commence? (4) And perhaps most vexing of all, if omnipotent Prospero can indeed hurl the thunderstone, what curious impotence kept him locked down in a gritty cell for twelve years? Why not waft thence to Milan on the wings of glorious magic? Did he prefer his island hideaway?

Despite these anomalies, Prospero is not embarrassed by his narrative mazes. Somehow this genial charlatan, like the Wizard of Oz, makes believers of everyone, including some of the most astute critics of

English literature. But be it noted: as it is self-evident that the chronicle he would impress on his subjects is fundamentally flawed and incoherent, we have no choice but to regard him as a dissembler. This does not mean the totality of his avowals is false; rather, his discourse is essentially problematic. Each word is suspect, to be taken *cum grano salis*. He should be presumed mendacious until proven otherwise.

Three remedial learners inhabit his realm: Miranda, Ariel and Caliban. Each is the victim of dedicated historical refurbishing. It is to them we turn once more.

II. Our Darker Purpose: Miranda

Jan Frans van Dijkhuizen writes:

The Tempest is . . . Prospero's attempt to undo the past by re-staging it. In this respect, Prospero is comparable to Hamlet, Richard II and Lear, who also employ a re-enactment of the past as a means of exerting symbolic power over it.

But any attempt to "re-enact" or "re-stage" which duplicates precisely the same bygone contours accomplishes nothing. We are not speaking here of a pointless and passive echoing. Rather, Prospero's re-stagings are active interventions in his personal narrative, ambitious and creative, and plainly designed to make a difference. As van Dijkhuizen says, this project is nothing less than a wholesale campaign to "undo" the past. This is a man with a positive itch to revise what has been.

On the occasion of the storm he foments, Prospero undertakes to instruct his only child, fourteen-year-old Miranda, on the most basic aspects of her life. The lesson is long overdue.

PROSPERO

Obey, and be attentive. Canst thou remember
A time before we came unto this cell?
I do not think thou canst, for then thou wast not
Out three years old.

MIRANDA
Certainly, sir, I can.

PROSPERO

By what? By any other house or person?
Of anything the image tell me that
Hath kept with thy remembrance.

MIRANDA

'Tis far off,
And rather like a dream than an assurance
That my remembrance warrants. Had I not
Four or five women once that tended me?

PROSPERO

Thou hadst, and more, Miranda. But how is it
That this lives in thy mind? What seest thou else
In the dark backward and abysm of time?
If thou rememb'rest aught ere thou cam'st here,
How thou cam'st here thou mayst.

MIRANDA

But that I do not.
(I, ii, 38-53 following *The Yale Shakespeare* in the use of "abysm"
not "abyss")

Prospero has waited over a decade to share with his only child essential information about who she is. But his lecture seems to take the form of an interrogation about which he, the questioner, betrays palpable anxiety. Repeatedly he challenges her and insists huffily on her attention, odd when the topic itself could not be more compelling. She is to "obey" him. The dialogue resonates not as a normal conversation, but rather as the intonations of a clumsy hypnotist. (See, Garber, 858) If information needs to be imparted, why not give it forthrightly and graciously, instead of cross examining the youngster who has been kept in ignorance? It is no small fact that Miranda dredges up a recollection of serving women, not her mother, whom Prospero mentions *en passant*. The omission is shocking. What has become of her - and Miranda's memory of her? We don't know, but the general impression is one of erasure. Does Prospero practice telepathic reprogramming? Can he press "delete" on brain cells? It cannot be disproven. In fact, their entire relationship is a complete mystery to us. Has he personally guided her through puberty - or just tossed her a book on the subject? Note that memory of time past is characterized by him as an exploration of the "dark." Why this particular metaphor? When Duke Orsino in *Twelfth Night* inquires about Cesario's sister's history, the memory is described as "a blank," not as darkness. (II, iv, 110) Prospero's early use of the conceit of darkness is reminiscent of King Lear's "darker purpose." Further, this use of "dark" looks forward to the characterization of Caliban as "this thing of darkness." What makes everything so dark?

PROSPERO

Twelve year since, Miranda, twelve year since,
Thy father was the Duke of Milan, and
A prince of power --

MIRANDA

Sir, are not you my father?
(I, ii, 53-55)

Good question. He might have said "I was Duke of Milan" but refers to himself slyly in the third person, prompting her question. And already in this strained fantasy the specter of paternity surfaces. It is raised with respect to Miranda, and will recur *a fortiori* in the case of Caliban. Unlike everyday life, where DNA tests rule, in a work of poetic fiction, a zone of inference, not actuality, paternity is insusceptible of proof. Yet the inquiry remains fraught with meaning. That Miranda can even ask this question is a sign of how little she has received to support the notion of Prospero's fatherhood. What has passed between them? Their conversation is formal to the point of being stilted. He sounds strangely peevish. At one point, he even addresses her as "wench." (I,ii, 139). His response inspires no confidence.

Thy mother was a piece of virtue, and
She said thou wast my daughter; and thy father
Was the Duke of Milan, and his only heir
And princess no worse issued.

(I, ii, 56-59)

This is the only mention of Miranda's mother in the play. She is not named or identified as his wife. Her rank in the society of Milan is not explained, nor are her parents identified. None of this is deemed sufficiently important for the former Duke of Milan to convey to his sole "heir and princess." Rather than affirm in affectionate terms his fatherhood, Prospero cites the authority of this shadowy maternal figure, doing so in such an abstract way that the question is sidestepped. Miranda is asked to accept (1) that Prospero's account of what her mother said is accurate, (2) that at the time of her birth, Prospero was married to this woman; (3) that Prospero had some sure way of telling that her mother was "virtuous"; and (4) that if indeed Miranda's mother affirmed that Prospero was the father, she was in a position to know that.

There follows the dubious tale of super-puissant Prospero's deposition by his brother. His manifest aim here is to persuade Miranda that he, the magnificent Duke of Milan, steeped in the mysterious lore of the universe, and capable of choreographing the sun, moon and stars, was somehow the dupe of coarse mortal stratagems. That is blatant chicanery. But there is another, overriding purpose behind Prospero's cant. That is to reinforce his image in her eyes as the caring and compassionate father who has always nurtured and protected her. What doubts compel such rationalization?

At the conclusion of this indoctrination, Prospero dons his magic garment to cause Miranda to swoon into sleep.

Here cease more questions.
Thou art inclined to sleep; 'tis a good dullness,
And give it way. I know thou canst not choose.
(I, ii, 185-187)

The linguistic mood is imperative. Ask no more. He renders her insensible so as to have private chat with Ariel. Is this the first time he has made her doze? There is no reason to think so. Clearly he can do it at will. But why? We have before us an almighty sorcerer possessed of an alluring young daughter. At any moment he can snap his fingers and render her unconscious. Even her waking hours have a dreamy, trancelike quality. What other transformations he might conjure up may well be wondered at.

Twelve years ago, despite his cosmic powers, these two were involuntary shipmates at sea. Was Miranda caused to slumber in their boat? If so, what happened then? Sadly, we must hearken to these words of Shakespeare:

> Great King,
> Few love to hear the sins they love to act.
> 'Twould braid yourself too near for me to tell it.
> Who has a book of all that monarchs do,
> He's more secure to keep it shut than shown.
> (*Pericles, Prince of Tyre*, i, 135-138)

Prince Pericles refers obliquely to the seduction by King Antiochus of his own daughter, with whom this King is still having a torrid romance when Pericles comes to seek her hand in marriage. Though the royal incest is papered over, it is recognized in the riddle which Pericles has no trouble resolving. There is no wife/mother at the court of Antiochus to interrupt the taboo intimacies of father and daughter. Pericles later becomes the father of Marina, and is chronically haunted by his original flirtations with incest at the court of Antiochus. A late play in the canon, *Pericles* brings out the incest theme which had always percolated beneath the surface.

According to Prospero, for a dozen years he and Miranda have occupied a desolate scrap of earth, uninhabited except for Ariel and the slave Caliban. There is no spouse to gratify his needs, or meddle in his activities. No busybody social workers can come snooping around. Though we are not shown a graphic picture of pedophilia, none is needed. The plain fact is that (1) opportunity and (2) motive dovetail perfectly with (3) uneasy *ad hoc* rationalizations. The signifiers line up with all the subtlety of a neon arrow. The stentorian, overbearing manner exhibited by our unwitting defendant is easily seen through. Van Dijkhuizen comments:

> Caliban may be said to embody Prospero's own repressed desires for Miranda. She is the only woman on the island and Prospero imagines his relationship with her as a kind of symbiosis. These desires are externalized and inscribed on Caliban. (van Dijkhuizen)

The question remains, however, to what extent were these desires effectively "repressed."

Think about King Lear. Again - no wife, no mother. He and Cordelia dwell privately, in what we may assume is an ample and secluded residence. We aren't told how long those circumstances have obtained. When Cordelia declines to deliver a contrived filial panegyric, why does Lear's temper flare so violently? If we attend to his demeanor before the daughters' speeches, we notice he's already in a bad mood. It has nothing to do with Cordelia's uncooperativeness. What are his first words?

Meantime we shall express our darker purpose.
(I, i, 36)

Why "darker"? Here we have the same trope employed in Prospero's "dark backward and abysm of time." What is lurking there in the dark? Partitioning a royal estate to provide legacies for one's grown children is not a melancholy moment, but cause for celebration. Stepping down presumably frees an aged king from cares of state, to relish the blessings of a merry retirement. What, then, is at the root of Lear's poorly concealed apprehension as he proceeds to dictate his will? He is worried about Cordelia, a ticking time bomb on account of his own illicit advances. A proclamation of love from her, no matter how perfunctory, would be accepted as a token of forgiveness for oppressions still festering in conjoined hearts. Will he be absolved? With Cordelia's "Nothing," his worst fears are realized. There is no other plausible explanation for his disproportionate anger and the rash disinheritance of his most beloved daughter.

Prospero labors with a parallel predicament. He too is stepping down, as ruler of the island. No longer will he be a magus, just a man. By implication, he, too, has tampered with his daughter. He must therefore harness all his paternal hocus-pocus to win her trust, to be for her a true father, if not a deity. Still, he nearly sinks under waves of guilt. And at the very end, when all are smiling, the assassination is foiled, Miranda has a fine husband, Caliban gets his island back, and Ariel is freed, Prospero is a bundle of misery. Sneaking sheepishly from behind the curtain, he asks us, the all-seeing audience, for . . . forgiveness.

> Let me not,
> Since I have my dukedom got,
> And pardoned the deceiver, dwell
> In this bare island by your spell;
> But release me from my bands

With the help of your good hands.
Gentle breath of yours my sails
Must fill, or else my project fails,
Which was to please. Now I want
Spirits to enforce, art to enchant;
And *my ending is despair*
Unless I be relieved by prayer,
Which pierces so, *that it assaults*
Mercy itself, and frees all faults.
As you from crimes would pardoned be,
Let your indulgence set me free.
(Epilogue, 5-20)

This is not Puck or Rosalind popping up to coyly beg for buoy-ant applause. These words are too personal, too keenly felt, too grave for that. What are these "faults," these "crimes"? Prospero knows that though he may have deceived the other characters, he has not deceived us. As he enslaved Ariel and Caliban, he has all along been himself a captive in the island of our imagination. And there he is held fast. As he craves the love of Miranda and her forgiveness, so he importunes ours. He feels our awareness of his abuse of power, and as the curtain descends we are weighing him in the scales of justice. I have drowned my book, he hastens to point out, and broken my staff. My magic gar-ment I cast off. From now on, he promises, I'll be just a human being, and a "no greater father." (I, ii, 21) Can we embrace him? While the jury deliberates, let's summon Ariel.

III. *Sweet Sprite, Bear the Burden*

Prospero's rhetorical position is that on account of having released Ariel from the cloven pine where he was lodged by Sycorax, he is not morally obliged to wholly discharge him until certain tasks are com-pleted. His on-going control of Ariel recapitulates and extends the rule of Sycorax. Prospero accuses Ariel of forgetting what favors he has done him. When Ariel denies ingratitude and inability to remember, Pros-pero flings at this most faithful of aides the charge of being a liar and a "malignant thing." (I, ii, 258) Then, in another brainwashing resem-bling the one forced on Miranda, Prospero gives a didactic recitation of what transpired on the occasion of his disembarkation. Yet there is never evidence that Ariel has overlooked anything or harbors resentment or ingratitude.

For Prospero, Sycorax was a "damned witch," appropriately banished from Argier for "manifold mischiefs," none of which are catalogued.

PROSPERO

This blue-eyed hag was hither brought with child,
And here was left by th' sailors. Thou, my slave,
As thou report'st thyself, was then her servant;
And for thou wast a spirit too delicate
To act her earthy and abhorred commands,
Refusing her grand hests, she did confine thee
By help of her more potent ministers,
And in her most unmitigable rage,
Into a cloven pine; within which rift
Imprisoned thou didst painfully remain
A dozen years, within which space she died
And left thee there, where thou didst vent thy groans
As fast as mill-wheels strike. Then was this island--
Save for the son that she did litter here,
A freckled whelp, hag-born -- not honoured with
A human shape.

ARIEL

Yes, Caliban her son.

PROSPERO

Dull thing, I say so; he, that Caliban
Whom now I keep in service. Thou best know'st
What torment I did find thee in. Thy groans
Did make the wolves howl, and penetrate the breasts
Of ever-angry bears; it was a torment
To lay upon the damned, which Sycorax
Could not again undo. It was mine art,
When I arrived and heard thee, that made gape
The pine and let thee out.

ARIEL

I thank thee, master.
(I, ii, 270-294)

This didactic rendition of days gone by seems to succeed in inculcating again indebtedness to Prospero, but stops well short of credibility. Angels have no need of bombast and braggadocio. Prospero avers that he possessed magic powers when he arrived. Why didn't he use them in Milan? His magic is suggested to be greater than that of Sycorax on the grounds that she was not able to release Ariel from his trap. Yet how does Prospero come by that information? When she landed on those shores, says Prospero, Sycorax was pregnant. Can this be fairly corroborated? If learned from Ariel, he need not lecture him about it. The father of the foetus is not identified. Apparently it is thought that this hypothesized unborn child became "the son that she did litter here," that is, Caliban. Yet premise and deduction hang in thin air, unsupported.

Prospero's powers seem closely associated with the wearing of a certain gown or cape, which he refers to as "my art." In first speaking with Miranda, he removes it, but puts it on to make her sleep. Without it he cannot influence events around him. How did he acquire it?

At this point it is best to clear the air with a supposititious exercise to achieve a more balanced and orderly accounting. Accept these premises for sake of argument:

1. The reason Prospero could be captured and evicted from Milan is because at that point he possessed no supernatural powers;

2. Prospero and Sycorax are both in the same business: sorcery;

3. Both are exiles in a strange land;

4. He is male, she is female;

5. While in Argier, Sycorax has already engaged in acts of witchcraft which have miscarried and caused her to be sent away;

6. The source of Prospero's strength is the magic garment;

7. That garment was not his on the day he first waded ashore.

Prospero alleges that when he arrived the only person on the island was Caliban (with Ariel caught in the tree). Sycorax had died. Had she? There are no witnesses for this claim. We can be certain of one thing: he wants to avoid any insinuation that he and Sycorax had a liaison. That is unthinkable. Yet he can glibly tell us that she had blue eyes and an "earthy" personality! What could that mean? Further, he exhibits a hearty dislike of her, as though he had been exposed to bitter interactions. We usually don't hate those we've only heard of. Moreover, Prospero says that in order to stuff poor Ariel in the cloven pine, she required help from "her more potent ministers." (I, ii, 276) Who are they? How is he aware of them? Are they her friends -- or his?

Prospero has told a tangled tale. While we cannot know what "really" transpired in a narrative which is fiction, we are bound by instinct and reason to reach a coherent reading. Here's one possibility.

The Tempest Reconstituted

When Prospero comes to the island, he meets a sorceress by the name of Sycorax. They have much in common, and enter into a complex and 'tempestuous' affair. It is she who is the more advanced wizard, for she can "control the moon, make flows and ebbs." (V, i, 273) Prospero has only book learning. As she is the more expert necromancer, she becomes his mentor. He progresses in her tutelage, and she rewards him with a magic garment, which confers on him paranormal capacities. She then becomes pregnant by him. But when the child is born, it is misshapen, badly deformed. This is Caliban, Prospero's natural son. As for Miranda, Caliban's older sister, who beheld these things, half graspingly, her memories are dangerous. Prospero has been improperly intimate with her. Using his newly-acquired art, he reduces her mind to a tabula rasa, the Renaissance equivalent of a prefrontal lobotomy. Ever after, he must be on his guard lest these troubling traces should sprout up and re-enter her consciousness. He continues to take advantage of her physically, but must now prepare her for married life, an awkward transition.

Early on, he tries to accept Caliban, but it's no use. He is repulsed. Sycorax and Prospero quarrel and go their separate ways, as did Titania and her Oberon, who squared off over the changeling boy. Needing assistance, he liberates Ariel from the cloven pine. Soon thereafter, Sycorax dies, and Prospero raises Caliban, allowing him to gradually lose track of what has happened. Sessions of acceptable recall are imposed. The "monster" loves his master, and soon has no ken of a paternal relationship. Gladly he shows Prospero the treasures of the isle. When he grows older, he begins to suffer resentment. He misses his mother and realizes that the island is his patrimony, misappropriated by a bizarre and manipulative magician. Caliban sexually assaults Miranda, already made vulnerable by the misbehavior of her father. At this point, Prospero demonizes Caliban, projecting all evil impulses on him. He becomes a master rather than the father he was.

As for Ariel, having been trapped in the pine so long, he is precluded from apprehending anything, and depends for information, for the most part, on what Prospero vociferously repeats.

If one objects, and insists that Sycorax died before Prospero's footprints were seen on those yellow sands, his word is taken as gospel, creating an intractable mass of lacunae and contradictions. But we have stipulated that Prospero enjoys no presumption of credibility. Only by firmly opposing him in letter and in spirit can we fathom the course of events implied by the play, appreciate his duplicity, and work our own way out of the moral labyrinth.

Now, come on, we'll visit Caliban, the slave, who never yields a kind answer.

IV. Ban, Ban, Caliban

In a book deserving greater attention, James Howe writes that Prospero's "acknowledgement" of Caliban may be "an acknowledgement of some darkness that he sees within himself," and that there is "perhaps some figural kinship with Caliban." (Howe, 196)

Jan Frans van Dijkuizen goes a tad further:

"Acknowledge" has a positive ring and may mean "to accept," or "to recognize." Caliban, initially branded as the ultimate, evil Other, is acknowledged as part of Prospero's own identity. (van Dijkuizen)

Van Dijkuizen goes so far as to suggest some "equation of Prospero and Caliban."

Marjorie Garber of Harvard writes:

> What Prospero acknowledges in this phrase is not only re-
> sponsibility (Caliban is my slave), but also identity (Caliban,
> the "thing of darkness," is part of me). (Garber, 853)

But what part? These writers all land in roughly the same place, but miss connecting the dots. Think of Trinculo's reference to Caliban as "such a natural." It is well known that "natural" in Elizabethan parlance meant an illegitimate child. (Oxford English Dictionary, "natural," defi-nition 15a) Significantly, in both civil and common law jurisdictions, to "acknowledge" an illegitimate child means to officially accept that child as one's offspring and as deserving of support and some portion of the estate. Thus, when Prospero says of this "bastard one," "This thing of darkness *I acknowledge mine*," he *ipso facto* admits he is the father of this illegitimate son, tacitly rendering to him the island which was actually the son's successive right from Sycorax. As there was no marriage to her, Prospero never had title thereto.

Prospero has stayed in the island to work through his neuroses in fear and trembling. His alchemy is dedicated to his own spiritual ob-structions and breaches. When he has finally overcome his demons, and can accept himself and others, there is no more need of magic, and he can return home a better individual.

The last act of Prospero signals the onset of his humanity. For the majority of the time, he has been in denial of Caliban, the wholly other. His inclination has been not only to rid himself of Caliban (to "ban Cali-ban"), but to eradicate all memory of his offspring's origins by traducing the past. While he does not state in so many words that he is the "father," the legal acknowledgement is binding and would be comprehended by his guests; someday Caliban may come to understand. Prospero has tak-en a stride forward in recovering himself through the partial recovery of his son. And as Gloucester says of Edmund, "the whoreson must be acknowledged."

V. Coda

It is on this fragile bond which knits Prospero to Caliban that we should focus our heuristic energies. It remains the very omphalos of this drama. Even at the level of popular culture, Hollywood, in *Forbid-den Planet*, the science fiction reprise of Shakespeare's play, makes of the "Krell Monster," nemesis of Dr. Morpheus, nothing but a projection of the mad scientist's own mind. The Freudian filmmakers got it right: the seemingly external monster is an expression of the reclusive genius (a madman whose temper flares at the prospect that he might lose his lovely daughter to some handsome American astronaut). But just as it is terribly difficult for Dr. Morpheus to come to the realization of his own complicity in the destruction raging around him, so it is difficult for modern criticism to gaze directly into the heart and mind of Prospero. Such is our collective Oedipus Complex: ever conspiring with the hero to seek an outward villain on whom to pin the blame. Hence the perpetual temptation to "ban Caliban." (II, ii, 183) He is still a fall guy allowed to "take the rap" for Prospero. Unable to sustain tragedy, we fall back into lazy and comforting melodrama.

Now, if Caliban is best understood as the son of Prospero, we should be able to point to some family resemblance. The predictive capacity of the theory would count in its favor. If we think back to cases of disputed paternity in Shakespeare, we find that he sometimes demonstrates resemblances between older and younger male figures suggestive of filiation. For example, he goes out of his way to offer striking resemblances between Julius Caesar and Marcus Brutus. And if you search carefully, you may find that Prince Hamlet is rather surprisingly like Uncle Claudius. But that is a story for another day.

With respect to Prospero and Caliban, it is language which unites them. Speech is given him by Prospero, from which Caliban acquires much more than a talent for cursing. (I, ii, 366) Though he is styled a savage and a brute, he is one of *The Tempest*'s most gifted orators. He has never stood in privy chamber, yet his verbal delivery is at times perfect courtier:

> Good my lord, give me thy favour still.
> Be patient, for the prize I'll bring thee to
> Shall hoodwink this mischance. Therefore speak softly.
> All's hushed as midnight yet.
> (IV, i, 204-207)

Of this utterance, Belarius might fittingly exclaim: "How hard it is to hide the sparks of nature!" (*Cymbeline*, III, iii, 79) A character even today disdained as a crude primitive somehow manages to express himself with enviable grace and eloquence. But wait, there's more. There are two veritable poets in this play, persons whose verbal mastery is so fine that it transmutes the base metal of words into golden art. These are Prospero ... and Caliban. Hear the elder first:

> Be cheerful, sir.
> Our revels now are ended. These our actors,
> As I foretold you, were all spirits, and
> Are melted into air, into thin air;
> And like the baseless fabric of this vision,
> The cloud-capped towers, the gorgeous palaces,
> The solemn temples, the great globe itself,
> Yea, all which it inherit, shall dissolve;
> And, like this insubstantial pageant faded,
> Leave not a rack behind. We are such stuff
> As dreams are made on, and our little life
> Is rounded with a sleep.
> (IV, i, 147-158)

Now Prospero, Jr.:

> Be not afeared. The isle is full of noises,
> Sounds, and sweet airs, that give delight and hurt not.
> Sometimes a thousand twangling instruments
> Will hum about mine ears, and sometimes voices
> That if I then had waked after long sleep
> Will make me sleep again; and then in dreaming
> The clouds methought would open and show riches
> Ready to drop upon me, that when I waked
> I cried to dream again.
> (III, ii, 138-146)

Schopenhauer says that it is the ability to conceive the world as a dream which is the *sine qua non* of the philosophical personality. This rare perspective is reflected in these enchanting soliloquies, arguably the most prominent passages in *The Tempest*. Both start with words of re-assurance ("Be cheerful, sir"; "Be not afeard"). Both sing of sleep and dream. Behind Prospero's professed dismantling of his dramatic apparatus lies a metaphysical message bearing on the nature of things: all is maya, passing illusion, and no harm to anyone. Caliban's consanguineous lesson is the same: many are the sounds erupting about us, which, though frightening, seem to emanate from a place of wonder. Sleeping, we have beatific visions, and awakening, we long to return from whence we came, still trailing our clouds of glory. At the core of these twin verses pulses that subtle *Sehnsucht* which, in F.H. Bradley's words, "draws the mind to wander aimlessly and to love it knows not what." (Bradley, 3) Like Prospero, Caliban is shackled to unworthy impulses, but in him there is no inveterate malice, only the bruised sensibility of an orphan. Even in the buzzing, blooming confusion of his oppression, in the midst of pinches and prodding which seem to come from all sides, there subsists something good. For Prospero, the challenge is within. The tempest he raises is a reflection of the storm in his soul, battered by foul deeds which no measure of regret can cancel. Finally, human once more, he begs our forgiveness - something most have previously granted him. If our portrayal is credited, however, he may have to add a healthy dose of patience to his penitence. Like Michelangelo's image of God and Adam on the vault of the Sistine Chapel, Prospero and Caliban reach out to one another - and almost touch. Whether, taking the full measure of the man, we ourselves are touched, is an open question.

WORKS CITED

F. H. Bradley, *Appearance and Reality*, Oxford University Press, Second Edition, 1897.

Philip David Collington, "O, Word of Fear: Imaginary Cuckoldry in Shakespeare's Plays," Doctoral dissertation, unpub., University of Toronto, 1998.

Wilbur L. Cross and Tucker Brooke, *The Yale Shakespeare: Complete Works*, Barnes and Noble, 1993

Marjorie Garber, *Shakespeare After All*, Anchor Books, 2004.

James Howe, *A Buddhist's Shakespeare: Affirming Self-Deconstructions*, Associated University Presses, 1994.

Oxford English Dictionary. (Thanks to Mr. Peter Kirwan for this reference).

William Shakespeare: The Collected Works, G. Taylor & S. Wells, eds., Clarendon, 2005.

Online Sources

Jan Frans van Dijkhuizen, "Prospero's Dream: The Tempest and the Court Masque Inverted," online text, no date.

6
Crown of Horns: Male Self-Betrayal in Shakespeare

I. The Self-Cuckolding of a Trojan

*T*here are passages in Shakespeare that seem to leap off the page as though composed yesterday. A good example occurs in *Troilus and Cressida*, where two lovers, about to launch an affair, cynically take the measure of male potency in relation to female desire. The results are revealing, and not particularly reassuring.

TROILUS:

O let my lady apprehend no fear. In all Cupid's
pageant there is presented no monster.

CRESSIDA

Nor nothing monstrous neither?

TROILUS

Nothing but our undertakings, when we vow to
weep seas, live in fire, eat rocks, tame tigers, thinking
it harder for our mistress to devise imposition enough
than for us to undergo any difficulty imposed. This is

the monstruosity in love, lady -- that the will is infinite
and the execution confined; that the desire is boundless
and the act a slave to limit.

CRESSIDA

They say all lovers swear more performance
than they are able, and yet reserve an ability that
they never perform: vowing more than the perfection
of ten, and discharging less than the tenth part of one.
They that have the voice of lions and the act of hares,
are they not monsters?

TROILUS

Are there such? Such are not we. Praise us as
we are tasted; allow us as we prove. Our head shall
go bare till merit crown it.
(III, ii, 71-89)

Though the dialogue is courtly, it may be questioned whether what
is wanted are quaint verses or melodies strummed on a lute. This is a
conversation about sex. That is how Troilus interprets Cressida's reference to the "dregs" of love, that is, as the wreck of intimate relations. (III,
ii, 65) What he proffers is not so much fidelity as athleticism *du cham-
bre.* Love here is not absolute, but aleatory, like a horse race. Implicit is
the realization that what ultimately may crown the lover's head is a pair
of cuckold's horns. For all his boldness in confronting the specter of
erotic failure, Troilus's wooing groans under a mountain of doubt. As he
raises the subject, (III, ii, 78-80) it is of his own devising. Yet it turns out
that the apprehension is not his alone, but belongs equally to skeptical
Cressida, who seems to be chiefly interested in sensuous gratification.
Despite his ardent oratory, Troilus's major premise ("desire is boundless
and the act slave to limit") defeats his own purposes. Woman, by the
very nature of things, is at risk of disappointment.

How different it stood with Juliet and her Romeo when they were
situated thus!

JULIET

My bounty is as boundless as the sea,
My love as deep. The more I give to thee
The more I have, for both are infinite.
(II, i, 175-177)

In contrast with the ersatz idealism of Troilus, the true chord of chivalric love is struck in *The Heptameron* of Marguerite de Navarre, Book Ten, in which Amador makes the following declaration to the Lady Florida:

All the efforts that I made five years ago were for no other end than to live my whole life by you. But you must believe me, my Lady, when I tell you that I am not one of those men who would exploit this advantage. I desire no favour, nor pleasure, from you, except what is in accordance with the dictates of virtue. I know that I cannot marry you. And even if I could, I should not seek to do so, for your love is given to another, and it is he whom I long to see your husband. Nor is my love a base love. I am not one of those men who hope that if they serve their lady long enough they will be rewarded with her dishonour. Such intentions could not be further from my heart, for I would rather see you dead, than have to admit that my own gratification had sullied your virtue, had, in a word, made you less worthy to be loved. I ask but one thing in recompense of my devotion and my service. I ask only that you might be my true and faithful Lady, so true, so faithful, that you will never cast me from your good grace, that you will allow me to continue in my present estate, and that you will place your trust in me above all others. And if your honour, or any cause close to your heart, should demand that a noble gentleman lay down his life, then mine I will gladly lay down for your sake. On this you may depend. Know, too, that whatever deeds of mine may be counted noble, good or brave, these deeds will be performed for love of you alone.
(de Navarre, 130-131)

From this chaste and lofty summit of medieval romance, we topple headlong in *Troilus and Cressida* into the pit of modern narcissism, where the other is viewed calculatingly as a utility. In the exchange economy of Cressida and her Troilus, virility can never match limitless concupiscence, as exemplified by the character of Venus in Shakespeare's masterpiece, *Venus and Adonis*. Later, when their fate is known, a coarse reality emerges:

> We two, that with so many thousand sighs
> Did buy each other, must poorly sell ourselves
> With the rude brevity and discharge of one.
> (IV, v, 38-40)

Troilus is the debtor, Cressida the demanding creditor holding no security. By contrast, for Juliet it is not desire which is infinite, but the superabundance of love, which receives each investment of male zeal and makes return with interest.

Poised on the brink of modernity, Shakespeare spans these two worlds. Amidst the "dregs" of love, he can still gaze back at all that has been lost. Despite his own principle that desire is boundless and "the act" a slave to limit, Troilus's libido prompts exaggerated promises. Aware that his lady is not a starry-eyed adolescent, but a sophisticated beauty mindful of her own prerogatives, he presses forward with a determination quixotic at best. And that is to embrace the prospect of defeat. It is therefore legitimate to wonder if this isn't what he craves. There's not much to guess at, as Cressida makes the hopelessness of his enterprise painfully plain.

TROILUS

What offends you, lady?

CRESSIDA

Sir, mine own company.

TROILUS

You cannot shun yourself.

CRESSIDA

Let me go and try.
I have a kind of self resides with you --
But an unkind self, that itself will leave
To be another's fool. Where is my wit?
I would be gone. I speak I know not what.
(III, ii, 140-147)

Is this the kind of woman with whom emotional bonds should be established? Her message is: "Yes, I fancy you, but there is an aspect of myself that longs to frolic with others." After that slap in the face does one turn the other cheek? What would we say of such a suitor except that he is hoisting himself with his own petard?

There follows another dubious pledge which rings so hollow that it could qualify as the Magna Carta of infidelity.

CRESSIDA

If I be false, or swerve a hair from truth,
When time is old and hath forgot itself,
When water drops have worn the stones of Troy
And blind oblivion swallowed cities up,
And mighty states characterless are grated
To dusty nothing, yet let memory
From false to false among false maids in love
Upbraid my falsehood. When they've said, 'as false
As air, as water, wind or sandy earth,
As fox to lamb, or wolf to heifer's calf,
Pard to the hind, or stepdame to her son',
Yea, let them say, to stick the heart of falsehood,
'As false as Cressid'.
(III, ii, 180-192)

Does not our lady protest a tad too much? Let us paraphrase: Better break things off now, for not only will I abandon you for another, that abandonment will be an epochal one for which I'll live in infamy; my name will be synonymous with perfidy.

The scene now shifts to a grim morning after. With weary steps, the embattled pair staggers into the harsh glare of day. Cressida would run off immediately, but her paramour tries to detain her. She seems unwilling. "Night hath been too brief," she complains. (IV, i, 13) The ambiguity is tantalizing. Does she mean, So great has been my delight that I must hate the dawn because it deprives me of an encore? Or, In that short night I found myself frustrated and miserable? It is obvious something is seriously wrong.

CRESSIDA

You men will never tarry.
O foolish Cressid! I might have still held off,
And then you would have tarried.
(IV, ii, 17-19)

Cressid is wretched because by yielding to Troilus's importunities she has lost a woman's tactical advantage. He has his conquest. She is still unfulfilled, just as she feared. Performance evidently did not "hit it." (See, *Love's Labour's Lost*, IV, i, 124-148) Troilus might have "tarried," deferred his gratification to ensure hers, but he has not. How else explain her sour mood? She has given herself away without the joys of which she dreamed. Even so, in a sense the edge still is hers, for poor Troilus is "in love," while she is disillusioned and quite ready to give free rein to her "unkind" self.

When Uncle Pandarus arrives to check on their progress, she tells him to go hang himself, a delicate indication of her distress. (IV, ii, 28) Rather than submit to his further matchmaking, Cressida invites Troilus back to the bedroom, not for fruitless embraces, but simply to avoid Pandarus. "You smile and mock me, as if I meant naughtily." (IV, ii, 40) She doesn't. It's over, but Troilus doesn't get it.

Now comes the dreadful news that she is to be given to the invading Greeks in a swap for Trojan prisoner, Antenor. Troilus panics, but is powerless to prevent the arrangement. And it is at this moment that the deeper wellsprings of his psyche begin to show through the fraying cloak of character. On the flimsy pretext of encouraging her to remain "faithful" in the enemy camp, he casts cold water on her ability to do so by positively singing the praises of the alluring and seductive Hellenes.

TROILUS

I will corrupt the Grecian sentinels

To give thee nightly visitation.
But yet, be true.

CRESSIDA

O heavens! 'Be true' again!

TROILUS

Hear why I speak it, love.
The Grecian youths are full of quality,
Their loving well composed, with gifts of nature flowing,
And swelling o'er with arts and exercise.
How novelty may move, and parts with person,
Alas, a kind of godly jealousy --
Which I beseech you call a virtuous sin --
Makes me afeard.

CRESSIDA

O heavens, you love me not!
(IV, v, 72-82)

The plea for fidelity has quite the opposite effect of the one seemingly intended. Cressida views it as an expression of distrust and therefore lack of love. And if loyalty is the objective, it can hardly be elicited through broadcasts on behalf of one's rivals. Such upside-down advocacy, particularly in the context of the ruin of the incipient affair, can only have one practical impact: to foreground the very attractions it professes to belittle. Troilus strains every nerve to bring himself to catastrophe. As we study this making of a cuckold, it's hard to avoid concluding that Shakespeare is illustrating the active and efficacious part we play in our own discomfiture. As there is an "unkind" self in her that would wander, so correlatively there is a self-destructive part of Troilus that craves humiliation. Not content with making the case for the Greeks, Troilus must put himself down directly.

I cannot sing,
Nor heel the high lavolt, nor sweeten talk,
Nor play at subtle games - fair virtues all,

To which the Grecians are most prompt and pregnant.
But I can tell that in each grace of these
There lurks a still and dumb-discoursive devil
That tempts most cunningly. But be not tempted.
(IV, v, 86-92)

Comes the exchange of captives. Cressida waltzes amongst the Greek tents and permits herself to be passed around for introductory kisses like a bottle of beer in boot camp. Her flirtation with Diomedes is unabashed, and soon enough there is an assignation. Meanwhile, Troilus, led by Ulysses, takes up a position of espial. Cressida's coquettish dalliance is agonizing to perceive. Ulysses urges Troilus to retreat, but he is caught in voyeuristic paralysis. Why does he stay, unless he sees what he wants to see? There is a cloying element here that seems to quicken him. If cuckoldry be the food of love, we almost hear him exult, play on! At last, overwhelmed by the gut-wrenching apparition, logic falters. If Cressid's vows are genuine, this cannot be her. And yet it is. Ergo: "This is and is not Cressid," (V, ii, 149) Perhaps more straightforward would be a recognition by the distraught fellow of his own part in cuckolding. But Troilus (like Marcus Brutus) cannot see himself. As emperor of duplicity, he sets the crown of horns on his own head. This self-deception is not lost on wily Ulysses, who questions Troilus's inflexible devotion to the "good" Cressid and his simultaneous condemnation of the "bad."

May worthy Troilus e'en be half attached
With that which here his passion doth express?
(V, ii, 164-165)

The hint is not taken. Troilus cannot perceive that there is something inside himself that is favorably disposed to this turn of events. To grasp that he has engineered his fate from beginning to end is beyond his ken. Instead, madness beckons.

II. The Self-Betrayal of Collatine

Let us attend to a portion of the Argument in *The Rape of Lucrece*.

[D]uring which seige the principal men of the army one
evening at the tent of Sextus Tarquinius, the king's son,
in their discourses after supper commended the virtues

of his own wife, among whom Collatinus extolled the
incomparable chastity of his wife, Lucretia. In that
pleasant humour they all posted to Rome, and,
intending by their secret and sudden arrival to make
trial of that which everyone had before avouched,
only Collatinus finds his wife (though it were late in
the night) spinning amongst her maids. The other ladies
were all found dancing, and revelling, or in several
disports. Whereupon the noblemen yielded Collatinus
the victory and his wife the fame. At that time
Sextus Tarquinus, being inflamed with Lucrece's beauty,
yet smothering his passions for the present, departed
with the rest back to camp, from whence he shortly
withdrew himself and was, according to his estate,
royally entertained and lodged by Lucrece at Collatium.
(*R/L*, Argument)

As everyone knows, Sextus Tarquinus will later attack Lucrece in
an horrific rape. And the question is: Absent the boasts of Collatine,
would anything untoward have happened? Assuredly not. Not satisfied
with his wife's dazzling appearance and unimpeachable virtue, Collatine
feels compelled to make of her a figure of public familiarity, an icon of
tempting allure.

> Haply that name of chaste unhapp'ly set
> This bateless edge on his keen appetite,
> When Collatine unwisely did not let
> To praise the clear unmatchèd red and white
> Which triumphed in that sky of his delight,
> > Where mortal stars as bright as heaven's beauties
> > With pure aspects did him peculiar duties.

> For he the night before in Tarquin's tent
> Unlocked the treasure of his happy state,
> What priceless wealth the heavens had him lent
> In the possession of a beauteous mate,
> Reck'ning his fortune at such high-proud rate
> > That kings might be espousèd to more fame,
> > But king nor peer to such a peerless dame.

108

O happiness enjoyed but of a few,
And, if possessed, as soon decayed and done
As is the morning's silver melting dew
Against the golden splendor of the sun,
As expired date cancelled ere well begun!
    Honour and beauty in the owner's arms
    Are weakly fortressed from a world of harms.

Beauty itself doth of itself persuade
The eyes of men without an orator.
What needeth then apology be made
To set forth that which is so singular?
Or why is Collatine the publisher
    Of that rich jewel he should keep unknown
    From thievish ears, because it is his own?
(*R/L*, 7-35, emphasis added)

Just as Troilus errs in touting the sensual qualities of the Greek youths to the smoldering Cressida, so we find Collatine crowing about his wife's virtue and loveliness to potential competitors in the emulous company. Notice that the tale of Lucrece might have been related without the thrasonical preface. There could have been ravishment without prior report, as there is of Lavinia in *Titus Andronicus*. Shakespeare underscores the question for us: why indeed does Collatine act as the toxic publisher of his wife's embellishments? A provisional answer occurs when Ulysses in *Troilus and Cressida* observes on the basis of a proto-Hegelian treatise he peruses that:

    man, how dearly ever parted,
How much in having, or without or in,
Cannot make boast to have that which he hath,
Nor feels not what he owes, but by reflection --
As when his virtues, shining upon others,
Heat them, and they retort that heat again,
To the first givers.
(III, iii, 90-97)

Achilles rejoins:

For speculation turns not to itself

Till it hath travelled and is mirrored there
Where it may see itself.
(III, iii, 104-106)

To which Ulysses chimes back:

[No] man is lord of anything,
Though in and of him there be much consisting,
Till he communicate his parts to others.
(III, iii, 109-112)

If we could exhume the mind of Collatine, we might well discover a masculine anxiety that cannot rest until its jewel is reflected in the eyes of cohorts. The difficulty is that while the urge to re-possess one's glory through the approbation of others may be fairly natural, Collatine's audience happens to be an assembly of professional fighters in the midst of war, all starved for female company. The bold display of her grace and beauty in this setting places Lucrece in peril. At some level Collatine must sense he is arousing the envy of his armed colleagues. When her virtues are ratified, and he wins the contest of spousal superiority, a palpable jealousy and resentment will ensue. In fact, the king's son is among the hearers when Collatine tells them that no king on earth is favored with such felicity as he enjoys with Lucrece. (*R/L*, 20-21) This is surely tempting fate. Over his victory in the spousal competition falls the shadow of his own cuckolding, a specter which he himself has conjured. How, then, avoid the inference that Collatine fashions his own undoing? We will return to this issue in more detail in Chapter 11, "Wanton Modesty."

III. *Posthumous Leonatus Consents to His Own Cuckolding*

The pattern of self-procured cuckoldry we have beheld in *Troilus and Cressida* and *The Rape of Lucrece* finds a strong reprise in *Cymbeline*. Posthumous, the foster son of the King of England, has married the monarch's daughter against the royal wish that she be given to his wife's son, the repulsive Cloten. Exiled from Britain, the universally acclaimed Posthumous travels to Rome for a period of enforced accommodation. There, at the house of Philario, he proclaims the splendors of his wife, Imogen. Among the guests is the lascivious and unscrupulous Iachimo, who champions the ladies of Italy as outshining any English beauty. As the temper of Posthumous flares, issue is quickly joined in the form of a wager. Any attempt to seduce his wife will be repulsed by her, says he, and so confident is he that he is willing to put her to the test. With husband's permission, Iachimo will go to England to make assault on the integrity of Imogen. If he prevails, Posthumous will sacrifice a ring, his parting remembrance from her. If he is rejected, Iachimo loses ten thousand ducats. Never occurring to him is that he is freely putting Imogen, his honor and their marriage all in harm's way. She may even be ravished, as was Lucrece. Of course, Imogen resolutely refuses to hear anything of intimacies with the serpentine Iachimo, but through stealth and guile, he is able to purloin the bracelet which Posthumous gave her on his departure, and also to observe her asleep in bed, noting facets of her body and bedchamber. On return to Rome, with the bracelet and confidential data, Iachimo persuades Posthumous of Imogen's disloyalty. In anguished soliloquy, he wallows in grief, neurotically condemning all women and rehearsing the concocted conquest in his mind.

> Is there no way for men to be, but women
> Must be half-workers? We are bastards all,
> And that venerable man which I
> Did call my father was I know not where
> When I was stamped. Some coiner with his tools
> Made me a counterfeit; yet my mother seemed
> The Dian of that time: so doth my wife
> The nonpareil of this. O vengeance, vengeance!
> Me of my lawful pleasure she restrained,
> And prayed me oft forbearance; did it with
> A pudency so rosy the sweet view on't
> Might well have warmed old Saturn; that I thought her
> As chaste as unsunned snow. O all the devils!
> This yellow [Iachimo] in an hour -- was't not? --
> Or less -- at first? Perchance he spoke not, but
> Like a full-acorned boar, a German one,
> Cried 'O'! and mounted; found no opposition
> But what he looked for should oppose, and she
> Should from encounter guard. Could I find out
> The woman's part in me -- for there's no motion
> That tends to vice in man but I affirm

It is the woman's part; be it lying, note it,
The woman's; flattering, hers; deceiving, hers;
Lust and rank thoughts, hers, hers; revenges, hers;
Ambitions, covetings, change of prides, disdain,
Nice longing, slanders, mutability,
All faults that man can name, nay, that hell knows,
Why, hers in part or all, but rather all --
For even to vice
They are not constant . . . .
(II, v, 1-30)

Posthumous sends word to his servant Pisanio to slay the strum-pet, forgetting that he attributes revenge to the female temperament, not the male. Implicit in his actions are precisely the terrible consequences he erroneously believes have been imposed on him. He has played the pandar and the victim. And in that respect, no matter his outward con-fidence, he has sought to bring about his own conjugal doom. Had he been truly confident in his wife's virtue, why bother to put it to proof? Prof. Philip D. Collington suggests that "Posthumous enters the wager because it is a way to elicit information from peers who cannot see past his obscure origins or status as a foreigner." (Collington, 178) But no man deliberately exposes his wife to ruin to "elicit information." Posthu-mous is an insecure husband, not an inquisitive sociologist. The perilous experiment shows that his possession of Imogen and trust in her were always troubled. Hence, to proceed with the wager is already to embrace his default. In fact, it is not too much to say that it is his own cuckolding he loves, not Imogen. For none of his words of affection comes close to matching the energy and intensity of this startling soliloquy, which car-ries within itself the fantasized particulars of his wife's adultery. Here lies his true center of spiritual gravity, as spectator rather than autonomous possessor. With Troilus, he is on the outside, looking in.

Anyone in the position of Posthumous Leonatus would be uneasy. He has been traumatized by a series of crippling losses, and is married to a quasi-sibling whose sexual unresponsiveness he has rationalized as virtue. Like Troilus, he worries privately that the lady has not returned his physical attentions on account of his own inadequacy. Great anxi-ety would be the expected result. On account of marrying her, he finds himself banished. Nursing his wounds in Rome, he defends her honor in quarrel, while burning with resentment over her physical remoteness. The willingness to permit the seduction by Iachimo, then, reflects (a) his deep-seated anger over her frigidity, (b) his own feared impotence, and (c) his hatred of the tyrannical Cymbeline. Away, then, and let her be seduced by Iachimo! By allowing himself to be cuckolded in this way, he will already have his revenge on Imogen for withholding herself from him, and on her father for his rage and unkind banishment.

IV. Notes Toward a Theory of Shakespearean Cuckoldry

Limitations of space preclude anything like a full treatment of Shakespearean cuckoldry. All that can be offered here are a few points for further exploration. Although there was without doubt a traditional revulsion over cuckoldry during the Renaissance, it is unrealistic in a culture so variegated and complex to expect complete unanimity. To presume that an unqualified and uniform cuckold-phobia prevailed throughout fifteenth and sixteenth century Christendom is to draw a caricature. And to ignore the possibility of a countervailing psychic undertow in the direction of cuckoldry is naïve. If today cuckoldry is a popular and affirmative sexual fetish (and it is), that is a significant piece of evidence which cannot be brushed aside. The roots of that fetish can be traced to medieval Europe. The Troubadour culture that descended from Catharism, for example, commonly saw the mating of rich old men to young ladies, the latter then being romanced by minstrels and courtly knights. As many of the husbands were in their dotage and either impotent or infirm, their apprehension of cuckoldry would naturally differ from that of a man in his prime. Wittols abounded. The feelings aroused in those venerable gentlemen over their young brides' trysts would certainly be worth inspecting. Could there have been a frisson or two of lascivious relish? This ambivalent Troubadour culture, with its simultaneous accents on virginity and indulgence, was still an influence in the time of Shakespeare.

In traditional Catholic theology the consent of the husband does not cancel the wife's sin of adultery. Rather, the willing husband sins also. We take note of this not to enter religious controversy, but as evidence that sufficient numbers of husbands acquiesced in spousal transgressions to come to the attention of ecclesiastical legislators. (*New Advent Catholic Encyclopedia*: "Adultery")

Medieval rigidity (as reflected in Dante) soon gave way to the metropolitan garrulousness of Giovanni Boccaccio, whose *The Decameron* is required reading for any student of the Renaissance. For example, in the tale of Pietro di Vinciolo (Boccaccio, Fifth Day, Tenth Story, 432-440), a husband with homosexual predilections is wedded to a lusty young female. When his wife's adulterous affair comes to light, he has nary a protest, as he manages to make his own arrangements with his wife's lover. Thus, being a cuckold commended itself to Renaissance husbands for a variety of reasons. Chaucer in *The Miller's Tale* makes light of it.

In Shakespeare the self-betrayal of husbands and suitors is not directly stated, but emerges perforce on any close reading. Furthermore, this theme is consistent with the self-responsibility of tragic heroes, a major Shakespearean leitmotif. Our behavior, he shows, is often destructive of our own personhood. Think of *Twelfth Night*. Isn't Duke Orsino a would-be self-cuckold? Rather than woo Lady Olivia face-to-face, he sends handsome young gents to plead in his place. Why? First, because in his heart he knows he cannot succeed, and second, if he should somehow win her, he fears that as an older male he would not be able to make her sufficiently happy for a marriage to endure. On the other hand, to be personally rebuffed is more than his fragile ego can tolerate. And so it happens that he sends as his ambassador the alluring and well-spoken Cesario (Viola in disguise). Why assume the risk that Olivia might fall for this artful go-between? Might he not "speak for himself"? That's what happens, after all, and when brother Sebastian takes Cesario's place, Orsino is *de facto* cuckolded. Will anyone contend that the unhappy Duke does not set the crown of horns on his own head? Orsino can console himself with the self-deceiving excuse that, after all, he was done in by the middleman, when in fact this was a foreseeable consequence of his employment of such an agent. The inevitable loss thus is reformulated to seem less of an insult, and more the product of a third party's insidious interference. In psychoanalytic jargon, that mental relief is the "secondary gain" of the neurotic behavior.

The conventional view is that cuckoldry arrives unbidden, as though it were a flowerpot landing on one's head. But the hand of the apparent victim always lurks in the background. A shallow reading would blame the machinations of Iago for leading Othello to believe that Desdemona has cuckolded him with Cassio, but ultimately Othello himself knows better. He is not a mere dupe. Well he recognizes that he has thrown away a pearl "richer than all his tribe." (V, ii, 357) By dawdling in his bizarre investigation, rather than promptly and rationally confronting Desdemona with his suspicions, he permits the imaginary affair to linger and balloon in his imagination, bringing the whole roof down on himself and his devoted spouse.

The action of the play takes place during a deferred honeymoon.

Marital consumption is supposedly put off on account of martial exigencies, when in truth there is no reason to temporize other than Othello's own insecurities. And it can hardly be overlooked that he is a minority person in a deeply prejudicial society, an aging black male tethered to a highborn Caucasian lass. From old cock to cuckold is but *ein Augenblick*. Othello has internalized not only the noble Venetian code of honor, but equally its pernicious racism. His acclaimed valor thus conceals an inevitable sense of guilt for having transgressed a significant social barrier. Beneath the gilded breastplate lies an inexpugnable disgust with the animal qualities ("an old black ram is tupping your white ewe") imputed to him by Venetian society. His sense of gnawing guilt can be expiated only by a form of self-punishment in which he permits his precious wife to be sullied. The betrayal he imagines affords a moral salve for his own sense of alienation and racial transgression. The murder of Desdemona confirms his moral deformity, an impression which has plainly haunted him throughout his expatriated career. The trickery of Iago succeeds, then, only because it exploits Othello's own vulnerability and emotional need to play the cuckold.

The vital significance of *The Winter's Tale* lies in the absence of any external villain. The jealousy of Leontes seemingly springs from nowhere at all. No sinister Iago or Iachimo leads him to such a baseless conclusion. Whence springeth, then, those lethal suspicions? Shakespeare's point is that jealousy (cuckoldry's nagging premonition) is a built-in defect in the masculine soul which can implode at any moment. Leontes himself is the problem. To his ravings we must hearken with a philosophic ear.

> Is whispering nothing?
> Is leaning cheek to cheek? is meeting noses?
> Kissing with inside lip? stopping the career of
> Laughter with a sigh? - a note infallible
> Of breaking honesty; - horsing foot on foot?
> Skulking in corners? wishing clocks more swift?
> Hours, minutes? noon, midnight? and all eyes
> Blind with the pin-and-web, but theirs, theirs only,
> That would unseen be wicked? is this nothing?
> Why, then the world and all that's in't is nothing;
> The covering sky is nothing; Bohemia is nothing;
> My wife is nothing; nor nothing have these nothings,
> If this be nothing.

(I, ii, 287-298)

These irrationalities reflect not an emotional hiccup, but a veritable existential upheaval. Notice that one item is missing from the paranoid inventory: Leontes himself. He is the principal Nothingness which reduces all else, including his marriage and friendship with Polixenes, to ciphers. He is his own blind spot, a black hole in inner space sucking in the universe. It is at this precise point that psychology must give way to ontology. In the classic metaphysical treatise, *Being and Nothingness*, Jean-Paul Sartre suggested epigrammatically that "nothingness lies coiled in the heart of being, like a worm." We are all infected. On phenomenological analysis, then, it is the very consciousness of Leontes himself, his vacant *dasein*, which renders his marriage alien and disposable. Leontes bursts out in hallucinatory rage over the supposed infidelity of Polixenes and Hermione because his inner need to be subjected to cuckoldry is embraced by his deeper self, and this in turn ignites an explosive reaction with his conscious horror of betrayal as he beholds "the spider." (II, i, 47)

But is it really possible that a man could crave the humiliation of cuckoldry? Professor Collington denies it, observing that cuckoldry is Renaissance man's "worst nightmare." If that were true, how explain the wittol? Renaissance man's worst nightmare was the iron maiden, not the unfaithful wife. And if, as remarked above, cuckoldry is indeed a contemporary sexual fetish, construing it narrowly as a medieval anathema seems a bit doctrinaire. Prof. Collington notes that most instances of cuckoldry in Shakespeare are imaginary, but strangely rejects out of hand the possibility that these imaginings directly express the intrinsic needs of masculine identity.

Interestingly, recent historical research shows that much of the stigma of cuckoldry seemed to disappear in seventeenth century England, which was rather exhibiting signs of its allure. (See, Turner, Chapter on Cuckoldry)

As for Shakespeare, he is at pains to demonstrate our profound ambivalence when it comes to cuckoldry:

> He that ears my land spares my team,
> and gives me leave to in the crop; if I be his
> cuckold, he's my drudge: he that comforts my
> wife is the cherisher of my flesh and blood; he
> that cherishes my flesh and blood loves my flesh
> and blood; he that loves my flesh and blood is my

friend: ergo, he that kisses my wife is my friend.
If men could be contented to be what they are,
there were no fear in marriage . . . .
(*All's Well That Ends Well*, I, iii, 44-51)

Behind this wry sorites lies rueful truth. The crux of the matter is that Leontes, like most men, is not content to be what he is, and as such, loses what appears to be his.

As Shakespeare is a philosophical poet, psychological expositions of his characters must inevitably fall short. The unsuitability of empirical psychology for hermeneutical tasks was demonstrated in 1943 by Sartre, a monumentally important writer not much mentioned these days in literary criticism. (Sartre, 712-734) For Sartre, cuckoldry is a species of masochism, which is in turn a form of "vertigo." Before human existence, Sartre says, an abyss of dreadful possibility may open up at any moment, a psychic sinkhole before which a surrender of ourselves can never be ruled out. The dizziness we experience perched on a precipice is not, according to Sartre, a function of our fear of falling, but of our apprehension that there is literally nothing to prevent us from hurling ourselves into space.

Interestingly, Shakespeare has his own Renaissance term for vertigo: the "giddy," to which he refers no less than thirty times. "*For man is a giddy thing,*" he opines through the mask of Benedick, "*and this is my conclusion.*" (*Much Ado About Nothing*, V, iii, 106-107) That means, *e.g.*, at the end of the day, Claudio's suspicions about the faithlessness of Hero say more about Claudio's lack of substance than they do about the machinations of Don John.

Let us close, then, with a brief but intriguing medley of giddiness. According to Rosalind (as Ganymede) in *As You Like It*, when married to Orlando:

I will be more jealous of thee than a Barbary cock-pigeon over his hen, more clamorous than a parrot against rain, more new-fangled than an ape, more *giddy in my desires than a monkey.*
(IV, i, 140-145)

"Tut, man," counsels Benvolio, in *Romeo and Juliet*:

one fire burns out another's burning,

One pain is lessened by another's anguish.
Turn giddy, and be holp by backward turning.
One desperate grief cures with another's languish.
Take thou some new infection to thy eye,
And the rank poison of the old will die.
(I, ii, 46-50)

And in *Twelfth Night*, poor Duke Orsino counsels Cesario that in comparison with ladies, men are more fickle because:

however we do praise ourselves,
Our fancies are more *giddy and unfirm*,
More longing, wavering, sooner lost and worn,
Than women's are.
(II, iv, 31-34)

Immediately before meeting with Cressida, Troilus confesses:

I am giddy. Expectation whirls me round.
Th' imaginary relish is so sweet
That it enchants my sense. What will it be
When that the wat'ry palates taste indeed
Love's thrice-repurèd nectar? Death, I fear me,
Swooning destruction, or some joy too fine,
Too subtle-potent, tuned too sharp in sweetness
For the capacity of my ruder powers.
I fear it much, and I do fear besides
That I shall lose distinction in my joys,
As doth a battle when they charge on heaps
The enemy flying.
(III, ii, 16-27)

As he awaits his first encounter with Cressida, the chasm of failure gapes at his feet, inducing in him a rush of confusion. What if he, the love-sick swain, is ill-equipped for the venture? Is that not monstrous? While he would roar like a lion, his actual call sounds more like that of "any sucking dove," (*A Midsummer Night's Dream*, I, ii, 77) for well he knows that "the act is slave to limit." How to deal with the angst? Seek refuge in the bosom of cuckoldry.

"Masochism," writes Sartre, "is characterized as a species of vertigo, vertigo not before a precipice of rock and earth but before the abyss of the Other's subjectivity." (Sartre, 492) All masochism, including cuckoldry, is for Sartre the "love of failure."

> It is sufficient . . . to point out that masochism is a perpetual effort to annihilate the subject's subjectivity by causing it to be assimilated by the Other; this effort is accompanied by the exhausting and delicious consciousness of failure so that finally it is the failure itself which the subject ultimately seeks as his principal goal. (Sartre, 493)

In cuckoldry we give our wife to the Other. This is not accident or error, but a stratagem.

> To give is to enjoy possessively the object which one gives; it is a destructive-appropriate contact. But at the same time the gift casts a spell over the recipient; it obliges him to re-create, to maintain in being by a continuous creation this bit of myself which I no longer want, which I have just possessed up to its annihilation, and which finally remains only an image. To give is to enslave. (Sartre, 758)

In strictly philosophical terms, then, cuckoldry is a masochistic ploy in which the male partner seeks to reduce himself to naught in the eyes of the Other, while maintaining himself as the indispensable ground of the satisfaction of the Other. The aim is to be the absolute and indispensable foundation of the Other's infidelity, the existence whose nothingness discloses the meaning and satisfaction of the disloyal act, without which it would be reduced to mere copulation.

Shakespeare is a metaphysical poet with an incomparably rich but unsparing insight into the human condition. Giddy in ourselves, we turn our oases into desert. We spin straw out of gold. Tomorrow makes hash of today. "O thoughts of men accursed! Past, and to come, seems best; things present worst." (*King Henry IV, Part II*, I, iii, 107-108) Upon this despondent bank and shoal of time, our most precious treasures morph into "gilded loam or painted clay." If, indeed, men could be contented to be as they are, all would end well in marriage. But the winter of our discontent has no summer. Sartre's dictum is that consciousness is riven with contradictions. It is not what it is. "I am not what I am," whispers Viola in our ear. (*Twelfth Night*, III, i, 139) Having "one foot in sea, and one on shore," we are contented least. If we do not stray ourselves, we must suppose that our beloved has. Thus the voice of the cuckoo echoes in our land: "O word of fear, unpleasing to the married ear." (*Love's Labour's Lost*, V, ii, 895-896) Losing touch with the substance of life, Troilus and his spiritual confrerès leap into the void, preferring to dispossess themselves giddily of what is theirs, that it may be regained vicariously in the firmer arms of others.

WORKS CITED

Giovanni Boccaccio, *The Decameron*, Second Edition., G.H. Mcwilliam, trans., Penguin Books, 1995

Geoffrey Chaucer, *The Canterbury Tales*, Peter Tuttle, trans., Barnes & Noble Classics, 2007

Philip David Collington, *"O Word of Fear": Imaginary Cuckoldry in Shakespeare's Plays*, University of Toronto doctoral dissertation, unpub., 1998.

Marguerite De Navarre, *The Heptameron*, P.A. Chilton, trans., Penguin Books, 1984

New Advent Catholic Encyclopedia (online version)

Jean-Paul Sartre, *Being and Nothingness*, Hazel Barnes, trans., Philosophical Library, 1956

William Shakespeare: The Complete Works, Second Edition, G. Wells and S. Taylor, eds., Clarendon Press, 2005

David M. Turner, *Fashioning Adultery: Gender, Sex and Civility in England, 1600 - 1740*, Cambridge University Press, 2002

Hank Whittemore, *The Monument*, Meadow Geese Press, 2005

Sincere thanks to Professor Philip D. Collington for making available his excellent dissertation for reference.

7
Shakespeare's Snobs

I. The Issue

*A*s the idea of snobbery often arises in contentions over Shakespeare, it may be well to pause to take stock of precisely what it is. The entry in The *American Heritage Dictionary of the English Language* is helpful and illuminating.

Snob. *n*. 1. One who overtly imitates, obsequiously admires, and offensively seeks to associate only with those one regards as one's superiors and who tends to rebuff or ignore altogether those one regards as one's inferiors. . . . 2. One who affects an offensive air of self-satisfied superiority in matters of taste and intellect. [Earlier *snob*, cobbler, lower-class person, person who aspires to social prominence.]

Word History: Snobs look down at their inferiors, but at one time snobs looked up at their betters. The word snob, the ultimate origins of which are uncertain, is first found in 1781 in the sense "shoemaker, cobbler," a regional and informal usage. The word is recorded around 1796 in a slang usage particular to Cambridge University, "a townsman as opposed to a gownsman." Both senses may have fed into the sense first found in 1831, "a member of the ordinary or lower classes." Along with this sense went another (1838), "a person without breeding or taste." From these two senses arose the sense first recorded in 1848, "a person who looks up to his or her social betters and tries to copy or associate

with them." We can see how this sense could blend into the other familiar sense, "one who looks down on those considered inferior" (1911).
(American Heritage, 1707)

A snob, then, is not a patrician, but a wannabe, a social climber
who puts on airs to be taken for more than what he actually is. Though
a king may regard himself as far above his subjects, he cannot be a snob
because his first rank is already satisfactorily established. His lofty demeanor is not put on, but a reflection of lifelong breeding and public
acknowledgement of his elevated station. For example, in *A Midsummer Night's Dream*, Theseus, Duke of Athens, considers allowing performance of Peter Quince's *Pyramus and Thisbe*. Objection is made by
the serving man Philostrate, who warns that this masque is the frui-
tion of mere "hard-handed men that work in Athens here, which never
laboured in their minds till now." (V, i, 72-73) As such, its reception
would represent an offense to the royal court. In overruling Philostrate's
protest, and allowing *Pyramus and Thisbe* to be put on, Duke Theseus
gives tacit indication of his unexcelled authority, sense of security and
freedom from affectation.

It may be replied by counter-example that the Count of Roussillon, Bertram, in *All's Well That Ends Well*, is an aristocratic snob, for
he emphatically rejects Helena on account of being the daughter of a
non-noble (physician). This is what he protests to the King of France
who would enforce the match. And many scholars have concluded that
Bertram is a Shakespearean snob for this reason. Yet it is not so. Difference in rank, though it may be the professed cause of Bertram's dislike
of Helena, is not its true explanation. For Bertram is a well-established
courtier, secure in his elevated station in life. And Helena could be easily
promoted by the King to make things even. No, what really rankles him
is that Helena is his step-sister, and, due to long propinquity, he has no
desire for her. Rather than admit this publicly, Bertram seizes instead on
the excuse of discrepancy in social position, leading him to have, perhaps, a worse reputation amongst the critics than he deserves.

In Elizabethan England, then, while the word was not yet born,
the idea itself was ubiquitous. It was of great interest to Shakespeare. In
several plays he gives amusing portraits of those we would dub "snobs."
Examining them is a pleasant way to gain better insight into his social
philosophy, and to prepare ourselves to address an important dimension of the authorship question. Here are a few of Shakespeare's better-
known snobs.

1. *Malvolio*

In the comic masterpiece *Twelfth Night*, Malvolio is major domo of Lady Olivia's manse. Some identify him as one of Shakespeare's withering re-creations of William Cecil, Baron of Burghley. Although only a servant, Malvolio is filled with an overweening sense of self-importance, so much so that it makes him ridiculous. Not only does he disdain his fellow domestics and Olivia's endearing jester, Feste, he cultivates a particular contempt for Olivia's cousin, the dissolute Sir Toby Belch. Feeling himself to be a lord by temperament if not by descent, Malvolio is galled that Sir Toby (and his foolish friend Sir Andrew Aguecheek) should enjoy the title of Knight, while he, the estimable and discriminating chief of domestic protocol, though far more distinguished in carriage and deportment, remains a lowly plebian. Here he is making comment on Feste:

> I marvel your ladyship takes delight in such a barren
> rascal. I saw him put down the other day with an
> ordinary fool that has no more brains than a stone.
> Unless you laugh and minister occasion to him, he is
> gagged. I protest I take these wise men that crow
> so at these set kind of fools no better than the fools'
> zanies.
> (I, v, 79-85)

Though Malvolio implicitly upbraids his own fair Lady, she responds moderately.

> O, you are sick of self-love, Malvolio, and taste
> with a distempered appetite. To be generous, guiltless,
> and of a free disposition is to take those things for
> birdbolts that you deem cannon bullets. There is no
> slander in an allowed fool, though he do nothing but
> rail; nor no railing in a known discreet man, though
> he do nothing but reprove.
> (I, v, 86-92)

When Sir Toby and his friends stay up late carousing, Malvolio reprimands them as though he were a reproving parent. He is at bottom a Puritan kill-joy disguised as proctor, a miserable snob too "good" to have a good time or grant that others might.

> MALVOLIO: My masters, are you mad? Or what are you?
> Have you no wit, manners, nor honesty, but to gabble
> like tinkers at this time of night? Do ye make an
> alehouse of my lady's house, that ye squeak out your
> cozier's catches without any mitigation or remorse of
> voice? Is there no respect of place, persons, nor time
> in you?

> SIR TOBY: We did keep time, sir, in our catches. Sneck up!

> MALVOLIO: Sir Toby, I must be round with you. My lady
> bade me tell you that though she harbours you as her
> kinsman she's nothing allied to your disorders. If you
> can separate yourself and your misdemeanors you are
> welcome to the house. If not, an it would please you
> to take leave of her she is very willing to bid you
> farewell.
> (II, iii, 83-97)

Toby's riposte is on target:

> SIR TOBY: Art thou any more than a steward?
> Dost thou think because thou art virtuous there
> shall be no more cakes and ale?
> (II, iii, 109-111)

By pointing out his humble place in the social hierarchy, Sir Toby punctures Malvolio's delusions of grandeur and authority. Later, in Act Two, Malvolio is tricked by a letter forged by Maria into revealing his dream of marrying Olivia and assuming control of her estate. Along with Maria, Sir Toby, Fabian and Sir Andrew, we overhear the bizarre reveries of the steward.

> MALVOLIO: To be Count Malvolio!

> SIR TOBY: Ah, rogue.

> SIR ANDREW: Pistol him, pistol him.

SIR TOBY: Peace, peace.

MALVOLIO: There is example for't: the Lady of the Strachey married the yeoman of the wardrobe.

SIR ANDREW: Fie on him, Jezebel.

FABIAN: O peace, now he's deeply in. Look how imagination blows him.

MALVOLIO: Having been three months married to her, sitting in my state --

SIR TOBY: O, for a stone-bow to hit him in the eye!

MALVOLIO: Calling my officers about me, in my branched velvet gown, having come from a day-bed where I have left Olivia sleeping --

SIR TOBY: Fire and brimstone!

FABIAN: O peace, peace.

MALVOLIO: And then to have the humor of state and -- after a demure travel of regard, telling them I know my place, as I would they should do theirs - to ask for my kinsman Toby.

SIR TOBY: Bolts and shackles!

FABIAN: O peace, peace, peace, now, now.

MALVOLIO: Seven of my people with an obedient start make out for him. I frown the while, and perchance wind up my watch, or play with my - some rich jewel. Toby approaches; curtsies there to me.

SIR TOBY: Shall this fellow live?

FABIAN: Though our silence be drawn from us with cars,

yet peace.

MALVOLO: I extend my hand to him thus, quenching my familiar smile with an austere regard of control --

SIR TOBY: And does not Toby take you a blow o' the lips, then?

MALVOLIO: Saying 'Cousin Toby, my fortunes, having cast me on your niece, give me this prerogative of speech' --

SIR TOBY: What, what!

MALVOLIO: 'You must amend your drunkenness.'
(II, v, 33-72)

Malvolio shows himself to be an insufferable prig and quintessential snob, contemplating his own promotion as a device allowing him to pull rank on his peers. He pictures the nobility as a phalanx of grey Puritans like himself, overlooking the notorious libertinism of the upper crust. And while he would impose a strict ascetic regimen on his superiors-turned-underlings, he would privately relish the favors of Olivia in bed. Such are the foibles of snobbery.

Before passing to other instances, let's reflect on what we may gather of the writer himself. After such brilliant vivisection of haughty Malvolio, it would be rather incongruous to conceive of its creator as anything other than snobbery's mortal foe, would it not? And that fairly rules out viewing Malvolio as anything like a self-portrait. For if Shakespeare himself turned out to be a Malvolio, he'd be a gigantic hypocrite as well. The more frequently he returns to the critique of the snob, then, the less likely it becomes that he himself ever exhibited such vain attitudes and behavior. This means that there is a rebuttable presumption that the author of the corpus was not himself a snob. Should any authorial candidate turn out to be one, he would by *modus tollens* be disqualified.

2. The Pedant and Don Adriano De Armado

Knowledge of classical languages in Renaissance Europe and England was not confined to members of the nobility. When a commoner acquired an education, he or she was not escorted into the ranks of the gentry, but often became a tutor in aristocratic households or a schoolteacher. Some of these prodigies fancied themselves as sophisticated and therefore well-bred as those for whom they toiled. The pedant Holofernes in *Love's Labour's Lost* illustrates such linguistically based snobbery. As there is no resemblance between the pedant and the notorious Babylonian general of that name, scholars have detected in the pedant a sly reference to Elizabethan contemporary Gabriel Harvey. Harvey was born the son of a rope maker, and in his youth attended Cambridge University, where he seems to have befriended and instructed Edmund Spenser. Holofernes indulges in the pretentious display of Latin and Italian to impress others with his erudition, a key sign of snobbery. During the sonnet frenzy of the King of Navarre and his amorous bookmen, the pedant scrutinizes Biron's verse and finds it wanting.

> You find not the apostrophus, and so miss
> the accent. Let me supervise the canzonet. Here are
> only numbers ratified, but for the elegancy, facility,
> and golden cadence of poesy - *caret*. Ovidius Naso
> was the man. And why indeed 'Naso' but for smelling out
> the odoriferous flowers of fancy, the jerks of invention?
> *Imitari* is nothing. So doth the hound his master, the
> ape his keeper, the tired horse his rider.
> (IV, ii, 120-126)

The pedant literally looks down his nose at Biron's sonnet, an *envois* intended for Rosaline, as being a poor imitation of Ovid, the eminent Latin poet whose work so influenced Shakespeare. Biron is essentially accused of scribbling a cheap and unworthy sonnet. But the charge is inappropriate and absurd. Biron's poem is in English, not Latin, and gives no sign of being an effort to outdo classical verse or rival Ovid. Rather, Biron is smitten by Lady-in-waiting Rosaline. His poem is an instrument designed to win her love. It is obviously not part of a scheme to impress third parties, editors of journals, compilers of anthologies or judges of poetry competitions. Thus, the pedant's technical objections backfire: in seeking to snootily dismiss Biron's private *billet-doux*, the pedant proves only how much of a fussy show-off he is.

As for that "refined traveler of Spain," Don Adriano de Armado, the king's houseguest, he too has a veneer of learning, just enough to render himself a thing of royal amusement. (I, i, 168-174) When, in Act

V, Don Adriano invites the pedant to participate in an afternoon theatrical performance, he does it thus:

> Sir, it is the King's most sweet pleasure and
> affection to congratulate the Princess at her pavilion
> in the posteriors of the day, which the rude multitude
> call the afternoon.
> (V, i, 82-85)

To which the pedant replies:

> The posterior of the day, most generous, sir,
> is liable, congruent, and measurable for the afternoon.
> The word is well culled, choice, sweet, and apt, I do
> assure you, sir, I do assure.
> (V, i, 86-89)

Don Adriano's own missive, intended for country wench Jaquenetta, but intercepted by the Princess of France and her ladies, sends them into peals of laughter. And in the concluding sequence of "The Nine Worthies" in Act V presented to the lords and ladies, Don Adriano becomes the target of stinging barbs. His half-learning, like his ill-fitting costume, renders him vulnerable to the merciless pillorying of his aristocratic audience. Contrast this prickly reception with the warmer embrace of *Pyramus and Thisbe* by Theseus and company. The difference is that the rude mechanicals are not snobs; they realize they are not cultured, but hope to make a good show through application and sincerity. As such, they are more kindly handled. But supercilious Holofernes and Don Adriano, with their shallow Latinisms, are excoriated. The gulf between the nobility and the commons is widened and deepened in *Love's Labour's Lost,* as Shakespeare demonstrates the grossness of any attempt of *hoi polloi* to morph into courtiers by the desultory reading of books.

3. Polonious

William Cecil was for most of her reign the chief advisor of Queen Elizabeth I. He was a commoner who in virtue of extraordinary services to the Queen was granted a peerage as "Lord Burghley." He had two children of note, Robert, who succeeded him, and his daughter Anne, who was given in marriage to the Great Lord Chamberlain, Edward Oxenford, the 17th Earl of Oxford. It is generally understood that Polonious is a mock on Lord Burghley, but few attempts have been made to detect other historical personages in the play, or explain how a mere yeoman from Stratford dared satirize the most puissant and lethal lord of the Realm. If we grant that Polonious in *Hamlet, Prince of Denmark* stands for Cecil, it follows as the night the day that Ophelia represents Anne, his daughter, and that Hamlet is Edward de Vere, who wedded her. Polonious cultivates King Claudius and Queen Gertrude assiduously in the hope of advantages not only for himself but also for his offspring, Laertes and Ophelia. Though a non-royal, Polonious associates exclusively with the nobility. The apparent madness of Prince Hamlet is a great embarrassment because his daughter Ophelia was destined to become Hamlet's bride. When the refractory Prince's behavior becomes totally unaccountable and bizarre, Polonious must scurry to undo what he has labored in the reign of King Hamlet the Dane to achieve: cement his rise in society by marrying his untitled daughter to the late King's son. His polite excuse to the King and Queen is that, as far as Ophelia is concerned, he has told her that "Lord Hamlet is a prince out of thy star." (II, ii, 142) Yet these words do not appear in the text as actually spoken to Ophelia. They are employed in private conference with Gertrude and Claudius to flatteringly and subtly cancel the match, not on account of Hamlet's odd manner, but on the grounds that, as heir to the Danish throne, his station is too far above hers for court protocol to sanction the union. In all of this Polonious never ceases to be the social climber and vain egotist, the symptoms of which are visible in his avuncular counsel to the departing Laertes.

> Costly thy habit as thy purse can buy,
> But not expressed in fancy; rich not gaudy;
> For the apparel oft proclaims the man,
> *And they in France of the best rank and station*
> Are of all most select and generous chief in that.
> (I, iii, 70-74)

He is possessed of a petty, literal-minded personality with limited intellect, and in conversation with the mordant, ironic Prince he is indeed out of his star. So tedious is his company that when he excuses himself from Hamlet's presence ("my honourable lord, I will most humbly take my leave of you,") Hamlet's witty and melancholy repartee ("You cannot, sir, take any thing that I will more willingly part withal - except my life . . . .") passes over his head like a meteor. In Polonious, then, we have yet another adroit and incisive Shakespearean profile of the snob.

4. Autolycus

Perhaps one of the more droll instances of the snob is the impersonation of a courtier put on by the thief Autolycus before the Old Shepherd and the Clown in Act IV of *The Winter's Tale.* To obtain information and continue to exploit these gullible rustics, Autolycus, a common thief formerly employed by Prince Florizel, assumes the guise of a lord. The contempt he feels for his victims is easily transmuted into the disdain of an imagined noble.

OLD SHEPHERD Are you a courtier, an't like you, sir?

AUTOLYCUS Whether it like me or no, I am a courtier.
Seest thou not the air of the court in these enfoldings?
Hath not my gait in it the measure of the court?
Receives not thy nose court-odour from me? Reflect I
not on thy baseness court-contempt? Thinkest thou,
for that I insinuate to toze from thee thy business, I
am therefore no courtier? I am courtier cap-à-pie . . . .

This wonderfully silly performance is made possible by the fact that Autolycus actually did serve in the court under Prince Florizel (IV, iii, 13) and can portray the courtier's style, which however, as a commoner, he cannot assume without becoming a laughable snob.

5. William of Stratford

There is, unfortunately, one more snob clamoring to be added to our list, that of William Shaksper of Stratford-upon-Avon. (Inasmuch as the name of the poet-dramatist is uniformly spelled "William Shakespeare" in his publications, this name will be reserved henceforth for that writer; as the name of the man from Stratford-upon-Avon was spelled variously, "Shaksper" will refer to him.) As the tale comes down to us, Shaksper stumbles into London as a poor and doubtfully educated youth who takes initial employment as an ostler outside a theatre, thereafter worming his way onstage. No records document his attendance at the Stratford Grammar School, and the claim that he studied there plainly begs the question where the evidence is the quality of the disputed works. One may object that it cannot be proved that Shaksper first hired on as an ostler, to which we can cheerfully assent. But our argument applies *a fortiori* to the gratuitous proposal that his initial employment was that of an actor, unless the parts he played were confined to Warwickshire bumpkins. An ostler in those days resembled a valet parking attendant today, except that in Elizabethan England the ostler looked after horses, not automobiles. The trade of ostler was as menial as any in Albion, requiring few, if any, skills. In the plays of William Shakespeare, the very term of "ostler" is one of denigration and contempt: Hal expostulates to Falstaff when asked to help the fat knight mount his horse, "Out, ye rogue! Shall I be your ostler?" (*King Henry IV*, Part One, II, ii, 42) In *Henry IV*, the ostler's rank is so low that while mere carriers are given speaking lines, the ostlers never appear onstage, and only once are given an utterance: "anon, anon," an expression of grudging drudgery. (II, i, 4) Indeed, the carriers (luggage handlers) speak nothing but abuse to the ostlers:

> God's body, the turkeys in my pannier are
> quite starved! What, ostler! A plague on thee,
> hast thou never an eye in thy head? Canst not hear?
> An 'twere not as good deed as drink to break the pate
> on thee, I am a very villain. Come, and be hanged! Hast
> no faith in thee?
> (II, i, 26-31)

This is the language William of Stratford would have heard and spoken on his alleged emigration to London, circa 1588. For had the man from Warwickshire possessed any mode of speech other than that employed by London carriers and ostlers, he would have been regarded as either a space alien, a spy, or an emissary of infernal Beelzebub - and treated as such. At this time the public knew nothing of anyone by the name of "William Shakespeare," a moniker which burst like a bombshell on readers in 1593 with the publication of the sensuous best-seller, *Venus and Adonis*. If we are to cleave to the conventional narrative, the plucky ostler of 1588 a scant five years later was publicly addressing a wealthy aristocrat in the mellifluous cadences of classical learning:

> *Vilia miretur vulgus; mihi flavus Apollo Pocula Castalia plena*
> *ministret acqua.*

To The Right Honorable Henry Wriosthesley, Earl of Southampton, and Baron of Titchfield

Right Honorable, I know not how I shall offend in dedicating my unpolished lines to your lordship, nor how the world will censure me for choosing so strong a prop to support so weak a burden. Only, if your honour seem but pleased, I account myself highly praised, and vow to take advantage of all idle hours till I have honoured you with some graver labour. But if the first heir of my invention prove deformed, I shall be sorry it had so noble a godfather, and never after ear so barren a land for fear it yield me still so bad a harvest. I leave it to your honourable survey, and your honour to your heart's content, which I wish may always answer your own wish and the world's hopeful expectation.

Your honour's in all duty,

William Shakespeare

In 1596, this son of an illiterate rural glover applied for and obtained a patent of nobility, a status that would later be generally proscribed by the Constitution of the United States of America as inconsistent with the principle of human equality. (US Const., Art. 1, Sect. 9, Cl. 8; Art. 1, Sect. 10, Cl. 1) Upon payment of a fee, an office of the Crown would research one's eligibility to possess an heritable coat of arms, and, depending on the facts (and various imponderables), grant or deny. There is no dispute then, that William of Stratford was a low "hedge-born swain that [did] presume to boast of gentle blood." (*King Henry VI, Part I*, IV, i, 43-44) There are considerable differences among scholars on the circumstances surrounding this request for a family escutcheon. Some commentators aver the original applicant was John Shaksper, William's father, in 1569. Yet twenty-seven years is a long time to wait to be called "gentleman." Others say John made serial applications. Still others claim that William made application on his father's behalf, or actually dragged John from Stratford to visit the College of Heralds in London. The explanation for the variation in these accounts is obvious: they are all narrative embellishment and sheer speculation. But one fact stands out: William of Stratford sought to invade the ranks of the nobility, true to his "upwardly mobile" pretensions.

Here is the fullest redaction of these events, reflecting a comedy-of-errors in miniature:

> In October of 1596, a grant of a coat-of-arms seems to have been made to John Shakespeare, doubtless at his son's instigation . . . The arms feature a spear in the diagonal of the shield and a falcon as the crest. In the upper left-hand corner of the draft of 1596 appear the words, *Non, Sanz Droict* ("No, Without Right"), this being evidently the Herald's judgment on the merits of the application. The words are crossed out but are again re-inscribed, just above the original notation. Then, in a larger hand and in upper-case letters the words NON SANZ DROICT are written across the top. Someone, it would seem, had taken the dismissal and by dropping the comma turned it into an endorsement: "Not Without Right." (Ogburn, 28)

Why was the rejection of the application rescinded in October of 1596? We will never know. But one possibility commends itself. In 1569, no one in London had ever heard of the villager John Shaksper, and his application to be recognized as one of the gentry was turned down. Then, in 1593 and 1594 the name "William Shakespeare" was suddenly up in lights as the acclaimed author of two exciting poems, *Venus and Adonis* and *The Rape of Lucrece*. If William Shaksper two years later (1596) knocked on the door of the College of Heralds, the similarity of his name to that of the now-celebrated and well-connected poet might have led the Herald to err on the side of caution and admit the petition for coat-of-arms.

In 1598, as is supposed, this same William of Stratford-upon-Avon, son of a village glover and erstwhile ostler, now a gentleman via retail purchase, would have his elegant play *Love's Labour's Lost* published, a work which makes fun of any commoner foolish enough to put on aristocratic airs on the basis of an inflated vocabulary.

The image we have of the Stratfordian "Shakespeare" is that of a nobody from the hinterlands who deserts wife and children to pursue a glittering theatrical life in London. While artfully dodging his creditors, he somehow manages to become exceedingly learned in many fields, and acquires, in addition to Latin, French and Italian languages as well. In no time at all he scoops up wealthy patrons whom he retains by "low-crookèd curtsies and base spaniel fawning," (*Julius Caesar*, III, i, 43) as reflected in the dedications of his long poems. Instead of focusing in his plays on the exploits of lowly folks who, like himself, allegedly rise from humble origins to accomplish triumphs and marvels, he chooses to write primarily about kings, queens and aspects of courtly life. Commoners get short shrift from this erstwhile commoner.

No sooner does the Stratford man succeed in clawing his way into polite society than he ostensibly devotes himself to the task of putting in their places those who would attempt to rise above their station in virtue of a mere fastidiousness of manners or knack for foreign languages. As we have already agreed that no dedicated snob would likely have sought renown by lampooning prominent public figures as vulgar snobs, William of Stratford is ruled out as the author's identity.

II. A Curious Twist

It is precisely at this point that the redoubtable defenders of Stratford rise to the occasion with a rhetorical novelty. There is no reason to heed those who have the audacity to challenge the legitimacy of Shaksper as the author, say they, because, ironically, such persons are just a bunch of "snobs." It is merely their inveterate and senseless prejudice against ordinary men and women, not the dictates of reason, which prevents them from recognizing and crediting the perfectly plausible accomplishment of Warwickshire Bill. Such an eristic gimmick wears its poverty on its shirtsleeve. We might say that it commits the fallacy of misplaced snobbishness, discovering snootiness not in certain Shakespearean characters, or in Wm. Shaksper, Esq., but in Oxfordian critics. Instead of apprehending and appreciating (a) the significant negative treatment of snobs in the works of Shakespeare, and (b) the plain evidences of snobbery in the threadbare biography of William of Stratford, and making the sensible inference that (a) and (b) rule out (c), the authorial candidacy of snobbish Shaksper, our traditionalist friends choose to ignore all this in favor of name-calling. It is an uncanny coincidence that the term of reproach they select happens to be "snob." It should be clear that there is a palpable tension between (a) and (b) that operates to exclude *homo Stratfordianus*. That is a matter of common sense, not bias, and seeing the implication is a function of rudimentary logic. In contemporary parlance, this is a slam dunk. There is zero evidence that this tension somehow arises because those who notice it are "snobs."

In fact, the shoe is quite on the other foot. Were we of a mind to leap into the *ad hominem* trenches with our Stratfordian brethren (and we are not), much stronger arguments could be advanced to show that it is the Stratfordians themselves who are the true snobs. We might observe, *e.g.*, that if Shaksper was himself an unchecked snob, his advocates and admirers must inevitably partake of that trait. The fans and devotees of Mr. Big Snob must be junior snobs themselves. The proof would lie in the fact that the overwhelming majority of those who employ the "snob" gambit are professors of English literature, the elbow patch crowd, who tend to regard such matters as their private playgound, dismissing challenges from persons beyond the groves of academe as unworthy of respect or consideration. We might then point out that their own doctoral coats-of-arms hang prominently in their faculty offices. After all, no one lacking a Ph.D. in English literature could possibly have anything of importance to say about Shakespeare or his identity. That is the exclusive prerogative of tenured English teachers. It's their turf. All of this we might urge, but do not so. We decline to descend to the level of *tu quoque* rebuttal.

Rather, it is sufficient for our purposes to simply remark that there has never been a showing on the basis of independent evidence that anti-Stratfordians suffer from bias of any kind. Nor are we persuaded that the Stratfordian use of the term "snob" comports with the definitions in such standard reference works as the *American Heritage Dictionary of the English Language,* cited above. That reference book tells us that a snob is, *inter alia,* "one who affects an offensive air of self-satisfied superiority in matters of taste or intellect." This definition fits the orthodox Stratfordian professoriate far better than it does the anti-Stratfordian rebels, at whom the epithet is thrown like a brickbat. In short, the argument that we should all be of the Stratfordian persuasion because those who dissent are just "snobs" is a *non sequitur* so coarse and ineffective that it deserves a place in the Guinness Book of World Records.

Most strange of all is that, despite their degrees and pedigrees, Stratfordians never consult Shakespeare himself on this subject. Should they trouble to do so, they would discover that he has a significant and relevant theory of knowledge: the general source of our understanding is our experience. It is within that realm that we function as artists. Recall the maxim of creative writing class: "write about what you know." And the scope of our knowledge is coterminous with our experience. To speak about the court authentically, we must have been there.

TOUCHSTONE: Wast ever in court, shepherd?

CORIN: No, truly.

TOUCHSTONE: Then thou art damned.

CORIN: Nay, I hope.

TOUCHSTONE: Why, if thou never wast at court thou
never sawest good manners. If thou never sawest good
good manners, then thy manners must be wicked,
and wickedness is sin, and sin is damnation. Thou
art in a parlous state, shepherd.
(*As You Like It*, III, ii, 31-43)

Hiding behind this satirical dialogue is an important truth: one cannot bring the Elizabethan privy chamber accurately to life as a dramatist without first-hand experience. The attempt to circumvent our ignorance lands us as writers in caricature and anachronism. In the "miracle at St. Albans" in *King Henry VI, Part Two*, Shakespeare gives vivid illustration of his rugged empiricism. When the sly peasant Saunder Simpcox claims to be blind from birth, he is interrogated by Duke Humphrey of Gloucester. Though he has acquired sight only minutes before, he presumes to know which colors are called "black," and which are called "red," something he could only grasp on the basis of additional information and patient instruction. In Humphrey's words:

If thou hadst been born blind, thou mightst as well
have known all our names as thus to name the several
colours we do wear. Sight may distinguish of colours
but suddenly to nominate them all, it is impossible.
(II, i, 131-135, following wording in *The Yale Shakespeare*)

Shakespeare's philosophical point is well taken, and has instant application to the authorship question. No matter how brilliant the imagination, it functions at all times on the basis of what we have ourselves passed through. Antony can tell us of the late and would-have-been king, Julius Caesar, because "he was my friend." And thus, "here I am to speak what I do know." (III, ii, 86; 102) Many have written about kings and queens, but most of it is wholly conjectural and external, failing to touch inner lives. A cat may look at a king, but not articulate his majesty's deepest fears and joys. It is this fundamental epistemological realism, and not so-called snobbism, which is the foundation of opposition to the authorial candidacy of poor William of Stratford-upon-Avon. When we see Shakespeare's sleepless King Henry IV envying the slumbers of the boy in the tall ship's crow's nest, or King Henry VI's similar envy of "homely swain" who keeps his flocks in peace, we behold a searching insight into the uneasy head that wears a crown, an insight reflecting actual acquaintance with royal sensibility.

At the end of *King Henry VI, Part Three*, the deposed monarch is captured by a couple of game keepers who, overhearing his musings on the vagaries of fate, question his identity.

> SECOND KEEPER: Say, what art thou that talk'st of kings
> and queens?
>
> KING HENRY: More than I seem, and less than I was born
> to: A man at least, for less I should not be;
> And men may talk of kings, and why not I?
>
> SECOND KEEPER: *Ay, but thou talk'st as if thou wert a king.*
> (III, i, 55-59)

And there is the point. For the "talker" in these lines is really Shakespeare himself, who can say with his character, "My crown is in my heart, not on my head." If Henry VI speaks like a king on the basis of having led a royal life, and those very words are given to him by the poet, it is no mean prejudice to acknowledge the nobility of the writer which his character exhibits.

WORKS CITED

Charlton Ogburn, *The Mysterious William Shakespeare: The Myth and the Reality*, Dodd, Mead & Company, 1984.

The American Heritage Dictionary of the English Language, 3rd ed., Houghton Mifflin Company, 1992.

William Shakespeare, The Complete Works, 2d ed., G. Taylor and S. Wells, eds., Clarendon Press, 2005.

8

Unreading Julius Caesar

Mars his true moving, even as in the heavens,
So in the earth, to this day is not known.
                         -- Charles, (*King Henry VI*)

Ein Buch ist ein Spiegel, aus dem kein Apostel
herausgucken kann, wenn ein Affe hineinguckt.
                         -- G. C. Lichtenberg

I. Introduction: A Tale of Two Critics

*I*n 1998 and 2004 appeared two of the most significant surveys of the plays of William Shakespeare: *Shakespeare: The Invention of the Human*, by Yale's Harold Bloom, and *Shakespeare After All*, by Marjorie Garber of Harvard. These critics are well-known and held in high esteem. Yet to examine them in tandem is to come away disappointed. Bloom is altogether omitted from Garber's General Index (Garber, 947), while his own volume contains no index at all. There seems to be a yawning disconnect between them. Worse, treatment of some of the best-known plays is uneven and often unsatisfactory.

Naturally, both have entries devoted to *The Tragedy of Julius Caesar*. Here are the opening lines of Harold Bloom's piece in 1998.

Like so many others in my American generation, I read *Julius Caesar* in grade school, when I was about twelve. It was the first play by Shakespeare that I read, and though soon after I encountered *Macbeth* on my own, and the rest of Shakespeare in the next year or two, a curious aura still lingers for me when I come back to *Julius Caesar*. It was a great favorite for school use in those days, because it is so well made, so apparently direct, and so relatively simple. The more often I reread and teach it, or attend a performance, the subtler and more ambiguous it seems, not in plot but in character. (Bloom, 104)

Garber opens her chapter this way.

For many years *Julius Caesar* was regularly taught in American high schools, often as the first play of Shakespeare assigned. One reason for this may have been the concurrent study of Latin. Caesar's *Gallic Wars*, taught in the sophomore year, would have introduced students to the legendary hero of ancient Rome. Another plausible reason for its favor among educators was that *Julius Caesar* is one of the few Shakespeare plays that contains no sex, not a single bawdy quibble. An equal and opposite relation to adolescent sexuality leads high school teachers today to assign *Romeo and Juliet* instead. Young love and eroticism, especially in a work deemed irreproachably classic - and available, in any case, on the movie screen - are perhaps a more enticing way to introduce the music video generation to Shakespeare than a play concerned, as *Caesar* is, with political rivalry, martial competition, and the disillusionment of ideals. (Garber, 409-410)

II. Shakespeare After Awl

One hardly knows which is more unsettling: to have failed to peruse Bloom's best-seller, which nestled conspicuously on American coffee tables six years earlier, or to have read it and forgotten the chapter on *Caesar* and the manner of its introduction. While it may have been popular with boards of education in part because it employed only muted allusions to sex, to claim that *The Tragedy of Julius Caesar* is absolutely void of suggestive references is wrong. What of the saucy cobbler's banter which commences just as the curtain rises?

> Truly, sir, all that I live by is with the awl.
> I meddle with no tradesman's matters, nor
> women's matters, but withal I am indeed,
> sir, a surgeon to old shoes . . . .
> (I, i, 21-24)

On one symbolic level, this loquacious fellow's "awl" prefigures the sharp daggers soon to be plunged into Caesar's body. I stick to my last, he slyly insinuates, and do not chase other men's wives. He is too Lilliputian for amorous escapades. Such phallic diminution hints at the masculine angst of the conspirators and the supporters of the deceased Pompey when contrasted with the apatosaurian Caesar. For if Caesar "doth bestride the world like a Colossus," while "we petty men walk under his huge legs," what indeed must we apprehend when we "peep about"? (I, ii, 136-139) (Cp., *Love's Labour's Lost*, IV, iii, 276-277: "O, vile! Then as she goes, what upward lies, The street should see as she walked overhead.") Any competent director will call for laughter from the crowd here. In Act II, sc. ii, in her desperate attempts to ferret out what husband Brutus is up to, whether an adulterous liaison or some graver intrigue, Portia charges that, in his refusal to take her concerns seriously, he is treating her more like an "harlot" than a wife. (II, i, 286) While we hope that twelve-year olds would not grasp the full implications of this accusation, it can hardly be claimed that it is without sexual significance. When Portia reminds Brutus that she "comforts [his] bed," it is presumed her meaning is not confined to changing the linens.

By the end of his initial paragraph, Bloom has put his finger on the crux of the play: the ineffabilities of character. Garber, on the other hand, readies us for a smattering of juicy topics: "political rivalry, martial competition, and the disillusionment of ideals." Focus is already lost.

Despite the redundancy of Garber's account of American lower schools' assignment of *Julius Caesar*, it serves a genuine purpose, for it reminds us of the standard rendition of this central Shakespearean text. According to that staid tradition, Brutus, "with himself at war" (I, ii, 48), is an exceedingly noble and honorable Roman who, fearing Caesar's growing power, is goaded by Cassius into leading the conspiracy. This determination conflicts directly with Brutus' professed love and admiration for Caesar, and his reluctance to commit homicide. Only too late, in the aftermath of the Battle of Philippi, does it dawn on him that the true spirit of this statesman is larger than life, and embodies the genius of the Roman people. As such, it is inextinguishable. In seeking to oppose it, he loses his way. That is the proverbial *precis* of the play, circa 1940. And despite its insufficiencies, this remains its basal significance in American education, as complacent thought continues to defer to habit. It is to Harold Bloom's credit that he at least challenges platitude. That is the purpose of scholarship, to excavate ever deeper towards what some might dare call truth. At least we can insist on a measure of intelligibility. The alternative is a legacy of nagging questions. Who is Brutus? How does Cassius really see him? Why is he selected to head the faction? Why does Brutus really slay Caesar? As Brutus was haunted by Caesar's ghost, so we remain haunted by Brutus.

To read we must learn first to *un*read, to find the gumption to shrug off the security of adolescent omniscience and view our literary self-representations with cleansed eyes. As Socrates called for an acknowledgment of ignorance, and René Descartes heralded the wholesale overthrow of archaic assumptions and ideas, so we must occasionally attempt to start afresh, taking nothing for granted in our Augean unreading of Shakespeare. Otherwise we risk construing things after our grandparents' fashion, clean from the purpose of the things themselves. (I, iii, 34-35) And though tragically there may be ultimately no text "in itself," the ideals of objectivity and insight still draw us forward, beyond the trite and the myopic.

Prof. Garber's treatment misses a critical opportunity to unread. Instead, it contents itself with repackaging the version of *The Tragedy of Julius Caesar* which has prevailed ever since the post-war New York State Board of Regents made the play mandatory. Norman Mailer once quipped that J.D. Salinger was the greatest mind ever to remain in prep school; if so, we might nominate Ms. Garber as class salutatorian. Gather, and surmise.

(1) "Brutus is torn by his own conflicting feelings, between his private friendship with Caesar and his public dislike of kingship and dictatorship -- of any absolute rule that approaches the condition of godhead." (Garber, 411)

(2) "Yet Brutus is consistently, indeed insistently, revealed as a man whose reason, whose trust in the power of order and discourse in the state, was his downfall. His sense of honor -- the word that above all typifies him to the time of his death, and beyond -- is unrealistic, in that

it is not an accurate gauge of the real world." (Garber, 412)

(3) "Brutus's interiority makes him judge everyone by his own standards, believe everyone to be as rational and as honorable as he is, and this leads directly to his catastrophe." (Garber, 415)

(4) "The fault in Brutus is that he convinces himself that his own sense of honor and reason, his private code, can be used to govern the state and to justify murder." (Garber, 417)

(5) "Brutus has too many scruples, too many principles, to think of trying to be clever." (Garber, 419)

(6) "Brutus speaks in prose, he appeals to reason, to the wisdom of the people, and he speaks, sometimes, in riddling syllogisms . . . ." (Garber, 421)

(Rather than for his "syllogisms," Brutus as a speaker, especially in his funeral oration, is remembered for his liberal reliance on classical rhetorical devices such as chiasmus, paradox, antithesis and metaphor.)

Each and every one of these six propositions is a restatement of the shibboleths of eleventh grade English, looking at Brutus as though he were, *e.g.*, a shy chess club president who inexplicably plots to rout the school bully with a Glock semi-automatic. But schoolyard snipers are neither brave nor honorable. By limiting the soul of Brutus to a brace of brittle virtues, Garber neglects other, more substantial, motives which might lead a man to act as he does. As his putative virtues shrink to vices, we lose comprehension not only of purpose, but of his actual full-bodied humanity as well. The closer we edge from character to caricature, the less we are able to hazard judgments of meaning and moral worth.

Four things seem absent from the proffered analysis. First, there is no interest in or explanation of who Brutus is. Second, in terms of criminal law, there is no showing of credible motive. No one commits bloody murder of a treasured friend because of anything as tepid and abstract as a "dislike of kingship." Third, there is a failure to explore the implications of the bonds linking Caesar and Brutus. How on earth could one start to fathom Brutus's action without a thorough understanding of the history of the interactions of these two men and what each meant to the other? Finally, to transcend the hackneyed acceptations of days gone by, it would be necessary to explore Shakespeare's sources, especially, Plutarch's *Parallel Lives* and *Life of Brutus*. Evidently such elementary research is not a part of pedagogical protocol at Harvard.

Ms. Garber dredges up momentous facts, but is curiously chary of putting them to use.

(1) "[Cassius] persuades Brutus that Brutus is like Caesar in a crucial way . . . ." (Garber, 425)

(2) "The play is at considerable pains, from the first, to demonstrate the resemblance between Brutus and Caesar." (Garber, 425)

(3) "Later on, after the assassination, the plebeians will suggest a substitution and a succession: 'Let him [Brutus] be Caesar. Caesar's better parts shall be crowned in Brutus.'" (Garber, 426)

These points are not taken up for serious discussion. As a result, characters and action slip through our fingers, leaving us bound in the shallows and miseries of the *status quo ante*. Or, to shift our metaphor, Ms. Garber charges right up to the mansion of understanding but neglects to ring the bell. Exactly how are Brutus and Caesar similar? What might that resemblance portend? What is implied about Brutus in the exclamations of the people that he become the principal leader of Rome in Caesar's place?

To express his personality in borrowed language, we might say of Brutus that he, "hath ever but slenderly known himself." (*The History of King Lear*, I, i, 283-284) Despite, or perhaps because, of his nightly lucubrations, Brutus lives in a perpetual fog of befuddlement. Self-ignorance allows Cassius to take advantage of him, rather as Iago dupes Othello. The disquieting reality is that often the victims of villainy become themselves villainous, as do Othello and Brutus. While Shakespeare scatters more than enough in the scenes to allow us to grasp the nature of Brutus and the basis of his actions, Ms. Garber, rather like an unripe psychoanalyst, forges an alliance with the neurotic aspect of her hysterical patient, recapitulating and re-inscribing his inexpugnable darkness within her own clinical exposition, the umbrageous spores of which are then disseminated willy-nilly to unwary students. As Antony notes, passion is catching. (III, i, 286) As "Brutus is more than any other character in this play the great man who 'falls,'" (Garber, 412) so is Prof. Garber herself, in virtue of her inexplicable refusal to look squarely at this tragic character, the great critic who falls, deserting the reader at the moment of greatest need.

III. *Looking Quite Past the Deeds of Men With Harold Bloom*

Where Marjorie Garber uses the play to serve up a scholastic smorgasbord, yet leaves the conceptual framework as it stood seven decades ago, Bloom, a scholar whose antennae pick up the slightest tremor of sensibility, tracks down a pregnant clue: Caesar has done no wrong. There is thus "no plausible complaint to make against [him]." Brutus merely speculates that Caesar, "contrary to his entire career, will become an unreasonable and oppressive tyrant, only because Brutus wants to believe this." (Bloom, 108) How so? Like a master sleuth, Bloom shrewdly delves into the "Brutish" psyche. (III, ii, 105)

> Brutus, the Stoic intellectual, is not affected by preternatural forces, but by his ambivalence which he has managed to evade. His love of Caesar has in it a negative element darker than Cassius's resentment of Caesar. (Bloom, 109)

Unlike those who content themselves with mere verbalisms like "honor" and "reason," Dr. Bloom performs a CAT scan of the psyche in search of something within Brutus which might account for his mixed sentiments as touching Caesar. This more fruitful line of analysis is made possible by Bloom's willingness to frankly anatomize Brutus and his actions in a way that the vast majority of scholars do not. He has the candor and perspicacity to recall the tradition that Brutus was Caesar's natural son, and confirms that "many critics have noted similarities that Shakespeare portrays between the two." (Bloom, 108-109) Garber, too, recognizes these congruencies, but raises no critical eyebrow, thus gaining nothing. Bloom, by contrast, finds Brutus to be "such a puzzle that he is wonderfully interesting." (Bloom, 112) That interest compels him to ask, "who and what is Brutus?" (Bloom, 112) He forces us to consider that the very idea of the introverted bookworm hacking Caesar to death on the basis of mere abstract ideals is a transgression of the principle of sufficient reason. And yet Bloom hesitates to conclude outright that Brutus dispatches Caesar on account of Oedipal aggression. For Shakespeare does not openly present this aspect of Brutus. This only deepens

Bloom's sense of fascination and intrigue. He is worth quoting at length. "I suspect," he says,

> that there is a curious gap in Julius Caesar, we want and need to know more about the Caesar-Brutus relationship than Shakespeare is willing to tell us. Caesar accepts death when Brutus, his Brutus, inflicts the final wound: "Then fall Caesar!" Plutarch repeats the gossip of Suetonius that Brutus was Caesar's natural son. Shakespeare surprisingly makes no use of this superb dramatic possibility, and surely we need to ask why not. (Bloom, 115)

> Antony, in his funeral oration, says that Brutus was "Caesar's angel," . . . and adds that the populace knows this, but gives no hint as to why Brutus was so well beloved by Caesar. (Bloom, 116)

> Shakespeare perhaps frustrated himself even as he baffles us by this evasion, and I wonder if the absence of the Caesar-Brutus complication does not help account for the baffled quality of the play. As things stand, the mysterious special relationship between Caesar and Brutus makes it seem as though Brutus and not Octavius is the authentic heir to Caesar. Certainly, Brutus has a very high self-regard, and a sense of destiny that transcends his own official descent from the Brutus who expelled the Tarquins. If he knows that he is not a Brutus but a Caesar, he would possess both a double pride and a double ambivalence. (Bloom, 116)

> [T]he explanation of a father-son relationship would illuminate the ambiguities of Brutus as nothing else does. (Bloom, 116)

> Shakespeare refuses to foreground why Brutus should be "Caesar's angel" . . . . By refusing to foreground or give any hint as to why Brutus should be "Caesar's angel," the dramatist allows an elite in the audience to assume that Brutus is Caesar's natural son. (Bloom, 117)

In a play weighted with magnificent ironies, the most ironical line may be "Brutus will start a spirit as soon as Caesar," since the Ghost of Caesar will identify himself as 'Thy evil spirit, Brutus'. And there would be a shrewd irony, an audacious one, when Cassius speaks of 'our fathers'. Brutus is an unfinished character because Shakespeare exploits the ambiguity of the Caesar-Brutus relationship without in any way citing what may be its most crucial strand. *Julius Caesar* has an implicit interest as a study in what shades upon patricide, but Shakespeare declines to dramatize this implicit burden in the consciousness of Brutus. (Bloom, 118)

As searching and helpful as these observations of the biological connection between Caesar and Brutus are, they stop short. The fact is that Shakespeare gives us everything we need to get inside Brutus's mind, "hints" and more, if only we will use what we are given. The fault, dear Harold, is not in the Bard but in ourselves that we are mystified. Insisting that we be hit over the head with an intellectual club before we can escape puzzlement is inappropriate and places unaesthetic demands on a poetic text, confusing it with a police report or news broadcast. Baffled by the delicate *chiaroscuro* of Shakespeare, Bloom calls for klieg lights.

IV. The Most Unkindest Cut of All

Had he scanned the script and its historical sources more resolutely, Bloom might have been emboldened to stride across the Rubicon and ratify his suspicion of the Brutus/Caesar filiation. Unfortunately, the jealous ghosts of middle school stood in the way, preventing that last crucial step. Since we know that Plutarch, on whose books Shakespeare based the play, clearly enunciates the tradition that Brutus was popularly regarded as the illegitimate son of Caesar, this account was undoubtedly in Shakespeare's view as he wrote. Reverberations of Brutus's direct descent from Caesar abound, as is admitted by Ms. Garber herself when she grants that "the play is at considerable pains, from the first, to demonstrate the resemblance of Brutus and Caesar." (Garber, 425) Why not, then, bring these items forward and make the appropriate deductions? Is it all so difficult?

If we jump in *medias res*, to the very apex of the narrative, the funeral speech of Mark Antony, we are suddenly brought face-to-face with a bastard. Mark Antony observes that Brutus chose to "unkindly knock" (III, ii, 178) with his poniard upon the body of Caesar. Lest there be any doubt about the stress he lays on this trope, Antony reiterates immediately and famously that Brutus's slash was *"the most unkindest cut of all."* (III, ii, 181) The word "kind" did not mean for the Elizabethans what it does for us ("friendly, generous, sympathetic"). It had multiple connotations - and it is in this recognition that we begin to transcend the banalities of secondary school. Crystal and Crystal, in *Shakespeare's Words, A Glossary & Language Companion*, inform us that "kind," as a noun, means: "nature, reality, character, disposition," citing the play *Julius Caesar*: "Why birds and beasts from quality and kind . . . change their ordinance." "Kind" also means: "breed, lineage, stock, family," as well as "nature, close natural relationship," citing Prince Hamlet's "A little more than kin, and less than kind." (Crystal, 251) Students of history will recall that when King Henry VIII and Anne Boleyn inscribed mottos in her *Book of Hours*, Anne's couplet suggestively employed this usage of "kind": "By daily proof ye shall me find, to be to you both loving and kind," which, in light of the term's significance may imply a filial relationship. It should be plain that the English word "kind" is a cognate of the Germanic "Kinder," referring to children, from which we get the word "kindergarten." As for "kindness," it can refer to "feelings of kinship." (Crystal, 252) When we turn to "unkind," we learn that in Elizabethan English, its meaning extended to "unnatural, abnormal, aberrant," and "lacking in family affection, with no respect for kinship." As an illustration, Crystal and Crystal cite *Titus Andronicus* and the murder of the protagonist's own daughter: "What hast thou done, unnatural and unkind?" (Crystal, 470) Compare this with Mark Antony's "This was the most unkindest cut of all," and the full dimensions of the usage emerge: to kill consanguineously, whether child or parent, is a sin which does violence not just to a human organism, but to the most keenly felt of human relationships. As patricide was the most unbecoming of all Roman sins, it is rather plain why Antony finds Brutus's thrust supremely reprehensible.

It is true that no one in the play ever expressly declares that Brutus is Caesar's son; the idea is all the more effective for its obliqueness. Shakespeare takes for granted that his audience is acquainted with Roman history, which reflects the belief of many, including Caesar, that Brutus was indeed his son. Thus when Antony exclaims before the Capitol that "Brutus, as you know, was Caesar's angel," it was expected that the bitter irony would be perceived instantly. But Antony couldn't just stand up and openly announce in Caesar's funeral that the previous speaker and self-styled executioner, Brutus, was the bastard son of the deceased. That option is ruled out by respect for the memory of the man whose corpse lay bleeding on the cold marmoreal platform. Not being able to make that statement, Antony could still allude to what "everyone knows," making the fact visible through figurative language. No wonder the crowd goes berserk.

And it is at just this point that things get interesting. Supposing Brutus was Caesar's "angel," how might this subtle Shakespearean phrase function beyond its employment as an euphemism for "beloved son"? For there does exist another facet of meaning. Crystal and Crystal advise that: "angel" means: "demon, evil spirit, attendant." (Crystal, 17) To read literally here, Brutus must be the evil spirit of Caesar, his illegitimate and wayward son. Fast forward to the civil war following the assassination. Brutus is reading in his tent at Sardis when the Ghost of Caesar appears to him. When Brutus demands of this apparition its identity, he is told:

> Thy evil spirit, Brutus.
> (IV, ii, 333)

Thus, most remarkably, Brutus is Caesar's evil spirit (angel), just as Caesar's ghost is the "evil spirit" of Brutus, a single malignant essence held in common.

V. Like Father, Like Son

Before passing on, let's enumerate a few key similarities of Caesar and his son Brutus which Shakespeare embeds in the narrative. We have already glanced at (1) the use of the adjective "unkindest" to show that Brutus's participation in the killing of Caesar exceeds in venality the wrongs of the other assailants on account of the implicit patricide. We have also noted (2) Mark Antony's use of the locution "Caesar's angel," as strongly pointing in the direction of a shared animus of Caesar and Brutus. The following may be added.

(3) In back-to-back, parallel scenes, Brutus and Caesar both confront distraught wives, who kneel before them to try to head off the looming disaster. Neither Brutus nor Caesar heeds his wife's pleas.

(4) Brutus's principal preoccupation is with his "honour," a quality he is sure he enjoys in abundance, and which forms the basis of his appeal to the commons at the funeral. What about Caesar? Though he may

not use this particular term, he leaves no doubt about the predominant role of *dignitas* in his life. "Shall Caesar send a lie?" he queries rhetorically when Calpurnia prompts him to inform the senators that illness detains him at home. Caesar sees himself as decisive and unwavering, a citadel of probity, invulnerable to flattery and emotional appeals. He is as "constant as the Northern Star,/ Of whose true fixed and resting quality/ There is no fellow in the firmament." (III, i, 60-62) Marjorie Garber observes that there are "two Caesars," one private, the other public, (Garber, 413 ff.) and that Caesar's center of gravity is in the public self, composed of pure virtue. What is overlooked is that this "public self" of Caesar is restated in Brutus's overzealous prizing of "honour" and the general good.

(5) As a corollary of their shared invocations of virtue goes a titanic sense of *amour propre* which easily qualifies as hubris. This classically dramatic quality supports the argument of Prof. James Howe, who demonstrates that Brutus and Caesar act in such a way as to fashion theatrical roles for themselves which foreclose sane alternatives and thus conduce to the tragic end. (Howe, 100 ff.)

(6) Along the same lines, Brutus, who adheres ardently to Stoic rationality, is yet constrained to admit of Caesar that "I have not known when his affections swayed more than his reason." (II, i, 20-21)

(7) Shakespeare deliberately puts into the mouths of Caesar and Brutus congruent speeches about the folly of fearing death.

i. CAESAR

Cowards die many times before their deaths;
The valiant never taste of death but once.
Of all the wonders that I yet have heard,
It seems to me most strange that men should
Fear, seeing that death, a necessary end,
Will come when it will come.
(II, ii, 32-37)

ii. BRUTUS

That we shall die, we know; 'tis but the time,
And drawing days out, that men stand upon.

CASSIUS

Why, he that cuts off twenty years of life
Cuts off so many years of fearing death.

BRUTUS

Grant that, and then is death a benefit:
So are we Caesar's friends, that have abridged
His time of fearing death.
(III, i, 100-106)

(8) Both Caesar and Brutus are eulogized by Mark Antony, who employs in both encomia noticeable sarcasm and irony. This becomes painfully evident when, after calling Brutus a "butcher," (III, i, 258) and terming his "the most unkindest cut of all," (III, ii, 181) at the conclusion of the play Antony declares that "his life was gentle," (V, v, 72) and "this was the noblest Roman of them all." (V, v, 67)

(9) And finally, as we shall show momentarily, Brutus exhibits one overriding trait in common with Caesar which makes a unique contribution to the outcome of the play: ambition.

VI. Plutarch's Brutus: Fall of a Prodigal Son

Any fair reading of Plutarch's chapters on Brutus and Caesar will leave no doubt that they form the precise historical background of the actions to which Shakespeare gives dramatic life. For example, the appearance of Caesar's ghost at Philippi, and its gnomic utterance that it is none other than the evil spirit of Brutus himself, is adapted directly from Plutarch. The resemblances of Caesar and Brutus to which we alluded above thus function in the play as illustrations and reinforcements of the implicit premise that Caesar is in fact the father of Brutus by Servilia. It is of the utmost importance to understand that for both Plutarch and Shakespeare this is not mere anecdote or window dressing, but the indispensable template that permits us to finally understand the attitudes and behavior of these men towards one another. After detailing the facts surrounding Brutus's participation in the war on the side of Pompey (in 49 BC) against Caesar, and his capture by Caesar's army at the Battle of Pharsalus, Plutarch writes:

It is said that Caesar had so great a regard for him [Brutus] that he ordered his commanders by no means to kill Brutus in the battle, but to spare him, if possible, and bring him safe to him, if he would willingly surrender himself; but if he made any resistance, to suffer him to escape rather than do him any violence. And this he is believed to have done out of tenderness to Servilia, the mother of Brutus; for Caesar had in his youth been very intimate with her, and she passionately in love with him, and considering that Brutus was born about that time in which their loves were at the highest, Caesar had a belief that he was his own child. (Plutarch, *Parallel Lives, Life of Brutus*, par. 5, p. 137)

It should be noticed here that Plutarch does not undertake the thankless task of attempting to prove that Brutus was in fact by blood and law the illegitimate son of Julius Caesar. And it would be similarly naïve, indeed absurd, for any student of literature, to aver, as to the play, *The Tragedy of Julius Caesar,* that Brutus is in some metaphysical sense the son of Caesar. For any tough-minded scrutiny of the documents will discover that "Brutus" and "Caesar" are never at any moment more than those spots of ink on a page which we scan in fear and trembling. But having assiduously unread the text, and faced with its reassembly through active decipherment, it is respectfully submitted that the best construction is the one to which Prof. Bloom is hesitatingly partial, that Brutus is indeed Caesar's son, at least in the sense that this is the perception of (1) Caesar, (2) Cassius and (3) many others in Rome. As to Brutus himself, the situation is more complex, and will be addressed below. What counts for Plutarch is the explanatory power of the hypothesis of Brutus's filiation: that is, embracing the proposition that Caesar felt himself to be the biological father of his beloved Servilia's son explains the extraordinary solicitude with which he regarded him, ordering that this treacherous young man be shielded from harm, and, if necessary, even allowed to escape. Thus it happened that Brutus was not slain by Caesar's troops. Instead, he penned a letter of apology to Caesar, who fast embraced him. Remove the linchpin of paternity and all these elements clatter down in disarray.

Once reconciled with Brutus, Caesar's favors to him continued.

Caesar, being about to make his expeditions into Africa against Cato and Scipio, committed to Brutus the government of Cisalpine Gaul, to the great happiness and advantage of that province . . . , insomuch that it was a most welcome and pleasant spectacle to Caesar, when in his return he passed through Italy, to see the cities that were under Brutus's command, and Brutus increasing his honor and joining agreeably in his progress. (Plutarch, *Life of Brutus*, par. 6, p. 139)

After being appointed Governor of Gaul by Caesar, Plutarch records that Caesar, in competitive bids for the coveted position of *Praetor Urbanus* of Rome, conferred this judicial plum on Brutus.

Now several praetorships being vacant, it was all men's opinion that that of the chiefest dignity, which is called the Praetorship of the City, would be conferred either upon Brutus or Cassius .... Brutus had only the reputation of his honor and virtue to oppose to the many and gallant actions performed by Cassius against the Parthians. But Caesar, having heard each side, and after deliberating about the matter among his friends, said "Cassius has the stronger plea, but we must let Brutus be . . . Praetor." So another Praetorship was given to Cassius, the gaining of which could not so much oblige him, as he was incensed for the loss of the other. And in all other things Brutus was the partaker of Caesar's power as much as he desired: for he might, if he pleased, have been the chief of all his friends, and had authority and command beyond them all, but Cassius and the company he met with drew him off from Caesar. (Plutarch, *Life of Brutus,* par. 7, p. 141)

What do we learn from Plutarch? The "honorable" Brutus to whom we are introduced in Act I of the play is not a mere idler wandering the cobblestones of Rome, but a Caesarean scion, the only "stem of that victorious stock" upon whom positions of renown were lavished by Caesar, most likely because he regarded him as his son. That all of this was happening to him because of that presumed descent from Caesar can hardly have escaped Brutus's notice. Brutus was borne aloft in Rome on the wings of Caesar's affection, and at every step took full advantage of promotion and augmentation of power. Yet it appears he was discontent. As an unacknowledged illegitimate, his path to the summit of power was occluded. No successor had been designated, but Caesar had named his nephew Octavius in his will. What, then, was Brutus's true fear? Caesar at the time of his assassination was already "Dictator for Life." Brutus had little to fear from dynastic succession, so long as he was first in line to inherit. And it was this of which he could not be certain. It is at just this ticklish moment that Shakespeare's Cassius, trumped in career and burning with the resentment of an Iago, approaches Brutus to act as his "mirror." And what does he say to Brutus?

CASSIUS

Brutus and Caesar: what should be in that 'Caesar'?
Why should that name be sounded more than yours?
Write them together: yours is as fair a name.
Sound them: it doth become the mouth as well.
Weigh them: it is as heavy. Conjure with 'em:
'Brutus' will start a spirit as soon as 'Caesar'.
(I, ii, 143-149)

Can there be any question as to Cassius's actual aim here - or Shakespeare's? Harken unto Plutarch: "When Cassius perceived that the *ambition of Brutus* was somewhat stirred by these things, he was more urgent than before and pricked him on . . . ." (Plutarch, *Life of Caesar*, par. 62, p. 589)

The appeal to "honour" and "the general good" was but a mask allowing Brutus to fool himself as to his real *terminus ad quem*: the diadem of Rome. He must act quickly, while his tide is at its height, lest Caesar pass the baton to a rival. It is this worry that prompts him to launch a pre-emptive strike against his benefactor and progenitor; the crown with which Caesar toys is but a bauble of no practical significance. Any lingering doubts are blown away after Brutus has given his funeral address and descends the pulpit. The "universal shouts" of acclaim he longed for at last ring out all about him.

ALL THE PLEBEIANS

Live, Brutus, live, live!

FIRST PLEBEIAN

Bring him in triumph unto his house.

FOURTH PLEBEIAN

Give him a statue with his ancestors.

THIRD PLEBEIAN

Let him be Caesar!

FIFTH PLEBEIAN

Caesar's better parts shall be crowned in Brutus.
(III, ii, 48-51)

The great achievement - and irony - of Brutus's speech is that in chiding Caesar as "ambitious," attention is deflected away from his own raging political drive. Mark Antony has to maintain a fine balance in his rebuttal, finding a way to turn the people against Brutus without too bluntly flinging the charge of "ambition" back upon its originator. No childish taunts here. The surer way is to refute factually Brutus's accusations against Caesar, profiling him as a sophist and demagogue whilst letting the crowd draw its own conclusions. The proletarians are not stupid. "You are not wood, you are not stones, but men," says Antony (III, ii, 143), contradicting the insults of the tribunes. (I, i, 35-36) As men of experience, the people know well enough that the wolfish lords who rule the roost, including Caesar, Cassius, Brutus, Casca, Cicero, Antony, Octavius and the rest, are all embodiments of *der Wille zur Macht*. After Antony's clever response, then, the shrill cry of Brutus that Caesar was "ambitious" appears to have all the elocutionary impact of calling a fish wet.

The historical fact is that Caesar was cognizant of his son's inclement inclinations, but contented himself with the expectation that Brutus would grasp that he was Caesar's *de facto* heir.

Neither was Caesar wholly without suspicion of him, nor wanted informers that accused Brutus to him; but he feared, indeed, the high spirit and the great character and the friends that he had, but thought himself secure in his moral disposition. When it was told him that Antony and Dolabella designed some disturbance, "It is not," said he, "the fat and the long-haired men I fear, but the pale and the lean," meaning Brutus and Cassius. *And when some maligned Brutus to him and advised him to beware of him, taking hold of his flesh with his hand, "What," he said, "do you think that Brutus will not wait out the time of this little body?" as if he thought none so fit to succeed him in his power but Brutus. And indeed it seems to be without doubt that Brutus might have been the first man in the commonwealth, if he had the patience but a little time to be second to Caesar.* (Plutarch, *Life of Brutus*, par. 8, p. 143)

Despite the illegitimacy of Brutus, Plutarch submits that it was Caesar's intention to place him in line to inherit the kingdom of Rome. The pre-emptive strike of the faction was a fatal miscalculation on the part of Brutus, who only needed to bide his time in order to stand in Caesar's place. Instead of waiting for destiny, Brutus leaped to his doom. Applying the *Parable of the Prodigal Son* (Luke 15:11-32) to take the measure of *The Tragedy of Julius Caesar*, we might say by analogy that if, after the prodigal son returned home, and if, after his father forgave his wandering and squandering, prepared the fatted calf in celebration, and put a ring on his son's finger and his finest robe on his body, if, after all this, in the very midst of his father's joy, the son, to seize his patrimony, had risen against his father, stabbing him in the heart with a sword, we might have before us a model of the wickedness of Brutus in slaying *Julius Caesar*.

VII. Et Tu Brute

Most of the historical content *The Tragedy of Julius Caesar* is an emanation from Plutarch. It is therefore not difficult to reconstruct what Shakespeare knew as he went about transforming his material into dramatic verse. Julius Caesar regarded Brutus as his beloved son by Servilia. So great was his affection for him that, even though Brutus fought with Pompey against him, Caesar did not seek retribution, but forgave him his folly. Soon thereafter, Caesar went out of his way to confer high office on him, making him governor of Gaul. Later, setting aside the superior qualifications of Cassius, Caesar dubbed Brutus *Praetor Urbanus*, chief judge of Rome itself. This is the disposition in Act I. Though news of Brutus's scheming reached Caesar, he brushed any threat aside, presuming from advantages already bestowed that it would be obvious to Brutus that the supreme reward would soon enough be his. Were it not for Shakespeare's brilliant staging, one could hardly imagine Caesar's shock to see this very Brutus among his assailants, indeed as their very captain. The depth of ingratitude and perfidious treachery is measureless, breathtaking. It is for this reason that Dante in *The Inferno* consigns Brutus, along with Judas, to Cocytus, the frozen lake in the very bottom of hell where Satan, caught in eternal ice, flails his wings of desolation. Yet this is the man remembered by legions of modern scholars as a patron saint (and pathetic victim) of "reason" and "honor," as though he were the John Stuart Mill of the ancients. So fearful is our age of authority, that a sour rebel of Brutus's ilk can be presented as a Technicolor hero, struggling against impossible odds to bring liberty to an oppressed people. Out of such valorous loins spring the likes of John Wilkes Booth and his brave progeny.

The problem with Brutus is that he cannot distinguish reason from rationalization and casuistry. Though some, *e.g.*, Allan Bloom, have argued that Brutus evinces the rationality of a Stoic philosopher, this idea has less than zero support in the text. Though he has studied Stoic writings, these are seeds cast on the stony ground of his heart. When in Act 4, sc. ii, he complains to Cassius of being "sick of many griefs," his friend correctly diagnoses intellectual duplicity:

> Of your philosophy you make no use,
> If you give place to accidental evils.
> (IV, ii, 197-198)

This impression of hypocrisy is given graphic confirmation in Act 5, sc. i, when, in the shadow of military defeat, they parlay for the last time, speaking of philosophy and death. Though Brutus leaps reflexively to Stoic condemnation of Cato, who committed suicide rather than be captured by Caesar, almost immediately he reverses course, confessing that he would indeed choose self-destruction under similar circumstances. And so he does, traducing the Stoic ideals he'd professed for so long. (V, i, 95-113)

It is hardly necessary to add that the whole point of Stoicism is the taming of the passions. A man who would succumb to unruly impulses to such an extent that he might actually stoop to killing his own patron and father is as far from "Stoicism" as can possibly be conceived.

VIII. Conclusion

Traditional readings of Julius Caesar seem to unconsciously adopt Brutus's own perceptions of himself, almost as though by sheer iteration of epithets ('noble', 'honourable', 'reasonable') we succumb at last to the view that Brutus is indeed a supernal being, light years removed from personal desires. Because, as Antony says, "passion is catching," we may find ourselves infected with Brutus's delusive image of himself. Our tacit premise is: "He who nobly accuses Caesar of ambition must surely be modest." That is what we have been taught. It never occurs to many of us that Brutus may be tarred with his own brush.

Similarly, in the case of the Thane of Cawdor, it is all too easy to suppose that Macbeth kills King Duncan out of personal ambition, a premise which a critical unreading may not support. In short, we may never discover that he who seems ambitious is really not so, while he who seems content might have the vulture of ambition gnawing at his innards.

The Tragedy of Julius Caesar, then, is not about honor, nor is it about "political rivalry, martial competition and the disillusionment of ideals." It is about self-deception and bad faith. It concerns a man who, like his father, embraces his own advertisements, who so flatters his ego with honorific maxims and principles that he no longer need be troubled by his deeds. He is the man "stuffed with all honourable virtues" so mocked by Beatrice. (*Much Ado About Nothing*, I, i, 54-57) In short, the subject of the play is Brutus -- and, thereby, ourselves. Shakespeare is always about us, not them. Cassius's mirror is through Brutus held up to the audience.

Though Brutus seems to have been discreetly regarded as the off-spring of Caesar, this is never acknowledged. He was always nominally of another family, and could no more feel confident of his bond with Caesar than he could of Caesar's beneficent intentions. His life was always half doubt, and one can guess that more than once he winced at perceived smirks, retreating like Prince Hamlet into a world of books - that is to say, words, words, words. As Lord Northumberland ruefully remarks in *King Henry IV, Part Two*:

> See what a ready tongue suspicion hath!
> He that but fears the thing he would not know
> Hath by instinct knowledge from others' eyes
> That what he fear'd is chanced.
> (I, i, 84-87)

As unacknowledged illegitimate, Brutus had "one foot in sea, and one on shore," and might well have suffered the sort of queasy anguish explored by Jean-Paul Sartre in *Being and Nothingness*. Lashing out at Caesar may have been for him a clumsy reaction to an existential predicament, but it remains nonetheless at the antipodes from the commendable. Feeling like a nothing, it still matters what sort of something one tries to become - and how. The fault, dear Brutus, is not in the stars, but in ourselves that we are blunderers.

We may add that because *The Tragedy of Julius Caesar* is a study of self-deceit, it is equally an examination of self-forgetting and self-betrayal. For the ancient Romans, virtue was conceived not as the decency of restraint, but as "virtu," meaning martial forwardness. The month of March, in the middle of which Caesar is put to death, is in fact the first month in the Roman calendar, named after Mars, the Roman god of war. The play shows what happens when the reservoir of testosterone bursts: men run amok. Brutus, the quintessential Roman, follows Caesar in spurning the feminine aspect of the psyche, rejecting wifely counsel, intuition, heavenly portents, and warmth of feeling in favor of rigid stratagems and unyielding calculations. This *modus operandi*, coupled with the grisly struggle for prestige, creates the perfect storm of chaos which Antony invokes in his cry of "Havoc." (III, i, 276 ff.) Here he echoes Northumberland, again in *King Henry IV, Part Two*:

> Let heaven kiss earth! Now let not nature's hand
> Keep the wild flood confined! Let order die!
> And let this world no longer be a stage
> To feed contention in a ling'ring act;
> But let one spirit of the first-born Cain
> Reign in all bosoms, that each heart being set
> On bloody courses, the rude scene may end,
> And darkness be the burier of the dead!
> (I, i, 153-160)

Confronted with a massive historical record, to make his "two-hours traffic of our stage," (*Romeo and Juliet*, I, i, Chorus) Shakespeare had to leave much on the cutting room floor. What remains is enough, however, to convey to the astute viewer the utter vacuity and craven cynicism of the play's chief protagonist - enough, that is, if reading is first preceded by unreading. Sadly, it almost never is. Yet it can be argued that it is unreading which is the very *nodus* of the play. What prevents Prof. Bloom from affirming Caesar's paternity is not any lack of textual evidence, but his inability to extricate himself from the hoary lessons of his youth. He must cling to the "noble" Brutus so admired of the Board of Regents, or risk unmasking not the heroical "human," but an avaricious minotaur lurking in the political labyrinth.

In order to win the approbation of the commons at Caesar's funeral, Mark Antony must undo the spell, unread the oration of Brutus, the speech in which he drapes himself in the flags of "honour" and patriotism. Antony's unreading is our cue to follow. Dismantling the fulsome rhetoric, he leaves not one stone standing on another. Brutus is not honorable. On the contrary, he is a double-dealing knave. Yet, some still tell their students that Brutus is honorable. (Garber, 412) After all, he litters the stage with "honour." Here was "the noblest Roman of them all." (V, v, 67) If so, then honor must be indistinguishable from talk of honor, for that is all he gives us, mere lip service. And in that long-faced babble about honor there is not one honorable deed. Nobility should be made of sterner stuff. Brutus begs that we credit him for his honor, defer to him as Rome's *Praetor Urbanus.* "Believe me for mine honour, and have respect to mine honour, that you may believe," (III, i, 14-15) he wheezes. In other words, assent is solicited on the basis of our sheer credulity, in response to nothing more than self-serving assertion and rhetoric. Mark Antony makes short work of that. Brutus was no more noble than Caesar was the North Star. And yet today the tide has turned the other way. Our hearts are there in the Capitol, with Brutus.

WORKS CITED

Harold Bloom, *Shakespeare: The Invention of the Human*, Riverhead Books, 1998

Marjorie Garber, *Shakespeare After All*, Anchor Books, 2004

James Howe, *A Buddhist's Shakespeare: Affirming Self-Deconstructions*, Associated University Presses, 1994

Jean-Paul Sartre, *Being and Nothingness*, Hazel Barnes, trans., Philosophical Library, 1956.

William Shakespeare: The Complete Works, Second edition, G. Taylor and S. Wells, eds., Clarendon Press, 2005

Online Sources

Plutarch, *Parallel Lives, Life of Caesar, Life of Brutus*

9
Indices of Divinity in Shakespeare's *All's Well That Ends Well*

I. Introduction

*W*hat does Shakespeare think about God? These pages present a modest contribution to the discourse concerning this question. It is not our purpose to delve into the private views and practices of the poet. They are unavailable, and cannot be reliably deduced. (Bloom, 7-8) Enough ink has been spilled in that singularly unrewarding venture, one we gladly leave to others. As the very identity of the author has become a topic of contention, arguments about his credal and ecclesiastical affiliations can only generate more heat than light. Rather, our task must be to fix upon expressions of transcendence in his verses. There, if anywhere, must reside the working convictions of our *magister*.

A thorough study of the role and meaning of religion in the plays and poetry of Shakespeare would be the campaign of a lifetime, and test sorely the enervated attention spans of the twenty-first century. Fortunately, a shorter route exists. Instead of laboriously surveying the totality of Shakespeare's oeuvre to gain a comprehensive appreciation of the place of religion in his art, it may be more efficient to focus on a single work, where we can behold, as in a speculum, the way in which devotional ideas, themes and expressions function and advance his poetic and dramatic agendas.

All's Well That Ends Well (hereinafter "*AWEW*") is elected on account of its centrality and relative straightforwardness. In its composition, Shakespeare embellished an anecdote of Giovanni Boccaccio's *The Decameron* (1353): Third Day, Ninth Story. What is striking and most useful about the relationship of these two writings is that the Italian's version is entirely secular; it contains nary a drop of religion or theology. Thus every note of religiosity found in *AWEW* was added by Shakespeare, providing an instructive contrast which lays bare his own religious vocabulary and associated concepts. In what follows we will anatomize those Shakespearean accretions, reconstructing in the process an overview of his syncretistic vision. We will then turn our attention to the way in which one contemporary school of thought, cultural materialism, approaches the same subject.

II. Boccaccio's Tale: Summary and Analysis

In France there lived an alluring young lady by the name of Gilette of Narbonne, daughter of an illustrious and recently deceased physician, Master Gerard of Narbonne, who was the personal attendant of Isnard, Count of Roussillon. The Count had one child, a son named Bertrand, reared as Gilette's playfellow. As she neared adulthood, she found herself hopelessly in love with him. At about this time, the boy's father died, causing responsibility for him to pass to the King of France, triggering his transfer to Paris. Shortly thereafter, Gilette's own father passed away, leaving her a fortune and much medical knowledge. Despite their separation, she remained obsessed with Bertrand.

There now came to her news that the King was suffering from a serious disease, one which court doctors could not mend. She resolved to go to there to try to restore the royal health, and possibly induce Bertrand to marry her. Having prepared medicine based on her father's formula, she rode to Paris and approached the stricken monarch. Though he was skeptical, in the end a bargain was struck, under the terms of which, if she could banish his illness, he would reciprocate by using his authority to provide her with a husband.

In a short time Gilette did in fact make the King well, and requested Bertrand be made her spouse. Though the young man protested that she was far beneath his social station, the King, acknowledging his promise, insisted on obedience and the two were married. However, instead of living with her as man and wife, Bertrand fled to Florence to fight in the wars in which that city was embroiled.

Gilette traveled to the Count's estate, where she learned that Bertrand had declared he would never return to be her husband unless and until she wore the ring he kept on his finger and carried his child in her arms. Telling everyone she would spend the rest of her days as a mendicant, Gilette departed from Roussillon, but instead of setting forth on the advertised journey to an undesignated sanctuary, she went straight to Florence dressed as a pilgrim.

There she was surprised to learn that Bertrand was himself infatuated with a poor Florentine girl whom he was trying to seduce. Gilette lost no time paying this girl and her mother a visit, offering them help in return for their cooperation. It was proposed that the girl communicate to Bertrand that she would gratify his wishes if he would send her his ring, which would then be secretly turned over to Gilette. He would then be allowed to enter her house, and in the dark unwittingly lie not with the unfortunate girl but with Gilette, possibly getting her pregnant.

Boccaccio notes that this scheme made the girl's mother uneasy.

> In the eyes of the gentlewoman, this was no trivial request, for she was afraid lest her daughter's name be brought into disrepute. But after due reflection, she came to the conclusion that it was right and proper for her to assist the good lady to retrieve her husband, and *she would be acting in pursuit of a worthy objective.* (Boccaccio, 271, emphasis added)

That is, the honorable and desirable ends, marriage and family, appeared to justify the means. And so she gave her consent. The umbrageous affair between Gilette and her nominal husband Bertrand commenced forthwith, and in fact continued over the course of "many encounters," until two sons were simultaneously conceived. (Boccaccio, 272) At no time did Bertrand ever understand that he was giving his caresses to Gilette, and each morning he would leave for her "beautiful and precious jewels" as a token of his affection. When the objectives of "the Countess" (Gilette) were accomplished, she bade farewell to the gentlewoman and her daughter, leaving them with five hundred pounds in cash and some of the jewels deposited by Bertrand. The mother then sent her daughter away to cut off any further supposed contact with Bertrand, who himself had been called back to Roussillon. Gilette remained in Florence where she gave birth to twins who much resembled their father. She then set out on her return, and reached Montpelier, where she learned that the Count (Bertrand) would be holding a feast at Roussillon "on All Saints' Day." Thither she traveled at once, arriving there on the holy day dressed in pilgrim garb, but carrying two infants in her arms. (Boccaccio, 273) Confronting Bertrand before the assembled celebrants and showing him his ring and two young sons, she confessed all that had happened, entreating him to accept her as his wife. With the encouragement from the others, and faced with his look-alike offspring and ring, Bertrand was overwhelmed, and in a sudden volte-face, embraced Gilette as his own bride, from that time forward faithful and true.

* * *

This amusing vignette was written by Boccaccio in the aftermath of the great plague which ravaged Florence in 1348. It is, in effect, a shot across the bow of the medieval conception of marriage. Its accent is on the imperatives of life rather than outward forms and ceremonies. It features a determined, pro-active heroine who knows what she wants and refuses to be cheated of her earthly patrimony by artificial rules and theological niceties. The experience of the plague taught the beleaguered people of Europe that life is too short to tolerate indefinite postponementof the few joys it affords. As the survivors of the Black Death crawled out of their cellars and burrows, they sought the gratifications of the sublunary sphere, and in art celebrated their natural right to do so. At that very moment the Renaissance was inaugurated. The sophisticated narrators in *The Decameron*, all refugees from the plague, pass their time telling bawdy, cynical tales tending to present the canniness of life as superior to medieval conceptions of pious virtue, asceticism and martyrdom. As such, although set within "Christendom," the stories in *The Decameron*, and the tale of Gilette and Bertrand in particular, are expressions of a naturalism and humanism which function as an implicit critique of the prevailing ethos. Though Gilette and Bertrand are finally united on a Church holy day, All Saints' Day, the selection of that feast is intended as heavily ironical. What is important to Gilette (and Bertrand also) is not veneration of the dead (*i.e.*, the canonized faithful of the Church) but celebration of the living, and by implication, acknowledgement of the prerogatives of succeeding generations. For it cannot have escaped the attention of the sapient survivors of the Black Death, including Boccaccio, that that catastrophe did not usher in the end of the world and Last Judgment, but rather wiped the slate clean, inviting Europeans to contemplate not only their own immediate exigencies, (pointedly expressed by the lascivious Lavatch (I, iii, 27-55)) but also the prospect of ages yet unborn (as we sense in the jeremiad of

Parolles against virginity). (I, i, 109-160)

Of course, viewed from the point of view of medieval Christian theology, the union of Gilette and Bertrand is not virtue but mortal sin. To have marriage there must be consent. Since Bertrand was coerced to marry Gilette it would be argued this critical element was withheld and so lacking. That is proved easily enough by his abrupt departure and refusal of cohabitation. Further, under customary law there must be consummation in order that a declared marriage be regarded as anything more than a sham. But Bertrand refused. Absent mutual consent and consummation, such putative matrimony is null and void, and either party could have successfully petitioned for annulment. Third, when Bertrand has intercourse with Gilette he believes he is embracing the young lady he has tried to seduce. Therefore, the act is adulterous per *Matthew* 5: 27-28. Bertrand commits adultery in his heart, a peccancy unrelieved by the adventitious fact of Gilette's duplicitous participation. Gilette is a fedary thereto and shares equally in the wrong with Bertrand, whom she has suborned via an extravagant ruse. Finally, as they are neither legally nor spiritually bound to one another at their reunion at Roussillon, for the reasons cited above, any intercourse between them is adultery and mortal sin. Such children as are born of their union are illegitimate. Boccaccio's narrative of Gilette of Narbonne, then, is not a mere bagatelle, but a hostile paradox, an engine of rhetorical war, a casuistic exemplar which strikes at the very root of Christian dogma. In fact, Boccaccio's book was eventually banned.

> While in seclusion and escaping from an outbreak of the plague, a group of young men and women divert themselves by telling stories to each other. These tales form Boccaccio's *Decameron*.... [I]t was placed on the Roman Index of Forbidden Books in 1559 by order of Pope Paul IV, with objections centered around 'offensive sexual acts' in which clerics, monks, nuns, and abbesses in the work engaged. However, its popularity was so great that an expurgated version was printed in 1573. (*Heresy, Sedition & Obscenity*)

Nor could this portion of *The Decameron* be rehabilitated by contending that consent and consummation had been achieved *ex post facto*, that is, at the time of the reunion of Gilette and Bertrand. For consent must be present at the ceremony of marriage, with sequent consummation. Instead, what occurred was Bertrand's spiritual adultery, which could only be viewed as consummation of the union with Gilette by gross sophistry and delusion.

The ultimate thrust of Boccaccio's story is that, despite the contrived precepts of Christian doctrine, actual good may come out of a deed technically bad, rescuing the dubious act from immorality. In an early example of utilitarianism, Boccaccio shows that the praiseworthy end can justify the meretricious means; hence the title Shakespeare affixes to his dramatic reprise of Boccaccio's story, "*All's Well That Ends Well.*" Professor Harold Bloom prefers the term "pragmatism." (Bloom, 354) What matters is that by cleverly circumventing any illicit congress with actual third parties, a man and a woman find enduring conjugal love for one another through a deception, and produce children to carry on the human enterprise. In the eyes of Boccaccio and his admirers, this represents a palmary victory for the human spirit. As we will see, Shakespeare, who gives that title to his amplified version of the story, seems to concur: if the end be well, all is well. His play carries on the deconstruction of Christian theology begun by Boccaccio.

It may be remarked in passing that what Boccaccio - and perhaps Shakespeare - seem to regard as an auspicious ending is nothing of the sort. To the contrary, it is an ill beginning. For, despite contemporary and all-too-fashionable strictures on the notion of literary character, to the extent one takes such a story seriously, as more than alphabet soup, it is impossible to avoid the inference that Gilette (or Helena) will inevitably remember the callow attitude and churlish behavior of a husband, who, on the eve of married life in France, was chasing wildly after some pretty face in Italy. (See, II, i, 19-22) From such anticipated reflections one might expect nothing but bitterness and misery. The day of ultimate reckoning, after all, is not the honeymoon. Better to heed the maxim of Solon, who is reported to have commented that we should regard no man as happy until he is dead.

III. Indices of Divinity in All's Well That Ends Well

In adapting Boccaccio's story for Elizabethan audiences, Shakespeare perforce crafted something of an hybrid: a 14th century Florentine tale re-set in a 16th century France inhabited by speakers of the English language. A secular plot in which a daughter of a prominent physician goes to extreme lengths to trap the nobleman on whom she has set her heart becomes a scaffold supporting a bizarre welter of devotional figures, tropes, expressions and other usages, comprising Catholic, Protestant and pagan traditions. By transposing an early Renaissance plotline willy-nilly to the fractious Elizabethan era, Shakespeare opens the floodgates, pouring into his captious and intenable vessel the antagonistic spiritual confluences of his epoch. The situation was far simpler for Boccaccio: his book was an anti-clerical satire of a single unified Christendom which had been compromised by the plague. Instead of recreating that more homogeneous world of the *Respublica Christiana*, as he does, for example, in *Romeo and Juliet*, Shakespeare in *AWEW* chooses to inscribe the sectarian strife of Elizabethan England within a 14th century narrative, retaining the same contrived resolution of the bed trick. The result is an aesthetically endearing but heady concoction, in which newly introduced elements of Christianity clash with Helena's unscrupulous devices.

Despite its heavy doses of Christian terms and ideas, then, *AWEW* remains as resolutely non-Christian as its Italian predecessor. It is in no sense a Christian play, but by the inclusion of so much Christian content becomes in a sense a comment on Christianity. The placing of *The Decameron* on the Index of proscribed books as late as 1559, one year after Elizabeth's coronation, shows the judgment of the Church, a judgment which was surely shared by English Puritans who would take *Matthew* 5: 27-28 with grave seriousness, and view its traducing as anathema. (Paglia, 207) And as diverse a phenomenon as Christianity has become, it would be hard to think of any denomination which would sanction a marriage founded on the sort of mendacious intimacy we find practiced by Helena and Bertram. At the very least, such a couple would need to be shriven, counseled, and fortified in the faith, after which they might be permitted to marry properly and legitimate their misbegotten offspring. If, then, we are searching for the tenor of religion in Shakespeare, and look to *AWEW* for insight, it becomes immediately clear that not only is Shakespeare writing without Christian intention, his aim is in part to show that the Church is actually inimical to human fulfillment, and that it is precisely by artful manipulations of its protocols that we can best achieve our ends.

In a single trope, Shakespeare sets aside altogether the Christian viewpoint. After delivering his amusing paean to cuckoldry, the clown Lavatch remarks on the commonalities of Catholic and Protestant:

If men could be contented to be what they are,
there were no fear in marriage. For young Chairbonne

the puritan and old Poisson the papist, howsome'er their
hearts are severed in religion, their heads are both one:
they may jowl horns together like any deer i'th' herd.
(I, iii, 50-55)

The reference to a Catholic as a "papist" is bluntly disparaging, and,
set opposite "puritan," suggests the other side is no better. Such language
is sufficient to rule out authorship by either a practicing Catholic or a
serious Reformer. The division of Christianity into two species is held
up as artificial and absurd, and a negative reflection on the faith. The
Catholic on fast days consumes only fish, while the Reformer or Protestant ("puritan") contents himself with meat. Yet both may be cuckolded,
and, by implication already are so by churches, which, while making
oeillades at the laity, serve in truth the interests of the clergy.

While a great number of the plays in the canon feature priests,
ministers, nuns, bishops, monks, saints, and cardinals, there is in
AWEW not one ecclesiastical personage. Jesus of Nazareth himself is
never mentioned. Further, there are no houses of Christian worship, no
cathedrals, churches or temples of any Christian sect. No religious rites
are depicted, nor does anyone utter anything that might be regarded as
a prayer directed to God. No one acts from any identifiably Christian
motive. Insofar as appearances of genuine Christian piety or divinity
are concerned, there is a complete void. The reason is not far to seek:
AWEW recapitulates the secular story of Gilette of Narbonne. It is true
that she declares her intention to make a "pilgrimage," but only because
that is the most expedient excuse she can invent to travel, and in fact she
makes no "pilgrimage" at all. Helena is literally cut from the same cloth.
The so-called "pilgrimages" of Gilette and Helena are charades, as false
as Richard III's public pretensions of sanctity, put on to disarm the authorities and march ruthlessly towards the crown. (*The Tragedy of King
Richard the Third*, III, sc. vii, 95-235) In declaring their intentions to go
on a pilgrimage, both heroines tell the same lie. The fact is that Helena
shows not a trace of conventional sanctity. Were she endowed with anything like that, the "bed-trick" would be ruled out.

AWEW is Christian, then, not in substance but in its language.
And it is in this respect that it differs from *The Decameron*. The characters in *AWEW* are inveterate word droppers, whose sentences are laced
with expressions and locutions drawn not only from Christianity but
from older traditions as well. Aside from its setting in France and Italy,
what is Christian about this play is its vocabulary. For example, the term

"heaven" occurs 24 times. Yet that term is never taken seriously in any doctrinal or metaphysical sense. It is a mere perfunctory, vacuous invocation or declamation, a pleasant sounding euphemism for Whatever-Powers-May-Be. An informal frequency count of usages in *AWEW* which may be associated with the Christian religion is as follows:

Heaven	24
God	20
Holy	8
Saint	6
Devil	6
Pilgrim	6
Prayer	6
Flesh	5
Sin	4
Blessing	3
Hell	2
Puritan	2
Papist	1
Priest	1
Nun	1
Friar	1
Christian	1
Christendom	1
Satan	1
Limbo	1

For example, in her Polonious-like address to the departing Bertram, his mother the Countess concludes her litany of maxims with a valediction:

> What heaven more will
> That thee may furnish and my prayers pluck down,
> Fall on thy head.
> (I, i, 65-67)

While these sentiments may appear well-intended and sincere, they are sufficiently bland and euphemistic, lacking in specific content, that to be considered Christian is impossible. The term "heaven" is too general to refer to something in particular, and reminds one of the "unknown god" of the Athenians famously derided by St. Paul. (*Acts* 17:23) Helena too expresses herself in these amorphous terms.

> Our remedies oft in ourselves do lie
> Which we ascribe to heaven. The fated sky
> Gives us free scope, only doth backward pull
> Our slow designs when we ourselves are dull.
> (I, i, 212-215)

When St. Augustine in his *Confessions* wrestles with the problem of free will in relation to the omniscience of the Creator of heaven and earth, that is a deliberation which occurs as part of a Christian discourse. Helena, taking up the same issue, does so as a secular thinker, and uses the vague term "heaven," a nebulosity selected precisely for its imprecision and lack of identifiable meaning. If this comedy were written in the Christian tradition, Helena would be shown praying to God through Christ to help her. This is not done. Instead, the emphasis is on bold action by the individual through which the self is liberated as her purposes find fulfillment.

Or, consider the intellectual confusion over the healing of the King's fistula. As the courtiers await the outcome of the treatment administered by Helena, they lament the skepticism of the times.

> They say miracles are past, and we have our
> philosophical persons to make modern and familiar
> things supernatural and causeless. Hence it is that we
> make trifles of terrors, ensconcing ourselves into seeming
> knowledge when we should submit ourselves to an
> unknown fear.
> (II, iii, 1-6)

This profound observation needs to be put in context. The general opinion of the court is that, based on the medical books of Galen and the applications thereof by the royal physicians, the King's disease cannot be cured. To do that would require a miracle, defined by the courtiers as "a showing of a heavenly effect in an earthly actor." (II, iii, 24-25) It is that miracle which Helena would have to provide. But whatever religion she may possess has nothing to do with the cure. That is based on the practice of her father, who wrote his prescription for the cure of such a sickness. While some small, unknowing persons in the court might view the King's remarkable recovery as a "miracle" in the Christian sense, (II, iii, 30-32), we know that it is no such thing, but the result of the correct use of empirical knowledge. That same skepticism about "miracles" was shown at the very outset of Shakespeare's career in the so-called "miracle at St. Alban's," in *King Henry VI, Part Two*, (II, i, 64-159), which is exposed as a fraud.

There is no need to multiply examples. The interested reader can examine the use of the indexed terms above as they are used in *AWEW* and will find that none of them entail or support the presence of a genuine Christian point of view.

What then? Are we thus thrust into the cold arms of secularism, humanism or atheism? No. For the sacral dimension of *AWEW* is not limited to its Christian vocabulary. There is a vitally important pagan subtext which must be reckoned with. That is not altogether surprising in an author as heavily influenced as Shakespeare was by Ovid's *Metamorphoses*. As the biblical scholar Roger Stritmatter concedes, the influence on Shakespeare of Ovid probably exceeds even that of the *Geneva Bible* of his time. (Stritmatter, 19) Further, we can hardly ignore the monumental commentary of England's poet laureate, Ted Hughes, who after more than a decade's study concluded that Shakespeare's entire corpus is a sustained illustration and elaboration of the ancient matriarchal mythos. The pagan subtext, non-existent in Boccaccio's original opus, is superimposed quite deliberately by Shakespeare.

Consider this word frequency count.

Diana	18
Mars	10
Love	4
goddess	3
god	3
Jove	2
Cupid	2
Iris	1
Plutus	1
Hesperus	1
Furies	1
Nessus	1

What do these figures portend for our comprehension of *AWEW*?

Close reading will show that while Helena is not animated by any aspect of the Christian deity, she is very moved indeed by members of the pagan pantheon, who are not concealed by generic terms but mentioned by name. Particularly compelling for Helena is the goddess Diana.

At the opening of the play, Helena engages in badinage with the rogue Parolles on the topic of virginity. The spicy dialogue is interesting because it is the one moment in the play in which she is portrayed as a three-dimensional and thus sympathetic human being rather than an hysterical monomaniac. (Bloom, 351) Here for the first and last time she displays a clever wit, flirtatious manner, and at the same time, an attractive commitment to an ideal unrelated to (even opposed to) her quest for the churlish young Count of Roussillon. Despite the armada of rational arguments rolled out by Parolles, Helena remains stubbornly loyal to chastity. In this she surpasses the many conventional female characters in Shakespeare who are mere "maids" who have not yet found suitable mates, *e.g.,* Hero in *Much Ado About Nothing.*

Of virginity, at the end of the debate, she concludes modestly, "I will stand for't a little, though therefore I die a virgin." (I, i, 131-132) No words such as these are ever uttered by Boccaccio's Gilette, furnishing Helena with a depth associated with an inner tension of inclination and principle.

It might be supposed that Helena's chastity is held by her as a precept or value in her alleged Christian faith. But the text shows something else. Helena is a votary of Diana, the goddess of chastity. But, as passionately obsessed with and desirous of Bertram, she is an uneasy disciple, and therein lies the rub, the true crux of this masterful drama and exploration of the feminine psyche. In confessing to the Countess of Roussillon her love for Bertram her son (who is also Helena's stepbrother), Helena pleads that the Countess consider the dilemma in which this overwhelming ardor places her in relationship to her prized chastity.

> My dearest madam,
> Let not your hate encounter with my love,
> For loving where you do; but if yourself,
> Whose agèd honour cites a virtuous youth,
> Did ever in so true a flame of liking
> Wish chastely and love dearly, that your Dian
> Was both herself and Love, O then give pity
> To her whose state is such that cannot choose

> But lend and give where she is sure to lose,
> That seeks to find not that her search implies,
> But riddle-like lives sweetly where she dies.
> (I, iii, 203-213)

Helena's impossible dream is that somehow Diana might allow her to win the love of Bertram and yet retain her prized virginity, in much the same way that Cinderella can enjoy the physical intimacy of the ball with Prince Charming, yet have her fragile "glass slipper" returned, unspoiled and intact. In this respect Helena somewhat resembles the beautiful young Amazon Emilia in *The Two Noble Kinsmen*, who prefers female company to male. She is to be given as wife to the victor in the battle of Palamon and Arcite. "I am bride-habited," she cries to the Goddess Diana,

> But maiden-hearted. A husband I have 'pointed,
> But do not know him. Out of two, I should
> Choose one and pray for his success, but I
> Am guiltless of election. Of mine eyes
> were I to lose one, they are equal precious --
> I could doom neither: that which perished should
> Go to't unsentenced. Therefore, most modest queen,
> He of the two pretenders that best loves me
> and has the truest title in't, let him
> Take off my wheaten garland, or else grant
> The file and quality I hold I may
> Continue in thy band.
> (*The Two Noble Kinsmen*, V, iii, 14-26)

Since she has allowed her love to settle on just one man, while her transcendent loyalty is to a single divinity, Helena's predicament is even more poignant than Emilia's. Can Diana really play two roles, as Helena desperately wants, that of Eros and chastity, simultaneously? Here is a prayer that tests even the potency of the gods.

It is in this conflicted situation that Diana enters the text, when Reynaldo first alerts the Countess that poor Helena is in love with Bertram.

> Her matter was, she loved your
> son. Fortune, she said, was no goddess, that had put

such difference betwixt their two estates; Love no god,
that would not extend his might only where qualities
were level; Dian no queen of virgins, that would suffer
her poor knight surprised without rescue in the first
assault or ransom afterward.
(I, iii, 108 -113)

Here we see the echo of a distressed soliloquy in which Helena
complains to the gods of her plight, particularly to Diana, accusing her
of deserting "her poor knight" (meaning Helena) by failing to protect
her from a romantic attachment having its roots in childhood. The
gauntlet is thrown down even at the very feet of Diana. And this challenge is immediately followed by the almost petulant wish that Diana
might maintain the very chastity she seems prepared to take away. In
other words, we might say that Helena is suffering from a "Diana Complex," in which she is caught between two poles of the Goddess, that of
Diana on the one side and Venus on the other, an opposition we find
repeated in *The Two Noble Kinsmen*.

After Helena has healed the King of France of his ulcer and is
about to declare her choice of husband comes Helena's third invocation
of Diana.

Now, Dian, from thy altar do I fly;
And to imperial Love, that god most high,
do my sighs stream.
(II, iii, 75-77)

In this third and critically significant call to her patron Goddess,
Helena openly characterizes herself as leaving the realm of the Moon
Goddess and flying to the realm of Venus and her son Cupid. Yet from
what we have seen to this point, it is understood that she is loath to leave
Diana behind. In fact, we know all too well that in her heart she never
does.

Now it is at just this point that Shakespeare does something truly remarkable. Following the flight of Bertram to the wars and Helen's
desperate plan to find him in Florence, she encounters quite by happenstance the young lady who in Boccaccio had no name, that is, the
woman whom Bertram is seeking to seduce, and who will be an accessory to the bed trick. And what Shakespeare does is give her the name
"Diana." Three times we hear the Goddess called, and she then steps

forth, disguised as an innocent maid whose most precious possession is her chastity. Just as Aristophanes in his play Ploutos has the god of wealth enter the action disguised as a blind beggar who is brought into a poor man's home, so Shakespeare by mentioning Plutus (V, iii, 103) hints at his *deus-ex-machina* in which the goddess Diana comes to personally rescue Helena without revealing her identity to anyone. So it is that when she introduces herself to Bertram as "Diana," he exclaims, with unwitting insight:

> *Titled goddess, and worth it with addition!*
> (IV, ii, 3-4)

Though Bertram may be more focused on getting Diana in bed than reflecting on her identity and role in the drama, this telling exclamation reveals and confirms Shakespeare's dramaturgical strategy: to have the summoned divinity descend and break through into the human sphere in her own right and name. Diana does not join her devotee anonymously or pseudonymously, but eponymously, with much greater impact. While lip service is paid to "heaven" and "God" at various junctures, these pious ejaculations remain at all times elements of rhetoric. Contrary to Christian, Catholic and humanistic exegeses, what moves Helena as a character (beyond her passion for Bertram) are: (1) her devotion to the goddesses of chastity and love, that is, to elements of the pagan pantheon, and (2) the goddess's subtle entrance into the plot to take a hand in Helena's well-being and difficult transition from her order to that of Venus and Cupid (Love). Notice that Helena's biological mother is never alluded to in *AWEW*. Diana's caring action resembles the maternal solicitude of the Countess, a foster mother, who reaches out to Helena. (See, I, iii, 132-180) Although Diana might well have been offended at Helena's passion and desertion of her order to join the ranks of Eros, she has surely witnessed such desertions many times. Instead of resenting Helena's ardor for Bertram, she recognizes that this unique young lady still longs for chastity even in the midst of her romantic imbroglio, and, putting selfish feelings to one side, she too willingly becomes a mother for Helena. But unlike the coarse and boisterous *deus-ex-machina* staged by Jupiter in *Cymbeline, King of Britain* (V, v, 185-216), her incarnation is a whisper of affection, as gentle as a mother's touch. She is content that her presence be felt, not known.

Thus, guided by Diana, who agrees to the curious substitution which places Helena and not herself in the bed with Bertram, Helena's duplicitous tryst is a trauma from which the girl emerges seemingly unscathed. Yet it takes little imagination to put ourselves there in that darkened chamber, and hear the Count of Roussillon calling out, ironically and his ignorance, to - of all people - Diana. This is one reason that *AWEW* is a comedy. Helena must force herself to accept that on the occasion of what is taken to be her marital consummation, her husband is not only thinking of another woman, but actually believes he is possessing her, and that it is in this ambiguous instant that her child is conceived. And though we may suppose a youth such as callow Bertram would speak to the woman in his arms using another's name, Helena might find consolation in the fact that the name she hears belongs to her beloved goddess of chastity.

IV. *Shakespeare's Paganism*

From a purely empirical perspective, looking at the totality of the works, one would have to say that Shakespeare's religious outlook is a potpourri of multiple traditions. It is child's play to detect expressions here of Protestantism, Catholicism, and humanism. And it is not difficult to see why various commentators have focused on one or the other of these as either the outlook of the author personally or as the dominant leitmotif of the texts taken as a whole. If we leave aside the biographical self, which, as we noted at the start of this discussion, tends to be viewed as a vexed *Ding an sich*, and confine ourselves to the creative writings facing us, certain observations commend themselves to our consideration. The first is that writing realistically about folks in the Christian lands of the British Isles and Europe, with an historical purpose in mind, it was inevitable that large swaths of that faith would find their way into the discourses of Shakespeare's characters. And the question is, whether those Christian locutions should be regarded as significant. There are good reasons to think not. For Christianity in Shakespeare is merely the background noise left over from the "big bang" of Roman expansionism. At the summit of his art lie dramatic poems which feature a humanity bereft of any religious consolation, a race for which God has effectively fallen silent. *Lear, Macbeth,* and *Titus Andronicus* come to mind. But the pagan note is always audible. There are others, but the territory is too vast to encompass in this space. If one familiar with the full range of Shakespeare's oeuvre determines that his eclecticism rules out Christianity as the center of gravity, it is natural to characterize the corpus as an expression of Renaissance humanism. This has often been done. Yet, the seething mass of pre-Christian deities and supernatural events which overwhelms any long-term visitor to the Shakespearean landscape is difficult to dismiss as mere decoration, and, if taken at face value, it is inconsistent with any smug secularism.

For example, in the English history play *King Henry VI*, whose three parts taken together make it the longest in the canon, we can see that the nodal event is not the quarrel in the temple garden sparking the War of the Roses, but the seance organized by Dame Eleanor Cobham, the Duchess of Gloucester (See, *The First Part of the Contention of the Two famous Houses of York and Lancaster*, Act I, sc. iv), a seance disrupted by a group of Yorkist lords seeking to undermine Duke Humphrey. Here the regnant spirit through a medium predicts the fates of the King, the Duke of Suffolk and the Duke of Somerset. And while the skeptical lords dismiss this heathen oracle as a cheap fraud, Shakespeare goes far out of his way to demonstrate the accuracy of its prognostications. Doing so tends to align the history pageant with the tragedies and comedies so freely populated with a variety of ghosts, witches, goblins, fairies, spirits, gods and goddesses. The tendency of Shakespeare is at all times to place the dramatic hero and his social and political world against an electrified spiritual template which forms the intellectual horizon of the action. Taking up the brave new world of secular humanism in all its many manifestations as the critical standpoint from which to approach the works means that such exegetes will occupy the position of the deluded lords York and Buckingham in *King Henry VI*. Brutus in *Julius Caesar* is a student of cool philosophy who in the midst of his reading encounters a ghostly visitor which defies every bit of logic and knowledge. Here is something that simply cannot be, he feels. And then he learns that this is his own "evil spirit." Shall his clumsy sophistication be ours?

Perhaps that the most candid and adequate acceptation of the texts is to take Prince Hamlet at his word when he tells Horatio that there are more things in heaven and in earth than are dreamt of in his complacent philosophy. It is not the God of Abraham and Moses, not the saints, who visibly appear in the plays of Shakespeare, but rather the denizens of the so-called pagan pantheon, and there is every reason for us as students of Shakespeare to take these figures as seriously as they seem to be intended. Was Shakespeare just catering to the sensationalism of the groundlings in presenting such *disjecta membra*? No, not when our very understanding of the works is essentially bound to them. Those sapient sensibilities which presume that Shakespeare was the P.T. Barnum or

Ripley of his day turn out to be themselves already inscribed in the very art they seek to emasculate.

It is fashionable in academic circles when encountering the figure of Diana or Cynthia in Shakespeare to simply treat these as flattering references to Queen Elizabeth I, or as cryptic replies to Spenser. Indeed, it is important to note that King Henry VIII suffered famously from the identical illness which hobbles the King of France in *AWEW*: a fistula. (Hurren) Henry's eventual replacement on the throne by his allegedly virginal daughter, Elizabeth, is recapitulated by the rhythm of the play. Such topical signals are always possible. But to maintain that the meaning of dramaturgical apparitions is wholly exhausted in their function as sociopolitical or literary allusions is not plausible, if for no other reason than the fact that the sheer variety of divinities found in Shakespeare goes far beyond Diana (i.e., Artemis) and her Olympian peers. Shakespeare shows repeatedly that his characters never fathom what the spirits are with whom they have contact. It is much easier and more reassuring to be informed by lofty authorities that the ghost in *Hamlet, Prince of Denmark* is an escapee from "Purgatory" (that is, a place on a map) than occupy the queasy position of the Prince himself, who never quite manages to reduce that ominous phenomenon to any common and pedestrian category. To speak of the Christian "God," on the other hand, is already to totter on the brink of theological rationalism, that is, *gnosis*. But when we speak of something as "god" ("theos") in the context ancient Greek, we mean the antithesis, that is, something which in its very unfathomable strangeness stands outside the comfortable region of our little taxonomies. Theos is uncanny, *unheimliche*. In Anglo-Saxon, it is Wyrd. It is what raises the hair on the back of the neck, that for which we have no precedent or analogy. This unruly animus was that against which Christianity struggled in launching its campaign to annihilate the gods, a vendetta of two millennia in which it was later reinforced by its offspring, scientific naturalism. The works of Shakespeare stand as an antidote to such deicide. They serve as a home, a refuge in which the gods may dwell. Roberto Calasso observes:

> But how does a god make himself manifest? In the Greek language the word is theos, "god," has no vocative case, observed the illustrious linguist Jakob Wackernagel. Theos has a predicative function: it designates something that happens. There is a wonderful example of this in Euripides Helen: - "*O theoi. theos gar kai to gignoskein philous*" - "O gods: rec-

ognizing the beloved is god." Kerenyi thought that the distinguishing quality of the Greek world was this habit of "saying of an event: it is theos." And an event referred to as theos could easily become Zeus. (Calasso, 5)

Much has been said in our modern age about the disappearance of the gods, but Calasso has the courage to point out the obvious: "the gods are still among us." (Calasso, 21) Where? "[T]his composite tribe of gods now lives only in its stories and scattered idols." (Calasso, 21) He goes on:

And this, one might say, has become the natural condition of the gods: to appear in books - and often in books that few will ever open. Is this the prelude to extinction? Only to the superficial observer. For in the meantime all the powers of the cult of the gods have migrated into a single, immobile and solitary act: that of reading. (Calasso, 22)

He concludes,

The world . . . has no intention of abandoning enchantment altogether. (Calasso, 23)[1]

If we turn briefly to *Macbeth* we find the same intriguing pattern. Just as Helena invokes Diana, who later responds by appearing on her behalf, so Macbeth refers to goddess Hecate twice, at II, i, 49-56 and III, ii, 40-45, well before she finally slithers in to join the witches. Is such efficacious precognition consistent with either the tenets of Christianity or the skepticism of contemporary secularists? Indeed, it is interesting to note that both Macbeth and Banquo speak of the "weird sisters" without ever having been privy to the witches' prior use of that term. How did they acquire it? A few hours' research will verify that Diana and Hecate are polar aspects of the Great Goddess who preceded Christianity by many centuries. She - and not dumb "Nature" - is the regnant

---

1 Compare F. H. Bradley: "And so, when poetry, art, and religion have ceased wholly to interest, or when they show no longer any tendency to struggle with ultimate problems and to come to an understanding with them; when the sense of mystery and enchantment no longer draws the mind to wander aimlessly and to love it knows not what; when, in short, twilight has no charm - then metaphysics will be worthless." *Appearance and Reality* (1893), p. 3.

(and pregnant!) first Principal of Shakespeare's universe.

Harold Bloom reminds us that not only does Helena unscrupulously subject Bertram to the "bed trick," she also later pretends to be dead, so as to increase the stage effect of her resurrection with child, behavior which Bloom unflinchingly identifies as "singularly unwholesome." This unsavory aspect of Helena's conduct must be offset. For Bloom, "The play protects Helena from our skepticism by presenting her monomania in heroic proportions." (Bloom, 355) But this will not do. Vice writ large is all the more unpalatable. It is only Helena's sincere affiliation with Diana and chastity that allows her to remain above a cesspool of expedience and opportunism as bad as Bertram's. She is redeemed not by "Heaven" but by the original Queen of Heaven. Professor Bloom might take seriously his own words:

> Though G. K. Chesterton liked to think that Shakespeare was a Catholic, at least in spirit, Chesterton was too good a critic to locate Shakespeare's universalism in Christianity. We might learn from that not to shape Shakespeare by our own cultural politics. Comparing Shakespeare with Dante, Chesterton emphasized Dante's spaciousness in dealing Christian love and Christian liberty, whereas Shakespeare *"was a pagan,* in so far that he is at his greatest in describing great spirits in chains." (Bloom, 10, emphasis added)

The figure of Helena is easily misconstrued on account of her (1) occasional Christian vocabulary and her (2) secular orientation in the profession of physical medicine. It is only by patiently tracing her actions and sentiments throughout the course of the entire play that we come to appreciate her actual native piety.

V. *Footnote on Cultural Materialism*

Those who have troubled to follow the argument this far may wish to become acquainted for contrast with one of the dominant schools of orthodox textual interpretation, Cultural Materialism. Firmly entrenched at major universities, it approaches "Shakespeare" as a mere literary epiphenomenon, a side-effect of historical-cultural emanations rather than individual design. If one wants to understand why English literature in schools has fallen on hard times, a glance at the volumes of Stephen Greenblatt or Richard Wilson will reveal much. What matters in this context is a creeping, subterranean Catholicism whose insidious forces excrete the intellectual and artistic works of Renaissance figures, even those who seem at furthest remove from Rome.

Thus, for Mr. Wilson, Helena's subterfuge of letting on that she is going on a pilgrimage to the shrine of Saint Jacques le Grand (III, iv, 4-7) shows that she (and Shakespeare) are "reconnecting the audience with the [Catholic] Europe they have repressed." (Wilson, 2-3) Nothing could be further from the truth. The idea of the daughter of Gerard of Narbonne telling everyone she is going on a pilgrimage is taken directly from *The Decameron*. (Boccaccio, 269) Gilette needs a handy excuse to politely disappear so that she can trail Bertrand to Florence. As the making of pilgrimages was one of the few reasons ladies traveled in late medieval Europe, it was natural for Gilette to seize upon this as her rationale for leaving Roussillon. Thus, for Boccaccio, there isn't even any reason to identify the shrine to which she was going. It's irrelevant. Gilette proceeds directly to Florence.

Shakespeare, in composing a more ambitious poetic work on the same subject, but set in the 16th century and featuring a religious atmosphere splintered by doctrinal conflicts, gives to Helena's destination a local habitation and a name: the Shrine of Saint Jaques le Grand at Compostela. Like Gilette, Helena ignores the false destination, and runs off straight to Florence. It is rather obvious that for purposes of verisimilitude Shakespeare needed a Shrine name to be given in Helena's letter. For this purpose, on account of its popularity, he chose the one at Compostela. It has no more significance than that. Yet on this slender reed Mr. Wilson erects an entire cathedral of speculation, turning Shakespeare's Helena into a heroine of "the Counter-Reformation." Historical records are strip mined to prepare us to learn that "With Spanish gold behind them, nothing was more apt than that the new King's Men should stage a play set on the Jacobean Road to Spain . . . ." (Wilson, 8) What? Helena never thinks for one nanosecond about going to Spain, nor does she head in that direction. (Asimov, 603) Yet we are told that she has made a "detour" and that she "shies away from Spain." (Wilson, 10) We also learn that not only did "Shakespeare's" putative father "John" (who originally applied for a British Coat of Arms) make a pilgrimage to Compostela, but so did Helena's father Gerard of Narbonne! Hypostatization of character is taken here to dizzying heights.

The great irony in all this is that even if there were evidence that Shakespeare attached any significance to the Catholic *terminus ad quem* of Helena's false pilgrimage, it is well shown by Ted Hughes and many others that Catholicism itself is an elaborate restatement of the pagan myth of the Great Goddess. It is also worth recalling that William Shakespeare wrote one of history's most stridently anti-Catholic plays, *King John*, in which the antagonist is the vermiculate Cardinal Pandolf.

We are reminded of Harold Bloom's admonitions on materialist criticism as "arbitrary and ideologically imposed contextualization, the staple of our bad time":

> In "French Shakespeare" . . . the procedure is to begin with a political stance all your own, far out and away from Shakespeare's plays, and then begin to locate some marginal bit of English Renaissance social history that seems to sustain your stance. Social fragment in hand, you move in from the outside upon the poor play, and find some connection, however established, between your supposed social fact and Shakespeare's words." (Bloom, 9)

Bloom's diagnosis of literary vampirism is well illustrated and confirmed by the example of Mr. Wilson's coarse and overbearing mistreatment of *AWEW*.

VI. Coda

It is little noticed that when Harry falls on his knees in the dim grey light before Agincourt, his cry is to Mars, the god of battles. (*The Life of Henry V*, IV, i, 286) It might have been otherwise. There could have been no prayer at all. Or, it might have been addressed to some abstract God of whom he had no ken. Instead, at the moment of greatest human need, the god of war is invoked. Though Harry tells the "Lord" that he has commissioned phalanxes of "sad and solemn priests" to "sing for Richard's soul," Harry's own soul has revealed itself to be a soldier's. His God must be the particular god of war, whatever those sad and solemn priests may suppose. This one scene takes the mask off Shakespeare's own authorial faith. The "Muse of Fire" has heard his prayer, too, and answered, carrying him aloft to the brightest heaven of invention. We may not be able to follow there, but of his sense of transcendence no question exists. True Divinity comes to us in our own form: a Muse for the poet, a Captain for a soldier. To appreciate this is to finally understand the subtle syncretism of Shakespeare's religious vision.

Think of Pericles in his hour of doom, aboard a failing ship. His daughter has just been born in the midst of the tempest, but his beloved wife has perished in the struggle. His cry goes up:

> O, you gods!
> Why do you make us love your worldly gifts?
> And snatch them straight away? We here below
> Recall not what we give, and therein may
> Vie honour with you.
> (*Pericles*, III, i, 23-26, citing not Taylor & Wells, but the Stratford Town Edition of 1904 published by Barnes and Noble, 1994)

These are the words of a tormented polytheist, in his grief hurling a challenge to the company of heaven. Will there be an answer? Yes. As in *AWEW*, it is Diana who responds for Olympus. It is she who shields Marina from the devouring sea, from the psychopathic Queen Dionyza, from the desperate pirates and the perils of the brothel, where Marina magically preserves her chastity. It is Diana who takes in Pericles' wife, Thaisa, brought back to life by the magus Cerimon. And it is Diana who descends from heaven in Scene 21 to comfort Pericles and give back to him that which was snatched away.

> My temple stands in Ephesus. Hie thee thither,
> And do upon my altar sacrifice.
> There when my maiden priests are met together,
> At large discourse thy fortunes in this wise:
> With a full voice before the people all,
> Reveal how thou at sea didst lose thy wife.
> To mourn thy crosses, with thy daughter's call
> And give them repetition to the life.
> Perform my bidding, or thou liv'st in woe;
> Do't, and rest happy, by my silver bow.
> Awake, and tell thy dream.
> (*Pericles*, xxi, 225-235)

At the end of the play, Pericles takes Marina and Helicanus to Diana's temple at Ephesus, (one of the most stupendous wonders of the ancient world) where he is reunited with Thaisa.

Further support for our thesis is provided by *The Comedy of Errors,* which features that temple. Going beyond *Pericles*, Elizabeth Howell Brunner argues in a painstaking and comprehensive analysis of *Com-*

edy of Errors that, though Shakespeare does not mention Diana by name in this early play, the temple therein is most certainly that of Diana / Artemis. Thus Diana's is the saving hand behind the restoration of the characters in that play too.

Shakespeare's unabashed paganism is perhaps most clearly realized by Bloom's student, Camille Paglia in her masterful *Sexual Personae*. (Paglia, 198-207) Though she does not explore *AWEW* directly, extrapolation of her argument is compelling and fruitful. Helena's otherwise inexplicable love for her adopted sibling lays the incestuous foundation for adult desire to seek alchemical union with its other self, that is, with the Adonis figure Bertram. (Paglia, 198-199) Helena, whose animus is a reflection of her physician father, in her fidelity to the man-excluding Diana, exudes an homoerotic sensibility which renders her a sympathetic companion to the Goddess. The love of Helena for Bertram is thus an Ovidian metamorphosis in which Diana merges through Helena into Venus and appropriates Adonis by feminine guile. Though she must perforce lose in the end the intimate friendship of the moon goddess, Helena offers up to her through her conquest of Bertram an appropriate sacrifice.

But in the final analysis, what redeems Helena -- and thereby the play itself -- is neither Helen's single-minded quest for Bertram nor her sexual audacity. It may not even be her devotion to Diana. Rather, it is Diana herself, in whose singular compassion Helena receives her true humanity.

Though the gods may have retreated, we live in their shadow. In metaphysical terms, the "airy nothing" of which Theseus speaks to Hippolyta (*A Midsummer Night's Dream*, V, i, 16) has no name, and waits to be refracted by the poet's art -- and heart. Until then, we dwell in the Nameless, in expectation and in hope. The Greeks called this "airy nothing" "chaos," the inchoate and sacred mother of all things. Chaos is the nameless, the Void. As Heidegger says, "Chaos is the sacred itself." (Calasso, 40) Out of its numinous womb are born the gods of whom Hesiod rhapsodizes. Their queen is Diana (or Hecate on a bad day). The dream is Shakespeare's, and, faithful to Diana's instructions, he sings it to us in his temple of verses. It is appropriate, then, to leave to him last words.

> Laud we the gods,
> And let our crookèd smokes climb to their nostrils
> From our blessed altars.
> (*Cymbeline*, V, vi, 477-479)

WORKS CITED

Isaac Asimov, *Asimov's Guide to Shakespeare*, Wings Books, 1970

Harold Bloom, *Shakespeare: The Invention of the Human*, Riverhead Books, 1998

Giovanni Boccaccio, *The Decameron*, Second Edition, G.H. McWilliam, trans., Penguin Books, 1995

Elizabeth Howell Brunner, "Restoring Goddess Diana: Subtexts of Jealousy in Shakespeare's *The Comedy of Errors*," posted online, 1999

Roberto Calasso, *Literature and the Gods*, Tim Parks, trans., Alfred A. Knopf, 2001

Ted Hughes, *Shakespeare and the Goddess of Complete Being*, Farrar Straus Giroux, 1992

Camille Paglia, *Sexual Personae*, Yale University Press, 1990, Vintage Books, 1991.

William Shakespeare, The Complete Works, Second Edition, S. Wells and G. Taylor, eds., Clarendon Press, 2005

The Complete Works of William Shakespeare, Stratford Town Edition, Barnes & Noble, Inc., 1994

Richard Wilson, "To great St Jaques bound: All's Well That Ends Well in Shakespeare's Europe," *Shakespeare et l'Europe de la Renaissance*, Edite par Yves Peyre et Pierre Kapitaniak, 2005, pp. 273-290. Societe Francaise Shakespeare.

Online Sources

"Heresy, Sedition, Obscenity: The Book Challenged," courtesy of Special Collections, University of Ortago Library, 2010

Elizabeth T. Hurren, MD, "King Henry VIII's Medical World," Senior Lecturer, History of Medicine, Oxford Brookes University

10
Woodstock and the Invention of the Human

For he is but a bastard to the time,
That doth not smack of observation.

-- *Sir Richard Plantagenet*

I. A *Volume of Forgotten Lore*

*T*here is in the British Museum an old and sere manuscript, long abandoned, just now coming to the attention of scholars. (Alexander) It may hold the key to the formation of the modern self. A mere sheaf of paper bearing no title, it is one of a group of anonymous Tudor plays classified impersonally as "Egerton 1994." (Jimenez) It is, in fact, an English renaissance drama set in the era immediately preceding the events depicted in Shakespeare's *King Richard II*. Scholars dub it either "*Thomas of Woodstock*" or "*Richard II, Part One*." We will refer to it simply as "*Woodstock*."

Near the end of this neglected gem is a scene of such remarkable singularity as to cause any true Shakespearean to sit bolt upright in his armchair. Thomas of Woodstock, Duke of Gloucester, and son of King Edward III, is the Lord Protector, a loyal guardian but outspoken critic of the excesses of his nephew King Richard II. As this interlude opens, the plucky and loquacious Thomas is hunkered down in his manse as a posse of Richard's supporters closes in on him. All is hushed and full of foreboding. In this grim situation one of the attendant lords, Cheney, announces that an octet of "country gentlemen" is at the gate with a merry diversion to present. Of course this is not a moment to frolic. But Thomas is no ordinary patrician; despite the shadow of doom hovering about him, he has sufficient *savoir faire* and sense of irony to welcome a recreation. And so we have, briefly, a play within a play, that dramatic device of which Shakespeare was especially fond.

WOODSTOCK

> Are they so near? I prithee let them enter.
> Tell them we do embrace their loves most kindly,
> Give order through the house that all observe them.
> We must accept their loves although the times
> Are no way suited to masques and revels.
>
> What ho, within there.
> Prepare a banquet: Call for lights and music.
> They come in love and we'll accept it so;
> Some sport does well, we're all too full of woe.
>
> They all are welcome; Cheney: Set me a chair.
> We will behold their sport in spite of care.

These guests are not itinerant players, but rather lords incognito. Though Thomas is savvy enough to realize he's probably noosed by his enemies, who might use such a stratagem to capture him, his largeness of spirit and sense of pride outweigh his nagging fears. He admits these strangers.

A trumpet sounds and the goddess Cynthia (that is, Diana) appears as Prologue. Her advent is an established Shakespearean marker. In cadences which ring familiarly in our ears, she speaks:

> From the clear orb of our Ethereal Sphere
> Bright Cynthia comes to hunt and revel here.
> The groves of Callidon and Arden woods
> Of untamed monsters, wild and savage herds,
> We and our knights have freed, and hither come
> To hunt these forests where we hear there lies

A cruel and tusked boar whose terror flies
Through this large kingdom, and with fear and dread
Strikes her a massed greatness pale and dead.
And having viewed from far these towers of stone,
We heard the people, midst their joy and moan,
Extol to heaven a faithful prince and peer
That keeps a court of love and pity here.
Reverent and mild his looks: If such there be,
This state directs, great prince, that you are he.
And ere our knights to this great hunting go,
Before your grace they would some pastime show
In sprightly dancing. Thus they bade me say,
And wait an answer to return or stay.

Diana, goddess of the moon, addresses Thomas directly and ingratiatingly, yet there can be little doubt in his mind that the "tusked boar" whom her minions would assail is none other than he himself. Scarcely believing that his peril could come in such gentle weeds of fancy, Thomas's outward demeanor remains amiable and bright.

The "Callidon" mentioned by Cynthia (that is, Diana) in her introit is, of course, the ancient Greek city of Calydon in Aetolia, where stood the temple dedicated to the twin Greek deities, Artemis (Diana) and Apollo. The Calydonian Boar was sent by Artemis/Diana to punish Calydon, whose king failed to honor her in its rites. The Calydonian Hunt, in which an ensemble of Greek heroes went forth to slay this Boar, was featured in Greek art and poetry. The reader will naturally recall that Calydon is referred to by Shakespeare in a later history play, *King Henry VI, Part Two*, (I, i, 235) in one of the soliloquies of Richard, Duke of York. Typically the Calydonian Boar is a figure of Nemesis, as is made abundantly clear by Ted Hughes in *Shakespeare and the Goddess of Complete Being*. Its most memorable appearance occurs in Shakespeare's first long poem, *Venus and Adonis*. And, in light of the contested question of "Shakespeare's" actual identity, it may be worth observing that the Boar was the personal emblem of Edward de Vere, 17th Earl of Oxford.

The telling locution "joy and moan" occurs in one of Shakespeare's last plays, *Cymbeline*, (IV, ii, 274).

Thomas speaks:

Nay, for heaven's pity, let them come, I prithee.

Pretty device, i'faith, stand by, make room there.
Stir, stir, good fellows, each man to his task,
We shall have a clear night; the moon directs the masque.

Here, however, we have not the bumbling and innocent moon-shine of *A Midsummer Night's Dream*'s "Pyramus and Thisbe," but a more ominous nocturne. As music fills the chamber, we behold none other than a masked Richard, His Majesty, King of England, and three of his base sycophants, clad as "Diana's knights." These are "led in by four other knights with horns about their necks and boarspears in their hands."

As Falstaff in *King Henry IV, Part Two*, (II, iv, 286 ff.) recognizes Hal and Pointz dressed as drawers, so we infer that Thomas suspects that this is his nephew, the King of England, and three of his court epigones, stumbling about like dancing bears. The scene astonishes in its forthright blend of the simple and the fantastic. We are reminded of Falstaff's wish in *King Henry IV, Part One* that he and his thieving companions be known as "Diana's foresters." (I, ii, 25) And we are put in mind of Act V, sc. ii *Titus Andronicus* in which old Titus detects the despicable Chiron and Demetrius, though they are flamboyantly arrayed as "Rape" and "Murder." (V, ii, 64-65)

Taking note of Diana's impersonation by a boy, and teasing his suspected gentlemen callers, Thomas indulges in a bawdy pun, which parallels the one delivered by Prince Hamlet as he dallies at "The Mousetrap" with Ophelia. (III, ii, 111) Then he proceeds to boldly take the King to task right to his face.

WOODSTOCK

Ha, country sports, say ye? 'Fore God 'tis courtly.
A general welcome, courteous gentlemen,
And when I see your faces, I'll give it each man more particular.
If your entertainment fail your merit,
I must ask pardon: My lady is from home
And most of my attendants waiting on her.
But we'll do what we can to bid your welcome;
Afore my God, it joys my heart to see,
Amidst these days of woe and misery,
Ye find a time for harmless mirth and sport.
But 'tis your loves, and we'll be thankful for't: Ah sirrah,

Ye come like knights to hunt the boar indeed.
And heaven, he knows we had need of helping hands:
So many wild boars root and spoil our lands
That England almost is destroy'd by them.
I care not if King Richard heard me speak it;
I wish his grace all good, high heaven can tell,
But there's a fault in some, alack the day:
His youth is led by flatterers much astray.
But he's our king, and God's great deputy,
And if ye hunt to have me second ye
In any rash attempt against his state,
Afore my God, I'll never consent unto it;
I ever yet was just and true to him
And so will still remain. What's now amiss
Our sins have caused, and we must bid heaven's will.
I speak my heart: I am plain Thomas still.
Come, come, a hall and music there; you dance being done
A banquet stands prepared to bid you welcome.

Thereupon the "country gentlemen," including the concealed King Richard, unleash their rustic Bergomask, mimicking the poorer classes which Richard's taxes are bleeding white.

Thomas now realizes his dilemma. If this is actually Richard, his speech will be used to confirm political blasphemy, a capital offense. Though loyalty is professed, the King's policies are roundly condemned. But if these boar-hunting guests are King Richard's foes, allowing them to put on their masque in his home is tantamount to aiding and abetting. And his announced refusal to aid their supposed rebellion could only spark enmity. In short, Thomas has provided plenty to outrage either camp.

The answer is not long in coming. The gambol concluded, Richard and the others reveal themselves.

RICHARD

Guard fast the doors and seize him presently.
This is the cave that keeps the tusked boar
That roots up England's vineyards uncontroll'd.
Bagot, arrest him; if for help he cry,
Drown all his words with drums confusedly.

Thomas is promptly led away and will soon be dispatched in prison by Richard's henchmen.

An understanding of these events is indispensable for an informed reading of Shakespeare's *King Richard II, Part Two*, which arises in the context of unspecified abuses by the king and a mystery as to the identity of Gloucester's killer. *Woodstock's* subject is precisely Richard's exploitation of the commons through taxes, appropriations and "blank charters," and Gloucester's stalwart opposition thereto. As these are not explained in *Richard II: Part Two*, absent acquaintance with *Woodstock*, the abuses to which John of Gaunt alludes in his famous soliloquy can be neither understood nor appreciated. (*King Richard II, Part Two*, II, i, 31-68) And the King's studied perplexity over who put "Gloucester" to death, impossible to comprehend for those who begin with the latter play, is seen as the height of hypocrisy once we know full well from *Woodstock* who the real culprit is.

Our present purpose, however, is to focus on Thomas as dramatic character. It is clear that he is a colorful colossus among grey Lilliputians. What other qualities does he exhibit?

1. Transcendence of the Immediate

Although he knows full well that the flattering lords have turned Richard against him, and that he is, in effect, a marked man, Thomas is sufficiently secure in himself to be able to sit through a bit of musical mirth. That is, his identity is not exhausted in terms of the dark events swirling about him. As such, he is no mere ideologue. Thomas inhabits a felt moral universe; he is the only figure in the play with one foot in a higher dimension. Further, the Prologue of Cynthia (Diana), designed as it is for Thomas's ears only, strongly implies an acknowledged affinity on his part with this Olympian deity, a frank expression of transcendence.

2. Sense of Humor and Wit

Compare Hamlet's "Do you think I meant country matters?" (III, ii, 111) with Thomas's "Ha, country sports, say ye? 'Fore God 'tis courtly." The Hamlet-like bawdry reflects a wit which serves Thomas well in distressing circumstances. All other characters in the play are straightlaced dullards, barren of jest or jibe. Thomas possesses sufficient depth to not only tolerate a masque (something Claudius fails to manage in

Hamlet) but take momentary delight in it. There is more than a trace of irony in Thomas's gallows humor.

3. Honesty

Thomas "speaks [his] heart." So outspoken is he that he is known to all as "Plain Thomas."

In virtue of such salient characteristics, Thomas of Woodstock stands head and shoulders above everyone else, overshadowing the whole text, in which he is *sui generis*, the unrivalled personality. It is interesting in this regard to read the *obiter dicta* of contemporary authorities who overlook not only *Woodstock*, but other early Shakespearean efforts, such as *King John*, which feature towering and incommensurable heroes. Writing of *The Tragedy of King Richard the Third*, for example, the estimable authors of *Essential Shakespeare Handbook* (2004) gush that "In this history play, Shakespeare *for the first time* creates a character who is larger than the narrative." (Dunton-Downer, 85, emphasis added) This assertion would be significantly true were it not so abysmally false. Over the course of his literary career Shakespeare fashioned a whole tribe of dramatic giants, of whom Thomas, Duke of Gloucester, is the prototype. Moreover, the gulf between the medieval *Richard II, Parts One and Two* and the shockingly modern *Richard III* is wide enough to swallow Pharaoh and all his chariots. Shakespeare's *Richard III* is an accomplishment which rests on much earlier experiments in fashioning the human.

Let us return to the text of *Woodstock* to note a few more features of its courtly hero. In Act I, sc. iii, we see that King Richard has just wed the illustrious Anne-a-Beame, princess of Bohemia, making her his Queen Consort. While the other nobles are perfunctorily effusive in their congratulations, Thomas gives a more candid greeting. In frustration he interrupts them.

WOODSTOCK

Let me prevent the rest for mercy's sake;
If all their welcomes be as long as thine
This health will not go round this week by th' mass.
Sweet Queen, and cousin, now I'll call you so
In plain and honest phrase, welcome to England;
Think they speak all in me, and you have seen

All England cry with joy, "God bless the Queen";
And so afore my God I know they wish it.
Only I fear my duty not misconst'red,
Nay, nay, King Richard, 'fore God I'll speak the truth:
Sweet Queen, y'have found a young and wanton choice,
A wildhead, yet a kingly gentleman,
A youth unsettled, yet he's princely bred
Descended from the royal'st bloods in Europe,
The kingly stock of England and of France;
Yet he's a hare-brain, a very wag i' faith,
But you must bear, madam: 'las, he's but a blossom,
But his maturity I hope you'll find
True English bred, a king loving and kind.

At this more-than-frank upbraiding, Richard is livid, and must fight to maintain his composure.

RICHARD

I thank ye for your double praise, good uncle.

But Uncle Thomas is just getting started. After a lovely and sincere response from Queen Anne, who politely begs to "be Englished," he shifts into high gear.

WOODSTOCK

Afore my God, sweet queen, our English ladies
And all the women that this isle contains
Shall sing in praise of this your memory
And keep records of virtuous Anne a Beame
Whose discipline hath taught them womanhood.
What erst seemed well by custom, now looks rude;
Our women till your coming, fairest cousin,
Did use like men to straddle when they ride,
But you have taught them now to sit aside.
Yet by your leave young practice often reels;
I have see some of your scholars kick up both their heels!

Thomas uses his praise of new Queen Anne as an opportunity to ridicule Richard's sybaritic court and the crude manners of its ladies, and with such directness that we might be offended were he not so amusing.

Even Gloucester's wife is caught off guard at this.

DUCHESS OF GLOUCESTER

What have you seen, my Lord?

WOODSTOCK

Nay, nay, nothing, wife.
I see little without spectacles thou know'st.

We can gather that Thomas the Lord Protector in these speeches is attempting to use public humiliation to corral young Richard and force him to send the money hungry flatterers packing. It is a dangerous tactic. Before the entire assembly he refers to the King in quick succession as: "wanton," "a wildhead," "unsettled," "hare-brained," "wag" and "blossom." Though these may be apt terms to describe Richard's conduct, they are hardly the sort of epithets a judicious courtier would select to cultivate his sovereign. Not content with these verbal slaps in the face of the King, Thomas, in heaping compliments on Anne-a-Beame, likens the ladies of conventional English royalty to females who ride horses astride, as men do, meaning that their manners have been coarse and provocative until Anne came to set a higher tone by "having taught them now to sit aside," that is, to practice a more refined deportment. While the full sense of the concluding line, "I have seen some of your scholars kick up both their heels," is not quite clear, what emerges beyond peradventure is that Thomas is aggrieved by Richard's failure to heed wise counsel. Indeed, at the outset of the play it appears that members of Richard's clique have tried to poison Thomas and his conservative friends. Being absolutely assured of his own moral probity, Thomas feels free to use the most flagrant and suggestive language to either jolt Richard to his senses or so shock the consciences of the peers as to push them to restrain their headstrong monarch. In this declamatory onslaught Thomas rises far above anyone else in the play, including King Richard II. Later, after Woodstock catalogues in detail Richard's abuses, the King vainly objects:

"Why is our Lord Protector so outrageous?"

Answer comes swiftly.

WOODSTOCK

Because thy subjects have such outrage shown them
By these flatterers. Let the sun dry up
What th' unwholesome fog hath choked the ground with.
Here's Arundel; thy ocean's Admiral
Hath brought thee home a rich and wealthy prize,
Taken three score sail of ships and six great carracks
All richly laden; let those goods be sold
To satisfy those borrowed sums of coin
Their pride hath forced from the needy commons,
To salve which inconvenience I beseech your Grace
You would vouchsafe to let me have the sale
And distribution of those goods.

This colloquy leads to Woodstock's charge that the King has committed malfeasance in office.

In Act III, sc. ii, there comes a uniquely piquant event in which the character of Thomas is laid bare. After another review of Richard's harsh and unscrupulous taxation of the commons and his luxurious lifestyle ("Thirty fat oxen and three hundred sheep / Serve but one day's expenses."), we see that Richard sends a "very fantastic'ly" attired courtier to summon the Duke to appear before the King for explanation. As Woodstock himself eschews court finery in favor of rustic hemp, the contrast is stark. Mistaking dowdy Gloucester for a servant, this overbearing lord commands him to stall his horse, pledging a gratuity later. Thomas, son of King Edward III, and peer of the realm, rather than take issue with this unwitting behavior, agrees to care for the lord's horse.

We then hear his eloquent soliloquy and address to this beast!

WOODSTOCK

Oh strange metamorphosis. Is't possible that this fellow
that's all made of fashions should be an Englishman? No
marvel if he know not me being so brave and I so beggarly.
Well, I will earn money to enrich me now, and 'tis the first
I earn'd by th' rood this forty year.

[To the horse]
Come on, sir, you have sweat hard about this haste,
yet I think you know little of the business. Why so I say;
you're a very indifferent beast, you'll follow any man that
will lead you. Now, truly, sir, you look but e'en leanly on't.
You feed not in Westminster Hall adays, where so many
sheep and oxen are devour'd. I'm afraid they'll eat you
shortly if you tarry amongst them; you're pricked more
with the spur than the provender, I see that: I think your
dwelling be at hackney when you're at home, is't not?
You know not the duke neither, no more than your master.
And yet I think you have as much wit as he: Faith, say a
man should steal ye and feed ye fatter, could ye run away
with him lustily? Ah, your silence argues a consent, I see.

When the obtuse courtier returns and is informed of the "ostler's" true identity, Duke Thomas of Gloucester asks payment in full for walking the horse! This animal is cleverly compared to the exploited commons, and then again to the foppish courtier who failed to recognize the Duke. Insisting on being paid for the mundane chore of stalling the horse indirectly mocks the profligate excesses of a reign which has been reduced to something on the order of a saloon. Thomas's address to the courtier's horse is, in effect, a soliloquy in which ironic interiority is displayed. Speaking to no one except an uncomprehending steed, Thomas in effect aims his words at himself, becoming the kind of "self-overhearer" which is for such critics as Harold Bloom the *sine qua non* of the tragic hero and the pith of human existence.

II. Attribution of Woodstock

The definitive work on the Woodstock play is Michael Egan's four volume *The Tragedy of Richard II, Part One: A Newly Authenticated Play by William Shakespeare,* published with extensive commentary by The Edwin Mellen Press (2006). A fine summary and review of Egan's masterpiece is "Richard II. 1: Another Early History Play Is Added to the Shakespeare Canon," by Ramon Jimenez, *Shakespeare Oxford Society Newsletter,* reprinted online in *Shakespeare Fellowship.* Egan's avowed purpose is the demonstration in over 2,100 pages of painstaking scholarship that the anonymous *Woodstock* is the real McCoy, one of the very first plays by the author of *Hamlet* and *Macbeth.* "The core of Egan's case for Shakespeare's authorship," writes Jimenez,

> is the swarm of images, thoughts, words, phrases, and rhe-
> torical and dramatic devices found in *Thomas of Woodstock*,
> of which there is some sort of echo, parallel or strong resem-
> blance in Shakespeare's plays. There is no Shakespeare play
> without them, and Egan cites more than 1600. (Jimenez, on-
> line source)

Jimenez then adds this Parthian shot: "It is hard to imagine that there will be much more to be written about *Thomas of Woodstock* than what Egan has included in these 2100 pages." (Jimenez, online source)

Nonetheless, what follows is a small footnote to the work of Mr. Egan. Taking as our point of departure the argument of Harold Bloom that in the poetic *oeuvre* of Shakespeare the modern self is first created through the crafting of larger-than-life personae exhibiting an interiority founded on "self-overhearing," we will add another log to Mr. Egan's fire by linking *Thomas of Woodstock* to Bloom's analysis of the Bastard in *King John*. Considering his claim that the first Shakespearean character to manifest the peculiar characteristics of "the human" is Richard Plantagenet (née Faulconbridge) in *King John*, we are compelled to draw attention to the much earlier sketch of Thomas of Woodstock, a character showing many of the same qualities as the Bastard, and who obviously precedes him by a considerable span of time. It is Thomas of Woodstock rather than the Bastard of *King John* which is the model and prototype for Sir John Falstaff. While disagreeing with those who attribute *Woodstock* to Marlowe, their suggestion of a date of composition of 1582 is likely accurate, placing it well in advance of the more sophisticated and polished *King John*.

III. Harold Bloom, King John and the Invention of the Human

At a time when Shakespeare criticism is putting the finishing touches on a complete exorcism of both author and character, Harold Bloom, a robust contrarian, has marched in another direction. An intellectual onslaught from modern movements such as existentialism, Buddhist analytics (James Howe), post-structural studies, deconstruction, historical and cultural materialism, and feminism, has had a withering impact on the self in literature. Authorial intention has been swept aside in favor of social energies (Greenblatt). Character has become a suspect class. Bloom's response has been to turn up the egological volume through a series of essays and books which focus on precisely those features of human life most denounced by what he terms "the school of Resentment." Bloom proudly traces his critical lineage back through Harold Goddard to the grand-daddy of all modern Shakespearean readers, A.C. Bradley, who located the meaning of the tragic plays in their appreciation and assessment of characters whose dimensions rival the figures of Mt. Rushmore. Starting with the ground-breaking 1933 essay, "How Many Children Had Lady Macbeth?" by L.C. Knights, the hypostatization of character came under attack, as students of Shakespeare rebelled against the tendency to psychologize speakers in terms of past experiences which, in light of their fictional status, must be ruled out *a priori.* Eighty years of sustained battering of the very notion of self-directed agency have led to a taboo under whose aegis any writer who betrays interest in self risks accusations of "patriarchy," the cardinal sin of politicized literary studies.

For Harold Bloom, on the other hand, not only are author and character foregrounded, they have followed a critical evolution which can only be described as deification. Shakespeare is a god (Bloom, 3), and we, walking in the footsteps of his immortals, *e.g.,* Falstaff, Rosalind, Cleopatra, Prince Hamlet, *et al.,* have become lesser deities ourselves, endowed with the talisman of Delphic self knowledge.

Nowhere is this tendency of Bloom's to supersize character more in evidence than in his 1998 opus, "Shakespeare and the Invention of the Human," in which he argues that the modern self, reflecting autonomy, irony and inwardness, was literally invented by William Shakespeare in his plays and poems. That is our legacy, as life imitates art. For any innocent souls who might not have realized what Professor Bloom was up to, this book hoists the Jolly Roger. It is not the purpose of the present discussion to mediate the debate on this issue which has had such a polarizing impact on our Shakespearean conversations. Rather, our interest lies in taking Bloom's thesis seriously so as to able to place the *Woodstock* play in proper perspective. For if Thomas of Woodstock turns out to be a forerunner of Falstaff, the thesis of Egan gains enormously in strength, credibility and efficacy, and suggests that the editors of "*William Shakespeare: The Complete Works*" would be well advised to include *Woodstock* in the next edition.

Our task is made more practical by limiting consideration to Chapter Five, which inspects *The Life and Death of King John*. Bloom dates this composition at anywhere from 1590 to as late as 1596. (Bloom, 51) The protagonist in this less-than-prominent play is "the Bastard," that is, the illegitimate son of Richard the Lion-Hearted by Lady Faulconbridge. Bloom cheerfully admits that, in comparison with Hamlet or Falstaff, the Bastard "is only a vivid sketch." Yet that little is more than enough to credit him with initiating the tradition of modern humanity. Bloom observes:

> Readers are likely to feel that the natural son of Richard the Lion Heart deserves a better play than the one in which he finds himself, and a better king to serve than his wretched uncle, John. (Bloom, 51)

Might we not say the same of Plain Thomas of Woodstock in his relation to his own play and in his connection to his troubled nephew, King Richard II? Indeed, we have. Bloom continues:

> The Bastard's greatness is not of the order of Falstaff's or of Hamlet's, but it is authentic enough to dwarf everyone else in King John. (Bloom, 51-52)

He adds:

> There is already a touch of Falstaffian wit and irreverence in Faulconbridge; he is the first character in Shakespeare who fully can charm and arouse us, particularly because no one before in a Shakespearean play is so persuasive a representation of a person. It is not too much to say that the Bastard in King John inaugurates Shakespeare's invention of the human which is the subject of this book. What made Faulconbridge's startling reality (or, if you prefer, the illusion of such a reality) possible? The other characters in King John, including John himself, still have upon them the stigmata of Marlowe's high, vaunting rhetoric. With Faulconbridge the Bastard, Shakespeare's own world begins, and that originality, difficult as it is now to isolate, has become our norm for representation of fictive personages. (Bloom, 52)

It may be well to itemize the traits which Bloom associates with "the human." The following is offered as a representative sample.

1. Speaking in a frank and candid manner;
2. Combining heroic intensity with a comic flair;
3. Exhibiting a manner too large for the inhabited play;
4. A conspicuous inwardness;
5. Capacity for self deprecation;
6. An overabundance of vitality;
7. A matchless wit;
8. A capacity for "self overhearing" rendering soliloquy a dialogue rather than a monologue;
9. Moral sensibility;
10. Acute perceptiveness;
11. A sense of transcendence;
12. Theatricality.

Writes Bloom:

> The Bastard . . . stands in *King John* for all the popular virtues: loyalty to the monarchy, courage, plainspokeness, honesty, and a refusal to be deceived . . . . (Bloom, 53)

But we have seen already that, on account of his blunt manner, Thomas of Woodstock earned the sobriquet of "Plain Thomas." In his speech before the disguised King Richard he demonstrates fierce fidelity, despite his objections to aspects of his sovereign's conduct. Bloom quotes the Bastard's lines:

> But from the inward motion to deliver
> Sweet, sweet, sweet poison for the age's tooth:
> Which, though I will not practise to deceive,
> Yet, to avoid deceit, I must to learn.
> (Bloom, 54)

"'Poison' here is not flattery but truth," comments Bloom, "and both the Bastard and Shakespeare assert their refusal to be deceived." (Bloom, 54) But notice that it is this opposition which is the very heart of *Woodstock*! Plain Thomas has taken as his mission the ousting of the "flatterers" who are leading the young king astray. King Richard is so threatened by what he regards as Thomas's subversive stance that he arranges to poison him and those lords in his camp. For his part, Thomas resolves to cleanse the foul body of the infected world by administering his own form of verbal "poison" designed to rid the state of those imps who are busy tainting Richard's mind. And it is not surprising, then, that at the conclusion of *King John*, the overreaching monarch should find himself poisoned by a monk.

Both the Bastard and Plain Thomas are overtly theatrical characters, but it should be noted that this theatricality, ironically, flows from a pronounced inwardness of disposition. That interiority severs the bond between prescribed social role and the individual, setting the actor free to assume the postures necessary to awaken the people about what is rotten in the state of England.

Bloom quotes the Bastard:

> By heaven, these scroyles of Angiers flout you, kings,
> And stand securely on their battlements,
> As in a theatre, whence they gape and point
> At your industrious scenes and acts of death.
> (Bloom, 55, citing II, i, 373-376)

"No one before Faulconbridge in Shakespeare is overtly theatrical in this way . . . ," touts Bloom, pointing to the fact that the contemptuous act of the lords on the battlements is self-evidently theatrical, and the Bastard's response joins in that theatricality and exploits it. France and England can act as partners to defeat the belligerent city of Angiers; once that objective is accomplished, they may contest their own differences.

> Do like the mutinies of Jerusalem:
> Be friends awhile, and both conjointly bend
> Your sharpest deeds of malice on this town.
> By east and west let France and England mount
> Their battering cannon, chargèd to the mouths,
> Till their soul-tearing clamours have brawled down
> The flinty ribs of this contemptuous city.
> I'd play incessantly upon these jades,
> Even till unfencèd desolation
> Leave them as naked as the vulgar air.
> That done, dissever your united strengths,
> And part your mingled colours once again,

Turn face to face, and bloody point to point.
Then in a moment Fortune shall cull forth
Out of one side her happy minion,
To whom in favour she shall give the day,
And kiss him with a glorious victory.
How like you this wild counsel, mighty states?
Smacks it not something of the policy?
(II, i, 378-396)

This is the Bastard's surprising counsel. It comes from one who has learned that all the world's a stage, and that it is we who choose to be friends or enemies as mood and purpose strike us. For partisans bound to rigidly adversarial roles, mutual assistance and cooperation with one's "enemy" is unthinkable, even though it be to the advantage of both sides. Only a gifted thespian, a natural scene stealer, could stand forth and so direct the Kings of England and of France.

Is it true that no one before Faulconbridge in Shakespeare is overtly theatrical in this way? If so, then *Woodstock*, obviously the earlier work, was not scripted by the same hand that wrote *King John* and *King Henry IV*, in which case it was not Shakespeare who invented the human, but some unidentified predecessor. And this is quite gratuitous and unacceptable. Plain Thomas's theatricality is no less than the Bastard's. We have confirmed this in looking at his own "wild counsel" at the marriage feast of Richard and Queen Anne-a-Beame. We saw it again in his admitting to his home the country gentlemen and their lethal Burgomask. Further, by interrupting their performance to deliver a speech defying both Richard and his rebellious adversaries, Plain Thomas inscribes his own personal theatricality within the solemn masque of King Richard and the flatterers. Finally, when taken for an ostler by an apish lord, Thomas has the perspicacity to give free rein to his theatrical nature, accepting the role of an ostler and then demanding payment for the performance. His staging savors of both tragedy and comedy, manifested markedly in his conversation with the courtier's horse. Here was ironic self-overhearing born.

IV. *Woodstock and the Invention of the Human*

Thus, for Professor Bloom to aver that no one before Faulconbridge in Shakespeare manifested the Bastard's type of showmanship is, in light of new evidence, no longer defensible. To make that claim, one would presumably need to consider who wrote *Woodstock*, and be able to show internally that aspects of *Woodstock's* style are inconsistent with Shakespeare's. This has not and cannot be done. Shall we chalk up *Woodstock* to Marlowe? But the very features Bloom seizes on to distinguish the Bastard in *King John* would also effectively remove Plain Thomas from the Marlovian realm. And this is the point. The creation of the human is the apex of Shakespeare's art, his most significant contribution to us, his heirs. To find those uniquely potent features in a character who stands logically at the threshold of all Shakespeare's Henry plays creates a presumption that the author is Shakespeare and that the institution of the human begins at that point, not with the later Bastard in *King John*.

It is true that the *Woodstock* manuscript is only a sketch. But it is a seminal sketch, a first step on a phenomenological journey that will pass through King John on the way to Falstaff. Bloom's own argument in *Shakespeare: The Invention of the Human*, when applied to *Woodstock*, shows that his claims for King John's Bastard are premature, and that it is Plain Thomas of Woodstock who deserves to be recognized as heir of first invention. Indeed, it could be argued that Thomas, whose modesty suggests a concomitant sense of his own incapacities, savors of that critical self-evaluation whose ultimate exemplar will be the rogue and peasant slave, Prince Hamlet. The Bastard, with his boasts of virile physique and cameo visage, swaggers just a bit too much for the top spot on the leader board. No one will take him for an ostler - nor would he permit it. We will hear that manly baritone later in Petruchio, a characterological cul-de-sac. Faulconbridge's braggadocio catapults him to the pinnacle of English nobility. Yet he is not a tragic personality, and, importantly, lacks the poignant fall from grace which we shall always associate with Falstaff. Woodstock, on the other hand, in pursuit of honor, candor and his private moral code, is undone, a man sacrificed in the machine. In this respect Plain Thomas is tragic, and the consequences of that tragedy resound through *King Richard II, Part Two* and the *Henriad*.

Accepting *Woodstock* into the canon fills a gap between the now secure *King Edward III* and *King Richard II*. While not as whole and polished as the former, suggesting a youthful inspiration, the character of Plain Thomas evinces a full-blooded humanity and largeness of spirit denied to Edward III, who lurches awkwardly from shameful lubricity and overreaching to nobility in arms and the chivalric idealism of the Order of the Garter. Though Professor Melchiori in his editorial comments on *Edward III* neglects *Woodstock*, and dubs *Edward III* the "natural prelude to the second Shakespearean cycle, from *Richard II* to

Henry V" (Melchiori, 3), exclusive reliance on *Edward III* as prologue will leave the reader in the dark as to the meaning of key events in *Richard II*.

In *Woodstock* we witness not talent but the birth of genius. A Promethean figure, hewn from the cliffs of feudal England, dormant for centuries, re-awakens and steps forth. Though the textual remnants are occasionally naïve, abbreviated or left fallow, these imperfections are to be expected in what is, after all, the tattered draft of an apprentice poet. Understanding here is not provoked by channeling a mysterious "social energy," but by discovering and acknowledging the true primal character who was to serve as model for all Shakespeare's "free artists of themselves," and, at the last, for us, who in our sad strivings are sometimes touched with genuine humanity. The text of *Woodstock* commends itself, then, not just to specialists, but to those who may take an interest in the scope of Shakespeare's art and the significance of dramatic character.

WORKS CITED

Harold Bloom, *Shakespeare: The Invention of the Human*, Riverhead Books, 1998

Leslie Dunton-Downer, Alan Riding, *Essential Shakespeare Handbook*, DK Publishing, Inc., 2004

Michael Egan, ed., *The Tragedy of Richard II: Part One*, The Edwin Mellen Press, 2006

L. C. Knights, "How Many Children Had Lady Macbeth," from *Explorations*, reprinted in *Modern Shakespeare Criticism*, Alvin B. Kernan, ed., Harcourt, Brace & World, Inc., 1970

William Shakespeare: The Complete Works, G. Taylor and S. Wells, eds., Clarendon Press, 2005

Online Sources

Justin Alexander, ed., "Richard II: Thomas of Woodstock," *American Shakespeare Repertory*, September 14, 2010

Ramon Jimenez, "Richard II: 1: Another Early History Play Is Added to the Shakespeare Canon," in *Shakespeare Fellowship*

11
Wanton Modesty: Lucrece and Elizabeth

But from thine eyes my knowledge I derive,
And, constant stars, in them I read such art,
As truth and beauty shall together strive,
If from thyself to store thou wouldst convert;
Or else of thee this I prognosticate:
Thy end is truth's and beauty's doom and date.

-- *William Shakespeare*

Wherein is contained how she [Elizabeth] (beholding and
contemplating what she is) doth perceive how of herself and
of her own strength she can do nothing that good is, or pre-
vaileth for her salvation, unless it be through the grace of
God, whose mother, daughter, sister and wife by the scrip-
tures she proveth herself to be.

-- *Princess Elizabeth Tudor*, age 11, (1544)

He's father, son, and husband mild;
I mother, wife, and yet his child.
How this will be, and yet in two,
As you will live, resolve it you.

-- *Pericles*

I. The Problem

At the heart of Shakespeare's *The Rape of Lucrece* is a moral paradox. If, in virtue of being forcibly violated by Sextus Tarquinius, "Lucrece the chaste" is innocent of adultery, what accounts for her swift and dramatic suicide, and how are her actions, including self-annihilation, to be appraised? Does not the lady protest too much? On the basis of the historical record (Livy, Ovid), well before Shakespeare, this was debated. One of the first non-Romans to take up the topic, Augustine, in Ch. 19 of *The City of God*, writes to refute the opinions of his pagan predecessors. He argues that it is beyond our capacity to decide whether she at some point gave inner consent, which, if present, would explain her chosen end as mortification and misguided penance. On the other hand, if there never was a shred of complicity, and she slew herself out of consideration for her reputation only, then in his eyes she must be set down as vain and unworthy. Immanuel Kant, too, in the eighteenth century, in his *Lectures on Ethics*, took a dim view of Lucretia, maintaining it is better for a woman to die resisting rape than suffer the dishonor of submission. More recently, under the influence of feminism, some contemporary partisans take umbrage at "patriarchal" rationalizations of rape, and lament Lucrece's failure to personally pursue revenge.

What is needed at this point is a patient and thorough re-examination of this nearly abandoned poem, and in particular the vexed theme of consent. Only when the moral minotaur lying at its heart is squarely confronted can we hope to pass to a mature and balanced assessment of its stanzas, both internally, and in relation to their setting in Tudor England.

II. Answerability

It is presumed by not a few that Lucrece is a pure victim, never accepting in any sense what befalls her, as she avows before her husband. (*RL*, 1656) The danger in this is a tendency to reduce poetry to melodrama: good guys versus bad. Oversimplification boils a subtle and complex tragedy down to the juvenile. For Augustine, Lucrece's non-consent was an unresolved issue, not a self-evident dogma. There is much to be said for such reservations. For her fate is a series of events in which at least three persons participate, not two. What are we to make of this unholy trinity? Are we sure of the relative contribution of each? Though the record has been allowed to fade, facts ignored are easily restored. Let us go and make our visit.

(a) Collatine's Responsibility

At the very outset, Shakespeare assigns substantial responsibility to Collatine. In jural categories, while the act of Sextus is the proximate cause of Lucrece's initial injuries, the bold publicity afforded by her spouse remains a significant "but-for-cause." The "Argument" tells us that Collatine, standing before his assembled brethren-in-arms, "extolled the incomparable chastity of his wife, Lucretia," a misstep savoring of hubris.

As a crystal window tempts a stone, so the rubric "chaste" invites violation. In stanzas 2-6, of "Lucrece the chaste" Shakespeare writes:

> Haply, that name of chaste unhapp'ly set
> This bateless edge on his keen appetite,
> When Collatine unwisely did not let
> To praise the clear unmatchèd red and white
> Which triumphed in that sky of his delight,
> Where mortal stars as bright as heaven's beauties
> With pure aspects did him peculiar duties.
>
> For he the night before in Tarquin's tent
> Unlocked the treasure of his happy state,
> What priceless wealth the heavens had him lent
> In the possession of his beauteous mate,
> Reck'ning his fortune at such high-proud rate
> That kings might be espoused to more fame,
> But king nor peer to such a peerless dame.
>
> O happiness enjoyed but of a few,
> And, if possessed, as soon decayed and done
> As is the morning's silver melting dew
> Against the golden splendour of the sun,
> An expired date cancelled ere well begun!
> Honour and beauty in the owner's arms
> Are weakly fortressed from a world of harms.
>
> Beauty itself doth of itself persuade

The eyes of men without an orator.
What needeth then apology be made
To set off that which is so singular?
Or why is Collatine the publisher
Of that rich jewel he should keep unknown
From thievish ears, because it is his own?

Perchance his boast of Lucrece' sov'reignty
Suggested this proud issue of a king,
For by our ears our hearts oft tainted be.
Perchance that envy of so rich a thing,
Braving compare, disdainfully did sting
His high-pitched thoughts, that meaner men should vaunt,
That golden hap which their superiors want.
(*RL,* 8-42)

This is "but-for causation." Had Collatine not unwisely advertised his wife's marvels and modesty, bringing the entire officers' club, including Sextus, to view them, never would she have been molested by anyone. Posthumous Leonatus in *Cymbeline* repeats the same pattern with devastating consequences. (I, iv, 52 ff.) In drawing so tempting a verbal portrait of his wife's attributes, and then, like a barker, hawking them to an envious mob, Collatine casts a subtle hex over "Enchanted Sextus," (*RL,* 83) a web of misapprehended *Sehnsucht* which short circuits judgment and restraint, well illustrating René Girard's theory of mimetic desire.

(b) *The Confession of Sextus Tarquinius*

Everyone agrees that Sextus Tarquinius deliberately ravishes Lucrece (though one or two insouciant souls still cleave to the notion that the offender is the king, Lucius Tarquinius). Yet in criminal law the background, condition and attitude of the accused are relevant to the sentence imposed, bearing on the gravity of the offense itself. Acknowledgement of fault, remorse and willingness to make reparation are all taken into account by courts in meting out punishment. In Shakespeare's poem, most of the comments made by Tarquin demonstrate recognition that (a) his conduct is entirely and profoundly discreditable, and (b) it will lead to the worst, not only for his prey, but also for himself. When Lucrece begs that he refrain, her appeal strangely echoes what has already been admitted by him. While no one will go so far as to contend that he is in any sense an accomplice, it can be argued that Collatine's declamations and imprudent exhibition of her virtues place the King's son in a kind of mesmeric miasma in which his conscience stalls. (Girard) To inquire whether the intent of Sextus was full or somewhat diminished is a legitimate enterprise. There is no indication of previous felonies, nor is there anything to suggest he later became an habitual stalker, sexual predator, or performer of other outrages. On the contrary, both before and afterwards, he shows the most lucid appreciation of his egregious misbehavior. His revealing words are worth review.

> 'Fair torch, burn out thy light, and lend it not
> To darken her whose light excelleth thine;
> And die, unhallowed thoughts, before you blot
> With your uncleanness that which is divine.
> Offer pure incense to so pure a shrine.
> Let fair humanity abhor the deed
> That spots and stains love's modest snow-white weed.

> 'O shame to knighthood and to shining arms!
> O foul dishonour to my household's grave!
> O impious act including all foul harms!
> A martial man to be soft fancy's slave!
> True valour still a true respect should have;
> Then my digression is so vile, so base,
> Then it will live engraven on my face.

> 'Yea, though I die the scandal will survive
> And be an eyesore in my golden coat.
> Such loathsome dash the herald will contrive
> To cipher me how fondly I did dote,
> That my posterity, shamed with the note,
> Shall curse my bones and hold it for no sin
> To wish that I their father had not been.

> What win I if I gain the thing I seek?
> A dream, a breath, a froth of fleeting joy.
> Who buys a minute's mirth to wail a week,
> Or sells eternity to get a toy?
> For one sweet grape who will the vine destroy?

Or what fond beggar, but to touch the crown,
Would with the sceptre straight be strucken down?

If Collatinus dream of my intent
Will he not wake, and in a desp'rate rage
Post hither this vile purpose to prevent? --
This seige that hath engirt his marriage,
This blur to youth, this sorrow to the sage,
This dying virtue, this surviving shame,
Whose crime will bear an ever-during blame.

'O, what excuse can my invention make
When thou shalt charge me with so black a deed?
Will not my tongue be mute, my frail joints shake,
Mine eyes forego their light, my false heart bleed?
The guilt being great, the fear doth still exceed,
And extreme fear can neither fight nor fly,
But coward-like with trembling terror die.

Had Collatinus killed my son or sire,
Or lain in ambush to betray my life,
Or were he not my dear friend, this desire
Might have excuse to work upon his wife
As in revenge or quittal of such strife.
But as he is my kinsman, my dear friend,
The shame and fault finds no excuse nor end.

Shameful it is -- ay, if the fact be known.
Hateful it is -- there is no hate in loving.
I'll beg her love -- but she is not her own.
The worst is but denial and reproving;
My will is strong past reason's weak removing.
Who fears a sentence or an old man's saw
Shall by a painted cloth be kept in awe.
(*RL*, 190-245)

It is plain that of the evil aspect of his plot Sextus is painfully aware.
If we glance at the immediate aftermath of the deed, we learn that his
opinion never varies.

He like a thievish dog creeps sadly thence;
She like a wearied lamb lies panting there.
He scowls, and hates himself for his offence;
She, desperate, with her nails her flesh doth tear.
He faintly flies, sweating with guilty fear;
She stays, exclaiming on a direful night.
He runs, and chides his vanished loathed delight.
(*RL*, 736-742)

As far as his rational mind is concerned, the view of Sextus as to the depravity of his crime is congruent with Lucretia's estimation. Only as he wavers, gives in to the spell, and loses all objectivity does he momentarily affirm his malicious design, in the weak name of "youth." (*RL*, 278) But in the main he hates the thing he does. His vicious battery, then, seems as opaque as does his victim's suicide. Defendant and plaintiff manifest parallel self-loathings.

To gauge the extent of Sextus's mental lapse, consider the circumstances that bring him to Collatium. The previous evening he was boasting to Collatine and others of the sobriety of his own wife, and suffered shame and envy when the regiment discovered that Lucrece far excelled her in that quality. Obviously he placed a premium on his marriage. How may he fare when his spouse inevitably learns he has thrown caution to the winds and ravished Lucrece, the spouse of Collatine?

Consider that he leaves Lucrece whole and alive, free to identify him as her assailant, which she does. There is no severing of her tattling tongue, as we find in Ovid's myth of *Philomela and Tereus*, and again in *Titus Andronicus*, where Chiron's and Demetrius's pillaging of Lavinia includes amputation of her hands and tongue. ("Nay then, I'll stop your mouth." II, iii, 184; II, iv, 26-56) Failure to mute his victim shows his utter discombobulation. So far as he knows, Lucrece will go straight to Collatine and his troops to retaliate. His actions guarantee that his gross disloyalty will be discovered by the woman to whom he is married. Is this a recipe for domestic tranquillity? When Sextus acts, then, he does not think - or sweeps away his ruminations in the heat of action. In other words, his impulsiveness is more akin to rashness than cold-blooded premeditation. While defense counsel today in such a case of aggravated rape would not urge acquittal on the grounds of temporary insanity, the circumstances and manner of Sextus's actions imply sufficient mitigation to render a guilty plea coupled with petition for modification of penalty reasonable. Or, in classical ethics, he would most likely be viewed as significantly incontinent (acceding to the promptings of lust which he judges wrong) rather than intemperate (deliberately -- that is, habitually -- aiming at excess). However, Aristotle would caution that what Sextus does is indeed heinous, and, if following related misconduct, would evince a radical decay of character.

(c) *The Riddle of Lucretia's Suicide*

As Augustine cannot be certain whether she consented, he rests his disapproval of Lucretia on the suicide and what that implies about her *amour propre*. And while one might do away with oneself on grounds of nothing more than sullied reputation, perhaps before jettisoning the notion of consent altogether, we might have one more go at the text. For a host of self-critical epithets leaves little room to question, not just her embarrassment, but the sense of real guilt under which Lucrece languishes after her despoilment. Here is a cross section.

1. "chastity's decay" (808)
2. "my loathsome trespass" (812)
3. "I [wronged] Collatine" (819)
4. "Yet am I guilty" (841)
5. "my crime" (931)
6. "In vain I cavil with mine infamy" (1025)
7. "my foul defiled blood" (1029)
8. "yielding" (1036)
9. "my trespass" (1070)
10. "my sable ground of sin" (1074)
11. "My life's foul deed" (1208)

It is with such self-pillorying locutions as these that Lucrece marks her private anguish. Yet when her husband rushes in to see what has transpired, a changed vocabulary is adopted:

'O teach me how to make mine own excuse,
Or at least this refuge let me find:
Though my gross blood be stained with this abuse,
Immaculate and spotless is my mind.
That was not forced, that never was inclined
To accessory yieldings, but still pure
Doth in her poisoned closet yet endure.

213

(*RL*, 1653-1659)

"What is the quality of my offence . . . ?" she cries rhetorically before plunging a dagger in her chest. Well might she ask, for there seems a tension between the long rhapsody of guilt and the edited account Collatine receives.

Since Lucrece bequeaths to us her challenge, let's take it up. She is "the chaste," yet a beauty whose husband boasts of the joys he finds in her arms. She is not "chaste," then, as Isabella, Emilia and Helena were. In their Shakespeare glossary, Crystal and Crystal give a second meaning: "of allowed love-making [because married]." (Crystal, 72) The example is from *The Two Noble Kinsmen*: "By all the chaste nights I have ever pleased you." (Hippolyta to Theseus) "Chaste" here does not denote virginal or ascetic, but merely non-wanton, giving pleasure exclusively to one's mate. Though we cannot be sure, it is difficult to avoid assuming that this brand of chastity is consonant with some measure of female gratification. In other words, this is a woman equipped with sexual instincts and responsiveness. The person raped is not maid but matron. And early on Shakespeare uses the telling oxymoron "wanton modesty" to describe her physical attributes. (*RL*, 401) What might this convey?

Lucrece is a *saftig* wench and knows it. It is therefore appropriate to ask how this fair lady and Sextus Tarquinius, the lusty young scion of the ruling clan, happen to be spending the night under the same roof, a domicile from which its lord is conspicuously absent. Having first laid eyes on her the previous evening, Sextus returns inflamed to make his conquest. As he is royal, she welcomes him. (*RL*, Argument) On sudden notice she arranges a lavish dinner, during which he becomes more and more smitten. Yet he coolly bides his time, regaling her with reports of her husband's derring-do in battle. She sighs in elation. After supper, the *tête-à-tête* continues as these two "*[wear] out the night*," (*RL*, 123, emphasis added) in cozy palaver, after which "Tarquin is brought unto his bed." (*RL*, 120) Do these courtesies betoken a mind "immaculate and spotless" - or just self-deceiving? Is this lady not the most renowned ornament of Rome? Is this not a candlelight dinner *a deux* catered by obedient domestics? Doesn't the chit-chat go on until nearly dawn? What is there to talk so much about? Gossip, perhaps? During this secluded repast, does gaze not meet gaze? Quoth he: "*She took me kindly by the hand, and gazed for tidings in my eager eyes.*" (*RL*, 253-255) Let us not be naïve. This is flirtation. Hence, not entirely without reason, Tarquin charges: "*the fault is thine*, for those *thine eyes* betray thee unto mine."

(*RL*, 482-483) What is intended by the blackguard here is not the lame excuse that he is compelled by her beauty to do her wrong, as the disingenuous Richard of Gloucester would excuse his destruction of King Henry and his son Edward to Lady Anne in *King Richard III*. (I, ii, 121-212) What is meant is not the orbs themselves, decked in exotic maquillage, but rather the use made of them, the subtle, sidelong glances, the rolling (see Sonnet 20, line 5), fluttering of lashes, and all the oeillades which must inevitably accompany such an assignation. Lucrece situates herself in what tort lawyers aptly refer to as "the zone of danger." (cp. Paglia, 1-39)

At approximately the same time that Shakespeare composed *The Rape of Lucrece* he also penned *King Edward III*, which, like *Lucrece*, like *Measure for Measure*, features a woman whose speech and behavior exhibit seductive overtones. In *Edward III*, it is the wife of the long-absent warrior, the Earl of Salisbury, who, in her provocative language entreating an extended visit, gives her royal male listener the wrong impression. Locutions with a suggestive meaning are underscored in a speech designed to keep under her roof a royal guest who can barely contain his desire for her.

> Let not thy presence, like the April sun,
> Flatter our earth and suddenly be done.
> More happy do not make *our outward wall*
> Than thou wilt grace *our inner house* withal.
> Our house, my liege, is *like a country swain*,
> Whose habit *rude*, and *manners blunt and plain*,
> Presageth *naught*, yet *inly beautified*
> With *bounty's riches* and *fair hidden pride*.
> For *where the golden ore doth buried lie*,
> The ground, *undecked with nature's tapestry*,
> Seems *barren, sere, unfertile, fruitless, dry*;
> And where the upper turf of earth doth boast
> *His pride, perfumes* and parti-colored cost,
> *Delve there* and find *this issue* and their pride
> To spring from ordure and corruptions stied.
> But, to make up my all-too-long compare,
> These ragged walls no testimony are
> *What is within, but like a cloak doth hide*
> From weather's waste *the under garnished pride*.
> More gracious than my terms can, let thee be:

Entreat thyself to stay a while with me.
(Scene II, 141-161, emphasis added)

Is it surprising that Edward found nothing in this to prevent him from making his indecent proposal? Was there anything more prohibitory in the intimate evening to which Lucrece treated her royal gentleman caller? Notice, too, that the suicide of Lucrece follows her rape, while the wife of Salisbury in *Edward III* threatens suicide to avoid Edwards' illicit embracements, and does so successfully. (Scene 3, 165-185)

The imputed integrity and probity of Lucrece is, of course, meant to evoke scripture's "virtuous woman" whose price is "far above rubies." As Lucrece is found "spinning amongst her maids," so *Proverbs*' virtuous woman "seeketh wool, and flax, and worketh willingly with her hands." (*Prov.* 31: 13) Would Solomon's ideal homemaker stay up to the wee hours in her husband's absence entertaining a forward youth? It is unimaginable. The problem with Lucrece, then, is that she is an uneasy combination of two quite different biblical female personae: (1) the virtuous woman of *Prov.* 31: 1-31, and (2) the temptress of *Prov.* 7: 1-27. One evening she is up late toiling for her *oikos*, while the very next she dallies at an impromptu supper party thrown for the dashing son of her husband's boss. This is virtue with a sensual twist.

Into her boudoir now creeps Tarquin, ogling his sleeping hostess. In visual art she is always depicted at this moment like Bathsheba, as nude. He places a resolute hand on her breast. She awakens, startled. Brandishing his falchion, he whispers his intention to force her into intimacy unless she submits. What is her reaction? She attempts to dissuade him, declaiming with Ciceronian unction the several reasons known full-well to him why this scheme is a moral nightmare. As might be expected, these protracted verbalisms only exacerbate his ardor. (*RL*, 645-646)

Faced with imminent death, Lucrece refuses to submit. But when he threatens to kill one of the servants and place the corpse in bed alongside her, suggesting infidelity on her part, her defenses crumble. (*RL*, 512-518)

Does she remind him he is a married man, that his libido is somewhat misdirected, and that his violent infidelity will hurt his wife and marriage? No. As long as conversation is taking place, wouldn't that have been helpful?

Does she offer physical resistance at any time? No.

Does she scream or call for help? No.

She does not even scratch at him, but "yields." (*RL*, 1036)

The act itself is decorously omitted. By censoring the scene, Shakespeare makes its content a matter of supposal. Not until intercourse commences does she cry out, but it's too late then as her face is muffled by her nightgown. (*RL*, 678-681) Had she raised her voice in peril, would anyone have heard her? Might she have been saved? Indubitably. After Tarquin slinks miserably off and Lucrece somewhat regains her composure, "she hoarsely calls her maid." (*RL*, 1214) It turns out this girl was already up and about before dawn and would have noticed any signal of distress. (*RL*, 1280) If a "hoarse" summons is audible, wouldn't a shriek have brought her scurrying? Fact is, to hear the "hoarse" call of her mistress, this servant must have occupied the adjacent chamber.

Now ask, Were there any others in the household? Affirmative again. Collatine is a military attaché of ample retinue. This is not speculation. As noted above, we learned in "The Argument" that when he and his fellows showed up unannounced at his residence, they found Lucrece "*spinning amongst her maids.*" This is a country seat with a large, live-in staff. At the slightest disturbance everyone would have come running. And are all of these domestics female? No, for Collatine maintains his own personal SWAT team.

Lucrece confusedly requests writing material to send an urgent message to her husband in his bivouac. A courier must be used.

> 'Go, get me hither paper, ink, and pen;
> Yet save that labour, for I have them here.
> What should I say? *One of my husband's men*
> *Bid thou be ready* by and by to bear
> A letter to my lord, my love, my dear.
> Bid him with speed prepare to carry it;
> The cause craves haste, and it will soon be writ.
> (*RL*, 1289-1295)

The messenger appears. In fact, this is one of the sullen grooms Tarquin mentioned in his extortive attempts to win her cooperation. As she gives orders to the man, Lucrece is overcome by an uncanny feeling that he can perceive her shame in her countenance.

Collatium, then, is actually a small military outpost, replete with servants, orderlies and soldiers. As there isn't a microwave oven, who prepares the late night feast shared by Tarquin and Lucrece, if not one of the cooks (most likely male)? Who escorts Tarquin, and lugs his belongings to his room, if not a valet or *aide-de-camp*? Had Lucrece called Tarquin's bluff, it's far more likely that he would have been dispatched by these guards than that he could have slain one of them.

What have we established?

1. Her asseverations to the contrary notwithstanding, Lucrece feels heavy responsibility for the sexual encounter with Sextus Tarquinius;
2. She freely admits him to her home, where she dines with him, making small talk until nearly sunup;
3. Well aware of her physical magnetism, her behavior is patently seductive;
4. There is never the slightest physical resistance;
5. Though a mere yelp would have brought instant aid, no distress is sounded. Instead, Lucrece engages *sotto voce* in a long-winded and fruitless dialogue hoping to discourage him;
6. On the premises of the estate are numerous soldiers and other male figures who could rescue her.

It is difficult to see how this scenario is consistent with unqualified refusal. In reply, then, to Lucrece's rhetorical "What is the quality of my offence?" (*RL*, 1702), we are constrained to observe that it appears to be unwitting complicity in her own undoing, something confirmed by multiple expressions of blameworthiness. It is that which triggers the otherwise inexplicable suicide. Even if one wanted to say that the conduct of Lucrece was passive and not a positive "but-for" cause of her undoing, as she failed to prevent it her role remains instrumental and cannot be gainsaid. (Gontar, 18)

The awful moral plight of Lucrece is that she advertises herself as helpless victim of rape yet cannot evade the sense of complicity in what has seemingly befallen her courtesy of fate. We can appreciate her deeper remorse when we think back to the reaction of Queen Margaret in *King Henry VI, Part Three*, when King Henry tells her that he has agreed to be succeeded by the Duke of York, thus disinheriting their son. He had no choice, he explains, because he was "enforced" to do so. Margaret's answer is direct and uncompromising:

Enforced thee? Art thou King, and wilt be forced?

I shame to hear thee speak!

Had I been there, which am a seely woman,
The soldiers should have tossed me on their pikes
Before I would have granted to that act.
    (I, i, 230-246)

There is no doubting her. Unlike Lucrece, whose actions all imply an acquiescence in sexual disgrace, Margaret would never under any circumstances have tolerated a bargain entailing the disinheritance of her son, though refusal were at the cost of her very life.

But again, this philosophical analysis should not be construed as a contention that Sextus is "innocent" and that he could expect exoneration in, say, a contemporary two-week jury trial. Though criticism can tease the consent of Lucrece from out the tissue of her behavior, in the "real world" such a gossamer thread could never trump the coarse significance of Sextus's upraised falchion.

III. How Many Children Had Shakespeare's Lucrece?

Grant for the sake of discussion that, as long suspected, Lucrece, in spite of herself, did in some sense implicitly consent to sexual relations with Sextus Tarquinius. We then face ancillary questions. What might have driven her to such self-subverting behavior? Or, what about Tarquin? Given the obtuseness of his plan to rape the wife of his colleague in his fully staffed and guarded house, was he led on exclusively by demented lust, or were deeper forces at work? These troubling issues cannot be taken up until we first consider the relationship of Collatine and his dama. What is her age? How long have they been married? Do they have children? True, we lack information, but still these are pertinent questions which cannot be circumvented.

It will be complained that such queries are not only conjectural, but that the very nature of the poetic enterprise precludes empirical treatment of its content. We cannot take fanciful personages so literally. In a notorious 1933 essay by the title "How Many Children Had Lady Macbeth?" L.C. Knights argued that it was a critical gaffe to speak of literary characters who inhabit a poetic medium as though they were flesh-and-blood folks with actual histories and formative experiences. It is certainly beyond peradventure that wholesale fantasy about people in books cannot form part of the critical discourse. Where anything is possible, nothing is interesting. On the other hand, to attempt to read an artistic narrative concerning credible characters without making inferences and judgments about their past is impossible. A literary character is by definition a meaning mass, a temporal arc embedded in an implicit past and moving into the horizon of the not-yet. We as readers connect the dots. That is what literature is all about. To attempt to come to terms with such imaginatively fashioned individuals as though they sprang to life *ex nihilo* and fully formed is to trample on nature and the manner of common understanding. To scan a book, and mentally transform its alphabetical shuffle into an account of women and men about whom we can care and with whom we may identify, is already to have taken a quantum leap into another world. Once there, the demand for both satisfaction and intelligibility requires an incessant deductive process. The positivist, skeptical of such a business, might just as well object that there is no warrant for passing beyond the spotted page. Anyone can see it's just ink. But once the business of reading is in hand, the human mind will assemble the data *comme il faut*, treating them as if they bodied forth actual persons. Were that not possible -- indeed necessary-- no one would trouble with poetry or drama.

The reason it is idle to wonder "how many children had Lady Macbeth" is not because it is somehow inappropriate to reconstruct a narrative past in poetry, but because the number of children she had is altogether unrelated and irrelevant to the narrative. Taking up such a topic is like asking what Mrs. Macbeth has for breakfast the day the Thane of Cawdor arrives at Inverness. We can easily distinguish that kind of gratuitous reverie from the sort of discussion we have when, suspending disbelief and taking the character as aesthetically real, we attempt an understanding of a salient act based on some natural construal of the "past."

The poem under inspection teems with references to offspring, and its central feature is a sexual act whose natural telos would be conception and childbirth. To persuade Lucrece to welcome his embraces, Tarquin, as we have seen (*RL*, 515-518), threatens to kill her and place a slain groom beside her in bed, giving out that he discovered them *in flagrante delicto*. This will mar her children, who will be "issue blurred with nameless bastardy" (*RL*, 522) Tarquin must of course refer to existing children, for a murdered Lucrece, even if newly pregnant, cannot give birth. But how does he presume she is already a mother? No toddlers appear, nor are there any references to them. Further, if Lucrece is a mother, it's strange Collatine doesn't boast of her maternal qualities to his friends. Does Lucrece proudly show her sleeping babes to her distinguished houseguest? No. It is also curious that, in pleading for her life and honor, she doesn't ask Sextus to spare her so as to avoid leaving her children motherless. Here is the clincher: would "Lucrece the chaste" commit suicide with nary a thought of her babes? Verily, no. Had she any kids, we'd be notified. Tarquin appears to be making an unwarranted assumption, namely, that Collatine and Lucrece are parents. This premise is insufficiently justified by what we find in the text. Why, then, does he make such a bizarre threat, unless his thoughts are already focused on ultimate prospects: the pregnancy of Lucrece and the possibility that she might bear his child? If he is forced to kill her, the hypothesized children she already possesses would be of questionable legitimacy. But if she yields and bears *his* child, he will not disclose its illicit origin. *Pace* L.C. Knights, is not this *quid pro quo* percolating somewhere in Tarquin's mind?

It is in the thinking of Lucrece as well. Indeed, this is her problem. After the rape, as she rummages about her rooms for a lethal blade, we hear these anguished words:

> Well, well, dear Collatine, thou shalt not know
> The stainèd taste of violated troth.
> I will not wrong thy true affection so
> To flatter thee with an infringèd oath.
> This bastard graft shall never come to growth.
> He shall not boast, who did thy stock pollute,
> That thou art doting father of his fruit.
> (*RL*, 1058-1064)

Minutes after suffering the impositions of Tarquin, Lucrece fears, nay, fervently believes, she is with child by him. Here we find the other key to the suicide enigma. Tarquin's awful boast that her issue will be "blurred with nameless bastardy" is now construed by an hysterical Lucrece to mean that he intended to and has in fact impregnated her. There is no scientific foundation for her conviction that she is carrying the germ of Tarquin's genotype. This idea is rather the picture of Tarquin's fantasy - and her own.

Push the analysis one step further. Suppose that, as the text would have it, Collatine and Lucretia are childless. It may be pointless to wonder why. But it is not pointless to ask whether, at some level, she hopes to have a child. After all, these characters, while developed as fictional in the poem, are also historical individuals discussed in Livy and Ovid, and were familiar to Augustine. This is another reason why Prof. Knights' abstract approach to character in literature must be set aside; for often literary persons have actual historical analogues or namesakes, and learning about the latter may shed light on the former. And so we return to our interrogatories. How long have these two been married? Is conjugal pregnancy being avoided? Does Lucrece perhaps yearn for a baby?

In the nineteenth century, when writers were not too squeamish to peer beneath the surface of things, Arthur Schopenhauer (1788-1860) published one of the most influential of all philosophical works, *The World as Will and Idea* (1819). His thesis, as profound in 2012 as it was two centuries ago, is that our phenomenal surroundings are the expression of the primal and irrational Will-to-Live, a vitalistic Darwinian precursor. Individuals count for very little in the larger scheme of things. The Will-to-Live has as its exclusive mission the propagation of the race; the fate of the particular organism is of no moment. The Will impels the individual organism to engage in reproduction of its kind. Once that is accomplished, we are, as this person or that, eminently dispensable. That is why young people are so often seized with an urge to commingle with unsuitable partners. They are puppets of the Will-to-Live rather than masters of their own destinies. The Will demands the next generation. That is its obscure and non-negotiable object of desire, in Aristotelian terms, its Final Cause. Moreover, it demands certain qualities in the next generation which promote succession. What counts is the genetic structure of the potential zygote, which beckons *sub rosa* to man, and, perhaps even more strongly, to woman.

When Sextus is swept up in an irresistible passion for another man's spouse, that desire is actually a complex of wishes. Beneath (1) the veneer of simple lust is (2) the anger he feels at Lucrece for besting his wife in virtue. Rape is his way of punishing her and refuting her purity by seeking to reduce her from saint to slut. Beyond that, he is (3) keenly aware of her condition as the potential bearer of his child. The connection of the sexual act and its biological consequences seeps into his consciousness. For consider: no one knows better than he that in abusing his friend's wife he is committing a self-defeating act. We have reviewed his candid mea culpa. And what he cannot fathom is why he feels an ineluctable urge to bring about his own downfall. No student of philosophy, he. Infected, then, with (1) mimetic desire, (2) the resentful urge to expose Lucretia as base, and (3) the reproductive bacillus, Sextus raps fatefully on the door of Collatium. There he finds that warm and engaging lady to whom only hours ago he was first introduced, but now unencumbered and alone. She has been wife to Collatine for an unspecified number of years without offspring. Would it be too much to wonder if she craves a child? Might there be just a tiny speck of resentment that she has been denied this?

The reason *The Rape of Lucrece* is misunderstood, then, is that our exegeses are so uniformly shallow. We are asked, in effect, to be contented with maudlin cliché: Lucrece is the innocent and unsuspecting heroine, Tarquin plays the lascivious villain and Collatine the witless and deceived cuckold. The idea that someone could have an unconscious agenda, or be a self-deceiver, or toil in the service of a power greater than himself, these obvious possibilities are excluded from view. Let there be a *Gedankenexperiment*. Would not an increment of comprehension and clarity be gained if we perceived these poor, awkward creatures as stumbling in spite of themselves towards something just beyond their ken, the production of a new and perhaps singular human being?

Lucrece, of course, is not a metaphysician or psychoanalyst. These are not ideas over which she can deliberate. Yet when she finds herself ravaged, the idea of pregnancy suddenly leaps in her brain. She doesn't know why. The remedy at which she lunges is self-murder. That will somehow expiate the sin of her dimly felt consent, and at the same time eliminate the child for which she secretly longed and which she neurotically believes now grows within her body. But as Augustine would observe, self-liquidation and sequent abortion are not equivalent to penance and absolution. Lucrece knows not what she does, nor do her bungling accessories, Collatine and Sextus Tarquinius.

At the poem's end, after she stabs herself, we meet her father, who hobbles across the threshold after Collatine. Horrified and grief-stricken at the loss of his daughter, he bewails not only her demise, but his own as well, for, says he, "that life was mine which thou hast here deprived." (*RL*, 1752). Pater Lucretius had seen his own visage flourishing in his comely daughter, a life he obviously hoped would be continued in his grandchildren. That dream shatters when he witnesses her end. Were any child of hers alive, Lucretius's tragedy would have struck a different note, for he would yet endure in that.

IV. Portrait of the Artist's Mother as a Young Lady

And it is just here, at the fifty yard line, that we must scrimmage, rather than rest contentedly. For it is now all the more important to learn why these curious, tumultuous, verses were written and published in 1594, and presented to, of all people, Henry Wriothesley (pronounced "rosely"), the Third Earl of Southampton. We are told by authoritative commentators that he was Shakespeare's "patron." Is that enough? What was Lucrece to him, that he might weep for her? Where might we turn in Tudor England for someone who might have been figured in the otherwise archaic character of Lucrece?

The logical suggestion comes from Professor Michael Delahoyde, whose paper "Devere's Lucrece and Romano's Sala di Troia" appeared in 2006. Mr. Delahoyde draws attention to the passages in which despairing Lucrece comes upon a mural of the Trojan War. The detail of the treacherous Greek, Sinon, leads to the insight that *RL* is really about England, and stands as a warning to Queen Elizabeth of some threat lurking in her Byzantine court. Unfortunately, Mr. Delahoyde is unable to make his claim stick by identifying the particular danger to Elizabeth symbolized by Sinon and Tarquin. What use could such a supposed "warning" be to her, whose life had been imperiled from the hour she first occupied the throne? When *RL* was published she was 61 years old and had been Queen of England for 35 years. Her network of spies, headed by Burghley and Walsingham, was omniscient and had no need of a woolly-headed poet's allusions. Without a way to put her finger on any person who might be intriguing against her, such a "warning" would be futile. Second, waving a camouflaged cautionary banner in a publication Her Majesty might not even read would be a poor service indeed. Why not send a letter, or pay a discreet visit? And if *RL* were a message to the Queen, why is it dedicated to Wriothesley? Oddly, Delahoyde never even considers whether Elizabeth was sexually battered.

Mark Anderson, another Oxfordian writing at about the same time (2005) in his *Shakespeare by Another Name*, has the perspicacity to connect Lucrece with Elizabeth, yet conceives the poem as a warning to Southampton about the tyrannical powers of Lord Burghley. (Anderson, 279) Anderson muddies the water by simultaneously identifying Lucrece with Burghley's daughter, Anne Cecil. In one place we learn that "Lucrece is Elizabeth as the Virgin Queen," (279) but elsewhere Lucrece is Anne. "Could Anne have been raped and then have covered it up? *The Rape of Lucrece* and *Titus Andronicus* present this scenario." (147) That it was Elizabeth who may have been actually raped isn't on Mr. Anderson's radar.

Yet it is well known that Elizabeth as a young girl was indeed physically transgressed. Moreover, she seems to have had an unhealthy relationship with sex, and a bizarre obsession with incest. (Shell, 16 ff.) Harvard University's Marc Shell writes:

> Elizabeth's own familial liaisons were tinged by incest. *Her uncle-father Thomas Seymour seduced the thirteen-year-old Elizabeth, or tried to.* (Shell, 17, emphasis added)

Think about that.

In fact, an entire book was written on incest by the precocious eleven-year-old Princess Elizabeth (1544), a painstaking, handwritten translation of the minor French classic of Marguerite of Navarre, *Le Miroir de l'ame pecheresse*, the thesis of which is that human existence is inextricably mired in consanguineous desire, a sinful condition which can only be transcended by cultivating an equally intimate and multivalent relationship with God. Elizabeth's title was *"The Glass of the Sinful Soul."* The significant words composed by the eleven-year-old Elizabeth (which appear at the head of this paper) reflect her sense of her own already illicit eroticism. Elizabeth, the illegitimate child of the (most likely) incestuous relationship of Henry VIII and Anne Boleyn, was drawn to incest as a moth to flame. (In truth, incest is coterminous with the career of King Henry VIII, which began with his incestuous marriage to his late brother Arthur's wife, Catherine of Aragon. Shakespeare's play *Hamlet* stands in the shadow of Prince Arthur's mysterious death and young brother Henry's appropriation of poor Catherine.)

According to Harvard's Prof. Shell, Elizabeth had a tryst with a highly libidinous older relative, and even in the solicitous opinions of orthodox historians dedicated to preserving the honor of Queen Elizabeth I, she came as close to being raped as anyone might. In fact, there is scant reason to deny that she had sex (whether consensual or not), and as a result became pregnant and gave birth. But note the equivocation of Professor Shell: Elizabeth was "seduced" - but maybe not . . . .

Following the death of Elizabeth's father, King Henry VIII, his widow, Catherine Parr, the last stepmother of Princess Elizabeth, was caring for the girl in her home. At this time, the monarch was (like Henry VI before him) a feckless minor, Edward VI, supervised by the Lord Protector, Edward Seymour, the King's uncle. Thomas Seymour, Edward's infinitely ambitious and aggressive brother, was scheming to wrest control of the state from Edward by marrying niece Elizabeth and staging a palace coup. In addition to Elizabeth, his differential wedding plans had included Mary Tudor, Anne of Cleves, and Catherine Parr. Unable to prevail with Elizabeth and some others, he consoled himself with wealthy Catherine Parr, wedding her in a clandestine ceremony. (Erickson, 61) However, none disputes that his first choice was the "nubile" Elizabeth. (Erickson, 62) Immediately upon the tying of this nuptial knot, Thomas Seymour installed himself in Parr's estate at Chelsea. (Erickson, 69) This led to some unusual escapades.

> As soon as he was moved into his new wife's house, Seymour began coming into Elizabeth's bedchamber very early in the morning, before she was fully dressed. As she gasped in surprise, he would shout out a hearty good morning and ask her how she was, then "strike her upon the back or on the buttocks familiarly" while she struggled, red-faced, into her petticoats. He took to coming even earlier, before she was up. He would burst into the room, throw open the bed curtains and jump at the girl (who was very likely naked, nightclothes being a rarity in the sixteenth century for anyone out of childhood), making her squeal in delicious fear and dive down under the bedclothes. Once he tried to kiss her while she was in that vulnerable state, and Kat Ashley (who slept with her), seeing that he was going too far, "bade him go away for shame." (Erickson, 69)

Then there was "a strange incident in the garden" in which Catherine Parr used a pair of shears to assist Seymour in slashing Elizabeth's gown to pieces.

> As the months went by Seymour became more provocative, and the game grew more elaborate. He took to coming to Elizabeth in his dressing gown, "barelegged in his slippers," and pestering her while she was studying. When Kat complained to him that "it was an unseemly sight to come so barelegged to a maiden's chamber," he lashed out at her angrily, and then went away without making any more of it. But when one morning he beseiged Elizabeth and all her waiting maids, who took refuge behind the bed curtains, and [he] refused to leave until Elizabeth came out, there was such commotion that the servants shook their heads over the gross impropriety and complained vociferously to Mistress Ashley.

(Erickson, 70)

Things continued to escalate in this manner, with the Admiral becoming ever more carefree and assertive. Now seemingly apprised of the risks, Catherine Parr sought to take charge and supervise the situation. She was suffering from acute jealousy over the attentions being paid to her step-daughter by her new husband. (Erickson, 71) Early in 1548, she learned that she herself was pregnant. Shortly thereafter she was shocked to discover Elizabeth and Thomas Seymour in an especially steamy (but never described) embrace, from which historians politely avert their eyes - and would divert ours. (Erickson, 73) Professor Erickson notes that "*what had passed between [Seymour] and Elizabeth cannot be known for certain.*" (Erickson, 74) Compare the terse Alison Weir: "How far [Seymour] became involved with Elizabeth is not known . . . ." (Weir, 15) But, from ignorance of the end result, inference of non-consummation is a gross *non sequitur*. That is special pleading and bad faith.

Elizabeth and her staff were packed off to Cheshunt. (Erickson, 74) There she took up studies with the brilliant Roger Ascham. (Erickson, 74-75) Latin and Greek drills were soon interrupted by a mysterious "illness" whose precise nature could not be established. She could not put Seymour out of her mind. (Erickson, 77) Elizabeth began to suffer from peculiar "rheums" and:

> other pains in the head which sometimes confined her to bed and generally reduced her capacity for concentrated study. It could be that study itself had brought them on, for she was nearsighted and may have suffered eyestrain. Or, more likely, the recent emotional upheaval had begun to take its toll. (Erickson, 77)

Catherine Parr had died a few weeks after giving birth under suspect circumstances, deliriously accusing Seymour of mischief. His poisoning of her has never been ruled out. Parr's infant daughter simply vanished.

Though the scandal was investigated, Elizabeth stood up to her accusers, who tarried just long enough for her to dispose of any remaining signs of pregnancy, labor and delivery. For that is indeed what everyone understood had occurred. Thus, in his deposition, Thomas Parry, who was tangentially involved in the affair, testified about comments made by Catherine Champernowne, later known as Kat Ashley, Elizabeth's governess:

> "She sighed, and said, as I remember," Parry deposed, "'I will tell you more another time,'" becoming anxious afterward and swearing Parry to absolute secrecy lest Elizabeth "be dishonored forever, and she likewise undone."
>
> *"Clearly there was more to hide."* (Erickson, 82, emphasis added to Prof. Erickson's remark)

Elizabeth, no doubt ably counseled, stonewalled.

> After a week of constant demands and queries Elizabeth was resilient to the challenge. Steadfast denials had given way to righteous indignation, which flared when she learned . . . that farfetched rumours were circulating among the people, deepening the stains on her reputation. She wrote to [Edward Seymour, the Lord] Protector, thanking him for his great "gentleness and good will" and . . . came to her main purpose for writing.
>
> "Master Tyrwhitt and others have told me that there goeth rumors abroad, which be greatly both against my honor and honesty (which above all other things I esteem)," she wrote, "which be these: that I am in the Tower, and with child by my lord Admiral."
>
> In truth, the rumors went further. A midwife, it was said, had been brought from her house blindfolded to attend a mysterious birth. She came into a candlelit room, and saw on a bed "a very fair young lady" in labor. In the darkness she could not tell whether she was in a palace or a hovel, or whether the beauteous young lady was Elizabeth or not . . . .(Erickson, 88-89)
>
> "My Lord," she went on in her letter, "these are shameful slanders, for the which, besides the great desire I have to see the king's majesty, I shall most heartily desire your lordship that I may come to the court after your first determination,

that I may show myself there as I am." (Erickson, 89)

The bluff succeeded and the investigation as to Elizabeth was dropped. But Thomas Seymour, who had been caught trying to abduct the boy King, was promptly beheaded. No proof of the falsity of the "rumors" was ever made. Historian John Guy adds:

> By Christmas 1548 gossip was rife that she was pregnant by the admiral, who did nothing to quash these rumours; he even encouraged them. (Guy, 201)

Why would Seymour have encouraged these "rumours" and "gossip" unless he planned to succeed in fact -- indeed, had already prevailed? Calling the impression of the public "rumours" and "gossip" does not show unreliability; rather, these circulating tales are elements of oral history and enjoy a rebuttable presumption of correctness. Shall we allow the smoke to obscure the fire?

From later events we know that in situations representing the slightest peril to her life or career, Elizabeth would freely and instinctively dissemble. Indeed, no English ruler could keep her head fixed to her shoulders or her derriere to the throne without frequent pretence. The wily daughter of Henry VIII was no exception. Recall, for example, the sham profession of Roman faith she put on during the heyday of her sister Mary. No martyrdom for Bess. Her zeal for the Mass was every bit as phony as the piety of Richard III which had wafted him to supreme power. (*King Richard III*, III, vii, 90-230) Elizabeth's self-serving and uncorroborated protestations of chastity proved nothing, but were instrumental in tamping down the investigation aimed at her. It was a shrewd and calculated bluff, daring those who would convict and condemn her to sacrifice a potential non-Catholic heir to the English crown. Such royal animadversions were in themselves plainly not to be taken seriously. The doctrine of the "virgin queen" was a related fabrication, used to rationalize Elizabeth's suspicious disinclination to marry.

Had any child come of the sexual assault upon Elizabeth by her Uncle Thomas, there was an expedient device at hand, for the Lord Protector had in his employ a most astute and discreet secretary, Mr. William Cecil, later to be appointed principal advisor of Elizabeth when she came to the throne November 17, 1558. It would have fallen to Cecil to dispose of the infant, a child who would inherit the fiery temperament of his father and the supreme intellectual gifts of his mother. Conveniently enough, there was at the time a certain nobleman indebted to and under the thumb of Edward Seymour, one John de Vere, the 16th Earl of Oxford, who could be compelled to accept the child as his own. John's new "son," Edward de Vere, inherited the title of 17th Earl of Oxford. If this chronicle is on target, we may expect that Elizabeth, who came to the throne a decade later, would have longed to see the boy she had born a decade earlier and reluctantly set aside. How could this be choreographed? In 1561, two years after her ascension, Elizabeth, with foresight and generosity, conferred upon Cecil (Lord Burghley) the lucrative office of Master of the Court of Wards. The ostensible purpose of this beneficent institution was to provide for aristocratic lads who lost their progenitors, such affluent youngsters being ruthlessly taxed for the privilege of being lodged in Cecil's home. More likely, Cecil House served as an asylum for those privileged lads who were in fact the embarrassing consequences of royal indiscretions. Edward de Vere was the first of Cecil's wards; importantly, others later included Henry Wriothesley (Shakespeare's "patron" and our dedicatee) and Robert Devereux, The Earl of Essex (note the linguistic coincidence that "Devereux" is a compound of "De Vere" and "ux," Latin for 'wife'). Kicked upstairs to London from the ancestral de Vere estate, Edward became available for Elizabeth's unique brand of love and affection. 1561 was also the year that Elizabeth would have first seen this splendid young man at the de Vere estate at Castle Hedingham in Essex. (Ogburn, 407) Edward's father John, who had always enjoyed robust health, graciously died in August of 1562 under the sort of dubious circumstances that frequently attended the deaths of those who had become inconvenient for the high and the mighty in Tudor England. This melancholy loss was more than compensated, however, by Edward's prompt and glorious promotion to Cecil House, where as royal ward he received a superlative education under the watchful eye of William Cecil, later Lord Burghley, and some of the realm's best tutors (Ogburn, 407), thereafter becoming a recognized habitué of the Court.

As everyone knows, it is this Edward de Vere, the 17th Earl of Oxford, who is the leading candidate in the authorship controversy and the most likely author of the works of William Shakespeare, works which feature multiple images and symbols of Queen Elizabeth. One of those works, *The Rape of Lucrece*, is still before us.

V. The Nymphet and the Wanton

Assisted by these portions of the historical record, we can perhaps better understand how and why it is that scholars perceive in the figure of Lucrece a fitting emblem of Queen Elizabeth I, whose public relations machine held her out as the "virgin queen." Contrary to conventional wisdom, both Lucrece and Elizabeth exhibited provocative conduct which elicited male sexual aggression upon themselves. In both cases the ideas of pregnancy and childbirth lurked in the background. With Elizabeth, the obstetrical dimension became a reality. For the historical Lucrece, whether she may have conceived or not is not established. What is known is that Thomas Seymour's avowed intention was to get Elizabeth with child, as he succeeded in doing with her step-mother Catherine Paar. In the case of Shakespeare's Lucrece, an unacknowledged longing for a child apparently plays a part in prompting her to place herself in jeopardy and then fail to alert others of her predicament. Is there a basis to say otherwise with respect to Elizabeth? One word from her to Catherine Paar or Somerset and Thomas Seymour would have been banished from her presence. Yet this was never attempted. On the contrary. Altogether, Elizabeth's passion for Thomas Seymour was animated by at least nine overriding elements:

a) by Semour's notorious virility and swashbuckling (bad boy) demeanor;

b) by his determined Don Giovanni campaign to seduce and ravish her;

c) by her well-documented obsession with incest and the incestuous allure of her uncle and step-father, Seymour;

d) by her unconscious desire to get a child, in particular one with Seymour's genetic constitution;

e) at first, by Catherine Paar's turning a blind eye to what was happening between her step-daughter and her new husband, followed by a brief *ménage à trois*;

f) later, by Elizabeth's participation in a heated sexual triangle in which she and Catherine Paar competed for the attentions and affection of Seymour;

g) by the not-unimportant fact that at this point in her young life, Elizabeth was blossoming and, in the description of Prof. Erickson, was "nubile," and becoming increasingly aware of her appeal to the opposite gender;

h) by her own libido, which had lain dormant during years of repressive tutelage, and which now came rushing to the surface under the onslaught of Seymour's ardent and insistent visitations;

i) by the fact that she was, simply and briefly, in love with him.

With respect to (d) above, it is suspected that Elizabeth sensed instinctively that a child born to such extraordinarily endowed parents would be a remarkable specimen of humanity. In the language of Schopenhauer, she was being guided by her species being, not the prospect of immediate gain. From herself, the child would inherit an off-the-charts IQ and matchless linguistic gifts, while through his father (Seymour) he would possess a volcanic spirit and iron determination of purpose. And it is respectfully submitted that it is this rarer-than-rare combination of combustible qualities which explains (what no one else has ever explained): the advent of the world's greatest genius in cinquecento England. In other words, "William Shakespeare" was the fruit of that "composition and fierce quality" that might fuel the accomplishment of the ages, rather than being one of those dull "fops got 'tween a sleep and wake." (*King Lear*, I, ii, 14-15)

The Rape of Lucrece, then, is a delicate portrait of feminine vulnerability which draws aside the veil of false modesty for just a moment to examine the way in which the forces of life impinge on human behavior. As Elizabeth was the most commonly represented figure in the literature of her day, famously known as the "virgin queen" who was resolutely married to her country, in the late sixteenth century *The Rape of Lucrece* would immediately be understood as a restrained yet daring commentary on her. In empathetic but unsparing terms it strips away the husk of fabled innocence and shows us a noble Roman woman who, suddenly confronted with brute male sexuality, succumbs to the needs of her own deeper nature. The poem, then, far from being a warning about the future, is a reminder and affirmation of the past, the checkered past of Elizabeth. And in connecting the rape of Lucrece with the concepts of pregnancy and childbirth, the poem gives subtle confirmation of those "rumors" that Elizabeth had, in fact, conceived and given birth in 1548/49.

It must be understood that the previous year, 1593, was the first time that the public had even heard of "William Shakespeare," the now famous poet whose *"Venus and Adonis"* had been a best-seller in London. There Elizabeth had been symbolized as a wanton goddess who pursues a cold and indifferent youth. In *The Rape of Lucrece* the obviously pseudonymous "William Shakespeare" returns to his theme, showing Elizabeth's minority in classical guise. Lucrece's reaction to her complicity in sexual battery and possible pregnancy is self-destruction and the erasure of any issue her intercourse had fostered. The fate of Elizabeth is analogously oblique: rather than slay herself, she went forward, bore the child of her assailant, assured his caretaking by surrogates, and in a short while took her rightful place on the English throne. It would be years before subtle and not-so-nice maneuvers could bring them together. Cat's-paw John de Vere, for example, had to be disposed of, as planned. The child, grown to become an immeasurably talented artist, in looking back, had much to celebrate, yet much to censure. In depicting the heroical Lucretia, he reaches back to his mother's youth and her nearly fatal affair which ushered him into the world. His love and gratitude are palpable. And yet, at the same time, the portrait of Elizabeth as Lucrece is not flattering, but rather unflinching in its realism. Consider again the rape of Lavinia in *Titus Andronicus*, published anonymously in 1594, the same year as *The Rape of Lucrece*. Is she entirely blameless? Doesn't she speak contemptuously to Tamora, Queen of the Goths, whose son has just been hacked to pieces by the sons of Titus? (II, iii, 66-87) Do not Lavinia's haughty insults steel Tamora's heart against cries for mercy? Isn't the silencing of Lavinia a fitting symbol of the rape and silencing of Elizabeth, whose mouth was stopped not by violence but by her position as Queen?

VI. *The Mysterious Dedicatee*

When John Keats wrote that "Beauty is truth, truth beauty, that is all you know on earth and all you need to know," the world was impressed, but baffled. What did it portend? T.S. Eliot termed the lines "meaningless," and "serious blemish on a beautiful poem." Keats wrote, of course, under the pervasive influence of William Shakespeare, whose bust was in his study. It was Shakespeare who first conjoined these terms, not Keats, in Sonnet 14. Is Sonnet 14 equally "blemished"? Or do "truth" and "beauty" have correlatives hidden from view?

For Shakespeare, truth and beauty are closely related. In the scintillating eyes of his beloved, "truth and beauty shall together thrive." But if the sonnet's lad shall have no issue, the poet predicts "thy end is truth's and beauty's doom and date." How so? We saw above that magnificent Lucrece is mourned by old father Lucretius not only because of his love for her, but because she carried his own life and qualities forward. That is a central Shakespearean theme, not only in the "procreative sonnets," but also in the plays. Thus does Viola in *Twelfth Night* say to Olivia, "Lady, you are the cruell'st she alive, if you will lead these graces to the grave, and leave the world no copy." (I, v, 230-232) That is, you should marry Duke Orsino and have children as lovely as yourself.

There is a general consensus that the "Mr. W.H." to whom the Sonnets are dedicated was none other than Henry Wriothesley, Earl of Southampton and Baron of Titchfield, to whom *The Rape of Lucrece* was dedicated in 1594. And the question is, why would William Shakespeare in *Lucrece* and in the Sonnets be urging Wriothesley to beget children? If "Shakespeare" hailed from an obscure sheep village there is no solution. For a low-born commoner such as Shaksper to have the chutzpah to lecture an English peer in public about his duty to beget children would merit drawing and quartering sooner than grateful compliance. Change the major premise, however, and things come into focus. "William Shakespeare" is the pen name of Edward de Vere, the 17th Earl of Oxford, the son of Princess Elizabeth in 1548/49. Wriothesley (another of Cecil's wards) is his Oxford's son. Like old Lucretius in the poem under consideration, Oxford wishes to extend his substance through his grandchildren, courtesy of Southampton. As for "truth," that is the code word for de Vere ("veritas" in Latin).

And what of "beauty"? Wriothesley's end is "truth's and beauty's" doom and date. The answer must again be . . . Elizabeth. But how? Certainly one fact will be denied by no one: William Shaksper, hedge-born swain of Warwickshire, never entered a mesalliance with the daughter of King Henry VIII. We can rule that out. And yet it must be Elizabeth. The sonnets begin with her: "From fairest ["vere-ist"] creatures we desire increase, that thereby beauty's Rose [Elizabeth] might never die." That is, Elizabeth will live in thee and thine.

Well, could Elizabeth have had a son by her own son? An affirmative answer may come as no surprise. The "Prince Tudor" theory has been around for a long time. Elizabeth herself was most likely the product of an incestuous relationship. Attempts at this late date to sweep this under the carpet are embarrassing. One can hardly contend, *e.g.*, that contemporaneous accounts of Henry's affair with Anne Boleyn's mother were all attempts to "blacken" Henry's reputation and should be discounted on that basis alone, when it is self-evident that such gratuitous doubts are entirely subjective and designed to shore up the reputation of Elizabeth in the face of the reports of Henry's universal philandering.

Elizabeth translated an entire book on the subject of universal incest at age eleven in which she confessed her fallen state and her personal fascination with the subject. And her partner in her first love affair at thirteen was her stepfather/uncle. When she finally became acquainted with her love child, Edward de Vere, the 17th Earl of Oxford, the two had long been separated. She was denied the experience of being a mother to him. Instead, she encountered him afresh as a young and preternaturally dazzling courtier. Further, as first son of the Queen, Oxford had a strong claim to the English throne. Is it any wonder that, denied this prize, he would wish it to pass to his descendants? Skeptical readers may wish to consider (1) whether there was any effective impediment to Oxford and Elizabeth creating a child and (2) whether there is any more cogent explanation of the Sonnets and *The Rape of Lucrece* than the provenance here suggested.

Today's mainstream media and press unflinchingly acknowledge that the image of the "virgin queen" was actually nothing more than a public relations stunt. Mr. Nigel Cawthorne in his 2009 treatise *Kings & Queens of England* provides a handy roster of Elizabeth's actual paramours, which includes Thomas Seymour, Robert Dudley, Sir William Pickering, Sir Christopher Hatton, Thomas Heneage, Sir Walter Raleigh, Robert Devereux, Earl of Essex, and . . . Edward de Vere, 17th Earl of Oxford, who "showered her with gifts from his [continental] travels." (Cawthorne, 114) This romantic activity took place over a span of decades in an age lacking any effective form of birth control. After a lifetime of serial liaisons, trysts and assignations, are we to suppose that Elizabeth remained childless? There is a natural presumption to the nayward. These offspring were known but never admitted. For always there was available to her "some stair-work, some trunk-work, some behind-door-work" to sweep away the consequences. (*The Winter's Tale*, III, iii, 72-73)

There is a preponderance of evidence that Elizabeth remained all her life in thrall to incest. Her affair with Oxford forms perhaps the keystone in that arch. Shakespeare's preoccupation with the subject is not accidental, but reflects his origins and legacy. While it might seem that *The Rape of Lucrece* stands outside the incest leitmotif, closer scrutiny shows otherwise. First, Livy states that Collatine and Sextus were cousins, as Collatine was the nephew of the king. Second, it was customary to regard members of an army as brethren. That is why King Henry V, exhorting his troops before Agincourt, refers to his legion as "we band of brothers." (*King Henry V*, IV, iii, 60) When Sextus has intercourse with Lucrece, he is thereby incestuously possessing his cousin's wife and his *de facto* brother's wife, as King Claudius in Hamlet, Prince of Denmark, by marrying sister-in-law Gertrude, "post[s] . . . to incestuous sheets." (I, ii, 156-157) In fact, incest is specifically mentioned in five works of Shakespeare, *The Rape of Lucrece* being one of them. (*RL*, 921)

It might be useful in this context to study anew Shakespeare's play *Pericles, Prince of Tyre*, in which the prince, fleeing the siren call of incest in Antioch, falls in love in Pentapolis with the king's daughter under nearly identical circumstances. In a storm at sea, his wife gives birth to a baby girl from whom the hero is parted, eventually believing that both infant and wife have died. The daughter survives, however; coming of age, she is abducted, and is transported against her will to a brothel in Myteline, to which Pericles later travels, thus staging the logical prospect of adventitious father/daughter intimacy. This is narrowly avoided by the daughter's compelling virtue and the intercession of the Goddess Diana (again channeling Elizabeth), in whose service the supposedly deceased wife now labors. The play suggests Shakespeare's conviction that the undertow of incest can drag one through an entire lifetime, flourishing tragically even in one's very struggle to escape its reach. Thus Pericles' exulting words of recognition to daughter Marina, "O, come hither, / Thou that beget'st him that did thee beget," are correctly diagnosed as symptomatic of Pericles' still smoldering incestuous desire. (Archibald, 99)

The incest theme is also prominent or discernible in *Cymbeline* (Imogen and Posthumous raised as sister/brother), *All's Well that Ends Well* (Helena and Bertram raised as brother/sister), *Measure for Measure* (Isabella / Claudio, III, i, 140-141), *The Tempest* (Miranda / Prospero / Caliban), *King Lear* (Cordelia / Lear), *The Winter's Tale* (Leontes / Perdita), *Much Ado About Nothing* (Beatrice, II, i, 57-58), *As You Like It* (Rosalind, Celia, I, i, 106-107), *Titus Andronicus* (Titus / Lavinia), *Hamlet* (Claudius / Gertrude / Prince Hamlet), *Romeo and Juliet* (Juliet / Capulet) and *A Midsummer Night's Dream* (Egeus / Hermia). (See, Ford, Barnes)

The plausibility of monarch / scion incest is explored by Shakespeare not only in Pericles but, importantly, also in *The Winter's Tale*. When the long-lost daughter of King Leontes returns to Sicilia with her fiancé, Prince Florizel, she does so as one who is (1) superlatively graceful and comely, (2) hauntingly reminiscent of Leontes' beloved wife, now presumed deceased, and (3) on account of absence since infancy, a young adult with no known filiation to the king. Under those circumstances, one would hardly be surprised if Leontes found himself moved to attraction by her. In fact, this is what happens, though the rejoining of Leontes with the wonderfully preserved Hermione cuts short his fascination with his unrecognized daughter. This gains in meaning when we learn that *The Winter's Tale* was based on a novel by Robert Greene, *Pandosto: The Triumph of Time*, first published in 1588. Though the plots are congruent, there is a vital difference: the royal father / daughter incest is given in the novel explicit treatment.

The editors of *The Yale Shakespeare*, in their Introduction to the text of the play, explain:

> The reception of the lovers at the court of Pandosto [= Leontes] and the discovery of Fawnia's [= Perdita's] identity run closely parallel to the same events in the play, save that Pandosto, before learning Fawnia's parentage, conceives an incestuous love for his own daughter. After Fawnia's marriage, Pandosto, grown melancholy with brooding over his sins against those whom he loved best, kills himself." (*Yale Shakespeare*, 1367)

Shakespeare adopts the plot, concealing its more raw aspects. For him to have openly depicted incestuous longings in a protagonist monarch would inevitably have been received as a slight upon Elizabeth, the regnant virgin queen. He therefore used his brilliant art to alter the conclusion, so that Leontes' spark of consanguineous desire for Perdita is doused by the highly emotional rapprochement with Hermione. All ends happily, as three couples are joined or restored in matrimony. Yet one cannot escape the uneasy sense that the bond is not sure, as the toxicity of Greene's earlier tale bleeds through the Shakespearean narrative. That helps us to understand why the prognosis for the Hermione/Leontes pairing cannot be favorable, as was pointed out, *supra*. Not only must Leontes atone for past misdeeds, the moment Perdita appears before him he is caught in the coils of incest, no matter how fleetingly. Objections to the incestuous affair of Elizabeth Tudor and her bastard offspring, "Edward de Vere," must overcome the prominence in Shakespeare's *oeuvre* of monarchical incest, a theme sufficiently iterated to be taken as one of personal significance to the author. Not only does *The Winter's Tale* illustrate the plausibility of such occurrences, its author was not a third party but, as history shows, was himself embroiled in intimacies with Queen Elizabeth I. (Cawthorne, 114) And as we all well know, such overly close relations are no less fecund than those more approved by society.

Return to the question. What was happening in the lives of Oxford, Elizabeth and Southampton around the time of publication of *Venus and Adonis* and *The Rape of Lucrece* that would explain "Shakespeare's" two fulsome dedications to Wriothseley? Indispensable reading here is Hank Whittemore's magisterial 861-page treatise *The Monument* (Meadow Geese Press, 2005), which dwarfs all other expositions of the Sonnets, putting organized fact in place of cant and empty formalisms. Whittemore details the point-for-point correspondence between key events in the lives of these three individuals and the systematic commentary we find in these famous but elusive poems.

By 1593/94 Henry Wriothesley had rejected the pleas from Oxford and Elizabeth to marry, and in particular he had rejected the suggestion that he wed Lady Elizabeth Vere. Southampton was in effect relinquishing any claim he might make to the English throne as the son of Elizabeth. As Lady Elizabeth Vere was Lord Burghley's grandaughter, his support was essential to advance Southampton to the seat of state. (Whittemore, xli) Wishing to free himself from the heavy hand of Lord Burghley, Southampton spurned the marriage proposal, the advancement of which was dropped in 1591. Nonetheless, Oxford continued to promote Southampton's right to the English throne. Whittemore writes:

> Oxford produced all these literary works [including *The Rape of Lucrece*] to support Southampton and to record his identity as a prince. (Whittemore, lxiv)

The end game of political struggle, aimed at controlling the succession, had publicly begun with the death of Walsingham in 1590. Burghley was already grooming his son, Robert Cecil, to fill the spymaster's post as Principal Secretary and eventually continue the Cecilian power behind the throne; but rising in opposition was another royal ward, several years older than Southampton, who had become a military hero and Elizabeth's newest court favorite: the tall, handsome, swashbuckling, brilliant, high-strung Essex, whose popularity rivaled that of the monarch herself. Southampton would take his chances with Essex; when he came of age, he would join his military adventures and, amid public acclaim, the two popular earls would eclipse the power of the Cecils to create England's policies and determine the nation's future.

Regardless of his disappointment over his royal son's decision to take matters into his own hands, Oxford would have given himself no other choice but to support him. Withdrawing from sight, he took the fateful step of issuing *Venus and Adonis* of 1593 and *Lucrece* of 1594 with their extraordinary dedications to Southampton as by "William Shakespeare," the name suggesting a mighty poet-warrior shaking the spear of his pen while striding onto the stage of history. In effect, Oxford might as well have publicly proclaimed his paternity in these open letters to Southampton; deliberately using the image of child-bearing, he wrote of Venus and Adonis that "if the first heir of my invention prove deformed, I shall be sorry it had so noble a Godfather, and never after ear so barren a land, for fear it yield me still so bad a harvest."

Henry Wriothesley was "the world's hopeful expectation," just as Henry IV reminds hs son, Prince Hal, that he must fulfill "the hope and expectation of the time." And in the Lucrece dedication, Oxford wrote as a subject vowing eternal servitude and bondage to his King:

> Were my worth greater, my duty would show greater; meantime, as it is, it is bound to your Lordship, to whom I wish a long life, still lengthened with all happiness. Your Lordship's in all duty, William Shakespeare.

He was boldly letting Elizabeth and the Court know where he stood and where he expected her and the other nobles to stand, regardless of Southampton's defiance of the marriage arrangement. He was also letting the Cecils know which side he was on. Meanwhile he was lifting Henry Wriothesley to the height of popular awareness; from here on, the names Shakespeare and Southampton went together in the public mind. (Whittemore, xlii)

Oxford would be disappointed. Essex's meteoric career ended with his "rebellion," after which, like Thomas Seymour, he was executed. And many still wonder if Essex too may have been yet another of the "virgin queen's" children. As for Southampton, he spent two long years in the Tower of London awaiting a beheading that always seemed just around the corner.

VII. Conclusion

Some may regret that much of what has been shown above seems too often sordid. But few things in life are as sordid as flattering mendacity through whose fraying fabric we catch glimpses of the truth. "William Shakespeare" was first and foremost a poet, one whose verses are inextricably bound up with his life and times. It is possible to study his poetry in a vacuum, without reference to biography and history, in which case the texts tend to become Rorschach inkblots on and through which clever readers project their own fancies and conceits. This gives us constellations, not stars and planets. So do those who dabble in bygone years under fancy names like historical and cultural "materialism." The past deserves better than that. The more strenuous but ultimately more rewarding path involves the systematic and comprehensive study of uncensored history, and the willingness to investigate the fruitful intersections of literature and life. That way meaning lies.

Our purpose in assimilating Renaissance poetry must somehow incorporate the purposes of the poet. While literary significance may never be reduced to the artist's intention, readings which omit those intentions are incomplete. As we read closely we can discern the criticism practiced in Elizabethan art. Lucrece is best viewed not as a saintly but helpless "heroine" tied down by a mustachioed villain onto the railroad tracks, but as a complex and vulnerable woman whose faults and frailties mirror Elizabeth's - and ours. As "pure victim" she would have no associated faults, and would be less, rather than more, human. Her fate would then be mere happenstance. This story was adapted by Shakespeare because through it he felt he could communicate indirectly and emotionally with Elizabeth, bond with their son, and influence events around him, not simply titillate and flatter a remote "patron." Already in 1593 and 1594 we can see a darkening of Oxford's feelings towards Elizabeth, as she fails to publicly designate Southampton as her successor. Thus *Venus and Adonis*, with its portrayal of her as a lascivious queen of heaven, is a gracious satire. Elizabeth as Lucrece is stronger medicine: England's "modest wanton" is seen as one whose incessant tides of suppressed eroticism come back to overwhelm her, requiring the mask of the "virgin queen." The reproductive dimension of the Will-to-Live, submerged at first, eventually asserts its prerogatives, forcing decisions not always wise, but always revealing of character. Through her peremptory suicide, Lucrece snuffs out the life of her imaginary child by rapist Tarquin. Elizabeth bears the bastard son of rapist Seymour, but later, having given that son his own son and royal heir, she betrays that trust. No wonder Oxford ruefully cries in Sonnet 147: "For I have sworn thee fair, and thought thee bright, Who art as black as hell, as dark as night."

WORKS CITED

Mark Anderson, *Shakespeare By Another Name*, Gotham Books, 2005

Elizabeth Archibald, *Incest and the Medieval Imagination*, Clarendon Press, 2001

Augustine, *The City of God*, Image Books, 1958

Incest and the Literary Imagination, Elizabeth Barnes, ed., University Press of Florida, 2002

Nigel Cawthorne, *Kings & Queens of England: From the Saxon Kings to the House of Windsor*, Arcturus Publishing Limited, 2009, Metro Books, 2010

Wilbur Cross, Tucker Brooke, *The Yale Shakespeare*, Barnes and Noble, 1993

David and Ben Crystal, *Shakespeare's Words*, Penguin Books, 2002

Michael Edmund Delahoyde, "De Vere's Lucrece and Romano's Sala di Troia," *The Oxfordian* 9, (2006): 50-65

Carolly Erickson, *The First Elizabeth*, St. Matin's Griffin, 1983

Jane M. Ford, *Patriarchy and Incest from Shakespeare to Joyce*, University Press of Florida, 1998

René Girard, *Theatre of Envy: Shakespeare*, St. Augustine's Press, 2004

David P. Gontar, "Permitting Harm: A Reply to Eric Mack," *The Southwestern Journal of Philosophy*, 1978, Vol. IX, No.3: 15-22

John Guy, *Tudor England*, Oxford University Press, 1990

Immanuel Kant, *Lectures on Ethics*, Cambridge University Press, 2001

L. C. Knights, "How Many Children Had Lady Macbeth?" from L.C. Knights, *Explorations*, reprinted in *Modern Shakespeare Criticism*, Alvin B. Kernan, ed., Harcourt, Brace & World, 1970

Charlton Ogburn, *The Mysterious William Shakespeare*, Dodd, Mead & Company, 1984

Publius Ovidius Naso (Ovid), *Metamorphoses*, A. D. Melville, trans., Oxford University Press, 1998

Camille Paglia, *Sexual Personae*, Vintage Books, 1990

Arthur Schopenhauer, *The World as Will and Representation*, Dover Publications, 1966

William Shakespeare: The Complete Works, S. Wells and G. Taylor, eds., Clarendon Press, 2005

Marc Shell, *Elizabeth's Glass*, University of Nebraska Press, 1993 [containing a complete transcript of Elizabeth's "The Glass of the Sinful Soul"]

Alison Weir, *The Life of Elizabeth*, The Ballantine Publishing Group, 1998

Hank Whittemore, *The Monument*, Meadow Geese Press, 2005

12
A Possible Elizabethan Model for the Droeshout Portrait

"William Shakespeare" by Martin Droeshout   Queen Elizabeth I, artist unknown, 1585-90

I. The Problem

The following comments represent a footnote to "Wanton Modesty: Lucrece and Elizabeth." It is presumed that the reader is acquainted with the historical issues and arguments taken up there, and also with the notorious Droeshout portrait. (See, *e.g.*, Ogburn, 71; 222-224) No attempt is made to trespass in the technical field of art history. Our purpose is simply to import into the scholarly conversation for the first time an hitherto unconsidered portrait which may have served as a

243

model for the face associated with the alleged author of the poems and plays of Shakespeare.

Above are shown details of the Droeshout portrait and an oil painting of Elizabeth of unknown origin.

Let's consider these two pictures in the most forthright terms possible. The melancholy clown with the mustache is the manifest content of the Droeshout Portrait in the First Folio of 1623. The other is - remotely - Queen Elizabeth I, created circa 1585-1590. (Cooper, 157) Assume that the one of "William Shakespeare" resembles William Shakespeare the poet, and that of "Queen Elizabeth" resembles Queen Elizabeth I. When we look more closely, we begin to spot strange similarities. Some features, *e.g.*, the noses, are indistinguishable, and the relationships of many parts are astonishingly homologous. The most immediate explanation for the likeness of the two portraits is that Queen Elizabeth I bore a physical resemblance to the great "bard" of her reign, Shakespeare of Stratford. But that would be a bizarre coincidence indeed. History provides no corroborative evidence for such an anomaly.

II. The Droeshout Provenance

According to Prof. Tarnya Cooper and the National Portrait Gallery in London, the First Folio illustration was probably the work of Martin Droeshout the Younger, born in 1601. (Cooper, 50) William of Stratford died in 1616. Hence, if Droeshout saw the subject of his etching, he would have been no older than 15, a mere apprentice. If the etching was executed in 1616, we have no way to explain why it remained unknown for seven years. But if it was crafted in 1623, at the time of the First Folio, we would have to believe that it was based on a recollected sighting of the subject seven or more years earlier, not too probable. On account of such considerations, art historian Tarnya Cooper declares that: "It is not clear what the original source of the engraving was, but the engraver must have based his likeness on an existing lifetime portrait, now lost." (Cooper, 48) With this momentous judgment we respectfully concur.

III. Portrait of the Queen as an Old Woman

Interestingly, although Ms. Cooper knows of no earlier image of Shakespeare which might have served as a model for artist Droeshout, in her book *Searching for Shakespeare* she provides a copy of a Queen Elizabeth I portrait dated, circa 1585-90 of unknown hand, a portion of which above bears an uncanny resemblance to the Droeshout portrait. Ms. Cooper writes:

> This image was painted towards the end of Elizabeth's reign, and was frequently copied in the 1590's. Yet, as with nearly all late images of her, it is not a portrait in the conventional sense. It was not painted from life: while her clothes followed the changing fashions over the decades, the Queen's face was frequently modelled on an earlier recorded likeness in portraits.
>
> This type of flat, almost diagrammatic style of representation, which makes little attempt at capturing figures in three dimensions, is typical of late Elizabethan painting. (Cooper, 158)

In fact, this style is particularly typical of portraits of Elizabeth. The aging process was not kind to her. In 1596, the Council, on her orders, "seized and destroyed a number of pictures that showed her looking old, frail and ill." (Weir, 239) "With the succession question unresolved, the government could not risk disseminating . . . any image of an ageing monarch." (Weir, 239)

> Virtually all we have to show us what Elizabeth looked like are stylised images. Painters throughout history have flattered and idealised royalty, but in her case this was a deception that was deliberately maintained over a period of forty-five years. (Weir, 239)

IV. Putting One and One Together

We thus have it on authority from the world of art history that neither the Shakespeare etching nor the Elizabeth oil was painted from life. As successive canvases of Elizabeth were copied, they became more like royal souvenirs than portraits. Proliferation of these coarse canvases would have made it relatively easy to use one as a model for a 1623 engraving of "Shakespeare." This would account for the Droeshout's own caricature-like appearance. Would there have been any reason to place a thinly disguised image of Queen Elizabeth I at the head of the First Folio? If, as some have argued, the author of the plays and poems of "Shakespeare" was associated with or closely related to the Queen, using a mustachioed image of Elizabeth as frontispiece would give nominal credit to "Shakespeare" while providing an adroit and amusing in-joke for those better acquainted with the facts.

V. The Controversy

In 1995 Lillian F. Schwartz published an article in *Scientific American* magazine in which she tried to show that the Droeshout Portrait was based on the "Armada" portrait of Elizabeth. This claim was then disputed by Mr. Terry Ross in a lengthy diatribe, available online. Discrepancies were gleefully observed. But if a schematic portrait of Elizabeth were used as the model of an etching of "Shakespeare," why expect identity? Whenever one work of art serves as the model for another there are inevitable differences. The odds of independently produced images purporting to represent "Elizabeth" and "Shakespeare" having the measure of correspondence and congruence seen above are infinitesimally small.

VI. Conclusion

So far as is known, the antecedent artistic visage most resembling the Droeshout portrait is not a depiction of "Shakespeare" at all, but rather a crude representation of Elizabeth I.

Though the suggestion that the author of the works of Shakespeare was closely related to Queen Elizabeth I is, to say the least, a much disputed point, it gains traction when we discover that the now-famous image gracing the first collection of those works resembles an image of this very Queen. Absent the sudden appearance of a trove of contemporaneous records, it is impossible to "prove" (where 'proof' means to establish a certainty not resting on inference, judgment and argument) (a) that the works of Shakespeare were written by a particular individual (now understood by many to have been the 17th Earl of Oxford), or (b) that Edward de Vere and the Queen were consanguineously related, or had intimate relations with one another, or (c) that the Droeshout portrait is in fact an altered icon of the Queen. These matters must forever lie shrouded in mystery.

But that very mystery, once acknowledged, rules out conclusory impressions given out as "facts," and rather invites further investigation. If it turns out that the 17th Earl of Oxford is a better fit for the role of author than the Warwickshire grain dealer / loan shark / show business producer and part-time literary genius, our job of inquiry has just begun. For it is only so long before we are brought to ask how and why this particular nobleman, out of all others, conceived and wrote the plays and poems. How is it that he had the burning desire, raw talent and Promethean determination to compose these works of celestial difficulty and "most humorous sadness"? Here no spooky "social energy" will come *deus ex machina* to our rescue. We must find the flint that struck this spark of nature. It is not insignificant that at this moment text and context point in the same direction: Elizabeth Tudor. Though we make no fell arrest, it is she who is our person of interest.

WORKS CITED

Tarnya Cooper, *Searching for Shakespeare*, Yale University Press, 2006, with illustration No. 67 from National Portrait Gallery, London, England (NPG 2471)

Charlton Ogburn, *The Mysterious William Shakespeare*, Dodd, Mead & Company, 1984

Lillian F. Schwartz, "The Art Historian's Computer," *Scientific American*, April, 1995, pp. 106-111

Alison Weir, *The Life of Elizabeth*, The Ballantine Publishing Group, 1998.

Online Sources

Terry Ross, "The Droeshout Engraving of Shakespeare: Why It's NOT Queen Elizabeth"

13
Speeches of Love in Shakespeare

The lunatic, the lover, and the poet
Are of imagination all compact.
One sees more devils than vast hell can hold:
That is the madman. The lover, all as frantic,
Sees Helen's beauty in a brow of Egypt.
The poet's eye, in a fine frenzy rolling,
Doth glance from heaven to earth, from earth to heaven,
And as imagination bodies forth
The forms of things unknown, the poet's pen
Turns them to shapes, and gives to airy nothing
A local habitation and a name.

-- *Theseus*

I. *Introduction: Shakespeare and the Moment of Love*

*I*t is worth observing that on more than one occasion Shakespeare audaciously presents the very instant when his characters are swept off their feet by love. This vivid transformation comes
not in response to mere physical comeliness, noble deeds or flattery, but
rather to improvised poetry. While written verses may function as to-
kens of affection, as when, *e.g.*, the amateur scholars in *Love's Labour's*

Lost scribble sonnets to capture a lady's heart, we do not find in the plays situations in which love is actually won through formal verse. It is only that more impulsive oratory occurring in the course of life, natural, unpremeditated and spontaneous, which, for the author in question, is capable of producing such a sea change. All the more momentous because unplanned, these utterances savor of inspiration. Their genuineness and strength are unmistakable and self-certifying. It is when native passion, the active soul, suddenly finds its voice, bursting forth as might a flame from smoldering embers, that the auditor is ignited and transported. Unique qualities, hitherto latent or submerged, manifest and impress with maximum impact. While well-established love may be conveyed in quiet hours when we "say nothing at all," expressing warmth or devotion by reassuring glance or gesture, the birth of romantic adulation in Shakespeare, by contrast, comes in a sudden aural immersion in the other's sublime reality. Dynamic, keenly felt words, received as in a tremolo, resonate, touch inner chords, triggering elusive reminiscences, summoning up long forgotten fragments of the past. And it is this quickening, this vital invocation, which constitutes Shakespeare's version of "Platonic love."

Of course, it is incontestable that every syllable in Shakespeare is, in fact, already prescribed, even those lively passages in which the speaker appears to be inventing his lines. But the purpose of the dramatic script is to emulate the free flow of speech. Shakespeare's poetry, in other words, is frequently an ideal representation of the efficacy of instinctive expression.

We will examine five cases of poetically induced ardor in Shakespeare:

1. Desdemona's for Othello;
2. Olivia's for Viola;
3. Angelo's for Isabella;
4. Romeo's for Juliet;
5. Phoebe's for Rosalind.

As we do so, it will be noticed that Shakespeare inscribes the speech of love within an abyss of tension, estrangement or pronounced opposition. On each occasion in which verbally induced love erupts, we find that speaker and listener are members of incommensurate groups which, by their very discrepancies, render love taboo. Othello and Desdemona are alienated by race and age, Viola and Olivia by homologous gender and amatory triangulation, Isabella and Angelo by a jurist's abuse of law, while Romeo and Juliet, the best known pair of the four, belong, of course, to antipathetic clans. Phoebe's predicament resembles Olivia's. Shakespeare shows that Cupid's dart is most fully and dramatically efficacious when it flies across a chasm to unite souls at the antipodes, those for whom any actual bond would be, in some sense, *malum prohibitum* or *malum in se*. Matches thus spawned are notoriously difficult to sustain.

II. Shakespeare and Plato

Though much in Shakespeare reflects the stamp of Plato, it has been denied that the English poet, with minimal Greek, could have digested the *Dialogues*. But the proposition that the author of the works of Shakespeare could not understand Greek is based on a conventional but suppositious view of his identity. One of the exegetical advantages of taking seriously the thesis that "William Shakespeare" is the pen name of Edward de Vere, 17th Earl of Oxford, is that Oxford's superlative curriculum included Plato. A couple of reminders may suffice.

Compare, if you will, the death of Falstaff recounted in *The Life of Henry the Fifth* with that of a certain ancient philosopher in Plato's *Phaedo*.

HOSTESS

"How now, Sir John?" quoth I. "What, man! Be
o' good cheer." So a cried out, "God, God, God,"
three or four times. Now I, to comfort him, bid
him a should not think of God; I hoped there
was no need to trouble himself with any such
thoughts yet. So a bade me lay more clothes on
his feet. I put my hand into the bed and felt
them, and they were as cold as any stone.
Then I felt to his knees, and so up'ard and
up'ard, and all was as cold as any stone.
(II, iii, 17-25)

Such is the end of Shakespeare's Falstaff.

Here is Plato describing the execution of his teacher.

Socrates walked about, and presently, saying that his legs were heavy, lay down on his back - that was what the man recommended. The man - he was the same one who had administered the poison - kept his hand upon Socrates, and after a little while examined his feet and legs, then pinched his foot hard and asked if he felt it. Socrates said no. Then he did the same to his legs, and moving gradually upward in this way let us see that he was getting cold and numb. Presently he felt him again and said that when it reached the heart, Socrates would be gone. The coldness was spreading about as far as his waist when Socrates uncovered his face . . . and said . . . "Crito, we ought to offer a cock to Asclepius. See to it, and don't forget."
(Plato, *Phaedo*, 98-99)

Could this degree of parallelism be consistent with anything but the most profound of influences?

Of course, well before the death scene in *Henry V*, Falstaff serves in *The History of Henry the Fourth* as Prince Hal's worldly mentor in the demimonde of Eastcheap. Falstaff, like Plato's Socrates, has filiations with Dionysus (Bacchus), as we can see by comparing (1) Plato's *Symposium*, the drinking party in which metaphysical toasts are given in praise of love (eros) with (2) Falstaff's paean to "sack" (brandy) in The Second Part of *Henry the Fourth*. (IV, ii, 83-121) In Falstaff's view the callow and perfidious Prince John lacks essential humanity precisely because "he drinks no wine." Falstaff rising on the field of battle at Shrewsbury as from the dead (*Henry the Fourth, Part One*, V, iv, 110) also is a reprise of Socrates sitting up, uncovering his face, and reminding Crito to make their offering to Asclepius. More importantly, Falstaff is a philosopher who raises questions about moral terms ("What is honor?" - *King Henry IV, Part One*, V, i, 134-135) and discusses them in the manner of Socrates' own dialectic.

In an ironic rhetorical flourish, and in typical Socratic fashion, Falstaff teasingly reverses the actual relationship when he exclaims in *The History of Henry the Fourth*:

Before I knew
thee, Hal, I knew nothing; and now am I, if a man
should speak truly, little better than one of the wicked.
(I, ii, 92-94)

This neatly inverts the usual statement of Socrates' interlocutors in Plato, who confess that before they met him, although they were confident in their knowledge, they in fact knew nothing. Meno's admission is typical.

> Socrates, even before I met you they told me that in plain truth you are a perplexed man yourself and reduce others to perplexity. At this moment I feel you are exercising magic and witchcraft upon me and positively laying me under your spell until I am a mass of helplessness.
> (Plato, *Meno*, 363)

It is thus helpful when dealing with a Platonic phenomenon like eros to read Shakespeare in that context. Elaborate musings on eros and the psyche can be found principally in two dialogues, *Phaedrus* and *Symposium*, with dilation in *Politeia* ("*The Republic*") and *Phaedo*. While the complex treatment of love in Plato does not lend itself to abstract summary, we can offer a thumbnail sketch of Plato's *mythos*. Prior to birth, the human soul dwells apart in a topos of ideal prototypes. This is not a solitary but a collective existence in which conjoined souls share the bliss of contemplation. At the moment of incarnation, souls, like spores wafted on the breeze, scatter in separate human bodies. Gradually the transplanted psyche comes to recollect aspects of the ideal forms with which it had commerce prior to birth. Souls extruded from the ideal realm in which they had been coupled now meet in the terrestrial zone, and may recognize one another, accounting for "love at first sight." Since the embodiment of souls is wholly unpredictable, recognition is in part a function of chance, and may occur in relation to an eminently unsuitable partner. That is, we may fall in love with the right soul but the wrong person. Shakespeare's contribution to the Platonic tradition is to substitute love-at-first-hearing for love-at-first-sight, and to trace the tragicomic consequences which ensue when, *e.g.*, a fairy queen finds herself enamored of an ass's "note." (*A Midsummer Night's Dream*, III, ii, 131)

Before proceeding, one caveat: it is well to keep in mind that Plato was *au fond* a poet and erstwhile dramatist; at all times his expressions are dialectical and figurative, not to be taken literally. It is one of the more frustrating aspects of life that its vital elements so stubbornly elude our ken. "*Physis* loves to hide" was the wise dictum of Heraclitus. That is why science -- and philosophy -- at a certain point yield to art.

III. Desdemona

As Meno jests that he has been put under a supernatural spell by Socrates, it may be best to begin with Othello's famous narrative in which he explains how it is that Brabantio's lovely daughter, Desdemona, came to love one so unlike herself. Here he seeks to defend himself against the paternal accusation that, like a wicked sorcerer, he used magic potions and witchcraft to arrogate to himself Desdemona's affections. Othello not only disposes of this rumor, but reproduces so faithfully the mood and manner of his first words to her that we can empathetically partake of her passionate reaction.

> Her father loved me, oft invited me
> Still questioned me the story of my life
> From year to year, the battles, sieges, fortunes
> That I have passed.
> I ran it through even from my boyish days
> To th' very moment that he bade me tell it,
> Wherein I spoke of most disastrous chances,
> Of moving accidents by flood and field,
> Of hair-breadth scapes i' th' imminent deadly breach,
> Of being taken by the insolent foe
> And sold to slavery, of my redemption thence,
> And portance in my traveller's history,
> Wherein of antres vast and deserts idle,
> Rough quarries, rocks, and hills whose heads
> touch heaven,
> It was my hint to speak. Such was my process,
> And of the cannibals that each other eat,
> The Anthropophagi, and men whose heads
> Do grow beneath their shoulders. These
> things to hear
> Would Desdemona seriously incline,
> But still the house affairs would draw her thence,
> Which ever as she could with haste dispatch
> She'd come again, and with a greedy ear
> Devour up my discourse; which I, observing,
> Took once a pliant hour, and found good means
> To draw from her a prayer of earnest heart

That I would all my pilgrimage dilate,
Whereof by parcels she had something heard,
But not intentively. I did consent,
And often did beguile her of her tears
When I did speak of some distressful stroke
That my youth suffered. My story being done,
She gave me for my pains a world of kisses.
She swore in faith 'twas strange, 'twas passing
strange, 'Twas pitiful, 'twas wondrous pitiful.
She wished she had not heard it, yet she wished
That heaven had made her such a man. She thanked
Me, and bade me, if I had a friend that loved her,
I should but teach him how to tell my story,
And that would woo her. Upon this hint I spake.
She loved me for the dangers I had passed,
And I loved her that she did pity them.
This only is the witchcraft I have used.
Here comes the lady. Let her witness it.

Nothing prepares one for words such as these. Despite his martial vocation, Othello has the delicate sensibility of a lover and a bard's silver tongue. These are not the syllables of stammering youth, but of seasoned maturity, self-possessed and having authority tempered by suffering and perseverance, courage tested in battle. Rich and sonorous in timbre, his sentiments are neither vainglorious nor seductive. Rather, Othello aims to furnish the Duke and company with a straightforward account of how he prevailed with Desdemona. These brawny anecdotes are intermittently overheard by her, until she gathers the courage to ask that he unburden himself to her privily. To her astonishment she discovers the accuracy of her feelings: this is the man. As she covers his face with ecstatic kisses, we witness through Othello's report the very moment when Cupid's arrow finds its object.

But consider the prevailing tension which precedes the arrival of love. Othello is a hero, yes, but a hero in a minor key. Disfavored in Venice on account of his race, he makes an unexpected and unwelcome son-in-law. Though the commonwealth depends on his military prowess, its backward and ungracious animus against dark-skinned peoples quickly comes to the fore in the scurrilous racial taunts of Rodrigo and Iago. (I, i, 79-142) Love in such an inimical setting arrives like a thunderclap, as though the parted waters of the sea had rushed together. There, to use

Eliot's trope, human voices wake us, and we drown.

It is a sign of Shakespeare's genius that Desdemona, in affirming her devotion to the Moor, speaks in stately measures which are consonant with the dignified rhythms of her lord's own deliverances. His puissant phrasings appear to empower her to adopt her own lexicon, a sibling dialect. Listen as she begs to accompany him to the wars.

> Most gracious Duke,
> To my unfolding lend your prosperous ear,
> And let me find a charter in your voice
> T'assist my simpleness.
>
> That I did love the Moor to live with him,
> My downright violence and storm of fortunes
> May trumpet to the world. My heart's subdued
> Even to the very quality of my lord.
> I saw Othello's visage in his mind,
> And to his honours and his valiant parts
> Did I my soul and fortunes consecrate;
> So that, dear lords, if I be left behind,
> A moth of peace, and he go to the war,
> The rites for why I love him are bereft me,
> And I a heavy interim shall support
> By his dear absence. Let me go with him.
> (I, iii, 248-259)

No, it is not the Duke's voice that assists here, but Othello's. Hearing her, he might exclaim with Ferdinand, "My language! Heavens! I am the best of them that speak this speech . . . ." (*The Tempest*, I, ii, 432-434) The poet's soul in Desdemona rises up to greet Othello's.

IV. Olivia

Castaway Viola, in the brilliant comedy, *Twelfth Night*, has disguised herself as a page and taken refuge in the household of Duke Orsino. She pines for him, but all his affections are directed to Lady Olivia, a beauty in the neighboring seat. Though many petitions of matrimony have been sent, they are refused on the grounds that she is in mourning for her late brother, grieving so she cannot lend herself to love. In truth she has no feeling for the Duke. On account of her forthright eloquence,

Viola, known to Orsino as the lad "Caesario," is appointed to bear his hopeless embassage. On several occasions this "Caesario," mourning her own brother, whom she thinks lost in shipwreck, goes to Olivia to dutifully plead on behalf of Orsino. Haughty Olivia takes scant notice of the message, which is old news, but is curious about the intriguing herald, who is described by the irascible steward Malvolio thus:

> Not yet old enough for a man, nor young
> enough for a boy; as a squash is before 'tis a peascod,
> or a codling when 'tis almost an apple.
> 'Tis with him in standing water between boy and man.
> He is very well-favoured, and speaks very shrewishly.
> One would think his mother's milk were scarce out of him.
> (I, v, 151-156)

After receiving from Olivia a wan catalog of her facial charms, Viola comments:

> I see what you are, you are too proud,
> But if you were the devil, you are fair.
> My lord and master loves you. O, such love
> Could be but recompensed though you were
> crowned the nonpareil of beauty.
> (I, v, 239-243)

After another sharp rebuff, Viola continues.

> If I did love you in my master's flame,
> With such a suff'ring, such a deadly life,
> In your denial I would find no sense,
> I would not understand it.
> (I, v, 253-256)

Even more curious, Olivia asks, "Why, what would you?" The versified answer is eventful:

> Make me a willow cabin at your gate
> And call upon my soul within the house,
> Write loyal cantons of contemnèd love,
> And sing them loud even in the dead of night;

Halloo your name to the reverberate hills,
And make the babbling gossip of the air
Cry out 'Olivia!' O, you should not rest
Between the elements of air and earth
But you should pity me.
(I, v, 257-265)

Olivia, breathless at these words, can only gasp "You might do much." (I, v, 266) It is the very lightning stroke of love. How has it happened? Olivia is now hugely infatuated with a member of her own sex. In male guise, Viola has given her an arresting portrait of an impassioned youth conjuring piquant anthems of unrequited love, singing them through the night, till all nature becomes a vessel of his desire. Yet what enraptures (and so captures) Olivia are not those referenced compositions, but the improvised vocalization of love, here and now. Such ardor is felt, not studied. Viola has thrown off her memorized script and chanted lyrics of the beating heart. And in this she has had an unwitting and unintended triumph: instead of seizing Olivia for her lonely lord, she has inadvertently obtained her in a far more personal way.

It is, of course, possible and indeed necessary to analyze the circumstances and emotional dispositions which lay the foundation for Olivia's metanoia. In doing so, we should stipulate that it is Viola's sympathetic love for Orsino which is the driving force behind her turbulent address to Olivia. Her true willow cabin lies at his gate. As he is impeded in his quixotic quest for the hand of Olivia, so is Viola equally tormented by her inability to appear before him as a woman to be desired and pursued. In advocating for Orsino, Viola is in emotional terms pleading for herself in relation to him. As Helena would remind us, women "should be wooed, and were not meant to woo." (*A Midsummer Night's Dream*, II, i, 242) This is Viola's quandary, as she woos not a man but a woman.

There is also the fraternal fixation to consider. Both ladies have apparently invested substantial oedipal libido in their relationships with brothers, one deceased, the other supposedly so. In the resolution of the dilemma, Olivia will eventually wed Viola's twin brother, Sebastian, whose imago is dimly apprehended through the personam of Caesario. In finally possessing Sebastian, Olivia will put to rest the painful loss of her brother and find a simulacrum of fulfillment in marriage. The comic irony, of course, is that it is not the dull Sebastian who provoked Olivia's love, but the gifted Viola/Caesario. We may legitimately wonder, then, how that conjugal pairing will "fadge" (to use Viola's endearing term) as the domestic conversation of Olivia and Sebastian unfolds. The point is that Olivia unconsciously detects in Viola's pulsing pentameters not simply the hunger for Orsino, but the shadow of a lost brother, which may be the critical element in her set of unconscious desiderata. In Platonic terms, may it not be the soul of that lost brother (a twin, perhaps) which is the other half of Olivia's being? (*Symposium*, Aristophanes' speech, 189c-193e) That spiritual complement could not be the soul of Viola, as she does not reciprocate Olivia's feelings.

Hence, the prognosis for both relationships must be guarded. Olivia is consigned to inevitable disappointment with the mental tortoise, Sebastian, while Viola will always be piqued that Orsino's love for her emerged only after Olivia was no longer available, that she was accepted on the rebound, not wined and dined. Nevertheless, it remains the case that the key to all these fortunate developments is Viola's powerful speech of love, which turns Olivia's head so wonderfully.

V. Angelo

In *Measure for Measure*, love is bedeviled by the pall of moral failure. Angelo is the appointed magistrate *ad hoc*, sitting in place of Duke Vincentio of Vienna, who has taken an obscure sabbatical. Old statutes making extramarital sex a punishable offense, having lain fallow for fourteen years, are without warning harshly revived by the deputy. Young Claudio has taken to wife *ex contractu* but in advance of public ceremony his lady friend, Juliet, now big with child. Intending to make of him an example to brothel patrons and other "fornicators," Angelo has thrown Claudio in prison where, faced with a maximum sentence, he languishes, awaiting execution. Isabella, sister to Claudio, is a Franciscan postulant in the Order of Saint Clare, in whose convent she will shortly take the strictest of vows. Learning of his plight, Isabella, renowned for her talents in philosophy and rhetoric, resolves to apply for the clemency of the austere Lord Angelo.

In what is, in effect, a post-trial oral argument for reconsideration of sentence, Isabella, accompanied by Claudio's friend, Lucio, contends that her brother should have mercy. Angelo will not relent, ostensibly on the grounds that deterrent steps must be taken to protect the public from a social menace. When Isabella retreats, Lucio prods her to be more aggressive in her entreaties. In a series of increasingly urgent remonstrations, Isabella tries in vain to "soften" Angelo. (I, iv, 69) Asked for pity, he replies sternly,

I show it most of all when I show justice,
For then I pity those I do not know,
Which a dismissed offence would after gall,
And do him right that, answering one foul wrong,
Lives not to act another. Be satisfied.
Your brother dies tomorrow. Be content.
(II, ii, 103-107)

Isabella now draws herself up to full homiletic height.

So you must be the first that gives this sentence,
And he, that suffers. O, it is excellent
To have a giant's strength, but it is tyrannous
To use it like a giant.

      Could great men thunder
As Jove himself does, Jove would ne'er be quiet,
For every pelting petty officer
Would use his heaven for thunder, nothing but thunder!
Merciful heaven,
Thou rather with thy sharp and sulphurous bolt,
Split'st the unwedgeable and gnarlèd oak
Than the soft myrtle. But man, proud man,
Dressed in a little brief authority,
Most ignorant of what he's most assured,
His glassy essence, like an angry ape
Plays such fantastic tricks before high heaven
As makes the angels weep, who, with our spleens,
Would all themselves laugh mortal.
  (II, ii, 108-126, as amended)

A startled Angelo blinks at words which seem to drop straight from the Empyrean realm. Something within has been jarred. "Why do you put these sayings upon me?" he groans, visibly taken aback. (II, ii, 137) This helpless ejaculation has the same significance as Olivia's "You might do much."

Isabella now plunges the poniard of eros to its hilt.

Because authority, though it err like others,
Hath yet a kind of medicine in itself

That skins the vice o' the top.
Go to your bosom; knock there,
And ask your heart what it doth know,
That's like my brother's fault; if it confess
A natural guiltiness, such as is his,
Let it not sound a thought upon your tongue
Against my brother's life.
(II, ii, 138-145)

Confesses the judge,

She speaks, and 'tis such sense
That my sense breeds with it.
(II, ii, 145-146)

Coincidentally, and thanks to Isabel's own verbal pyrotechnics, Angelo does in fact harbor in his bosom the very fault of desire which prompted the actions of Claudio for which he is being prosecuted. And though what he feels may be lust, to Angelo it is denominated love. Following her departure, his wrenching soliloquy lays bare a soul in perdition.

What's this, what's this? Is this her fault or mine?
The tempter or the tempted who sins most, ha?
Not she; nor doth she tempt; but it is I
That, lying by the violet in the sun
Do, as the carrion does, not as the flower,
Corrupt with virtuous season. Can it be
That modesty may more betray our sense
Than woman's lightness? Having waste ground enough,
Shall we desire to raze the sanctuary
And pitch our evils there? O, fie, fie, fie!
What dost thou, or what art thou, Angelo?
Dost thou desire her foully for those things
That make her good? O, let her brother live!
Thieves for their robbery have authority,
When judges steal themselves. What, do I love
Her, that I desire to hear her speak again,
And feast upon her eyes? What is't I dream on?
O cunning enemy, that, to catch a saint,

With saints dost bait thy hook! Most dangerous
Is that temptation that doth goad us on
To sin in loving virtue. Never could the strumpet,
With all her double vigour, art and nature,
Once stir my temper, but this virtuous maid
Subdues me quite. Ever till now
When men were fond, I smiled, and wondered how.
(II, ii, 168-192)

Isabella's petition for mercy has fallen on ears deafened by her own celestial eloquence. Angelo can hear only her, not the doctrine of mercy she imparts. The result is sin and bitter self-accusation.

When I would pray and think, I think and pray
To several subjects: heaven hath my empty words,
Whilst my invention, hearing not my tongue
Anchors on Isabel; God in my mouth,
As if I did but chew his name, and in my heart
The strong and swelling evil of my conceptions.
(II, iv, 1-6)

Here we find the same debased and debauched attitude exhibited by King Claudius, in *Hamlet, Prince of Denmark*, whose exasperated prayer, stymied by irremediable guilt, collapses: "My words fly up, my thoughts remain below. Words without thoughts never to heaven go." (III, iii, 97-98)

Though Angelo fancies that he loves Isabella, and so bluntly informs her ("Plainly conceive, I love you," II, iv, 141), he is and remains an emotionally shrunken personality and, as such, incapable of such a bond. What in the healthy soul would have blossomed as adoration, in Angelo's twisted psyche swells into a double toadstool of concupiscence and extortion. Isabel's words are like seed cast in a toxic waste dump. Instead of heeding the call of forgiveness, commuting the Draconian sentence imposed on Claudio, and then, at the appropriate time, approaching Isabella as a sincere suitor, Angelo proposes a shameful *quid pro quo*, in which she is to yield her body up to him in return for sparing her brother not only from death but gruesome torture. (II, iv, 165-167)

Observe that his usages include terms such as "breeds" (II, ii, 146) and "conceive" (II, iv, 141). Angelo's earthy inclinations betray him, no matter the lofty allusions to law and justice. Even as Isabella's declama-

tion reaches its crescendo, he never allows the "love" in his ample vocabulary to find its way to his will. This is the perfection of hypocrisy.
Words of such magnificence as would have melted the reserve of a Desdemona or an Olivia, issuing in true love, become tainted and perverted,
leading not to *caritas* but to lubricity, "seeming" and scheming. (II, iv,
150) And yet it is almost fitting that he professes love, for he might have
had it, had he been decent. Angelo has been trained in law and government. But in terms of Plato's spiritual taxonomy as set forth in *Politeia*,
his soul is of the lowest order of the appetitive class. As such, he is on-
tologically ineligible to rule. He is a cad, his professed valorization of
probity and honor a sham. In the relations of Angelo and Isabella, we
behold the complications that ensue, not when beauty comes to love
a beast, but rather when a moral brute, hearing the divine harmony of
kalon/agathon, fails to achieve the proper status of moral agent. Instead
of love we get crime. Later, after this corrupt deputy has been exposed,
cashiered, and stands before the wrath of the returned Duke, Isabella,
true to her compassionate nature, falls on her knees, and begs that he be
shown mercy. (V, i, 440-450) One almost detects in this a grain of love.

VI. *Romeo, Romeo*

At the opening of the play in Verona, not only do the protagonists
belong to feuding families, but Romeo is suffering depression after the
loss of unresponsive Rosaline. Meanwhile, young Juliet is fast becoming
a pawn in a paternally contrived marriage. What could be a less propi-
tious setting for the entrance of love? Romeo's friends urge him to give
liberty to his eyes and "examine other beauties" (I, i, 224), which he is
to hazard at the feast in the house of Capulet. Interestingly, perhaps the
worst peril is not Tybalt and his street thugs, but a certain *femme fatale*.

It is natural in light of the mutuality of the first conversation between Romeo and Juliet to assign verbal agency to them both, each
serving as the efficient cause of the other's craving. But there are countervailing considerations. When Romeo spots Juliet in the cotillion, he
believes he experiences love for the first time. (I, v, 50-52) If he does, Plato's original theory is correct; it's love-at-first-sight. Yet, is this so? When
he strode in the door of the Capulet residence, he would have sworn he
was still in the grip of love for Rosaline. That was his impression. But it
is soon disavowed. Now he has a similar conviction he's mad for Juliet
- after monitoring her for less than a minute. But we know from the
episode with Rosaline that that conclusion is unreliable. Only the most

sanguine adolescent could imagine that Romeo truly loves Juliet before they actually meet. What if she prove a shrew? Notice he doesn't actually say he's in love; rather, he asks rhetorically, "Did my heart love till now?" The answer, "Forswear it, sight, For I ne'er saw true beauty till this night." (I, v, 51-52) There is no absolute declaration of love at this point.

On the Shakespearean model, what is requisite is not a peek at beauty, but speech capable of disclosing the soul and turning the heart. Romeo makes his way to her and, boldly grasping her hand, improvises a delicate quatrain in iambic pentameter, to beg a kiss.

> If I profane with my unworthiest hand
> This holy shrine, the gentle sin is this:
> My lips, two blushing pilgrims, ready stand
> To smooth that rough touch with a tender kiss.

Kiss not granted. Instead, to his great shock, this pretty girl, whose name he doesn't even know, answers with a coquettish quatrain of her own.

> Good pilgrim, you do wrong your hand too much,
> Which mannerly devotion shows in this.
> For saints have hands that pilgrims hands do touch,
> And palm to palm is holy palmers' kiss.

And with that brief reply we are already eight lines deep in a shared sonnet. It is remarkable enough that this boy should begin the conversation with poetry, but that the young lady should answer in kind is nothing short of miraculous.

Thereafter, each pronounces a line or two until the fourteenth is reached, at which time Romeo has his reward.

> R)   Have not saints lips, and holy palmers too?
> J)   Ay, pilgrim, lips that they must use in prayer.
> R)   O, then, dear saint, let lips do what hands do:
>   They pray; grant thou, lest faith turn to despair.
> J)   Saints do not move, though grant for prayers' sake.
> R)   Then move not while my prayer's effect I take.
> (I, v, 92-105, following *The Yale Shakespeare*)

This miniature dialogue, unique in all literature, seems to hurl the interlocutors into a profound and impassioned romance. But is it actually instrumental, or more in the nature of an aesthetic prologue? Instead of one party's transcendent oratory precipitating a love response in another, we seem to find instead two equally gifted poets having an identical effect on each other. What are we to make of such fearful symmetry? It is short lived. By the time we get to Juliet's "Gallop Apace" soliloquy, which seems an antecedent of the soliloquy of Lady Macbeth, it dawns on us that Romeo is in way over his head. Her gallop easily outpaces his. As argued in an earlier chapter, unlike Romeo, Juliet is a genuinely tragic character who is rapidly imploding as a black hole in inner space. Romeo is occasionally plucky and enterprising, but just as often simply rash or down-at-heels. Of the malevolent aspect of life he is utterly innocent. Once un-reading and re-reading of *Romeo and Juliet* are undertaken, and the gross difference between these two seemingly twinned protagonists is grasped, we can return chastened to the primal sonnet in Act 1. It is one thing to warble a witty and flirtatious rhyme to impress a girl, but something else altogether to absorb such a ditty and, in a fraction of a nanosecond, send the poetic ball zinging back across the net. Such is genius, and such is Juliet. Romeo is, in contrast with her, nothing more than the small tethered bird to which she likens him, (II, i, 220-230), a clamoring, clambering pet. For Romeo, Juliet is a stand-in for Rosaline. She is the girl he loves. But that obsessive love comes from the web of words she weaves about him. And this he never realizes. For Juliet, on the other hand, Romeo represents, in relation to her life and social predicament, an existential challenge, a metaphysical crisis, an image of apocalypse. He is a bad boy, the call of the wyrd. Hence Juliet's Romeo is simultaneously all, and nothing at all. The pretence of symmetry vanishes in the orchard scene, which stations aspiring Romeo below, in the subordinate position of servant, one who attends to Juliet's confession and cannot decide whether to speak out. (II, i, 79) Here are the operative words.

> O Romeo, Romeo, wherefore art thou Romeo?
> Deny thy father and refuse thy name,
> Or if thou wilt not, be but sworn my love,
> And I'll no longer be a Capulet.

> 'Tis but thy name that is my enemy.
> Thou art thyself, though not a Montague.
> What's Montague? It is nor hand, nor foot,

Nor arm nor face, nor any other part
Belonging to a man. O, be some other name!
What's in a name? That which we call a rose
By any other name would smell as sweet.
So Romeo would, were he not Romeo called,
Retain that dear perfection which he owes
Without that title. Romeo, doff thy name,
And for thy name -- which is no part of thee --
Take all myself.
(II, i, 75-91, as amended)

By the time he summons up the nerve to interject, he is fast under her spell, remaining so for the duration of the play. His inferior position in the orchard scene tallies with his also-ran role in the initial sonnet. He is never the principal voice but at all times an accompanying *obbligato*. It is Juliet who actively inscribes herself in him. Hers is the speech of love.

VII. *Phoebe, Phoebe, Phoebe*

It is interesting to compare the diction of the loquacious shepherdess Phoebe in *As You Like It* with that of Audrey, the alluring goatherd. While Audrey's dialect is recognizably rustic and innocent, Phoebe expresses herself as a young lady strangely steeped in learning and poesy.

AUDREY

I do not know what 'poetical' is. Is it honest and
word? Is it a true thing?
(III, iii, 14-15)

Do you wish, then, that the gods had made me poetical?
(III, iii, 19-20)

I am not a slut, though I thank the gods I am foul.
(III, iii, 33-34)

PHOEBE

I would not be thy executioner.

I fly thee for I would not injure thee.
Thou tell'st me there is murder in mine eye.
'Tis pretty, sure, and very probable
That eyes, that are the frail'st and softest things,
Who shut their coward gates on atomies,
Should be called tyrants, butchers, murderers.
Now I do frown on thee with all my heart,
And if mine eyes can wound, now let them kill thee.
Now counterfeit to swoon, why now fall down;
Or if thou can'st not, O, for shame, for shame,
Lie not, to say mine eyes are murderers.
Now show the wound mine eye hath made in thee.
Scratch thee but with a pin, and there remains
Some scar of it. Lean upon a rush,
The cicatrice and capable impressure
Thy palm some moment keeps. But now mine eyes,
Which I have darted at thee, hurt thee not;
Nor I am sure there is no force in eyes
That can do hurt.
(III, v, 9-27)

The delighted audience can be as grateful that the gods chose to make Audrey as uncommonly common as they made Phoebe poetical. The soul of Phoebe, filled with the verbal kindling of love, is like a dry tinderbox waiting for a spark. It is soon in coming. Overhearing her peremptory rejection of the swain Silvius, her ideal companion for a cottage on Mt. Parnassus, Rosalind in the person of Ganymede steps forth with a sharp yet lofty rebuke.

ROSALIND

Who might be your mother,
That you insult, exult, and all at once,
Over the wretched? What though you have no beauty
As, by my faith, I see no more in you
Than without candle may go dark to bed --
Must you be therefore proud and pitiless?
Why, what means this? Why do you look on me?
I see no more in you than in the ordinary
Of nature's sale-work. - 'Od's my little life,

266

I think she means to tangle my eyes, too.
No, faith, proud mistress, hope not after it.
'Tis not your inky brows, your black silk hair,
Your bugle eyeballs, nor your cheek of cream,
That can entame my spirits to your worship.
(To Silvius) You, foolish shepherd, wherefore do you follow her,
Like foggy south, puffing with wind and rain?
You are a thousand times a properer man
Than she a woman. 'Tis such fools as you
That makes the world full of ill-favoured children.
'Tis not her glass but you that flatters her,
And out of you she sees herself more proper
Than any of her lineaments can show her.

To Phoebe:

But, mistress, know yourself, down on your knees
And thank heaven, fasting, for a good man's love;
For I must tell you friendly in your ear,
Sell when you can. You are not for all markets.
Cry the man mercy, love him, take his offer;
Foul is most foul, being foul to be a scoffer. --
So, take her to thee, shepherd. Fare you well.
(III, v, 36-64)

What is Phoebe's reaction to this unexpected and impassioned outburst from a mere passerby?

Sweet youth, I pray you chide a year together.
I had rather hear you chide than this man woo.
(III, v, 65-66)

Has not the bell of love been struck? "Why do you look on me?" asks Ganymede, with the accent on the last word. Shouldn't your astonished gaze fall upon the devoted swain who dogs your heels? Like Olivia, Phoebe has accidentally fallen for a gifted girl disguised as an eloquent youth. Ganymede realizes at once what has happened, and teasingly quotes the Marlovian line from *Hero and Leander*, Who ever loved that loved not at first sight? (III, v, 83) The joke here is that once more it is not vision which has done the trick, but the power of the spoken word.

The breathless Phoebe, still recovering from the surge of love, debates the cause with faithful Silvius. Can it be the mere appearance of this glib lad which has so captivated her, or, perhaps his command of speech?

Though she later considers the possibility that his looks have won her, it is his language to which she first turns to explain Ganymede's impact on her.

PHOEBE

Think not I love him, though I ask for him.
'Tis a peevish boy. Yet he talks well.
But what care I for words? Yet words do well
When he that speaks them pleases those that hear.
(III, v, 110-114)

There is the answer. Shakespeare parts company with Marlowe. Cupid's every dart's a word. Unlike mere visual appearance, language has within it the power to weave a spell around the hearer, and so even when, as here, the speech is a bit rough around the edges, it retains the power to transfix and transport.

VIII. Conclusion

Shakespeare is intellectually indebted to Plato. Yet the plays situate the moment of absolute love, not in beatific vision, but in the moment of hearing. Perhaps the ease with which the virile "spear" in "Shakespeare" is discovered obscures the whispered "ear." Where Plato is photocentric, Shakespeare revels in logocentricity. As he proclaims in *The Rape of Lucrece*, "For by our ears our hearts are tainted."

Whether in the soliloquies of despairing Hamlet, in Henry V's predawn meditations and rousing exhortations at Agincourt, or the poignant parleys of Olivia and Viola, he brings us to see language in its vital centrality. Harold Bloom is almost correct: in our overhearing of ourselves - and others - lies our humanity. It is how we make a difference to one another, and how those differences paradoxically make us one. Love, then, lives in our language and the way we verbally engage. In employing the speeches of love in these four plays, Shakespeare isn't making the outlandish claim that love always takes its beginning in an historically memorable oration; rather, he is simply drawing our attention to its magical power to do so.

What we say is what we are to one another. Hence to lose that capacity for whatever reason is in Shakespearean terms the worst of all possible fates. That's why the most severe penalty in Plantagenet England was banishment. When, for example, Thomas Mowbray, Duke of Norfolk, is ejected from the realm by Richard in *The Tragedy of King Richard the Second,* he bemoans exile as the ruin of his universe.

> The language I have learnt these forty years,
> My native English, now I must forgo,
> And now my tongue's use is to me no more
> Than an unstringèd viol or a harp,
> Or like a cunning instrument cased up,
> Or, being open, put into his hands
> That knows no touch to tune the harmony.
> Within my mouth you have enjailed my tongue,
> Doubly portcullised with my teeth and lips,
> And dull unfeeling barren ignorance
> Is made my jailer to attend me.
> I am too old to fawn upon a nurse,
> Too far in years to be a pupil now.
> What is thy sentence then but speechless death,
> Which robs my tongue from breathing native breath?
> (I, iii, 153-167)

In *The History of Henry the Fourth, Part One,* there is a scene deserving of more attention than it currently receives. In Act Three, Sc. 1, the rebels prepare to depart for the fatal battle against the forces of implacable Bolingbroke. Mortimer and Hotspur spend their last hour with their wives. But Mortimer is frustrated by a linguistic barrier. "This is the deadly spite that angers me: My wife can speak no English, I no Welsh." How, then, can they, tongue-tied, make a fitting adieu, there in the great drafty hall, as trumpets blast and horses neigh?

"O, I am ignorance itself in this!" he cries.

Glyndwr, his Welsh father-in-law, offers a translation.

> She bids you on the wanton rushes lay you down,
> And rest your gentle head upon her lap,

And she will sing the song that pleaseth you,
And on your eyelids crown the god of sleep,
Charming your blood with pleasing heaviness,
Making such difference 'twixt wake and sleep
As is the difference betwixt day and night
The hour before the heavenly-harnessed team
Begins his golden progress in the east.
(III, i, 209-217)

And so Mortimer rests his head where 'tis invited, as does the doomed Hotspur with his Kate. Instead of empty talk, Mortimer's Welsh wife intones to them her hymn of bygone days, of joys that are no more. Before the final coup, an interlude of conjugal intimacy infuses the couples with grace.

At the other end of the scale of language, at its full, lies for Shakespeare the speech of love, a storm of words in which we hear our "other half" beckoning to us. And yet, the poetry of the heart is forever like the song of the Sirens: we heed it at our peril.

WORKS CITED

Plato, *The Collected Dialogues*, Huntington Cairns, Edith Hamilton, eds., Bollingen Series LXXI, Princeton University Press, 1989

William Shakespeare: The Complete Works, S. Taylor and G. Wells, eds., Second Edition, Clarendon Press, 2005

14
The Quality of Portia

Tell me where is Portia bred,
Or in her heart or in her head?
How begot, how nourishèd?
Reply! Reply!
She's engender'd in our eyes,
With gazes fed while lovers cry.
'Neath the counterpane her treasures lie.
Let us all ring Portia's bell;
I'll begin it, -- Ding Dong Dell,
And welcome thee to Belmont Hell.

"Our house is hell," Shylock's daughter Jessica exclaims, but the description is a tad shy of detail. All we really know is that she elopes with a gentile boy, absconding with plenty of cash, and receives a generous award from the Venetian Court of Justice to boot. Whether she has been actually mistreated is anybody's guess. The other - and far greater - house in *The Merchant of Venice* is Belmont, the palatial country seat of beautiful Portia, who has inherited a bundle from Daddy, conditioned on her accepting a husband from the results of a bizarre lottery. Curiously, the girl who has everything appears to be down in the dumps. "By my troth, Nerissa," she confides to her handmaid in language reminiscent of American slaves, "my little body is a-weary of this great world." (I, ii, 1-2) But unlike Jessica's unhappy domicile, the hell of Belmont is of Portia's own devising. She alone is in control there, with none to oppress her. Delving to the root of her malaise is therefore a critical necessity. Now, it is of no small significance that the play opens with a parallel confession of melancholy from the merchant himself, Antonio.

> In sooth, I know not why I am so sad.
> It wearies me; you say it wearies you,
> But how I caught it, found it, or came by it,
> What stuff 'tis made of, whereof it is born,
> I am to learn;
> And such a want-wit sadness makes of me
> That I have much ado to know myself.
> (I, i, 1-7)

From our vantage point, we can easily answer his nagging question. Antonio's dearest friend has just fallen hopelessly in love with gloomy Portia, and is about to use Antonio's financial credit to woo her. As Bassanio's male bond shows signs of loosening, Antonio can already sense that something is wrong. Portia is fantastically rich and Bassanio is not. Why is he convinced that he needs so much money to win her? That premise comes from Portia, the Queen of Hell, whose portrait sits, ironically not in the casket of gold or silver, but lead. He has already found favor in her eyes, and choosing a casket is a pretty cheap date. Emanations of avarice and despair radiate out from her and infect the spiritual body of all Venice, including Shylock. His world belongs to her. The mood of Belmont resembles that of Dante's *Inferno*, in which the body of Lucifer rests in the deepest pit of all, frozen fast in ice which his own flailing wings have created. In symbolic terms, Antonio, Bassanio and Shylock are all denizens of the sublunary world of mortals who fall into the benighted clutches of Belmont. Portia, the lover of disguises, goes forth like a vampire, arrayed in the form of legal virtue to spy on men and lead them into temptation, rendering them her debtors. The spirit of transvestite concealment which absorbs Nerissa and Jessica has its metaphysical center in Belmont. In the end, as we shall see (V, i, 249-255), the very soul of Antonio, which had fluttered about in helpless anguish throughout the play, is finally snared by Portia as he numbly surrenders to her final and complete control. Shylock, a mere subaltern of her will, is traduced and tossed aside, his vital energies utterly sapped and drained.

Bassanio, a clueless dupe, along with Jessica, Lorenzo, Gratiano, are all taken captive, much as the Knight and his entire retinue are led dancing off by Death in Ingmar Bergman's masterful *The Seventh Seal*. In this way does the Queen of Hell pay back her Father for placing her in an uncomfortable little fiefdom instead of unconditionally yielding his whole kingdom to her.

It is interesting to note that in his masterpiece, *Shakespeare and the Goddess of Complete Being*, on which he labored for ten years, Ted Hughes, after an exhaustive philosophical analysis of Shakespeare, at the very summit, finally reaches *The Merchant of Venice*, which he characterizes quite accurately as a work of "anti-anti-Semitism," meaning that the ideological cant which would condemn the play as hostile to Judaism could hardly be more misguided. The spirit of revenge is Portia's sphere of influence, and Shylock, a pawn who sought to oppose the advocate of "mercy," is the one who suffers real vengeance. Shylock is like a fly embedded in the web of hate that is 16th century Venice, a web symbolically spun and operated by the arachnoid Portia and her ilk, and his hatred of the Christians is but a pale reflection of and reaction to the atmosphere of fear and loathing in which he must live, move and have his being each day.

If we want to take the measure of the misunderstanding of *The Merchant of Venice*, consider how many viewers, readers and critics have happily found in Portia and her crew a band of angels standing up in defense of love and law in defiance of Shylock's awful wickedness. Though a mere glance at the text is sufficient to dispose of such folly, and legions of commentators have been at pains to lead us to a more balanced view, the conventional wisdom prevails. After all, what about that quality of mercy? Doesn't it droppeth like the gentle rain from heaven? Why couldn't cruel Shylock see that? Isn't Antonio a loyal hero willing to lay down his life for his friend? It's all so simple, isn't it? Look at how he is regarded by his friends. Here is Salerio:

A kinder gentleman treads not the earth. (II, viii, 34)

And Bassanio:

The dearest friend to me, the kindest man,
The best-conditioned and unwearied spirit
In doing courtesies, and one in whom

> The ancient Roman honour more appears
> Than any that draws breath in Italy.
> (III, iv, 290-294)

Really. Contrast these testimonials with the painful but uncontradicted report of Shylock:

> Signior Antonio, many a time and oft
> In the Rialto you have rated me
> About my moneys and my usances.
> Still have I borne it with a patient shrug,
> For suff'rance is the badge of all our tribe.
> You call me misbeliever, cut-throat, dog,
> And spit upon my Jewish gaberdine,
> And all for use of that which is mine own.
> Well then, it now appears you need my help.
> Go to, then. You come to me, and you say,
> 'Shylock, we would have moneys' -- you say so,
> You, that did void your rheum upon my beard,
> And foot me as you spurn a stranger cur
> Over your threshold.
> (I, iii, 105-118)

Instead of denying these allegations, Antonio confirms and renews them in the instant:

> I am as like to call thee so [dog] again,
> To spit on thee again, to spurn thee too.
> If thou wilt lend this money, lend it not
> As to thy friends; for when did friendship take
> A breed for barren metal of his friend?
> But lend it rather to thine enemy,
> Who if he break, thou mayst with better face
> Exact the penalty.
> (I, iii, 128-134)

Thus speaks the kindest man in all the world. Is such a one not under some kind of malignant spell?

Let's take a closer at Portia, the herald of mercy. Close attention will show that she is a charter member of a female rogue's gallery, which includes such redoubtable figures as Lady Macbeth, the Queen in *Cymbeline*, Dionyza in *Pericles*, and *King Henry VI's* Queen Margaret. According to her late father's will, she must marry the suitor who passes the test of the three caskets. This imposition on her liberty has evidently triggered an attack of chronic *Weltschmerz*. She and her handmaid Nerissa recount with evident glee the roster of unappetizing candidates for the title of Signior Belmont. Everyone comes in for a drubbing, particularly the unfortunate Prince of Morocco, who makes an extensive apology for being a black man ("Mislike me not for my complexion . . . ."). Not to worry, Portia is free of bias:

> In terms of choice I am not solely led
> By nice direction of a maiden' eyes.
> Besides, the lott'ry of my destiny
> Bars me the right of voluntary choosing.
>
> But if my father had not scanted me,
> And hedged me by his wit to yield myself
> His wife who wins me by that means I told you,
> Yourself, renownèd Prince, then stood as fair
> As any comer I have looked on yet
> For my affection.
> (II, i, 13-22)

Unfortunately, this is nothing but cynical dissembling, as we learn in Act II, sc. vii, when, after the Prince of Morocco mistakenly selects the casket of gold, and graciously takes his leave, Portia gives the game away by muttering:

> A gentle riddance. Draw the curtains, go.
> Let all of his complexion choose me so.
> (II, vii, 76-77)

Portia is an inveterate liar and racist. Ironically, the gist of the casket game is to learn to make our choices not by superficial appearances but by true assessments of worth. But Portia dismisses Morocco (who chooses the gold casket) because he is black. Her maxim seems to be, What is like me is good; what is not like me is what I do not like. If her father had hoped she might learn something about values from the casket game, he obviously would have had his hopes dashed.

Of course, mindless Bassanio is a far more alluring aspirant, and would be the perfect complement to Portia's conniving self-seeking. Coveniently, he too enters the lists to play a round of pick-the-casket, and Portia cannot afford to let him fail. The solution? She cheats. As her picture is kept in the casket of lead, she arranges for a song to be performed during Bassanio's deliberations which contains subliminal clues in the form of five words rhyming with "lead." Portia watches his every move as he watches her. Can you guess who wins? One imagines her father squirming in embarrassment in his grave.

Liar.

Racist.

Cheat.

Where do we go from here? To court, of course. But why? Wouldn't it be easier for jet-set Portia to retain Dr. Bellario, rather than pretending to visit the convent while schlepping instead to Venice as a male lawyer? Equipped with the professor's costume and a crib sheet of legal pointers, Portia is ready to bedazzle the Magnificoes and baffle the Jew in the City of St. Mark. But impersonating an officer of the court is a grave offense in anyone's estimation and grounds for a mistrial. And it is hard to fathom why Portia would fraudulently deprive her unwitting client, Antonio, of competent counsel just to visit her new husband, Bassanio, when she never discloses her identity. But consider: if she is in disguise, Portia would have an opportunity to spy on Bassanio and his friend to appraise the nature of their unusually fervid affection for one another. And so it is that, disguised as junior partner, Balthasar, Portia is paradoxically triumphant to hear Bassanio say:

> Antonio, I am married to a wife
> Which is as dear to me as life itself,
> But life itself, my wife, and all the world
> Are not with me esteemed above thy life.
> I would lose all, ay, sacrifice them all
> Here to this devil, to deliver you.
> (IV, i, 279-284)

Anyone can see that Bassanio is unaware of his wife's presence in

276

the courtroom, and is simply posturing for the court. But rather than straightforwardly clear the air by private conference, Portia lets this slide to take advantage of it later.

As for the defense offered on cross examination, it is a palpable sophism.

> Tarry a little; there is something else.
> This bond doth give thee here no jot of blood.
> The words expressly are 'a pound of flesh'.
> Take thou thy pound of flesh.
> But in the cutting it, if thou dost shed
> One drop of Christian blood, thy lands and goods
> Are by the laws of Venice confiscate
> Unto the state of Venice.
> (IV, i, 302-309)

This legal gambit must be examined carefully. The strict construction of the language of the bond is absurd, since flesh contains blood as fruit must have juice. To take one is to take the other. Hair and skin are not named in the bond either, but who would dispute that they would go with the flesh to the creditor? The real point of Balthasar, then, is not the bond, but the anti-alien and anti-Jewish statutes of the Republic of Venice, which allowed capital punishment and confiscation of goods in the case of Jews who shed Christian blood. Further, although the trial took place before the Duke, behind him lay an ecclesiastical tribunal, the Inquisition of Venice, which also had jurisdiction over such cases. It had the power of torture, and those Jews, like Shylock, who were converted to Christianity, but withheld inner assent, or later abandoned the "true faith," could be sent to the galleys for hard labor. Half of these condemned oarsmen died or became disabled before their terms expired, as well explained in Brian Pullan's study, *The Jews of Europe and the Inquisition of Venice, 1550-1670.*

Note that Portia stipulates in open court that Shylock is legally entitled to his bond, but threatens criminal action against him to gain an advantage in the civil proceeding, an unethical tactic now universally proscribed by the bar. As for the "quality of mercy," of which she famously speaks so loftily at the outset, no relief is proposed by her in the damages phase of the trial. Shylock's plea that he retain his house is not honored. "Mercy" turns out to have been nothing more than rhetoric, to be demanded of the plaintiff but not granted to him. But as Portia refreshingly admitted earlier, "I can easier teach twenty what were good to be done than to be one of the twenty to follow mine own teaching." (I, ii, 15-17) Thus, *Weltschmerz* soon enough becomes *Schadenfreude*. Even though Shylock relents and abandons his suit for specific performance of the bond, the Duke finds that there has been an attempt on the life of a Venetian citizen by an alien, and awards half of Shylock's estate to our hero, Antonio, the moiety to pass to the general fund.

At this point, the defendant, that is, Antonio, is offered the option of amending the judgment. This he does as follows:

1. Shylock is relieved of the 50% fine to the State;

2. The other half of Shylock's estate (presumably including his house) will pass to Antonio, to be used until the death of Shylock, at which time it will pass "unto the gentleman that lately stole his daughter";

3. Under Venetian law, Shylock must cease being Jewish and must take up the public practice of Christianity;

4. Shylock must bequeath on his death the remainder of his fortune to Lorenzo, the same gentleman that lately stole his ducats and his daughter!

This travesty of justice is the final judgment. There is no appeal. Although the court to do equity should take judicial notice of the subornation of Jessica and the theft of Shylock's ducats, at least for credit or reimbursement, this is blithely ignored. And, since it is highly unlikely that Shylock, an observant Jew, is going to be able to become a convincing "Christian," the sentence of forced conversion entails either his death on the Galleys or his permanent injury.

Antonio, who chronically abused Shylock and who freely subscribed to the bond, avoids the legal terms thereof, escapes the loss of his flesh, and wins a great deal of property. Shylock, the lifelong victim of rabid discrimination in Venice, and whose anger against the gentiles was fueled by the abduction of his daughter and the burglary of his home, is handed a sentence of doom.

At the conclusion of Shakespeare's *Measure for Measure*, Isabella, whose own plea for mercy on behalf of her brother excels in heartfelt emotion and dramatic impact any words of Portia, kneels down before the Duke, and begs that mercy be extended to the rogue magistrate who sought to coerce from her sexual favors. (V, i, 440-450) But while Isabella is nobly willing to pardon Angelo, her enemy, Portia, who preached on the identical virtue of mercy, refuses to accord any to Shylock. In this she shows herself inconsistent, inclement and hypocritical. Worse, it would appear that her role in the civil trial of *Shylock v. Antonio* is not that of defense counsel for Antonio, but rather that of independent legal expert.

We come now to the last Act. The inconvenient Shylock is disposed of and quite forgotten. At the prompting of Antonio, Bassanio has acceded to "Balthasar's" request and surrendered to "him" the precious ring of trust he received from Portia. She now has that ring, and is nursing a grudge against Bassanio for his improvident courtroom remarks about his supreme love for Antonio. When he returns to Hell-mont, she asks to see the ring. Poor stammering Bassanio tries to explain he gave it as a token of appreciation to Balthasar, little realizing that he was actually returning it to his wife. At this point Portia accuses him of lying, saying he gave the ring to a woman (an amusing half truth for us, but a malicious lie in relation to her spouse). It was Portia who is responsible for Bassanio's loss of the ring. Under the guise of "Balthasar" she asked for it. Now, because he hasn't got it, she accuses the man who worships the ground she walks on of infidelity. And here is the virtue of the jest, the heart of the comedy. For though the couples will have a laugh as all these odds are made even through conversation before going to bed, Bassanio finds himself married to a manipulative schemer, who will not hesitate to harass him and make of his life an endless torment. The honeymoon is just getting under way.

But at the peak of the crisis, and before Bassanio learns that "Balthasar" was in fact his runaway wife playing lawyer-without-a-license, Antonio steps forward once more on behalf of his friend.

Antonio (to Portia)

I once did lend my body for his wealth
Which, but for him that had your husband's ring,
Had quite miscarried, I dare to be bound again,
My soul upon the forfeit, that your lord
Will never more break faith advisedly.

And Portia replies:

Then you shall be his surety. Give him this,
And bid him keep it better than the other.

(V, i, 249-255)

Hapless Antonio, the stooge of the anti-Semitic community in Venice, and puppet of Portia, here becomes a surety again, this time not in relation to Shylock as to his body, but in relation to Portia as to his very soul. Thus her fiendish enterprise is now complete, with everyone in subjection to her. One would say she has stepped into Shylock's shoes, except for the fact that he was walking all along in hers.

WORKS CITED

Ted Hughes, *Shakespeare and the Goddess of Complete Being*, Farrar, Strauss, Giroux, 1992.

Brian Pullan, *The Jews of Europe and the Inquisition of Venice*, I.B. Taurus Publishers, 1997.

William Shakespeare: The Complete Works, S. Wells and G. Taylor, eds., 2d Edition, Clarendon Press, 2005.

15
False Radicals

The Tao is called the Great Mother
Empty yet inexhaustible
It gives birth to infinite worlds
It is always present within you
You can use it as you wish.

When the great Tao is forgotten
Goodness and piety appear
When the body's intelligence declines
Cleverness and knowledge step forth.

All things have their backs to the female
And stand facing the male
When male and female combine
All things achieve harmony.

- *Lao Tse*

I.

There is a specter haunting Shakespeare studies today - the specter of the authorship controversy. Though countless exorcisms have been performed, the ghost hovers still, its chill breath fogging the laptops of the professoriate. "There is no question," they insist.

"It is a bogus non-issue, on a par with flying saucers and the Loch Ness Monster." But they are hoist with their own petards: non-existent demons need hardly be cast out, only real ones.

Let us pluck from the frothing sea of hermeneutical fecundity a single representative volume for inspection: *Alternative Shakespeares*, a collection of essays by prominent critics, edited by John Drakakis. What catches one's attention is that, despite a title hinting at authorship, there is not one alternative Shakespeare mentioned in its pages, a disappointing preterition. Rather, what is taken up, none too surprisingly, are various readings. "What is proposed," writes Mr. Drakakis, is:

> a series of explorations of the ways in which historically specific readings are generated, which acknowledge the existence of structures within the text as devices for exclusion and repression, while at the same time insisting that the process of 'making sense' of a Shakespearean text is itself determined by a multiplicity of forces. (Drakakis, 23-24)

For Mr. Drakakis and his colleagues, "criticism is now an openly pluralist activity, with proponents of particular positions contesting vigorously the intellectual space which it has occupied." (Drakakis, 1) Other than the outworn topographical trope, what have we here? It seems to be implied that everyone before Derrida spoke in one dreary dirge, a monotonous drone now suddenly replaced by symphonies of diversity. What kind of "readings" would be "generated" to "acknowledge" anything? Is it assumed that in any historical text there are "devices for exclusion and repression"? Beyond our own political desiderata, what warrants such presumption?

If a book is about various *discourses*, why call it "*Alternative Shakespeares*," unless somewhere in the recesses of the collective unconscious there is a lingering sense that it is precisely an alternative *Shakespeare* which is missing? Title belies purpose. In reality these are critics who accept only *one* Shakespeare, damn the "alternatives."

In the name of "pluralism" any voices raising actual literary rivals to William of Stratford are deposited in a dark and unmentionable oblivion. No decent, self-respecting "pluralism" would dare hazard the idea that the author was anything but the Warwickshire yeoman, as advertised. Yet, what these writers celebrate is complete openness. Let a thousand flowers bloom, a thousand thoughts contend! For in the "space" of competing discourses will arise an hitherto unsuspected paradise of forms and possibilities which hold the key to the future of the world. There will be no limit to edifying readings as we hurtle at the speed of thought into our brave new world of letters. Dogmatism and overbearing patriarchy will be relics of the dim and dying past. And though there is no "author," William be his name.

This is the sort of schizoid thinking that continues to dog contemporary criticism. In the shining firmament above, where post-structural eminences soar in vertiginous freedom, Shakespeare is at last whatever we make of him, as protean as Prince Hamlet's clouds. (III, ii, 364-370) He is all posture and attitude, the sophisticated stance we adopt in relation to the radically amorphous text. Watch in wonder as we scribble his name in the stratosphere and see it dissolve, as though writ in water. Meanwhile, William of Stratford crieth in the dank and dirty ground and will not be denied. He stealeth forth to stalk the land. He is like the picture of Dorian Gray, ugly and demented, chained in a dark house as a monument to the Neanderthal era when it mattered who wrote what. It is in his memory that so many exclaim in their tautological frenzy: "Shakespeare wrote Shakespeare." But you can't have it both ways. There cannot be a solution to a question if there is no question. As Hotspur would say, that's flat. You cannot simultaneously reduce Shakespeare to congeries of "social energies" while making pilgrimages in double-decker tour buses to Anne Hathaway's Cottage. Or . . . can you? William of Stratford is like a barnacled anchor in the cellarage of the sea, holding down a thousand bubbles of theory. He is the awful patriarch into whose emaciated arms we flee to escape authority. So long as we prattle about our "readings," William is mere absence, superfluous and unnoticed. But when that lodestone is threatened by pesky authorship gadflies, we quickly shift to the most hidebound literalism in order that the mummified begetter of our transcendence be preserved. He is the literary talisman we wear about our necks to drive away the ghost.

In the salubrious light of "pluralism," feminism, homosexual studies, and other modern splendors flourish. That is as expected. But the authorship question has been judged and found wanting; it alone is the pariah undeserving of the benefits of "pluralism." The authorship discourse is now the "Other," the unacknowledged, the Untouchable of literature. Its alien voices must not be admitted or tolerated. Hence, if they are mentioned, it can only be for ridicule. The logic is simple. It is self-evident that William of Stratford wrote the poems and plays. Anyone who chooses to doubt this is behaving irrationally, indeed indecently, leaving no alternative but to treat him dismissively and contemptuously, with ad hominem attacks, disrespect and name-calling. Once those who are seeking actual authorial alternatives to William Shagsper are firmly and finally suppressed, we can happily return to Project Ambiguity and the bestowing of peace and pluralism upon all. The ghost is banished.

It never occurs to these philosophical revolutionaries that by substituting a single remarkable authorial biography for the standard model, the kind of paradigm shift in reading which is plainly the contemporary desideratum might be achieved. Remaining with the Stratford man lies at the foundation of the unacknowledged reactionary nature of most Shakespeare scholarship from which these thinkers profess to have escaped. Somehow by clinging to the quintessential patriarch we will finally overcome all things patriarchal, seems to be the logic.

On the other hand, it may be that what these critics are after is not just any radical interpretation but one which serves their particular cultural designs. If we start with the intention of exhuming the text to find therein material consistent with or hostile to, say, feminism, or some other cherished point of view, if, like one who writes a flattering letter to himself, we frontload the text with what we intend to discover there, like Aaron burying his bag of gold, we must be prepared to answer those who might challenge our method on moral and intellectual grounds.

Mr. Drakakis writes:

> The following pages offer, across a wide spectrum, a series of *radical* transformations of the questions that can be asked of texts, a problematizing of the concept of the text itself, and a sustained critique of those critical discourses that have claimed for themselves the role of transparent mediators of the text. The objective common to all of these essays is the demystification of the 'myth' of Shakespeare. (Drakakis, 24, emphasis added)

One wonders in reading such a pompous manifesto how it is expected that a "problematizing" of the text can lead to any "demystification." Do these words imply that we plan to so obfuscate the printed words that we can then extract from them whatever we happen to want? Is that cricket? Can a fundamental interrogation be carried out if the stubborn question of the author's identity and his relation to that text are sedulously omitted? It has been proclaimed everywhere, shouted from the housetops, that the tale of William of Stratford-Upon-Avon is the biggest hoax ever foisted on a trusting public. Now comes a group of writers dedicated to the "demystification" of the "myth" of Shakespeare which manages a discreet silence on this very myth. Instead of genuine inquiry, what we find is a private conversation among a cadre of intellectuals altogether alienated from the concerns of the general readership. But the day has not yet arrived when polysyllabic jargon ('problematizing', 'demystification') can take the place of thought. There is indeed a Shakespeare myth but it is not one these essayists deign to notice. It is well to be radical if it takes one to the roots of things. But the root of every writing is the writer. When Shakespeare uses this word, it refers to the fathoming of a human being. "I cannot delve him to the root." (*Cymbeline*, I, i, 28) And the character referred to is plainly an image of the poet himself. One can certainly contemplate the poetry of Shakespeare without ever giving a nod in the direction of the fellow who dragged his pen across the page, a pen filled with blood, sweat and tears. One can do that. But to dub such business "radical" gives a new meaning to the word, and shows just how shallow one can be in the name of depth.

II.

We will look briefly at one of these writers, Catherine Belsey, in Chapter 8, "Disrupting Sexual Difference: meaning and gender in the comedies." (Drakakis, 166 ff.) Belsey, a post-structural feminist, seems to want to say something about the comedies, among which she counts *The Tragedy of Cymbeline* (1623). Though it has its fool, Cloten, *Cymbeline* is not concluded with marriage and is in no sense comic. On the contrary. The Queen's ignominious death is reminiscent of Dionyza and Lady Macbeth. The general idea is that in his comedies Shakespeare challenges binary sexual stereotypes and so points in the direction of relationships characterized by genuine partnership. (Belsey, 177 ff.) Along the way, however, a doctrinaire ideology wedded to a 1970's argot so encumbers the argument that it stalls in incoherence.

We begin at the beginning.

The problem with the meanings that we learn - and learn to produce - is that they seem to define and delimit what is thinkable, imaginable, possible. To fix meaning, to arrest its process and deny its plurality, is in effect to confine what is possible to what is. Conversely, to disrupt this fixity is to glimpse alternative possibilities. (Belsey, 166-167)

What is intended by these words? What are these "meanings"? It must be pretty plain as no examples are offered. How would one go about "producing" a "meaning"? We know how to speak and write, how to do things with words. Is this the "production" of "meaning"? Our actions have significance for ourselves and others. As we conduct our everyday affairs are we "producing" "meanings"? Might there not be an elucidation at this point so we know what is being claimed? When we look up words in the dictionary, we see multiple definitions. It is no secret that words have numerous employments and senses, and that usage and language are constantly evolving. If that is what Belsey refers to, it's true but trivial. If it's not, where is the necessary difference? Do dictionaries "arrest the process of meaning"? Deny plurality?

> A conservative criticism reads in quest of familiar, obvious, common-sense meanings, and thus reaffirms what we already know. (Belsey, 167)

What is "conservative criticism?" No example is offered. What, exactly, is wrong with affirming what we already know? Would it be better to affirm what we don't know? Does "conservative criticism" forbid the growth of language, proscribe metaphor? Who can tell? A straw man is so ill set up that it could be anything for anybody. It is notorious that as languages develop, some words and some meanings are irretrievably lost. Should such losses be applauded? Is it suggested that traditional meanings should be abandoned simply on the basis of having been once established?

> A radical criticism, however, is concerned to produce readings which challenge that knowledge by revealing alternative meanings, disrupting the system of differences which legitimates the perpetuation of things as they are. The project of such a criticism is not to replace one authoritative interpretation of a text with another, but to suggest a plurality of ways in which texts might be read in the interests of extending the reach of what is thinkable, imaginable or possible. (Belsey, 167)

Why must a reading be "radical" to identify ambiguity and choices of interpretation? Textual exposition has been going on for thousands of years. That is the business of every exegetical enterprise. If "meaning" were "fixed" and already known, why would we ever return to a text previously read? We all have had the experience of finding meanings on second and third visits we missed first time around. Why would the expansion of the range of our interpretation rely on something called "disruption," which connotes rude and untoward conduct? If Prof. Belsey delivered her paper at a Modern Language Association conference and a heckler jumped to his feet and disrupted the meeting, would that disruption be welcomed by the speaker as enlarging the "meaning"? The significance of words and meanings is always in process of change over time, and hardly requires "disruption" to continue.

Could it be that what is wanted by the new "radicals" is a preconceived significance that, tortuously extracted from the text, will serve ideological purposes? Shall we grab the book by the throat and throttle it until it disgorges what we demand of it, what we need to accomplish our "radical" agenda? Is Shakespeare like a prisoner to be subjected to intellectual waterboarding?

Pace Prof. Belsey, it should be fairly clear that the binary distinction between "conservative" and "radical" readings is emphatically not pluralistic, but dualistic. Narrowing the choices in that way sets up a false dilemma in which it appears there are only two options, one allegedly "conservative," the other "radical." What became of plurality? *Henry V*, for example, has been read as a dramatic celebration of English nationalism, monarchism, and the value and propriety of a charismatic and aggressive leader. A radical or post-structural interpretation, on the other hand, could view the textual tea leaves in a different light, finding therein a bold critique of arbitrary royal power presented on behalf of exploited masses shanghaied by anxious princes to serve as cannon fodder in "giddy quarrels" of dubious moral worth. Note that this second view just happens to be congruent with political liberalism, that is, of a piece with contemporary ideology.

The problem with such doctrinaire "reading" is that Shakespeare expressly observes that literature is not a "cheverel glove" in which we can demonstrate our wit by simply turning words inside out. (*Twelfth Night*, III, i, 12-13) Such oversimplification is a bootless enterprise which masks the true complexity of the interpretive art.

In a truly pluralist acceptation of the play, a variety of constructions are noted and considered. *Henry V* may then be understood more concretely, as neither fascist propaganda on the one hand, nor a call to the oppressed masses to storm the barricades on the other, but rather as a realistic, three dimensional dramatization of war in its hideous complexity and oppositional totality. Instead of ideology, Shakespeare gives us life in all its rich confusion, with villains and rogues on every side, each individual fashioning and refashioning his or her own wyrd. In such a conflicted context, to look for good guys and bad risks melodrama and fails to do justice to Shakespeare's art.

"I want to suggest," writes Prof. Belsey,

> that Shakespearean comedy can be read as disrupting sexual difference, calling in question that set of relations between terms which proposes as inevitable an antithesis between masculine and feminine, men and women. But in order to do so I need first to draw attention to the context of this disruption, the opposition in the sixteenth and seventeenth centuries between two distinct meanings of the family. Women then as now, were defined in relation to men and in terms of their relations with men. A challenge to the meaning of the family is a challenge to these relations and in consequence to the meaning of what it is to be a woman. (Belsey, 167)

How might "the sixteenth and seventeenth centuries" be the "context" of Shakespeare's comedies? This is never explained. Even on a Stratfordian reading, poor William dies in 1616. That would leave 84 subsequent years to form the "context" of comedies previously published. The introduction of "family" into the discussion is worrisome, as the relations between the sexes are larger than the family. To learn what this curious passage "means" we must go further.

> The place of woman in the dynastic family is clear and well known, and is perfectly defined in Katherine's final speech in *The Taming of the Shrew*: 'Such duty as the subject owes the prince / Even such a woman oweth her husband' (V. ii. 156-7) Sovereignty in marriage precisely resembles sovereignty in the state, and both are absolute. Men, Luciana explains in *The Comedy of Errors*, 'are masters to their females and their lords' (II. i. 24) Wives 'are bound to serve, love, and obey' (*The Taming of the Shrew*, V. ii. 165) The perfect wife is 'meek and patient', 'pliant and duteous' . . . . (Belsey, 173)

In the absolutist, dynastic meaning of marriage women were everything that men were not: *silent, submissive, powerless*.

(Belsey, 175, emphasis added)

Belsey selects four cross-dressing comic heroines, and one cross-dressing tragic heroine, to illustrate her thesis that art can shake patriarchal oppression, unfixing

> the existing system of differences, and in the gap thus produced we are able to glimpse a possible meaning, an image of a mode of being, which is not a-sexual nor [sic] bisexual, but which disrupts the system of differences on which sexual stereotyping depends. (Belsey, 190)

Very well, but if marriages in Shakespeare's time were typified by domineering husbands and silent, powerless, submissive wives, one would expect the vast majority of marriages depicted in his plays would reflect that description. Where are they? Where in the text is the silent, submissive and powerless wife? If we do not find her, we may want to re-evaluate Belsey's claim that Julia, Viola, Imogen, Rosalind and Portia "disrupt" an anterior male tyranny. A man may behave like a jackass (Proteus, Leontes) without being an habitual tyrant.

The idea of a submissive, silent, dutiful wife is expressly and forcefully rejected by Shakespeare, who not once in his plays or poems presents any such thing. On the contrary, the male/female relationship in Shakespeare is either one of rough parity of husband and wife -- or female preeminence. We need not timidly peer through the keyhole of a handful of cherry-picked and bowdlerized comedies to obtain a fair impression of Shakespeare's philosophy of sexual relationships because his works represent a collective monument to feminine primacy. In Table One below are placed husband wife pairings of arguable parity between conjugal partners, even in cases of monarchical households. (Note: these tables are presented not as exhaustive, but as representative.)

TABLE ONE   (Marital Parity)

	Wife	*Husband*
1.	Lucrece	Collatine
2.	Dionyza	Cleon

3.	Eleanor (Nell)	Duke Humphrey
4.	Lavinia	Bassianus
5.	Titania	Oberon
6.	Duchess of York	Duke of York
7.	Queen	King Richard II
8.	Lady Percy	Hotspur
9.	Lady Mortimer	Mortimer
10.	Hostess	Pistol
11.	* Beatrice	Benedick
12.	Hero	Claudio
13.	Mistress Ford	Ford
14.	Mistress Page	Page
15.	Gertrude	Claudius
16.	Helena	Bertram
17.	Desdemona	Othello
18.	Emilia	Iago
19.	Marina	Lysimachus
20.	Hermione	Leontes
21.	Perdita	Florizel
22.	Queen	Cymbeline

23.	Imogen	Posthumous
24.	Hippolyta	Theseus
25.	Paulina	Antigonous
26.	Isabella	Duke Vincentio
27.	Thaisa	Pericles
28.	Aemilia	Aegeon
29.	Adriana	Antipholus
30.	Cordelia	France
31.	Olivia	Sebastian
32.	Mary	Sir Toby Belch
33.	Lady Northumberland	Northumberland
34.	Duchess of Gloster	Thomas of Gloster, Woodstock
35.	Lady Macduff	Macduff
36.	Goneril	Albany
37.	Regan	Cornwall
38.	Julia	Proteus
39.	Silvia	Valentine

* = Arguably Dominant

TABLE TWO (Ux Superior)

1.	Juliet	Romeo
2.	Lady Macbeth	Macbeth
3.	Portia	Bassanio
4.	Rosalind	Orlando
5.	Viola	Orsino
6.	Queen Margaret	King Henry VI

TABLE THREE (Female Superior)

1.	Cressida	Troilus
2.	Cleopatra	Antony
3.	Venus	Adonis
4.	Rosaline	Berowne
5.	Princess of France	King of Navarre

TABLE FOUR (Dominant Female Solus)

1. Queen Elinor
2. Joan La Pucelle
3. Hecate
4. Diana

5. Countess of Auvergne

6. Emilia (Lesbian, Two Noble Kinsmen)

7. Volumnia

TABLE FIVE (Ux Inferior)

1. * Kate   Petruchio

* (subject to change)

Totals

Conjugal Parity   39

Dominant Female 18 = 57 Non-Submissive Females

*Submissive Female 1

(Note: Luciana argues for wifely submission but has not yet married. Her views are dicta, not judgment.)

In her discussion of *The Winter's Tale*, Prof. Belsey writes that Hermione "loses both her children through her husband's tyranny, bears it patiently and is finally reunited with her family, though in this case Florizel stands in for Mamillius." (Belsey, 173) It would appear that for Prof. Belsey, the picture painted of woman as spouse in *The Winter's Tale* reflects silence, submission and lack of power, and that this representation of the asymmetrical relation of husband and wife in *The Winter's Tale* is generally the disposition of marriage in sixteenth century England. It may even be hinted that, in presenting such an imbalanced social tapestry, Shakespeare himself is complicit through this re-presentation in this lack of reciprocity, as though through his authorship he were authorizing it. None of this has any foundation in the text.

The reasons may be quickly stated.

1.   There is no evidence that the jealous rage of Leontes which so suddenly explodes and brings such misery is characteristic of the tenor of the union of Leontes and Hermione generally. On the contrary, it is shocking because it is altogether surprising and utterly incommensurate with the affability and geniality which has previously prevailed, a sense of which is plain in the banter we hear just before the storm of jealousy breaks out.

2.   The claim that Hermione "bears patiently" her husband's discreditable accusations and the loss of her children is as false as a proposition can be. When she hears Leontes' mad allegations for the first time, she publicly rejects them. (II, i, 60-126) Her repudiation is firm, dignified and chiding of her husband, the King of Sicilia. Being thrown into prison is not "submission." Are these words "silence"?

> Should a villain say so,
> The most replenished villain in the world,
> He were as much more villain. You, my lord,
> Do but mistake.
> (II, i, 80-83)

Forthright denial at her arraignment is followed by her defense at trial in Act III, sc. ii. Too long to reproduce here and too well-knit to dismember, it is a model of probity, articulation and wounded pride which deserves patient study. Suffice it to say that it is one of the greatest protests on behalf of justice and humanitarian principles in history. It is the very opposite of silence and submission. No counselor could have done better. If this woman, untrained in law, could marshal facts and reasons so magnificently, she must be a figure not of "silence, submission and powerlessness" but of natural forensic genius. A captain's captain, she towers above the deluded and sputtering Leontes. In their concision and modesty the words of Hermione rival those of Socrates in Plato's *Apology*.

Thus, the picture of the place of woman in marriage afforded by the example of Hermione and Leontes is of domestic symbiosis interrupted by the inexplicable descent of one of the partners into raving dementia. This is shortly followed by a public defense in which the actual intellectual and moral superiority of Hermione over her husband is palpable.

Furthermore, any adequate consideration of the role of woman in marriage as witnessed in *The Winter's Tale* would need to take into account the response of Paulina to the misbehavior of the King. Though only the wife of one of his courtiers, Paulina assails Leontes directly and absolutely refuses to be muzzled by anyone, including her husband and the King himself. (II, iii, 27-130) Though she has seen her Lady hurled into prison, Paulina challenges Leontes to his face, accuses him of mortal error, fairly daring him to lay a finger on her. He does not. Where in literature is there such a moment of courage and sagacity? A small extract will suffice.

> What studied torments, tyrant, hast for me?
> What wheels, racks, fires? What flaying, boiling
> In leads or oils? What old or newer torture
> Must I receive, whose every word deserves
> To taste of thy most worst? Thy tyranny,
> Together working with thy jealousies --
> Fancies too weak for boys, too green and idle
> For girls of nine -- O think what they have done,
> And then run mad indeed, stark mad, for all
> Thy bygone fooleries were but spices of it.
> That thou betrayed'st Polixines, 'twas nothing.
> That did but show thee, of a fool, inconstant,
> And damnable ingrateful. Nor was't much
> Thou wouldst have poisoned good Camillo's honour,
> To have him kill a king -- poor trespasses,
> More monstrous standing by, whereof I reckon
> The casting forth to crows thy baby daughter
> To be or none or little, though a devil
> Would have shed water out of fire ere done't.
> Nor is't directly laid to thee the death
> Of the young prince, whose honourable thoughts --
> Thoughts high for one so tender -- cleft the heart
> That could conceive a gross and foolish sire
> Blemished his gracious dam. This is not, no,
> Laid to thy answer. But the last -- O lords,
> When I have said, cry woe! the Queen, the Queen,

The sweet'st dear'st creature's dead, and
Vengeance for't not dropped down yet.
(III, ii, 174-201)

In light of this it would seem that feminism could make a different use of *The Winter's Tale* than to hold it up as an illustration of the
silence and weakness of woman in marriage. If anything, the play should
be adopted as a showcase of woman's resilience and fighting spirit, her
indomitable will and supreme capacity for moral insight, intuition and
expression. Its lesson is not the weakness of woman but her strength.
If one sincerely wanted a "plurality of ways" of reading the text of *The
Winter's Tale*, we would naturally include both the image of woman as
(1) potential victim of masculine heavy-handedness and obtuseness,
and the image of her as (2) the being capable of combining personal autonomy and assertiveness with an inextinguishable capacity for compassion and nurturing. Ironically, we find Prof. Belsey giving us a one-sided
vision of the feminine as the weaker vessel, even though the dimensions
of Hermione and Paulina are self-evidently heroic.

If another example were needed, consider Volumnia's bold confrontation of the tribunes in *Coriolanus*. (III, ii, 1-55) Does this grandmother meekly defer? Does she, who publicly calls the mighty tribune
Sicinius a fool to his face, define herself "in relation to men" and remain
mute? Could any suggestion be more presumptuous, more base, or further from the spirit of Shakespeare? Later, in her plea that Coriolanus
refrain from joining Aufidius in a conjoint assault on Rome, Volumnia
gives one of the most stirring and heartfelt orations in the English language, easily eclipsing anything in such overdone tragedies as *Othello*
and *King Richard the Third*. (V, iii, 95-183) "*Should we be silent and not
speak . . . ?*" she asks, (V, iii, 95, emphasis added) as if directly putting the
challenge to Prof. Belsey and other skeptics of woman's social efficacy in
ancient history and in Tudor England. Must we not ask: Is Shakespeare
studied - or merely talked about? Go to *Coriolanus* first, dear reader. Go
there, and then, after acquaintance with Volumnia, make bold to comment on the weak, silent women in Shakespeare.

It is important to point out that female outspokenness in Shakespeare is not the exclusive prerogative of Roman matrons or English
dames. In *King Henry IV, Part Two*, Act II, we witness Mistress Quickly's
attempted arrest of Sir John Falstaff in the public square based on her
lawsuit against him for open account and breach of marriage contract.
She has the chutzpah to not only file that suit, but personally escort the

sheriff to one of Sir John's public haunts where she loudly accuses him of assorted perfidies. (II, i, 1-166) Yes, she is "fobbed off" again, (II,i, 141-167) but her words, though comical, still stand for the reality of female assertiveness and initiative in Renaissance England, where women possessed, enjoyed and exercised the right of legal remedy.

Recall that in *Twelfth Night* it is not the noble but perplexed Viola/Caesario who wins the palm for sheer brilliance, but rather the housemaid of Lady Olivia, Maria. It is Maria, not Viola, who devises the witty plot to deflate the snooty Malvolio and cause him to be confined by his mistress as a madman. So scintillating is her repartee, so quick her wit, that Maria wins the affection of Lady Olivia's kinsman, Sir Toby Belch, with whom she elopes. (V, i, 360-361) Where, then, are the silent, submissive and powerless women in this cross-dressing comedy, one in which even a female domestic may top all?

And if women in Shakespeare's time were dumb, how shall we account for the bold slogan of Rosalind?

> Do you not know I am a woman?
> When I think, I must speak.
> (III, ii, 244-245)

"But, what about Lavinia?" someone may object. "Surely she is a spouse silenced, and violently so, in *Titus Andronicus*. Does this not support Belsey's hypothesis?" No. It does not. Lavinia is the victim of rape by a pair of hoodlums, who cut out her tongue, and lop off her arms in revenge for the severing of their brother Alarbus's limbs by the sons of Titus. In relation to her husband, Bassianus, there is nothing to suggest anything disproportionate or lacking in equity. Further, though only a soldier's daughter, Lavinia has no difficulty speaking derisively to the Emperor's wife Tamora the Queen of the Goths, whom she bitterly mocks for her apparent assignation with the moor Aaron. (II, iii, 66-79; 80-84; 86-87) Lavinia is yet another bold female character crafted by Shakespeare. Finally, those sensitive to the intricacies of Tudor history may find a connection between the muting of Lavinia, and the silence of Queen Elizabeth I, who could never divulge the litany of her amours, or the curious consequences thereof.

III.

Just coming tentatively into view in the sixteenth century, according to Prof. Belsey, is a refined view of marriage in which the female half is anything more than a slave.

> But there begins to be . . . an alternative meaning for the family in the sixteenth century. In the intimate, affective realm which comes into being with the emergence of a set of differences between work and leisure, public and private, political and domestic, the place of both women and children is newly defined. The home comes to be seen as a self-contained unit, a little world of retreat from the conflicts of the market place, and at the same time a seminary of good subjects, where the wife enters into partnership with her husband in the inculcation of love, courtesy and virtue in their children. The affective marriage is necessarily founded on consent and harmony. (Belsey, 173)

Are we to understand from this that a caveman ethos wholly predominated in relations between the sexes until the dawn of sixteenth century Europe? This seems a tad overdrawn. Other than a few pieces of visual art tendentiously tossed about, Prof. Belsey presents no evidence for her dubious historical claim. The partnership of marriage is at least as old as Genesis 2:20-24, in which man does not stand in relation to woman as a lord over a vassal; on the contrary, they are made "as one flesh." (Genesis 2:24) The way Prof. Belsey views three or four scattered paintings and drawings, marriages of intimacy and partnership had a diffident emergence in 1527 (Hans Holbein the Younger), only to quickly vanish, re-appearing gingerly in 1628 (Rowland Lockey) and then retreating once more in 1640 (Cornelius Johnson). (Belsey, 167-177) The nature and development of matrimony is a topic better suited for a five-volume treatise; it can hardly be fathomed on the basis of a handful of early modern pictures hastily perused.

Further, Prof. Belsey's novel theory that true marriage had its origins in the seventeenth century is at odds with the testimony of Shakespeare. His poems and plays reach back into ancient Greece, and though it is inevitable that many of the customs and sentiments contained in these antiquarian settings reflect Anglo-Saxon and Norman cultures, as Shakespeare's plays were based on Plutarch *et al.*, there is little reason to doubt that, *e.g.*, the marriages of Julius Caesar and Lord Brutus were as intimate and shared as they are depicted as being.

Tables One through Five above indicate that the only husband /

wife relationship fitting the characterization proffered by Prof. Belsey is that of Petruchio and Kate, and that is based on a marriage of a few days' duration and the concluding paean to masculine supremacy of Kate. That speech is open to various interpretations, however (as any "pluralist" will agree), and the finale invites us to ponder the future of such an alliance. Petruchio selected the most independent and obstreperous gal in Padua to be his bride, and though he seems to have "tamed" her, it is, after all, a shrew which has been "tamed." How long will it be before she turns the tables on him? Has she not already found his weak spot?

The only example that comes to mind of a male / female relationship in Shakespeare in which the female is, in fact, wholly under the thumb of the male is not a spousal but a filial bond, between the magician Prospero and his daughter Miranda. As she wakes and sleeps at the snap of his fingers and takes his every word as gospel, she is altogether his puppet. But in cases in which the connection is one between spouses or lovers, Shakespeare gives us either parity or female supremacy.

Many more examples could be discussed, but limitations of time and patience allow only a few. *King Richard II* is about events which occurred around 1400 A.D., during the deposition of Richard by Bolingbroke of the House of Lancaster. After King Henry IV is crowned, the plot against the new King's life in which the Duke of Aumerle is involved is uncovered by Aumerle's father, the Duke of York. (V, iii, 72) Still a member of the group supporting the now crowned Duke of Lancaster, the horrified York condemns his son's treasonous folly and rushes off to expose his son's rebellion to the King. But before he can fly across the threshold, the Duchess of York strongly objects to exposing her son's plot, exchanging bitter words with her husband. Testily he commands her to be silent: "Peace, foolish woman," he cries, (V, iii, 81), but York's wife refuses to be mute. "I will not peace. What is the matter, son?" (V, iii, 82) It must be remembered that so far as we know, the House of York is not atypical; the marriage of York and his Duchess is an ordinary one. Although Prof. Belsey contends that before 1527 English wives were weak, submissive and silent, the Duchess of York puts the lie to that odd contention.

The moment an exasperated York is out the door, the Duchess sends Aumerle racing to the King, and then, despite age and gender, hops on her own horse in hot pursuit!

The scene shifts to the royal estate, where York is insisting that his son be punished for his disloyalty to Bolingbroke. Aumerle confesses the scheme, and while the King is deliberating his fate, the Duchess of

York pounds on the door. There follows a striking tableau in which Aumerle, York and the Duchess all kneel before the new King Henry IV, the father begging that his son be punished, while his wife sues desperately for pardon. As the Duchess of York's plea is several decibels more strident than her husband's self-serving argument, and as she refuses to rise until that pardon is granted, Henry relents and pardons the Yorks' son.

The episode is pertinent because it shows that in Shakespeare's view, partnered marriage was normal as early as 1400. The Duchess could not be silenced by her husband. Though of a grandmother's age, she rides a galloping steed in an emergency. She would not hesitate to oppose her mate's will, both privately and in the chambers of the King. If the thesis urged by Prof. Belsey were correct, that wives at that period were silent, submissive and powerless, how is it that York could not quiet his Duchess, could not make her obey, and in competition with her petition for clemency could suffer defeat in the royal chambers? Curiously, Belsey admits that "the period of Shakespeare's plays is also the period of an explosion of interest in Amazons, female warriors, roaring girls and women disguised as pages," (Belsey, 178), but she fails to attach any significance to this all-important contraindication.

Mention of "roaring girls" is important, as the virago personality was quite in vogue in early 17th century London, and found expression in Middleton and Dekker's popular comedy *The Roaring Girl*, whose swaggering heroine is modeled with historical verisimilitude on Mary Frith, a brash transvestite and heroical figure in London's demimonde. Plays and novels such as *The Roaring Girl* show that female loquaciousness grew to such a pitch in Renaissance England that the marriage option was expressly rejected by these most independent women, far too strong to ever accommodate themselves to even a partnered relationship with a male. Middleton's "Mad Moll Cut-Purse" shares some features with Rosalind in *As You Like It*; she has in addition to physical prowess, "wit, intelligence, intuition and imagination," and is "cast the sympathetic role of the agent through whom true love eventually finds a way," notes Professor Patricia Shaw. But the differences count heavily too. "For although Elizabethan drama, with Shakespeare at its head, is full of girls dressed as men, they are not counterfeit 'roaring boys' engaged sometimes aggressively, although always justifiably, in picking quarrels with unworthy men of all ages, nor do they possess the physique which would permit them so to do." (Shaw, 148) Unlike Middleton's Moll, Rosalind is not in any sense butch. Thus, while the virago is tethered to the mundane life of city, Rosalind preserves a femininty which is sufficiently angelic to allow her an aspect of transcendence, a quality to which Moll Cut-Purse could make no plausible claim.

Instead of taking an accurate measure of spousal relations in the sixteenth century and in Shakespeare, Prof. Belsey prefers to imagine a totalitarian sexual universe in which the door of equality can only be squeezed ajar symbolically a few inches through a "close reading" of those comedies which feature female transvestitism. For this was an age which "allowed women authority only on the condition that they seem to be men." (Belsey, 180) That is, a boy actor playing the part of a girl who dresses as a lad (who in the case of Rosalind plays the part of a girl), creates an ambiguous "space" in which a vision of a freer femininity could take momentary root, thus "disrupting sexual difference." Squinting through a tiny textual aperture, Belsey shrinks the female role to Lilliputian dimensions, and then, slipping it under the critical microscope, manages to recover it as a tender portent of things to come.

The problem with this gambit, as the above Tables show, is that for Shakespeare the *cinquecento* marriage was already a mutual pairing, and further, that in many cases the female partner tended to dwarf and dominate the male, as we find in the case of King Henry VI and Queen Margaret. Indeed, it is likely that Lewis Carroll's diminutive King and raucous Queen of Hearts in Alice in Wonderland represented the Henry / Margaret relationship. (For independent confirmation, See online C. W. Giles, *Punch*, August 15, 1928.)

Consider that although boy actors took on the part of females on the Elizabethan stage, there are nearly no instances in Shakespeare in which the male character disguises as female (with the qualified exceptions of Flute as Thisbe in *A Midsummer Night's Dream* and the serving-man as Sly's wife in *The Taming of the Shrew*, where both "female" roles are confined to the play within the play). In *The Merry Wives of Windsor* (IV, ii, 60 ff.) Falstaff briefly dons female costume to escape the wrath of Ford. Yet this act has no other significance except to suggest his emasculation and humiliation by the "merry" wives. As Prof. Roger Moss notes, "the disguising of Falstaff as a woman seems devoid of almost all interest." (Ross, 31) Prof. Moss astutely notes that: "*the power of women over men's lives is at the heart of* [*The Merry Wives of Windsor*]." (Moss, 33 emphases added) Given the fact that the theatrical troupes were all male, the simplest and most direct transformation to present on stage would have been boy taking on female identity. Yet what we find is just the opposite; it is Julia, Imogen, Rosalind, Viola and Portia who adopt masculine appearances. Hence, for Shakespeare and his Elizabethan audience, the theatrical male-playing-female is merely the actual or the real; female playing male is the fantasy and therefore the ideal. What is sought by the imagination is not the sacrifice of virility but its putative and ludic acquisition.

What all of this points to is the primacy of the feminine in Shakespeare. Human existence in relation to the transcendent gods is represented by the fragile male (Lear, Macbeth, Titus, Hamlet, et al.) who in seeking to rise above himself, perishes. That is tragedy. But the quintessential comic protagonist is woman, the female who takes on a mere codpiece to achieve an aspect of wholeness emblematic of the Mercurial gods themselves. (Paglia, 209 ff.) And this symbolic metaphysical integrity raises the prospect of the divinity in Shakespeare's female characters.

The politicized premises operating in Prof. Belsey's analysis preclude the full apprehension and appreciation of this dimension of what Paglia terms "sexual personae." Belsey's categories are uniformly mundane. Inevitably she is led to ask an unanswerable question: Who is speaking when Rosalind/Ganymede mocks women?

> [I]f we imagine the part played by a male actor it becomes possible to attribute a certain autonomy to the voice of Ganymede here, and in this limited sense the extra-textual sex of the actor may be seen as significant. Visually and aurally the actor does not insist on the femininity of Rosaline-as-Ganymede, but holds the issue unresolved, releasing for the audience the possibility of glimpsing a disruption of sexual difference. (Belsey, 183)

This will not do. Since it is always Rosalind, what is it that gives "a certain autonomy" to the voice of Ganymede? On the lines of political feminism offered by Belsey, the puzzle is beyond us. Never acknowledged by her is the not insignificant fact that Rosalind (with a little assist from Shakespeare) has selected the name of a god, the cup bearer of Zeus, as her alter ego. Why? Hints this broad always repay recognition. As Rosalind/Ganymede, this comic protagonist has not become a conventional transvestite, but rather a divine hermaphrodite bearing within her (in the manner of Tiresias) the essence and insights of male and female. To use Ted Hughes' pregnant phrase, Rosalind is "the goddess of complete being." The audience is not simply permitted to "glimpse" the "possibility" of a "disruption" of "sexual difference," but to behold in a single epiphanic figure the dramatic fulfillment of the ontological project of sexuality: a resplendent magus in which male and female have become one, *et hoc omnes intelligunt deum*. To be a woman yet to mock her, to be in love yet laugh at it, is a divine prerogative. And in all of Shakespeare, it is Rosalind's alone.

Though she is a unique figure in Shakespeare, and the comedies in particular, Rosalind in one important respect resembles certain other heroines. Think of Helena in *All's Well That Ends Well*. She is a virgin and committed to remaining so until death. (I, i, 132) That is, she is at least *de facto* dedicated to the goddess Diana. Unaccountably, she falls in love with her step brother, Bertram, a young cad and runabout quite unworthy of her. To win his affections, Helena, who has been married to Bertram by the King of France, employs the well-known "bed trick," substituting herself for a woman named "Diana" with whom Bertram has devised an assignation. Made pregnant by an unwitting husband, Helena presents herself to him and wins his love. To accomplish this feat (through "Diana's" intervention) Helena must sacrifice her prized virginity and personal devotion to the goddess.

In *The Two Noble Kinsmen*, Palamon and Arcite of Thebes are captured by Theseus and brought back to Athens to be imprisoned in a cell together. Though best of friends, these two warriors fall out with one another when, through their oriel, they spy Emilia, Theseus's sister-in-law, instantly and irrevocably desiring her. Emilia meanwhile reveals to her sister that she has been a lesbian since age eleven, when she was inextricably entwined with the beloved and now departed Flavina. At the time of that loss, when Flavina "took leave o' th' moon - which then looked pale at parting," (I, iv, 52-53) (meaning that she was mourned by the votaries of Diana) Emilia swore a solemn vow of chastity. (I, iii, 86) In order to put a stop to the feud of Palamon and Arcite, who manage to leave their cell, Theseus commands that Palamon and Arcite fight to the death, the winner to have the virgin Emilia as his wife. In a prayer to Diana just before the battle, Emilia, "bride-habited but maiden-hearted," (V, iii, 14-15), asks that either she be won by the competitor who loves her best, or else "grant the file and quality I hold I may continue in thy band," (V, iii, 25-26) that is, remain a votaress of Diana. Though the victor is Arcite, he is killed in a freak accident, and Palamon, who has survived, takes the maiden-hearted Emilia as his wife.

In *As You Like It*, this same pattern may be detected. Like Emilia and Flavina, Rosalind and Celia are cousins and childhood friends of whom it is said that "never two ladies loved as they do." (I, i, 106-107) Though blessed in their affection for one another, as an amusement they talk teasingly about the prospect of falling in love, that is, with a man. Soon thereafter, as they attend a wrestling match, Rosalind realizes she is deeply in love with Orlando, a serious athlete but no match for his savvy admirer. As the reader knows, after many misadventures in the green world of Arden, in which shepherdess Phoebe falls in love with Ganymede, Orlando and Rosalind marry. This leaves many to scratch their heads and wonder, why would she wed someone so inferior to herself? (Paglia, 202; Bloom, 205)

"Ganymede" is the key, a token of divinity. The female figure Helena/Emilia/Rosalind is a goddess, in fact, the principal deity of the ancient world. (Hughes, 4) Her form is hermetically sealed purity, and her regard is directed to herself and her devotees. Through woman, human beings apprehend a small sliver of the numinous. In Rosalind/Ganymede, then, we do not "glimpse" the "disruption" of "sexual difference;" rather, we are inundated by the radiant majesty of the *ens realissimum*. As we stand in Her presence, we do not measure out our lives with coffee spoons, but drink the milk of paradise.

Shakespearean iconography sends us back to a time before Marduk, Yahweh and the Babylonian warrior deities, when the divine was the autochthonous goddess of fertility. (Hughes, 1-44) How does all this bear on the relations between the sexes, our abiding sexual skirmishes? All three instantiations of the goddess fix upon distinctly mediocre males: Helena on Bertram, Emilia on Palamon and Rosalind on Orlando. What is the meaning? The answer lies on several planes, occupied by Adonis, Osiris, the child, and the dull male sex. In dialectical terms, the closed position implies an interior, which in turn implies a void. Diana entails Venus, not as in popular psychopathology ("the virgin whore") but dialectically. In ontological terms, being is not primary, but merely the existential condition of non-being, as the bark circumscribes the tree, as the frame girds the painting. The struggle to preserve virginity, over which Helena and Parolles banter, is, as Parolles cynically avers, a hopeless campaign, akin to building moats of sand before the waves. Nothingness demands its antithesis, being, in order to exist. But woman, the true fecundating sex, is the biological primary. Being the earthly image of the goddess, she is *ab initio* infatuated with herself. Her gaze is first inward, then later out to catch reflections of herself in others. *Non esse qua non esse bonum est.* Complete as such, she draws all to her orbit. In this respect, lesbianism (Emilia/Flavina, Rosalind/Celia) is best understood as symbolic self-gratification, the perfect Ouroboros. Rosalind and Celia, like Flavina and Emilia, form a little world of their own which wants for nothing.

> You talk of Pirithous' and Theseus love:
> Theirs has more ground, is more maturely seasoned,
> More buckled with strong judgement, and their needs
> The one of th' other may be said to water
> Their intertangled roots of love; but I
> And she I sigh and spoke of were things innocent,
> Loved for we did, and like the elements,
> That know not what, nor why, yet do effect
> Rare issues by their operance, our souls
> Did so to one another. What she liked
> Was then of me approved; what not, condemned, --
> No more arraignment. The flower that I would pluck
> And put between my breasts -- O then but beginning
> To swell about the blossom -- she would long
> Till she had such another, and commit it
> To the like innocent cradle, where, phoenix-like,
> They died in perfume. On my head no toy
> But was her pattern. Her affections -- pretty,
> Though happily her careless wear -- I followed
> For my most serious decking. Had mine ear
> Stol'n some new air, or at adventure hummed one,
> From musical coinage, why, it was a note
> Whereon her spirits would sojourn -- rather dwell on --
> And sing it in her slumbers. This rehearsal --
> Which, seely, innocence wots well, comes in
> Like old emportment's bastard -- has this end:
> That true love 'tween maid and maid may be
> More than in sex dividual.
> (I, iii, 54-82)

In *As You Like It*, what begins as a jest, Rosalind's and Celia's sport about falling in love, becomes a compelling reality. This way Orlando lies. We might with justice imaginatively revise the myth, such that after Actaeon stumbles clumsily into the bower of Artemis, her rage dissolves into love, so that the goddess of the moon should, like the deluded Titania, come to love a beast, that is, a man. There is, then, a certain *noblesse oblige* about woman's love for the poor male. When she conquers, she stoops to do so. It is a mission of mercy. As D.H. Lawrence asks, "Why couldn't a girl be queenly, and give the gift of herself?" (Lawrence, p. 9) Woman, the aristocrat of sex, with a magnificent condescension rivaling the Incarnation steps from her heavenly throne into the mire, betraying her matchless perfection for a clod of wayward marl. Thus, in the Troubadour tradition out of which the western notion of love blossoms, the lover is by definition unworthy of his lady, and must content himself with his lute and admiring glances from afar. In such a setting what could be more monstrous and absurd that a pining after "equality"? Are God and the angels envious of mortality? For Prof. Belsey, "romantic love" is the "cement of a life-long relationship, as men and women are alike . . . ." (Belsey, 175) But what in the world is "romantic" about likeness? Must the bride dress like the groom to be respected? Or is she not yet sufficiently "liberated" to prefer tuxedo, suspenders and top hat? Many "life-long relationships" are buried in "cement," to be sure, but few have identified that embalming adhesive as "romantic love."

For Prof. Belsey, women have always been "defined in relation to men and in terms of their relations with men." (Belsey, 167) As this proposition is self-evident, there is no need for citation to authority and none is given. Do Flavina and Emilia "define themselves" in relation to men? What about Rosalind and Celia? Does Lady Macbeth so define herself? Paulina? Hippolyta? Juliet? Cordelia? Joan of Arc? Marina? Volumnia? The Countess of Auvergne? Queen Margaret? Queen Elinor? Or are these simply the grand exceptions that prove the *soi disant* rule?

When the Princess of France comes to the Kingdom of Navarre with her retinue in *Love's Labour's Lost* she is not on any errand in relation to males who "define" or shall define what she is. She is an ambassador on a diplomatic mission regarding the possession of Aquitaine and payment therefor. It is a business trip. She hardly expects to be lodged in the field and then accosted by supercilious, concupiscent bookmen looking for any opportunity to seduce her and her ladies in waiting. The shoe is on the other foot. It is Biron, a man, who defines men by their relation to women, not the other way round: "Or [for] women's sake - by whom we men are men." (IV, iii, 336)

The elevation of women over men in *Love's Labour's Lost* and in Shakespearean comedy generally is plainly stated by the Arden editor.

> As always in Shakespearean comedy the women are cleverer and wittier than the men. That great exemplar of wit, "'honey-tongued' Boyet', has to admit that 'The tongues of mocking wenches are as keen / As is the razor's edge invisible': his

imagery inverts the punishment of losing her tongue proposed for any woman who homes within a mile of the court. The women are not just more verbally adroit than the men, they are constant. The men are fickle, not just in their sexual relations or their ability to keep their vows, but also in their grasp of the idea that words have a true value which must be maintained. The women weigh and value words, recognizing that they must not be viewed as open-ended in their signification if life is to go on. (Woudhuysen, 42)

At every turn, the bungling philosophers of Navarre are bested and pilloried by the ladies of France, who maintain power despite their grassy bivouac. "Sexual differences" are not daintily "glimpsed" here: they are gilded in five-fold blazon. (*Twelfth Night*, I, v, 283) Rosaline is particularly brilliant in her merry badinage with Biron, as she plays Beatrice to his halting Benedick. Though a gifted orator, in verbal jousts he stands in her shadow. Biron's presumptuousness in supposing that a few trinkets and words of affection might move her to love is in fact galling and offensive to Rosaline, in whose words we can still catch the flash of celestial rage of Artemis, as Actaeon is caught trespassing.

PRINCESS:

We are wise girls to mock our lovers so.

ROSALINE:

They are worse fools to purchase mocking so.
That same Biron I'll torture ere I go.
O that I knew he were but in by th' week! --
How I would make him fawn, and beg, and seek,
And wait the season, and observe the times,
And spend his prodigal wits in bootless rhymes,
And shape his service wholly to my hests,
And make him proud to make me proud that jests!
So pursuivant-like would I oe'rsway his state
That he should be my fool, and I his fate.
(V, ii, 58-68)

IV.

The fury of Rosaline, so little noticed by contemporary criticism, exposes her mythic origins, as does the irrepressible and self-mocking wit of hermaphroditic Rosalind / Ganymede. Are not these two figures bearing the same name different aspects of something more than human?

Ted Hughes writes:

> Shakespeare seems to have difficulty in making his women real . . . . One is more than a little aware that a new, much bigger, extra dimension has opened behind them. They [Helena and Isabella] both produce an uncomfortable impression, like a double exposure. Both seem willfully committed to awkwardly superhuman roles. The truth is, perhaps, that the secularized characters of Helena and Isabella, with their human histories which the audience observes from the outside, are inadequately insulated from their mythic roles, which continue to galvanize them from the inside. In other words, Shakespeare has some difficulty in bringing these women down to earth. This is evident in what they say, but it is visible too in various details. To perform her part, Isabella is snatched from the very gates of the nunnery, a creature 'ensky'd and sainted', just about to become (like mythic Venus) a bride of the sacrificed god no less. And Helena, who, having declared from the opening scene that her passion for Bertram is a 'holy' matter, goes on a pilgrimage, and materializes as Diana, in a shrine to consummate it. Helena and Isabella are flawed . . . by supernatural gleams from their mythic existence. This existence enfolds, after all, the highest idea of the Divine. Helena and Isabella, these prototypical Shakespearean heroines . . . blushing into hectic sexual life, are only just touching earth with their toes. (Hughes, 4)

The wonder is that these words could be written by a poet who was a lifelong Stratfordian, one who in his searching metaphysical analysis of the hermaphroditic boar, never considered that such profound theorizing could be carried out only by someone steeped to the gills in classical learning, and that the boar was the personal emblem of the 17th

Earl of Oxford.

Camille Paglia, too, is a traditionalist who inherits from her mentor, Harold Bloom of Yale, a congenital aversion to authorship ideas. The genius of Shakespeare, lavishly presented in *Sexual Personae*, is new wine which she must struggle to pour into the untenable sieve of William of Stratford-Upon-Avon, who so far as we know, never managed to write so much as a single missive to anyone, and who, on his death, owned no books to bequeath to his heirs.

The fundamental issue is stark:

1. For Catherine Belsey, "woman" is defined in relation to "man."

2. Yet, for Berowne in Shakespeare's *Love's Labours Lost*, quite to the contrary, "men" are defined in terms of their relation to "women." (IV, iii, 336)

3. Camille Paglia reads Shakespeare as saying that "sexual personae" (such as Rosalind in *As You Like It*) are the models of "self definition." (Paglia, 207)

4. For Ted Hughes, such figures as Isabella and Helena are mortal symbols of the "goddess of complete being" which holds in dynamic solution the sexual polarities of desire and chastity, from which masculine aggression emerges and circulates.

While it may not be possible to analyze these competing positions so as to make all odds even, it becomes apparent that the standpoint of post-structural feminism cannot compete with the foregoing radical alternatives which the contributors to *Alternative Shakespeares* never envisage. Post-structural feminism appears to rest on a host of assumptions which remain unidentified and undefended, and which would reductively interpret Shakespeare and his historical context in naïve political terms. In particular, the transvestite comedies for Belsey "disrupt" essentially social stereotypes, thereby providing a "glimpse" of gender relationships founded on domestic partnership. Unfortunately, no evidence is provided by Belsey to show that women and wives occupied in the sixteenth and seventeenth centuries a caste so base and helpless that they were akin to serfs and household chattel. The art of Shakespeare, on the other hand, gives us a world in which the marital bond and interaction are almost always exchanges of mutuality, while the social sacrifices of women related to work and childbirth are offset by the asymmetrical romanticism inherited from the Troubadours. Further, the elaboration and development of the female protagonist in many of the plays, including but not limited to the comedies, is sufficiently expansive to assimilate masculinity without sacrificing essential femininity, tending to give the impression of hermaphroditic divinity. Instead of rehearsing a tale of sexual exploitation of the female by the male, we see instead a model of organically founded feminine supremacy. "The liberated woman," writes Paglia, "is the symbol of the English Renaissance . . . . In Shakespeare, the liberated woman speaks, irrepressibly." (Paglia,199) She is not silent. "Wit, as Jacob Burckhardt suggests, is a concomitant of the new 'free personality' of the Renaissance." (Paglia,199) And what is "glimpsed" thereby, if anything, is not the possibility of a tepid egalitarianism, but the apotheosis of the feminine in a figure that transcends earthly limitations. As always, Shakespeare is pointing not only to myth, but to its metaphysical offspring, philosophy. (See: Plato, *Symposium*, 189 c - 193 d)

The more we read Prof. Paglia, the more we find that the Shakespearean heroine is not a second class citizen but a goddess-in-disguise whose purpose is to provide an ideal prototype for women.

> Rosalind, the alchemical Mercurius, symbolizes comic mastery of multiple personae. Viola and Rosalind discipline their feelings, while the minor characters are full of excess and self-indulgence. Both women patiently maintain their male disguise in situations crying out for revelation. They differ, however, in their speech. Viola is discreet and solicitous, Rosalind aggressive, mischievous bantering, railing. Riffling through her endless personae with mystical ease, Rosalind seems conscious of the fictiveness of personality. She theatricalizes her inner life. She stands mentally outside her role and all roles. [Ecstasy, *ekstasis*] Rosalind's characteristic tone is roguish self-satire: "Make the doors upon a woman's wit, and it will out at the casement; shut that, and 'twill out at the keyhole; stop that, 'twill fly with the smoke out at the chimney." Her own darting wit is this gusty draft in the closed household of Renaissance womanhood. Rosalind turns words to smoke, a spiritualistic emanation of her rest-

less motility of thought.

The Mercurius androgyne has the reckless dash and spon-
taneity of youth. Despite our racy modern bias, if Rosalind
were to keep her male disguise, she would cease to grow as
a character. Shakespeare's plays . . . esteem development and
process, Dionysian transformation. Rosalind transforms
herself by going to the forest, but she would stagnate if she
stayed there. Her valiant Amazon personality would be diminished and trivialized. She would turn into Shakespeare's
other mercurial androgyne, the cavorting sky-spirit, Ariel . . .

Rosalind is never madcap or flippant. Behind her playfulness
of language and personae is a pressure of magisterial will.
Multiplicity of mood tends towards anarchy. Shakespeare's
Renaissance wisdom subordinates that multiplicity to social
structure, containing its exuberant energies in marriage. In
the Renaissance as now, play must be a part of a dialectic of
work, or it becomes decadent. (Paglia, 208-209)

Unwitting corroboration of Shakespeare's profound feminism was
furnished as far back as 1972 by Leslie A. Fiedler, who tried to assimilate "woman" in the corpus to the same category of alienage reserved
for Shylock (a Jew) and Othello (a black). That is, Fiedler paradoxically sought to view woman, largely a creature of domesticity, as "the
stranger." Along the way, in a tortured exegesis that careens from one
misunderstanding to another like a drunken sailor in a windstorm,
Fiedler knocks against some surprising truths. He is constrained to
acknowledge that the treatment of woman in Shakespeare often functions at the level of myth, and that many of his heroines have roots in
the Great Goddess of antiquity. (Fiedler, 43-81) Further, he accurately
identifies that primal figure as the Triple Goddess associated with wyrd
(Fiedler, 73), and with Diana. (Fiedler, 69) But instead of making the
straightforward deduction that woman is the principal spiritual agency
in Shakespeare, Fiedler prefers to fall back on the weary subjectivity of
the Warwickshire yeoman, claiming that "Shakespeare" had a complex
when it came to the opposite gender and was "squeamish" about sex. His
male characters in their fear and loathing of all things feminine either
condemn women outright, or kick the feminine upstairs by making it
a divine adversary to be handled as one would enriched uranium. I

reading Fiedler we should bear in mind that his career in *belles-lettres* was launched by promoting the canard that Huck Finn and the Slave Jim were homosexual lovers. This obsessive sensationalism is plainly reprised in his botching of sexual relations in Shakespeare. The bulk of Fiedler's conclusions rest on an artificially narrow selection of texts hastily glossed. Overlooked is the fact that the witch in *Henry VI*, treated as a product of masculine fantasy and phobia by Fiedler, is taken in all seriousness by Shakespeare, who carefully demonstrates the subtle efficacy of her prognostications. It requires attentive reading to see it and integrity to make report. Fiedler's insinuation that boy actors prompted the poet's perverse lust is pure - and impure - conjecture, and, employed as confirmation of his homoerotic thesis, is a grotesque *petitio principii*. Fiedler shows in spite of himself that many of Shakespeare's female leads do in fact embody cosmic archetypes.

V.

There are, then, for our purposes, not one but two species of feminism. These are (1) modern political feminism and (2) the original, natural feminism. The former, nominal in substance, would deny the reality of anything natively feminine. It is a "feminism" in a Pickwickian sense only. Human females are treated as economic or demographic units, a set of entities equipped with physical attributes distinguishing them from the set of males. That anatomical structure is unrelated to intelligible behavior, the product of adventitious circumstances and experience. With no essential differences, all set members are fungible commodities, interchangeable with all others. This type of human equality, such as was promoted by the American *Declaration of Independence*, flows from premises derived from Descartes, Locke and other *philosophes* of that era, for whom consciousness and rationality are common all. Any form of gendered "essentialism" is rejected by modern po-
1 feminism. Original sexual ontology, emergent from *gemeinschaft*
s, is far older and can be traced back to Aristotle (*ousia*) in the
' Lao Tse in the East. For this originary metaphysics, what a
iust as much, if not more, to do with what it does than what
'ng. It follows that there is a basic connection, an internal
ill, between being female and acting as a woman. This
mean that feminine behavior cannot be imitated or
'od forbid. But mimesis, as important or entertain-
k of those Elizabethan boy actors in their dresses

- is not authentic being. As Belarius exults, "How hard it is to hide the sparks of nature!" (*Cymbeline*, III, iii, 79) Rosalind is quite emphatic on this point: "Do you not know I am a woman? When I think, I must speak." (*As You Like It*, III, ii, 244-245) This comes from the gut, not a course in feminine deportment. It is this inexpugnable link between being and doing which is denied by what calls itself "feminism" today in academe.

Thus, for Catherine Belsey, we are simply members of the male set or the female. Sexual differences are not significant, and have been dreadfully exploited by males historically to take unfair advantage of women, imposing inferior social positions upon even their own wives and daughters. For critics of this ilk, sexual differences can and should be "disrupted" to reveal the possibility of love and cooperation based on an underlying Cartesian commonality. Marriage henceforth will be a harmonious partnership. And yet, one fears the news that marital love must proceed in the absence of sexual differences may come as a disappointment to many couples at Niagara Falls or Waikiki Beach popping their bottles of Dom Perignon.

Furthermore, the feminism of Prof. Belsey is not a reflection of mere Cartesian premises. It emerges from the wholesale rejection of the very concept of human nature, which is characterized by her as "liberal humanism." (Dollimore, xxviii)

> Belsey begins with the proposition that *Man* is the subject of liberal humanism. Woman has meaning in relation to *man*. [sic] And yet the instability which is the result of this asymmetry is the ground of protest, resistance, feminism. (Dollimore, xxviii, ff., emphases added)

For these critics, though there be no such thing as "man," it would appear that "woman" does exist, as she remains the object of an hysterical, politicized feminism. "Man" is the metaphysical correlative of "God," and, with the fall of theology, "man" is to be extirpated from our vocabulary and our thinking. (Dollimore, xxix) Any valid criticism must therefore adopt a strident "anti-Humanism" (Dollimore, 249) on pain of appearing outdated. In the sixteenth chapter of Radical Humanism, Prof. Dollimore reviews the historical foundations for the assault of "essentialist humanism," an "ideology" which he finds has led to prejudice, racism, discrimination and oppression. It follows that there is no significant distinction to be drawn between (1) men and women and (2)

313

human beings and other life forms. And it is in this context that such critics propose to live, move, and read the poetry of Shakespeare.

There is, to be sure, a small truth here. Technically, the term "man" makes no linguistic sense. We do not speak of "tree" or "ant" or "tiger," but of trees, ants and tigers, and it is only habit and thoughtlessness that permits the nonsensical jabber about "man." But, in addition to individual men and women, there certainly is something else: homo sapiens, the human species, a scientific category unmentioned and unaccounted for by Belsey, Drakakis and Dollimore. That species has, if not a metaphysical "essence," an identity firmly rooted in deoxyribonucleic acid, which, in turn has a relationship to behavior, whether of the male or the female. Thus, while there is no way to disprove the notion that human beings are determined by a metaphysical essence, the mere absence of that "essence," would not herald the unreality of our species and all that it implies.

Remove (1) the significant differences between men and women, and you will be led to remove (2) the significant differences between human beings and other life forms. Would we then not want to say, for example, that it is an inexcusable and embarrassing prejudice which allows only human beings a seat in the classroom? The Prophet Noah was far more consistently democratic. On the theoretical grounds proffered by Belsey, Drakakis and Dollimore, would we not recognize that dogs, monkeys and crayfish have an equal right to be exposed to the poetry of Shakespeare - or, in a more contemporary vein, to be shielded from it? After all, there is no metaphysical "essence" which makes us special. But let us not make Shakespeare required reading for simians; it should naturally be an elective. Above all, let us be serious about our "anti-Humanism."

And indeed, in the field of elementary education, of late we see the "mainstreaming" of children suffering with extreme autism into the classes of children not so afflicted. Youngsters lacking bowel control, the ability to communicate through words or recognize the emotional states of others, are daily given "homework" assignments consisting of mathematics, history and literature, "homework" for them quite inconceivable which must be religiously done by their hapless parents. Of course, what these children desperately need is not math and science, but instruction in the activities of daily living, such as washing, dressing, using money and obeying traffic signals. But to do so would be to sanction an invidious distinction between handicapped persons and non-handicapped which offends against a political correctness derived from the premises

promoted by radical criticism. Do differences disappear when intellectuals dress us in the emperor's new clothes?

Now it is interesting to note that the views of "radical criticism"
and "anti-Humanism" were anticipated by Shakespeare himself, and
that its advocates are more than a little influenced by his articulation of
the standpoint. For the rejection of "man" as a creature of metaphysical
significance was first declared by Prince Hamlet.

> What a piece of work is man! How noble
> in reason in reason, how infinite in faculty,
> in form and moving how express and admirable,
> in action how like an angel, in apprehension
> how like a god -- the beauty of the world, the
> paragon of animals! And yet to me what is this
> quintessence of dust? Man delights not me --
> no, nor woman neither, though by your smiling
> you seem to say so.
> (II, ii, 305-312, as amended)

Here is encapsulated the entire philosophy of twenty-first century
"materialist criticism." "Man" is summarily demoted from a metaphysical prince distinguished by noble essence to a handful of dust. And true
to modern egalitarianism, woman too is brought equally low. Professors
Belsey, Drakakis and Dollimore are in effect miniature Prince Hamlets,
testily rejecting any elevated aspect of human existence, seeking instead
to tear our species apart and reduce it to the lowest common denomina-
tor in the universe, deducing political feminism as a corollary along the
way.

And yet, this insight is but a moment in Hamlet's phenomenology
of mind, a stage in his development. He does not rest in his "radical"
ideology, which is just as unstable as any of the philosophies set down as
inadequate by Mr. Dollimore. Hamlet changes, he grows, he develops,
and in the end his death is redeemed by precisely the tragic maturation
at which Mr. Dollimore scoffs. (Dollimore, 258-271)

The fact is that the distinction between human existence and other
life forms, embedded as it is in thought, custom and language, cannot
be transcended. This is the lesson of Shakespeare flouted by today's criticism which calls itself "radical." Even when Prince Hamlet puts down
human beings as so much "dust," he assigns our rank and role as that of
the "quintessence" thereof, reflecting the unique role we still play in the

larger scheme of things.

At some point in the unfolding of being, or what is termed "evolution," the question arises, the question itself, that is, not any particular question, but the capacity to hold things in abeyance, to bracket the facts and challenge them. As human beings we interrogate life, just as Prof. Dollimore seeks to interrogate essentialist humanism. In the advent of human existence we see the eruption of the question as such. As Heidegger observed, Dasein *is* the being that asks the question of being. *Sein oder nicht sein, das ist die Frage.* From a simply phenomenological perspective then, we are not defined by a metaphysical essence or DNA code, but by our existence as the question itself. Human existence transcends contingency in its gaze in the direction of a conceived but unknowable answer which gives meaning to our projects. Thus, the radical criticism which ostentatiously denies the reality of any human essence is but one of the latest expressions of that ineluctable inquiry that is coterminous with what we are.

For Shakespeare, men and women are different in kind, and that distinction is both positive and complementary. The union of marriage is grounded not in a legalistic meeting of "true minds," but in the organic and complementary features of a differentiated nature. These are not the products of learning, but the foundation which makes learning possible. When Ferdinand meets Miranda on their little island in the still-vex'd Bermoothes, he initiates amorous advances reciprocated by her. (*The Tempest*, I,ii, 428-429; 450-452) His seizing of the initiative is best understood as a reprise of his biological existence, which appears even at the cellular level when we observe all those tadpole-like spermatozoa swimming like mad to be the first to touch the one thing needful.

Aristotle taught, erroneously, that the male was the fundamental and predominant sex. His mistake was not in his "essentialism," but in giving top billing to the male. It has taken the West many centuries to recover from this fatal detour, a catastrophe from which the East was spared, as we can see in China's *Tao Te Ching* and *I Ching*. In fact, Western thought still struggles with this problem, caught between the occasional male domination on the one hand and the blandishments of a bland egalitarianism on the other.

Light filters in slowly from sources here and there. Ted Hughes affirms in his work on Shakespeare the goddess of complete being, a restatement of the primal spirit of the earth. As Hughes reads Shakespeare, his plays and poems reflect a deliberate schematism in which the Goddess, acting out the story of her transformations through literature, leads humanity beyond itself. For Paglia, it is the magically androgynous female such as Rosalind whose double but integrated sexuality resolves the contradiction of sexual differences, not by "disrupting" those variances, but through their transmogrification into one dazzling, supreme being.

Shakespeare's art is significant and valuable because it reflects the wisdom of life. To this wisdom, Professor Belsey appears untuned. The plays and poems we are reviewing show that cooperative marriage was firmly entrenched in the sixteenth and seventeenth centuries. As we have seen, the Duchess of York and her husband the Duke have a connubial relationship which is already a partnered conversation, founded not on a doctrinaire equivalence but on complementarity of function. She seeks to have her son spared the wrath of Bolingbroke because she feels a mother's affinity for her son, a feeling absent in the Duke. She is spontaneously compassionate and dedicated to the welfare of her child. "Hadst thou groaned for him as I have, thou wouldst be more pitiful," she remonstrates with York. (*Richard II*, V, ii, 103-104)

The stumbling block for modern political feminism, then, is not merely the Cartesian dualism lurking behind the egalitarian rhetoric, but the unquestioning allegiance to "anti-Humanism" and doctrines which, according to its own "radical" purposes should have been critically examined. It is Belsey's assumption that sixteenth and seventeenth century marriages were grossly lopsided, an idea not supported by citations, and effectively rebutted by the contemporaneous dramatic record furnished by Shakespeare. On the other hand, marriages in the twentieth and twenty-first centuries based on the "cement" of "romantic love" and "partnership" are foundering currently at around 60% in the United States. And no one seems to recall that the very notion of romantic love as it emerged from Cathar Europe and the Troubadours was one in which the female was placed on a pedestal, not in the kitchen.

Professors Drakakis, Belsey and their colleagues parade under the banner of the "radical." But it is hard to ignore that theirs is a comfortable radicalism which manages to do suspiciously well with the status quo. They remind one of H.D. Thoreau, who boasted of survival in the wilderness but had only to take a short stroll to his mother's house to fetch anything he wanted. "Radical" criticism fails to question its historically derived philosophical premises, fails to question its portrait of Jacobean marriage and fails to question its idea of Shakespeare. Is this radicalism or reaction?

Post-structural feminism is a coercive game in which language is manipulated to extract artificial meanings designed to accomplish the aims of a political ideology. In its program of thought and linguistic control, its politically correct implications are totalitarian. It may be likened to the shifting relationship with words displayed by the bookish suitors in *Love's Labour's Lost*. The inauthentic use of polysyllabic vocabularies to accomplish the seduction of the ladies of France tends to illustrate Shakespeare's distrust of indefinitely open meanings, which allow language to be put to any purpose. After their verbal whirlwind, the King and his sophistical followers, including Biron, are left with precious little to show for their efforts. Instead of being rewarded by love or amorous favors, the ladies of France impose penalties. As Shakespeare himself has already taken the measure of language, the attempt to "deconstruct" him for political profit is a bootless enterprise. The Arden editor, H.R. Woudhuysen, writes:

> The play combines these two themes in its dramatic investigation of the contractual nature of language: words and things, the signifier and the signified, do not have a natural but an arbitrarily imposed, purely socialized relationship. In their search for fixity and permanence, the male characters act as though language . . . is not a closed system of absolute values, but an open one in which words can be clipped, bent or melted down like coins to become something other than they are. [S]hakespeare wants to suggest that people who spurn closed systems of meaning in life, language and art will ultimately be disappointed: they will discover that there is one finally closed system they cannot avoid and that is death. The very open-endedness of the play's long last scene suggests the inevitability of death, the only conclusion in which anything is concluded. (Woudhuysen, 19)

The ease with which the King and his friends are deceived by the signs of the Princess and her ladies shows they make the same mistake about love as they do about learning. The mistake anticipates Hobbes' warning about words and *false learning*. 'For words are wise mens counters, they do but reckon by them: but they are the mony of fooles, that value them by the authority of an *Aristotle*, a *Cicero*, or a *Thomas*, or any other Doctor whatsoever, if but a man.' The inevitability of the inadequacy of their conversion from learning to love is laid deep within Biron's specious arguments that women's eyes will become their 'books', 'arts', and 'academes'.

The chief lesson of *Love's Labour's Lost* is that, as with stories in which we always want a definite end, so with love and life we want conclusions in which something is concluded. If we see and use language as an open-ended system of signs in which meaning is forever changeable, if we swear to oaths which we know we cannot keep, if our words are not our bonds, if 'Vows are but breath, and breath a vapour is,' then that closure, that 'world-without-end bargain' of which the Princess so fittingly speaks will constantly elude us. We shall have plenty of names, plenty of words, plenty of fun, but never the thing itself -- until death comes. (Woudhuysen, 32-33, emphasis added)

If, as Socrates taught, the philosophical life is a preparation for death, the wise person strives to avoid provocation, trading in ambiguities, choosing rather to address others authentically, trusting that it is possible to convey meaning directly, as in a touch. And bear in mind that on the subject of love, Socrates was the self-confessed disciple of Diotima, a woman, who taught him all things needful. (Plato, *Symposium*, 201d - 212b) To the extent to which our world becomes a battleground of uneasy doubletalk in which each tries to gain advantage over the other through linguistic guile and deceit, all quickly succumbs to chaos and confusion, and we and our professed values are found hollow. Women will not prosper by seeking to emasculate their counterparts, or exploit male errors to win the upper hand, but by teaching men to honor them by those very "russet yeas and honest kersey noes" (V, ii, 413) which Biron finally comes to acknowledge. The conversation of marriage is not, in fact, forever, but happens in a mutual recognition of mortality. The hours are long but the years are swift. It is in dedication to the task of saying what we mean and meaning what we say that our truest love must abide. Let us celebrate one another. Sexual difference is meant to be embraced, not disrupted.

WORKS CITED

Catherine Belsey, *Alternative Shakespeares*, John Drakakis, ed., Routledge, 1992

Jonathan Dollimore, *Radical Tragedy*, Duke University Press, 2d edition, 1993

Leslie A. Fiedler, *The Stranger in Shakespeare: Studies in the Archetypal Underworld of the plays*, Barnes and Noble Publishing, 2006

Ted Hughes, *Shakespeare and the Goddess of Complete Being*, Farrar, Straus Giroux, 1992

D.H. Lawrence, *Lady Chatterly's Lover*, London: Egoist Press, 2012

Roger Moss, "Falstaff as a Woman," *Journal of Dramatic Theory and Criticism*, Fall, 1995.

Camille Paglia, *Sexual Personae*, Vintage Books, 1991

Plato, T*he Collected Dialogues of Plato*, E. Hamilton and H. Cairns, eds., Bollingen Series, LXXI, Princeton University Press, 1996

William Shakespeare: The Complete Works, Clarendon, Oxford, 2005

Patricia Shaw, *Mad Moll and Merry Meg: The Roaring Girl as Popular Heroine in Elizabethan and Jacobean Writings*, University of Oviedo, online, 145-156, no date given.

H. R. Woudhuysen, ed., Introduction, *Love's Labour's Lost*, The Arden Shakespeare, 1998

Online Sources

C. W. Giles, in *Punch*, August 15, 1928 (online)

Lao Tse, *Tao Te Ching* (online)

16
The Measure of All Things

There is a trend in recent Shakespeare scholarship to assimilate his art to earlier thinkers, such as Michel de Montaigne and Niccolo Machiavelli. As such undertakings do not rest so much on documentation as they do on inference, discretion and speculation, they should proceed only with the greatest care. The admirably reserved and deliberate temperament we observe in Montaigne, for example, is wholly at variance with the passionate and venturesome spirit of Shakespeare. Even though there may be hints of skepticism in some plays, the epistemological mood of modern thought is alien to Shakespeare's realism and the inner turbulence of an Othello or a Lear. As for Machiavelli, we may suppose Shakespeare knew of his work, but makes no reference to him. There are three casual castigations of individuals as a "Machiavel." On the other hand, Shakespeare's characters freely mention by name Socrates, Aristotle (including a citation to his *Ethics*), and Pythagoras. Thus to suppose that any portion of Shakespeare's oeuvre was to a substantial extent prompted by or meant as a direct rejoinder to Niccolo Machiavelli is a proposition without foundation. And it is interesting to note paradoxically that the larger influence on Shakespeare of Castiglione seems to attract far fewer scholars.

In the following pages a recent attempt to come to terms with *Measure for Measure* as a reply to Machiavelli is examined and found to be flawed and misleading. Suggestions for reading Shakespeare more productively are offered, including a note on his employment of dialectic.

I. The Convent

1. In Act 1, scene 4, Isabella, a postulant in the Order of Saint Clare in Vienna, is in conversation with Sister Francesca, when a knock on the door is heard. It is Lucio, having come from town to alert Isabella of her brother's arrest and conviction by Lord Angelo of a capital offense. Isabella is to greet the messenger.

FRANCESCA

It is a man's voice. Gentle Isabella,
Turn you the key, and know his business of him.
You may, I may not; you are yet unsworn.
When you have vowed, you must not speak with men
But in the presence of the prioress.
Then if you speak, you must not show your face;
Or if you show your face, you must not speak.
He calls again. I pray you answer him.

This is plain enough. Just open the door. How could any misunderstanding arise? Yet in an erudite article Prof. Zdravko Planinc manages just such a feat. "When Isabella first confronts Angelo," he writes,

> she deliberately disregards the Rule of the Order, which specifies that *a novice* may only be in the presence of a man if the Mother Superior is also present, and that she might show her face or speak but not both. (Planinc, 155, emphasis added)

This is error. The rule is for the sworn, not the unsworn. Isabella is sent to the door because Francesca and the other nuns have taken a sacred oath ("When you have vowed . . . .") to accept and abide by the rules of the convent, including the regulation regarding communications with the opposite sex. As Isabella has not yet taken vows, she is exempt and so permitted to confer with the visitor normally. Few things are as clear as this. Hence, when Isabella later squares off against Lord Angelo there is no "deliberate disregard" of the Rule of the Order, as Prof. Planinc claims in direct contradiction of Shakespeare. An unsworn postulant, she is free to address men in a conventional manner.

The point is important because Prof. Planinc seeks in his essay to cast aspersions on the character of Isabella. She is "deceitful, vengeful, merciless and motivated by little more than a desire for recognition." (Planinc, 154) Her supposed flouting the rule of Saint Clare controlling speaking with males is a principal piece of evidence cited to prove her venality. But in light of the disclosed misrepresentation, it is clear at the outset that though Prof. Planinc would scrutinize "Isabella's intentions," (Planinc, 154) his own intentions towards her appear suspect.

Things are even more confused when we read that Isabella "seems about to become a novice." (Planinc, 154) What could this mean? Has she just wandered in off the street to try on the costume of a postulant? There is no basis to infer anything about her status except that she is a novice in the Order; that's why she is clad as one. It is recognized that "she has neither begun to live by the Rule nor has taken vows." (Planinc, 154-155) But if so, what rules could govern her? If she is an unsworn novice who hasn't "taken vows," what rules would restrict her colloquies with Lucio or Angelo?

According to Prof. Planinc, "Her first words show her balking at how few 'privileges' *the novices* are allowed, although she quickly recovers from the gaffe." (Planinc, 155, emphasis added) But her actual words, not quoted, are: "And have *you nuns* no farther privileges?" (I, iv, 1, emphasis added) Isabella's inquiry is about the nun's privileges, not the privileges of the novices. At any rate, is she "balking," complaining because the Saint Clares are too strict for her taste? No.

> I speak not as desiring more,
> But rather wishing a more strict restraint
> Upon the sisterhood, the votarists of Saint Clare.
> (I, iv, 3-5)

Where is the "gaffe"? While the Oxford editor has no problem confirming that Isabella is expressing the desire for greater strictness in the order, (Bawcutt, note, 105) Prof. Planinc, without either evidence or argument, tells us that she is "balking" at the confines of the convent, then dissembling by seeming to ask for even more imposing limitations. From a textual point of view, the interpretation is gratuitous and wildly off the mark. There is no showing that Isabella hankers after additional freedom and indulgence. The question "And have you nuns no farther privileges?" can only mean, "As you have explained your rules, there seem be so many liberties, more than I expected in an Order known for its severity. Are there, perhaps, even more laxities you may not have mentioned?" This obvious rendering is not even considered by Prof.

Planinc. As the samples examined show, she is not treated fairly by this critic. The "gaffe" is his, not hers. Tendentious and overbearing in his treatment of characters, he freely assigns meanings and interpretations which flow not from the text but from his own whims and preconceived ideas.

Having misconstrued everything so far, Prof. Planinc botches the meaning of Isabella's departure. Lucio has told her of her brother's fate and his request that she try to intercede on his behalf with Lord Angelo. She agrees, and after excusing herself with the prioress, departs posthaste to save her brother's life. According to Prof. Planinc, the news about her brother "provides a convenient excuse to leave. She never returns to the nunnery." (Planinc, 155) Again, "the moment she realized the extent to which her 'privileges' would be limited by the authority of the Mother Superior, she seized the first chance to leave the nunnery, citing the pressing authority of her brother's *worldly concerns* - and taking the habit with her." (Planinc, 166, emphasis added) What is behind the condescending characterization of Claudio's pending doom as her brother's "worldly concerns," as though he were, say, losing heavily at the casino and needed to borrow more cash from her? Needless to say, there is no textual support for these uncharitable assertions. Isabella must take care of a family emergency and notifies the prioress. There is no mention of a "Mother Superior" in the text. There is no evidence that her novice privileges would have been limited by the "Mother Superior," or that she was looking for an excuse to leave. By the way, the non-return to the convent is not shown in the text; it is an assumption made by Prof. Planinc. Taking her habit with her implies an intention to return, and to carry her religious identity back into a secular world she has provisionally renounced.

Since it is implied that there is something sinister in Isabella's leave taking to help save her brother's life, her wearing of her habit beyond the confines of the convent, and her failure to return, let's dwell a moment longer in this area. Isabella is not a nun, but a novice. The reason for the novitiate is to provide a reasonable time for young ladies to determine if they have a genuine religious vocation, and a constitution which can bear the sacrifices required of a monastic existence. As chastity and a rejection of biological motherhood are parts of this arrangement, the decision is a momentous one. Prayer, meditation and counseling over a certain period are all important in this process of self-discovery. It is natural for problems and inner conflicts to arise. Thus, if Isabella had discovered that the religious regimen was in fact beyond her endurance and departed for good, no shame would be attached to her action. But as it turns out, she is not troubled by the asceticism of the Sisters of Saint Clare, and believes she could accommodate even greater degrees of control. Nevertheless, she is in her novitiate, and has a perfect right to her deliberations. The religious house is not a prison. Many return home before a final decision is reached. In Isabella's case, she leaves on account of a family crisis. Wearing the habit beyond the convent is a sign of her intent, a reminder to herself and others of her application and spiritual sincerity. Yet for Prof. Planinc the habit is Isabella's "disguise." (Planinc, 154) Everyone knows it's possible that such a one may meet a special individual during this time and opt in favor of marriage and family. That is normal and to be expected. It is the purpose of the novitiate, which serves to prevent unpleasant discoveries after vows have been taken. If a postulant marries, there is cause for celebration, as it spares everyone the trouble caused by an unsuccessful and unhappy sisterhood. Finally, Isabella seems to accept a marriage proposal from Duke Vincentio. But that marriage may never be consummated, and so far as we know Isabella just might return to the convent.

Having said that, we should add that "Isabella," though descended from Cinthio's and Whetstone's dramatis personae, is a Shakespearean character, and one of some complexity. That is what makes her interesting and instructive. Further, she is not merely a particular self, but a symbol, as were the figures in the old Morality Plays. It may be acceptable to think of her role in the drama as representative of Religion. As a human being, Isabella is rather immature; she has an ample panoply of desires, wants, conflicts and insecurities which can easily be detected, and are well known to literary criticism. She is possessed of ample beauty, grace and libido, which thus far have proved beyond her capacity to manage comfortably. These emerge in symbolic form, as noted by Prof. Planinc and others. (Planinc, 156; II, iv, 99-104) It is thus likely that she has been impelled to seek the confinement of religious life to escape temptations which she fears may cause her to lose all dignity and propriety. And this is the meaning of her otherwise baffling comment that she is desirous of an order even stricter than the one of Saint Clare. Consider, too, that Isabella interprets her condemned brother's preference for her sexual relations with Angelo over his own death and torture as a sign of "incest." (III, 1, 140) This curious reaction, along with strident references to her father (III, i, 84-85; 141-142), might be profitably taken up by psychoanalysis (and probably have been) as symptomatic of an unresolved father complex which after the paternal death has been transferred to Claudio and thence to others. External force is therefore wanted to hold herself in check.

With respect to Religion, Isabella's internal contradictions are emblematic of the incoherence and internal tensions in Christianity itself. As so often happens, the secret lure of asceticism is its sadomasochistic appeal. (Planinc, 147, 156) At this late date it shouldn't be necessary to explain this. But on the social or institutional level, Shakespeare uses Isabella's ambivalence to deconstruct the form of religion as such, in the manner of F.H. Bradley's neo-Kantian critique of morality and religion in *Ethical Studies* and *Appearance and Reality*. Here ontogeny and phylogeny run on parallel tracks. In order to exist and fulfill their mission, morality and religion entail an adversary, and that entailment is expressed in a number of ways, including the establishment of evil. This is not to say that Shakespeare or Bradley condemns Isabella, or would seek the abolition of the Christian faith. Rather, in the manner of Kant's critical analysis of the categories in *The Critique of Pure Reason*, Shakespeare is simply drawing our attention to the ambiguity of many social categories, which by their very nature pull in opposed directions. His method resembles Plato's destructive dialectic in the last books of *Politea* (VIII, 546 - IX) Thus, Prof. Planinc is partially correct when he claims that *Measure for Measure* is a critique. Indeed it is, but not of any single political point of view (such as Machiavelli's), which would imply the assertion of a rival ideology. Rather, love, law, religion and morality are all chronically and intrinsically incoherent, and as such are subjected to dramatic categorial deconstruction by Shakespeare through close study of certain exemplars, the Duke, Angelo, Isabella and perhaps others. It is thus naïve and misleading to read this dialectical play in mundane or ideological terms, as though it were a vulgar melodrama complete with good guys and bad. Failure to appreciate its metaphysical standpoint is thus the reason why it is classed as a "problem play" so elusive in relation to our absurd attempts to boil it down to fit our preconceived ideas and expectations. In this respect, along with the characters in the play, we too serve comic purposes as we fail to apprehend. The dialectical dimension of the play is further discussed, *infra,* Section VII.

II. Meeting with Angelo

When Isabella first meets with Lord Angelo, the Deputy appointed to lead Vienna during the Duke's absence, she attempts to persuade him

to show mercy on her brother. He declines, despite some good arguments on her part. At a certain point in the conversation, her plea rises
to such a pitch of fevered eloquence that Angelo, finds himself violently
attracted to her. According to Prof. Planinc, this attraction is a part of
a scheme devised by Isabella to trap Angelo and compel him to release
her brother. The theory of a scheme is based on aspects of her language
that can be construed as seductive, and also on her willingness to appear
before the magistrate in her religious garb and uncovered face. This is
distortion.

Prof. Planinc writes that Isabella "keeps the novice's habit on; and
she is quite willing to use the misleading impressions it causes to her
own advantage." (Planinc, 155) What could this mean? Would it have
been better if she had taken the offending habit off and appeared nude?
The hour of her brother's execution is unknown to Isabella, and she
proceeds directly from the convent to the magistrate's office. There is
no time to change clothes. Further, she has not resigned from the Saint
Clares but has taken a brief leave of absence to try to save her brother.
While speaking to a man as a nun with unconcealed face would be a violation of the Rule, as a postulant it is permitted. That is not to deny that
there is a seductive aspect of her behavior. Isabella is aware of her beauty
and eloquence. It is true that the contrast between her alluring visage
and her habit is provocative, and some of her language contains erotical-
ly suggestive imagery. (Planinc, 155- 156; II, iv, 99-104, 153-154) What
those discrepancies point to are: (1) personal ambivalences and lack of
self awareness in Isabella as a woman, and (2) the self-contradictory aspects of the Christian religion, which has for centuries made uneasy
bedfellows of asceticism and piety on the one hand and sensuality on
the other. But what Prof. Planinc is claiming is far more ambitious and
overreaching. He alleges that Isabella has hatched a plot by which to
trap Angelo: she will entice him to some misdeed and then threaten to
denounce him unless he frees Claudio. And for this bizarre notion there
is simply no support in the text.

What we have is a somewhat neurotic postulant in flight from her
own sexuality who would try to hide from temptation behind a wall
of religious coercion. She is interrupted by news of her brother's own
sexual indiscretion and imminent execution. She goes straight to the
magistrate to plead on his behalf. There is no plot, nor any time to think
of one. There is no showing that she is by nature crafty or fond of guile
and deceit. On the contrary, she is impulsive and lacking in foresight.
Her artless arguments do not have their intended effect. Admitting on

the one hand the awfulness of unchecked sexuality while simultaneously attempting to play down the gravity of her brother's misdeeds shows beyond doubt that Isabella has not thought through basic aspects of her own philosophy or decided on what she sets a premium in life. Her fault is that she is young and confused, and learning by painful experiment, a common syndrome to be sure. But attempting to construe her hapless immaturity as deliberate manipulation will not do. So when we find Prof. Planinc charging her with "attempting to inflame Angelo's passions" so as to "ensnare" (Planinc, 154) and "trap" him (Planinc, 156-157), we can only suppose he has read Isabella's secret diary, unavailable to the rest of us. Shakespeare shows nothing like that.

At a certain point, as Isabella is repeatedly refuted and there is a rapid escalation of her poetic rhetoric, something suddenly snaps in Angelo's brain and he finds himself deeply drawn to her. We can put our finger on the exact moment. Instead of curt rebuff, or terminating a pointless conversation which has dragged on too long, Angelo falters: "Why do you put these sayings on me?" (II, ii, 137) This is followed by the aside: "She speaks, and 'tis such sense that my sense breeds with it." (II, ii, 144-145) Isabella departs, and in soliloquy Angelo confesses that he is captivated, and guiltily so. (II, ii, 168-192) Is it love or lust? He cannot know, so estranged is he from himself and others.

When Isabella returns, their verbal joust continues, but with painful conscience tugging at the magistrate for what he feels, for what he feels he must do. As he attempts to say guardedly what he has in mind, she seems to miss his point.

> And from this testimony of your own sex,
> Since I suppose we are made to be no stronger
> Than faults may shake our frames, let me be bold.
> I arrest your words. Be that you are;
> That is, a woman. If you be more, you're none.
> If you be one, as you are well expressed
> By all external warrants, show it now,
> By putting on the destined livery.
> (II, iv, 131-138)

What is sought to be conveyed so slyly here? Isabella, you have admitted women are weak, and if you be a woman, you also are weak. Though you fancy you are more than a woman, that would only make you nothing. (Note the pun on "none" and "nun," at line 135.) So, if you are a woman, accept it, your weakness and its consequences, "by putting on the destined livery." (II, ii, 138) Of course, this recalls, "the livery of a nun," one possible choice for Hermia in *A Midsummer Night's Dream*, (I, i, 70). Mr. Bawcutt renders "the destined livery" at p. 140, fn. 139 as "uniform of frailty, which women are destined to wear."

This prepares us for Prof. Planinc's interpretation. Quote:

> Angelo is naïve and inexperienced. Thinking that they have reached some agreement, Angelo takes the bait and asks her, not to disrobe, but rather to put on "the destined livery." He proposes marriage. (2.4.134-138). (Planinc, 156)

Let us bring things out of the ozone. There is no proposal of "marriage," neither by word or implication. To "put on the destined livery" is not the gnomic utterance it is made out to be. Isabella appears to Angelo attired in "the livery of a nun." (*MND*, I, i, 70) His aim is seduction, but he is chary still of the bluntest language, so although he doesn't say "take off your clothes," that is precisely what he means. That is, exchange your "livery of a nun" for the livery of weakness, woman's body, which is your destiny as woman.

We then find this:

> If she is willing to renounce the authority of the Church, he offers to join her in a minor rebellion of love against the world by showing himself willing to renounce the authority of the Duke: he will act against his commission and not have Claudio executed. (2.4.144) (Planinc, 157, emphasis added)

Need we point out that Isabella knows nothing of any "commission," nor is any "rebellion" against authority expressed or implied? The words written by Shakespeare at (II, iv, 144), not given by Prof. Planinc, but allegedly summarized above, are:

He shall not [die], Isabel, if you give me love.

This says nothing about renunciation, authority, the Church, rebellion, the world, the Duke or his commission. Not a bit of it. Rather, what we find is a blunt and demeaning *quid pro quo* under the terms of which, if Isabella will provide sexual gratification to Angelo, who professes his "love" for her (see, II, iv, 141) he will refrain from executing

Claudio, the same base proposal found in Cinthio and Whetstone. It is at this point that she reacts strongly, finally having understood his coarse proposal, as far from "marriage" as one could possibly imagine. She threatens to expose his grossly improper acts to the public. Heedless of righteous retaliation, (and Prof. Planinc seems to know this, see, Planinc, 157) Angelo doubles down: if Isabella will not cooperate and lay down the treasures of her body to him, he will torture Claudio and then execute him.

> Redeem thy brother
> By yielding up thy body to my will,
> Or else he must not only die the death,
> But thy unkindness shall his death draw out
> To ling'ring sufferance.
> (II, iv, 163-167)

Here Angelo quickly sinks to the very nadir of official conduct, attempting to extract sexual favors in return for lifting inappropriate, gratuitous and Draconian penalties imposed on a relative of the petitioner.

Not only does all this appear to Prof. Planinc to be the consequence of Isabella's alleged chicanery, he goes so far as to claim that Angelo is completely innocent. He has done no wrong. This claim is made at least three times. At the beginning of his article, in the first instance, we learn that in *Measure for Measure*, this "odd" play (Planinc, 144, 145), "despite our impressions to the contrary, no one [including Angelo] seems to do anything terribly wrong." (Planinc, 145) This is an astounding comment which totters on the brink of gibberish. If we have the "impression" that someone has done something wrong, how is it that no one "seems" to? An impression might reasonably be in conflict with a deeper reality, but can hardly be in conflict with what seems to be, for that seeming is the impression. How the audience might have gotten the "impression" that someone had done something wrong in the play is not explained. If that "impression" is delusive, there is no indication as to how or why. And what is meant by the sophomorically equivocal "terribly wrong"? Prof. Planinc's thesis is that Duke Vincentio is an utterly corrupt and devious leader who is willing to surreptitiously sacrifice innocent lives in various convoluted schemes and plots to achieve the respect of the citizens of Vienna. People like Claudio and Angelo are mere tools to be destroyed successively to accomplish his goal of power. Allegations which might have been directed to King Richard III get misapplied to

Duke Vincentio. Be that as it may, Prof. Planinc certainly attempts to make the Duke the Machiavellian villain of the play. Isabella, the natural ally of the Duke, selected for her possession of the worst kind of qualities, is "deceitful, vengeful, merciless and motivated by little more than a desire for recognition." (Planinc, 154) As for Angelo, not only is he an extortionist, but he is condemned by his own words of self accusation. Unlike Prof. Planinc, Angelo knows quite well that it is not Isabella who is the tempter but he himself, tempting her to the crime for which her brother was arrested.

> What's this, what's this? Is this her fault or mine?
> The tempter or the tempted who sins most, ha?
> Not she, she doth not tempt; but it is I
> That lying by the violet in the sun,
> Do as the carrion does, not as the flower,
> Corrupt with virtuous season. Can it be
> That modesty may more betray our sense
> Than woman's lightness? Having waste ground enough,
> Shall we desire to raze the sanctuary
> And pitch our evils there? O, fie, fie, fie!
> What dost thou, or what art thou Angelo?
> Dost thou desire her foully for those things
> That make her good? O let her brother live!
> Thieves for their robbery have authority
> When judges steal themselves.
> (II, ii, 169-173)

In a play in which Prof. Planinc reveals some of the very worst of human characteristics, plots and schemes worthy of Cesare Borgia and Machiavelli, up to and including conspiracy, attempted murder, torture, seduction, and various forms of distasteful duplicity, he yet finds that all is well. Here is the true puzzle. On page 157, for example, we read:

> When there was not a shred of evidence that Angelo was do-ing anything other than acting according to the law and the Dukes's instructions, Isabella threatened to denounce him publicly as a tyrant ... (Planinc, 157)

When Isabella indicated her intention to denounce Angelo publicly, it was in direct response to Angelo's extortion, abuse of office and

331

sexual harassment. Angelo himself confesses his wrong in soliloquy. In what sense he might be following law when he suggests that the execution of her brother could be avoided by the granting of sexual favors is hard to see. Nor is it shown that all of Angelo's actions are mere obedience to the Duke's orders. Even if they are, they are still grave civil wrongs. At the close of his article, Prof. Planinc returns to the same audacious pronouncement: "Angelo is pardoned before anyone realizes he has committed no crime." (Planinc, 165)

When Isabella declares she will expose his disreputable acts, Angelo doesn't deny that he is breaking his oath of office and the law, and that he is committing a wrong on her. Had that been the case, that would be his first line of defense: you can't denounce or expose me because nothing improper has transpired between us. He doesn't say this. Instead, he contends that no one would believe her. It would be a case of his word against hers, the standard ploy of today's rapists and child molesters. Is there then no wrong?

While we do not have access to the statutes of Shakespeare's Vienna, which in some ways represents 16th century London, we have our own statutes to consult. Consider Louisiana Revised Statute sect. 14: 134.3:

> No public officer or public employee shall knowingly and intentionally use the authority of his office or position directly or indirectly to compel or coerce any person to provide the public officer, public employee or any other person with anything of apparent, present or prospective value when the public officer is not entitled by the nature of his office to the services sought or the object of his demand.

Similar to Louisiana's law is the "Abuse of Office" statute of Texas, Title 8, Ch. 39, 39.03 (a) treating sexual harassment:

> A public servant acting under color of his office or employment commits an offense if he . . . (3) intentionally subjects another to sexual harassment.

Sexual harassment means:

> Unwelcome sexual advances and requests for sexual favors, submission to which is made a term of or condition of a per-

son's exercise or enjoyment of any right or privilege, power, immunity, either explicitly or implicitly.

Of course, modern statutes directed to corruption and malfeasance do not spring out of thin air, but rest on legal precedents stretching back in history. Thus, while the facts are slightly different, in scripture King David of Israel wrongly uses his power as monarch to seduce the wife of one of his soldiers. (II Samuel 11: 2-4) When the woman, Bathsheba, becomes pregnant, King David contrives to have her husband placed in the most dangerous part of battle and there deserted, so as to be slain. (II Samuel 11: 15) These actions are condemned by the Prophet Nathan. (II Samuel 12: 1-12)

It would be difficult to find in literary studies an idea more profoundly wrong than the claim that in *Measure for Measure* "no one seems to do anything terribly wrong." (Planinc, 145)

Prof. Planinc balances a whitewashing of Angelo against a cartoon distortion of Isabella which attempts to portray her in the malignant guise of Lucrezia Borgia. In summary, while the meetings with Lord Angelo reveal in Isabella an emotional vulnerability and unresolved conflicts over her sexuality, the record is void of those more deliberate vices of which she is accused. Shakespeare is at pains to portray a woman who, on account of early experiences only hinted at, has not yet integrated sex within her sense of self, and this ambivalence is reflected in the emblematic dichotomy of convent versus city. To achieve effective insight into our use of language, and the way our unconsciously chosen words and gestures are received by and affect others represents the challenge of maturation, a challenge we all meet in varying degrees. As Taylor and Wells note in their brief introduction:

> *Measure for Measure*'s subtle and passionate exploration of issues of sexual morality, of the uses and abuses of power, gave it a special appeal in the later part of the twentieth century. Each of the 'good' characters fails in some respect; none of the 'bad' ones lacks some redeeming quality; all are, in the last analysis, 'desperately mortal'. (4.2.148) (Taylor and Wells, 843)

In his zeal to drive a stake through the heart of Isabella, Prof. Planinc attributes to her intentional vices we would ordinarily reserve for the likes of Lady Macbeth or Dionyza of Tarsus. Given her importance in the play, it is doubtful that such a misjudgment of character bodes well for the appreciation of the play as a whole.

III. *Meeting with Claudio*

Someone like Portia, who teaches Shylock the quality of mercy while showing him only hostility, is plainly guilty of a crude hypocrisy. A nobler soul like Isabella, on the other hand, who surpasses Portia in her praise of mercy and forgiveness, though her conduct be not perfect, victimizes no one. Portia relishes the Draconian penalties imposed on Shylock; but as *Measure for Measure* comes to a close Isabella falls to her knees and begs forgiveness for the crimes of Angelo. (V, i, 440-450) Her faults tend to be inconsistencies of feeling and philosophy rather than outright selfishness and malice.

Having been sent by Claudio to plead for clemency before Lord Angelo, Isabella is in something of a quandary as she enters Claudio's cell on death row. Not only has she failed in her advocacy, she has been rudely propositioned by the judge himself, leaving her in an impossible dilemma. The only way to save her brother is to violate the sanctity of her body; and the only way to preserve that fleshly temple is to consign her sibling not just to death but torture as well. The task of having to relate this to unhappy Claudio makes her situation even more painful and awkward.

Of all these mitigating factors Planinc seems blissfully unaware.

> This novice, as [the Duke] supposes her to be, then shocks him again by mercilessly abusing her own brother the moment he shows a desire to be anything other than a martyr to her virtue. She cries out -- these might be the darkest lines Shakespeare ever wrote -- "Take my defiance,/ Die, perish! Might but my bending down / Reprieve thee from thy fate, it should proceed./ I'll pray a thousand prayers for thy death,/ No word to save thee . . . . 'Tis best that thou diest quickly." These are the last words she speaks to her brother in the play. (Planinc, 153)

Prof. Planinc comments that the Duke, overhearing this outburst, decides to "use" Isabella on account of her perceived "ruthlessness." (Planinc, 153)

It takes no great genius to see that, under intense pressure, Isabella reacts to Claudio's plea for life by losing her temper. We all know what that's like. We say things we don't really mean. But there's a big difference between a woman losing her temper in an immensely stressful situation and a woman making her brother the target of "merciless abuse" and "ruthlessness." The latter quality is customarily associated with ambitious people who let nothing stand in the way of their desires. But at this point Isabella has no plan, and though her speech to her brother is over-the-top hyperbole, it is most certainly not "ruthless." Notice that although Isabella has just been told by Angelo that he's going to subject Claudio to "ling'ring sufferance," her wish for Claudio is a quick (and painless) departure from this world. Even within her so-called "merciless abuse," then, Shakespeare's "darkest lines" of all, (Planinc, 153), there lies a hidden note of mercy and compassion. Portia lends "mercy" a hollow praise when it's expedient to do so, while Isabella stands for mercy throughout her ordeal. Perhaps her most severe sin, according to Prof. Planinc, is her charge that by begging her to sleep with Angelo, allowing her brother the gift of life, he is behaving towards her with forbidden intimacy. "When Claudio proves himself less of a man than she would have him be, Isabella invokes their dead father's authority and makes her mother an adulteress by denying Claudio's legitimacy." "To use her own words, 'is't not a kind of incest' to kill the mother in order to have the father to herself?" (Planinc, 166) If Isabella's meaning is hard to fathom, Prof. Planinc's rendering is even more obscure. It should be quite clear that Claudio betrays no incestuous wish in his desire to live. That is Isabella's personal preoccupation. And while it is neurotic, and makes her fearful (III, i, 72), it is in no way "ruthless." She manifests an unhealthy regard for her father whom she has idealized in order to conceal something troubling. What is it she flees? The reader will recall that Isabella is well acquainted with Claudio's fiancée/wife, Juliet. When Lucio informs her that Claudio "hath got his friend with child" (I, iv, 29), she guesses the girl in question is "my cousin Juliet." (I, iv, 44) Though she retreats from the idea of Juliet being her biological cousin (I, iv, 46-47), in terms of emotional intimacy, Juliet is indeed her sister or "cousin." That being so, Claudio's own intimacy with Juliet is felt by Isabella as a kind of incest, a feeling she has obviously had for some time. For any cousin of Juliet is a cousin of Claudio. And behind that feeling lies, more deeply, Isabella's attachment to her father, the incestuous nature of which becomes deflected to Claudio. In a few strokes of his pen, Shakespeare anticipates the whole of psychoanalysis. And this is the reason why it is so easy for Isabella in Claudio's cell to leap to the trope of Claudio's "incest" when he urges her to surrender herself to Angelo. The point is that what Prof. Planinc inappositely presents as "ruthlessness" and "merciless abuse" is better conceived as a symptom of hysteria associated with Isabella's father/brother complex and sexual phobia. At no time is she lacking in mercy. For if, as she says, "the poor beetle that we tread upon in corporal sufferance finds a pang as great as when a giant dies," (III, i, 76-79), it can hardly be denied that Isabella is painfully aware of the misery and fate of Claudio which she rushed to alleviate when she first learned of his plight. It is only when in extremis he urges her to save him by yielding to Angelo that her own prohibited urges come rushing to the surface in what some might construe as a lack of mercy. Had the conversation between brother and sister not been interrupted by the Duke at this sensitive juncture, Isabella's panic might have abated, with a corresponding return to her native compassion for her beloved brother. The idea that the eavesdropping Duke selects her at that moment for her "ruthlessness" is groundless. Her anguish and concern are palpable, and it is these which move the Duke to intervene, not nihilism or depravity. Wishing "to have the father to herself," then, is not deliberate "ruthlessness" but a psychological condition which Shakespeare himself anatomizes for us.

IV. *Isabella's Testimony at Trial*

Prof. Planinc continues his diatribe against Isabella in discussing the complex trial. For our purposes only one aspect need detain us: Isabella's testimony before the Duke, which must be briefly rehabilitated, as she is accused of perjury.

> Isabella's role in the proceedings raises disquieting questions for most commentators. It is undeniable that she is knowingly putting on a performance, but how much of what she says and does is an act? and does she perform already knowing that the Duke is Friar Lodowick? I think it is evident that there are only two things she does not know: the fact that Claudio is still alive and the Duke's ultimate intentions. She presents herself in public before the Duke, and charges Angelo with-- well, what exactly? "Angelo's forsworn . . ./ a murderer . . ./ an adulterous thief . . ./ An hypocrite, a virgin-violator." (5.1. 38-41) *He is innocent of all these charges* except the irrelevant one of being a hypocrite. More specifically, she

says she gave Angelo her maidenhead for Claudio's head, and charges him with not keeping his word. . . . (Planinc, 161, emphasis added)

To understand, one must know that in the traditional versions of the story on which Shakespeare modeled the play, the magistrate always takes advantage of the heroine and then, contrary to the bargain, kills the brother/husband anyway. In *Measure for Measure*, Isabella follows the counsel of the Duke, disguised as Friar Lodowick, and consents to sex with Angelo on the condition that Claudio be spared. This is the deal which is customarily traduced by the magistrate. At the trial, as Prof. Planinc notes, Isabella believes that Angelo has executed Claudio, though in fact he has received the head of a different prisoner as evidence of the completion of the deed. Meanwhile, a "bed trick" has been carried out in which Angelo has actually slept not with Isabella, but with Mariana, his former fiancée, still pining after him.

It is these circumstances which prevail at the time of trial. According to Prof. Planinc, Isabella is a liar (Plaininc, 161) and perjures herself. Angelo is "innocent of all these charges."

Is he?

1. *Angelo is forsworn.* This is correct. In demanding sexual favors in exchange for sparing the life of Claudio, Angelo has broken his oath of office. He is a corrupt office holder and a sexual predator. Further, so far as Isabella knows, he has broken his promise and executed Claudio. He is therefore in her mind forsworn. There is no lie.

2. *Angelo is a murderer.* This is not a lie. So far as Isabella knows, Claudio has been undeservedly and wrongly executed. By the way, it is unclear that the people of Vienna were apprised before the fact that laws condemning "fornication" would, after a lapse of fourteen years, be suddenly enforced. To be effective and valid, a law must be promulgated. In this case, there is no showing of proper and fair promulgation. Execution of any such arrestee would be immoral and illegal, and constitute a homicide. It would also be grounds for a civil action against the state and the magistrate in question. So far as Angelo knows, he has in fact killed Claudio under immoral conditions, as his soliloquy makes clear. One more thing. Under law, if one attempts to murder one person and in the act kills another by mistake, one is still guilty of homicide. Angelo is guilty of the attempted murder of Claudio, and in Isabella's eyes has

actually committed this crime.

3. *Angelo is an adulterous thief.* This is not a lie. Angelo believes he has had wrongful, coercive sex with Isabel. He has to himself confessed this wrong, lamenting his larcenous intentions. (II, ii, 180-183) Further, it could hardly be more evident that as Shakespeare is here writing about a time and place in which the predominant ethos is Christianity, "adultery" is broadly construed under the aegis of Matthew 5:28; it is a matter of the will and heart, not the mere deed. At the time of Angelo's attempted seduction and intercourse, he was under the impression that Isabel was a postulant with the Sisters of Saint Clare. She was a *virgin* on the brink of religious vows making her a bride of Christ. So far as he knows, he has violated that virgin. Further, although Angelo has in fact had sex not with Isabella but with his former fiancée, Mariana, his relationship to Mariana is point-for-point identical to the relationship of Claudio to Juliet. As Claudio is guilty of "fornication," and adultery, so is Angelo guilty of fornication with Mariana. Arguing that it was unknown to Angelo that it was in fact Mariana is unavailing when (1) his intention was deliberately adulterous and (2) the sexual partner was in fact someone other than his lawful wife. As for "thief," Angelo has appropriated by force and guile something not his own, making the metaphor of larceny a not unreasonable one.

V. The Vice of Recognition

In his attempt to fathom the fundamental sin which lies at the root of Isabella as character, Prof. Planinc locates this in her frenzied campaign for "recognition." (Planinc, 154, 157, 165) For example, we are told that despite her phony cry for "justice, justice, justice, justice" (V, i, 25), Isabella cares not a straw for it, but is obsessed rather with acclamation. (Planinc, 157) It is this shameful perversion which causes all her other manifold faults and misdeeds, avows Prof. Planinc. And what is interesting about this is that it has been argued by Shakespeare scholars that recognition is not only not a vice in the Shakespearean catalogue, it is the cardinal *virtue*. In fact, it is the principal virtue in the play under consideration, *Measure for Measure*. Hearken to Shakespeare speaking through Duke Vincentio to Lord Angelo, putting him on the path to "recognition."

> Angelo,
> There is a kind of character in thy life
> That to th' observer doth thy history
> Fully unfold. Thyself and thy belongings
> Are not thine own so proper as to waste
> Thyself upon thy virtues, they on thee.
> Heaven doth with us as we with torches do,
> Not light them for themselves; for if our virtues
> Did not go forth of us, 'twere all alike
> As if we had them not. Spirits are not finely touched
> But to fine issues; nor nature never lends
> The smallest scruple of her excellence
> But, like a thrifty goddess, she determines
> Herself the glory of a creditor,
> Both thanks and use.
> (I, i, 27-40)

The Duke's message to Angelo is that the nature and purpose of virtue is glory, and that to hold back, keeping one's light under a bushel, is a crime against oneself and a loss to others. (Matthew 5:15) It may be pointed out that this view of the public or acclamatory nature of virtue is common to both the so-called "pagan" philosophy of Aristotle and to the religious principles of Jesus of Nazareth. These two streams of moral analysis are of course inherited by Shakespeare. Students of Aristotle are familiar with his moral prototype, the "great-souled man." This individual, for whom philanthropy is the jewel of life's crown, possesses virtue in a fuller sense than do others because in his public achievements and works he can see reflected his own self. (Aristotle, *The Nichomachean Ethics*, Book IV) A like principle was also enunciated in the theistic context by Christ. Prof. Edward Hubler writes:

> There is no idea to which Shakespeare returns more often than the doctrine taught by the parable of the talents. It is referred to and expounded at length in the dialogue of the plays. It is often a major dramatic theme. In the sonnets it is no less prominent than in the plays. In both it is glanced at on innumerable occasions, when, most often, it is taken as correlative to an idea of more immediate importance. *None of Shakespeare's ideas is more fixed or serves more often as a measure of character.* The idea is, of course, the concept of

339

man's stewardship referred to in the discussion of plenitude. Shakespeare's use of it in connection with propagation will indicate to modern readers the pervasiveness of his belief in it. In the very first sonnet the young man was told that he consumed himself in not giving himself, and in the fourth he was warned that "Nature's bequest gives nothing, but doth lend." The point invariably made is that we hold our possessions in trust, that we are the stewards and not the owners of our excellence. (Hubler, 417)

In a discussion of Duke Vincentio's speech to Angelo, Prof. Hubler adds:

In this instance the idea is allied to another of his most pervasive convictions -- the belief that a virtue cannot finally be said to exist until it has expressed itself in action. (Hubler, 108)

The philosopher G.W.F. Hegel also stands in this tradition, memorialized in his dictum that "Spirit which does not manifest itself is not spirit."

It is therefore a bit difficult to know what to make of Prof. Planinc's accusation that Isabella hankers after recognition, when this is for Shakespeare and many other thinkers the essence of virtue. In fact, if *Measure for Measure* is read in such a way that Isabella's leave-taking of the convent is viewed as permanent, this should probably be construed not as betrayal but rather as dedicating her talents to her fellow human beings rather than wasting away "a barren sister all [her] life, Chanting faint hymns to the cold fruitless moon." (*A Midsummer Night's Dream*, I, i, 72-73) Perhaps by "recognition" Prof. Planinc means mere vanity (which Isabella does not manifest), or fame, which Shakespeare says "all hunt after in their lives," (*Love's Labour's Lost*, I, i, 1) but as he spends no time at all explaining what he does mean, it may be best to pass on.

VI. The Sources of Measure for Measure

Instead of trying to probe to the foundation of Isabella's character on the gratuitous supposition that it is tied to some nameless evil, it might be more useful to try to ascertain what primal error leads Prof. Planinc so deeply and consistently astray. The answer is not far to seek.

Professor Zdravko Planinc is Associate Professor of Religious

Studies at McMaster University in Canada. He has a Ph.D. in government from Harvard University. His paper, "Shakespeare's Critique of Machivellian Force, Fraud and Spectacle in *Measure for Measure*," has in its "References" (Bibliography) no citation to any edition of the Collected Works of Shakespeare, but only to the Signet edition of *Measure for Measure*, 1988, edited by S. Nagarajan. No other works by Shakespeare are cited, quoted or alluded to in his paper, as though cross references were not needed.

From his paper we learn that Shakespeare was a "political philosopher," indeed, "as good a political philosopher as Plato." (Planinc, 147) However, we also learn that "it is most likely" that Shakespeare did not read Plato (ignoring such telling markers as *King Henry V*, II, iii, 9-25, cp. *Phaedo*, 117e - 118; see also, *Timon of Athens*, V, ii, 71-72 and *Phaedo*, 118). Indeed, it is quite impossible to read a play like *Timon of Athens*, featuring an Athenian banquet, complete with Alcibiades, wine bibbing, dancing girls, Cupid, and attendant philosopher (Apemantus), and not perceive that the play is a frank reprise of Plato's Symposium. No dialogues of Plato are found in the bibliography. Yet we know that Shakespeare is "as good a political philosopher as Plato" because

> Shakespeare and Plato simply have comparable understandings of human nature, in both its comic and tragic aspects. More specifically, Shakespeare saw the largely corrupt erotic undercurrents of politics in much the same way as Plato did. (Planinc, 147)

No effort is made to clarify, as though it were not necessary. In other words, as Shakespeare's poems and dramas seem to evince political opinions consonant with those of Plato, and Plato is a good political philosopher, therefore Shakespeare is an equally good political philosopher. And does it not follow as the night the day that if Prof. Planinc agrees with the opinions of Plato and Shakespeare that he too is a "good political philosopher"? One could spend much time analyzing the smug and complacent logic of such a passage. Suffice it to say that (1) opinion of any kind (*doxa*) is for Plato a very low and unreliable form of "knowledge"; (2) whether Plato possessed political opinions in our sense of the term is open to debate; (3) perceived congruence between one philosopher regarded as "good" and a second philosopher doesn't mean the second philosopher is also "good"; (4) for Prof. Planinc the test of philosophical thinking appears to be ideological correctness rather than, say, the rigor of argument, efficacy of metaphor, scope, depth, coherence and dialectical acumen. In other words, Prof. Planinc is an ideologue whose metaphilosophy is itself shallow and ideological. To be frank, there is nothing in his present comments about Shakespeare and Plato to give a firm impression that he has read much or learned much from either of these thinkers.

There is nothing wrong with attempting to study Shakespeare from an intellectual point of view, or trying to distill philosophical ideas from his drama, provided that due deference is given to Shakespeare's fundamental role as poet, that is, as artist. It must be a large temptation for a student of "government" to come across a Shakespeare play which commences with words like:

> Of government the properties to unfold
> Would seem in me t'affect speech and discourse,
> Since I am put to know that in your own science
> Exceeds in that the lists of all advice
> My strength can give you.
> (I, i, 3-4)

But the fact is that, excepting Plato's disputed letters, neither Plato nor Shakespeare wrote an expository book or pamphlet on politics. And to fall upon any of their works and pretend to declare and compare their political doctrines is the height of presumption when these writers have eschewed intellectual manifestos in favor of living conversations. Had Prof. Planinc said Shakespeare was a good political philosopher because his dramas seem to extend Plato's dialogues to characters on the brink of the modern world, and that in the character of Falstaff we see the re-birth of Plato's Socrates, there would have been no offense. But to praise Plato and Shakespeare because they seem to hold political views which you yourself find congenial is quite the antithesis of philosophy, as any reading of *Euthyphro* or the other dialogues will show. Simply because a play of Shakespeare begins with a speech about unfolding the properties of government doesn't mean that it can be exploited by modern students of government as a source of the correct "understanding" of "human na-ture." What happens in such a case is that an ironic and dialectical work of art is debased and treated as though it were little more than a political advertisement or campaign platform.

This brings us straight to the heart of the problem. Prof. Planinc candidly admits that his approach to Shakespeare is guided by the writings of Harry Jaffa and Allan Bloom, in Shakespeare's words from *Measure for Measure*, "two notorious benefactors" of learning (II, i, 49) remembered as "political theorists." (Planinc, 146) It quickly becomes apparent that a background in "political theory" entitles one to ignore what literary criticism and Renaissance studies have to tell us about Shakespeare. What matters is political correctness. It also becomes apparent that insofar as political theorists read Plato as the granddaddy of political ideology, political philosophy itself is a failure. It is that failed appreciation of Plato's thinking which is then brought to bear on the ideas of Shakespeare, *obscuram per obscuris*.

From Mr. Allan Bloom, Prof. Planinc derives the tantalizing idea that Shakespeare "combines a Machiavellian critique of law and of those who use it with a classical . . . love of justice." [sic] (Planinc, 146-147) What this means is not explained. Does Shakespeare offer a critique of Machiavelli or a critique of law *a la* Machiavelli? Whatever it is, it is certainly impressive. Then we read:

> Jaffa and Bloom both mention that the Duke's political use of Angelo is similar to Cesare Borgia's use of Remirro de Orco, described by Machiavelli in Book VII of *The Prince*, but neither of them does much with the parallel. I think there is little doubt that Shakespeare modeled Duke Vincentio on Machiavelli's Borgia, the man whose more popular name was Duke Valentino. My reading of the play will attempt to uncover the full significance of the resemblance. How good, or perhaps it is better to ask, how thorough a Machiavellian is the Duke? And is there a critique of his political effectiveness underlying the play's happy ending? I think that until the "old fantastical Duke of dark corners" is brought entirely into the light, the profundity of Shakespeare's insight into the workings of Machiavellian politics will not be appreciated. (Planinc, 147)

What shall we make of this?

> 1. There is no argument or demonstration that Duke Vincentio resembles Cesare Borgia;
> 2. There is no argument or demonstration that if there were a similiarity between Cesare Borgia and Duke Vincentio, it would mean that Duke Vincentio was "modeled" on "Ma-

chiavelli's Borgia."

3. We are asked to accept Prof. Planinc's supposition that "there is little doubt" that Shakespeare modeled Duke Vincentio on Borgia on no other basis than that he, Prof. Planinc, "thinks" so.

4. There is zero discussion as to what other scholars have thought about Duke Vincentio, and what figures may have inspired his character.

5. If, as it seems, Prof. Planinc is making a new argument about the provenance of Duke Vincentio and thereby *Measure for Measure*, it is incumbent on him to review all that Shakespeare scholars have said about the origins of the Duke and the plot or story of *Measure for Measure*. This fundamental scholarly duty is scanted.

6. There is no evidence that Prof. Planinc is even aware of the fact that much scholarly work has been done on this play and its origins.

7. However, none of this matters because the "good political theorists," Jaffa and Bloom, have identified Machiavelli's Borgia as the likely model of Duke Vincentio, a prospect Prof. Planinc finds appealing.

And so, without further ado, we are launched on Shakespeare's critique of Machiavellian ideas in *Measure for Measure*. There's only one small problem. It's all wrong. Had Prof. Planinc conducted even a cursory investigation he would have learned that Duke Vincentio and the other characters were modeled not on figures in Machiavelli but on literary works by Giovanni Baptista Giraldi Cinthio and George Whetstone. This information is in most of the standard editions of the collected works. For example, in *The Yale Shakespeare*, 1993, the Introduction to *Measure for Measure* explains that the influential predecessors of Shakespeare's play are *The Right excellent and famous Historye of Promus and Cassandra: Divided into Commical Discourses*, 1578. (Yale, 403) The Yale volume makes no mention of either Machiavelli or the Borgia family. The standard academic edition of the complete works is the Oxford 2005 edition edited by Taylor & Wells. They write:

The story of a woman who, in seeking to save the life of a male relative, arouses the lust of a man in authority was an ancient one that reached literary form in the mid sixteenth century. Shakespeare may have known the prose version in Giambattista Cinzio Giraldi's Gli Ecatommiti (1565, translated into French in 1583), and the same author's play Epitia (1573, published in 1583), but his main source was George Whetstone's unsuccessful, unperformed two-part tragicomedy *Promos and Cassandra*, published in 1578. (Taylor & Wells, 843)

Taylor and Wells make no mention of Borgia or Machiavelli.

The most extensive introductory materials on the genealogy of *Measure for Measure* is in the *Oxford World's Classic, Measure for Measure*, edited by N. W. Bawcutt. It contains a minute analysis of the folktale that circulated in Europe well before Cinthio and Whetstone, and then proceeds to a thorough study of Cinthio and Whetstone in relation to Shakespeare. Again, Machiavelli and Borgia are not mentioned.

Thus, all of the claims made by Prof. Planinc about Shakespeare's critique of the "Machiavellian" Duke Vincentio are unsupported. Further, the uncharitable and even hostile theories which attribute pernicious motives to Duke Vincentio and Isabella, insofar as they are products of a Machiavellian contextualizing, are completely wrong. In other words, by adopting the doctrinaire stance of a "political theorist" rather than a student of Shakespeare, Prof. Planinc has produced yet another treatment of the poet which reveals little except the scholar's own political proclivities. In the process, there is displayed a shocking lack of understanding of political philosophy itself and a view of Plato which is largely ideological imposition masquerading as reading. The result is a series of blunders which, to be fully itemized and set right, would require twice the number of pages already consumed.

VII. Alternative Reading

What little of value remains in Prof. Planinc's approach to *Measure for Measure* is the notion of critique. But critique of what? And what is criticism? Does Shakespeare in *Measure for Measure* set out to "criticize" "Machiavellian" practices and ideals? It is not likely. For though there be "little doubt" in Prof. Planinc's mind that Machiavelli is intended, that confidence, unsupported by demonstration, does not carry over to the reader. An entire play dedicated to mocking one particular political viewpoint is of limited interest and utility.

And yet, the narrative line does strike us in its portrayal of moral confusion in Vienna as basically a critical enterprise. What, then, is its object? Here we return to the discussion of dialectic initiated above. If we go back to the later philosophy of Immanuel Kant (1724 - 1804), we recall that it was styled "critical," an attitude reflected in his three "Critiques." In the *Critique of Pure Reason*, Kant does not assail particular scientific theories, but connects the inability to establish a fundamental consensus of scientific knowledge to the instability of the "categories" of human understanding, including space, time (the forms of sensibility) and causality. Kant's close inspection shows these categories to be internally self-contradictory and therefore productive of opposed and irreconcilable points of view. Kantian criticism, then, was not so much directed at one theory or another, but at the human mind itself, which in seeking to understand the fundamental nature of things, ends in an antinomous predicament suggestive of intrinsic and unsurpassable intellectual limitations. As the categories themselves are Janus-faced, our use of them must eventually end in intellectual impasse. Reality remains beyond human understanding.

In the nineteenth century, G.W.F. Hegel employed the dialectical approach to a wider set of categories, harnessing their contradictions to generate a totalizing system expressive of and amenable to reason. Thereafter, post-Hegelian philosophers such as F.H. Bradley (brother of Shakespearean critic A.C. Bradley), Karl Marx, Jean-Paul Sartre and many others, used the dialectical method to launch attacks on the social and intellectual categories. This critical/dialectical philosophy can in fact be traced all the way back to Plato, the philosopher who probably originated it. Yet when Prof. Planinc and his colleagues bring the "good political philosopher" Plato into the conversation, it is not for his inception of the dialectic but rather, as it seems, for his "understanding of human nature," that is, for his imagined ideology. Thus it is that "political theorists" devote their time to debating the ideological meaning of Plato's thought, *e.g.*, whether the philosopher-king would be more like a Spinoza or a Cesare Borgia. (Planinc, 147) But if we actually read Plato's dialogues we find that their thrust is entirely exploratory and experimental, pushing ideas to their breaking point to reveal what they are and what they yield, much as scientists today accelerate sub-atomic particles, smashing them together to discover what remains of nature. After all, it was Hegel who wrote that Truth is the bacchanalian whirl in which all elements are intoxicated, not a set of expedient propositions which just happen to reflect our interests.

Beginning at *Politea* (*Republic*) VIII, 545d, Plato, who had built up in the dialogue a metaphysical vision of the ideal community, sets about showing the dialectical inevitability of that ideal community's fall through internal conflicts (*i.e.*, contradictions) in the body politic. That is, the ideal of the perfect political community turned out to be a mere regulative ideal, such that, even if the perfect state could somehow be realized on earth, the inner contradictions of human existence would step-by-step undermine its constitution, ravage its social harmony, disrupt its economy and bring its citizens to either tyranny or anarchy.

As we have suggested, Shakespeare was a student of Plato who read the writings of his ancient teacher, himself a former dramatist. Taking over from Cinthio and Whetstone the tale of a city riven by internal dissension, Shakespeare sought to illustrate the dialectical decay by having certain characters represent the flawed social categories. *Measure for Measure*, then, is only at one level the story of the Duke, Lucio, Isabella, Claudio, Angelo, et al.; beyond that is a dramatic representation of the intrinsic tensions which beset four fundamental social forms: (1) Morality, (2) Law, (3) Love, and (4) Religion.

1. Morality

Whereas writers such as Harry Jaffa allege to find in *Measure for Measure* a paean to morality, in which Isabella is the prototype of probity, the text shows a marked tendency in an entirely different direction. *Measure for Measure* provides the antidote to a Tillyardian reading of Shakespeare which overemphasizes Ulysses' speech on "degree" in *Troilus and Cressida*. (I, iii, 85-137) The reader will recall the bitter realism of Timon as he stands outside the city walls in *Timon of Athens* and rails against the sphere of social and political forms, including "instruction, manners, mysteries, and trades, degrees, observances, customs, and laws." (IV, i, 18-19) All such forms, compounded as they are, by "confounding contraries," (IV, i, 20) bear within themselves the seeds of their own undoing.

To see the essential problem stated in expressly philosophical terms, we must go forward to F.H. Bradley's 1876 analysis in *Ethical Studies*.

> So we see morality is negative; the non-moral and the immoral must exist as a condition of it, since the moral is what it is only in asserting itself against its opposite. (Bradley, 223)

Knowledge of morality is knowledge of specific forms of the will, and, just as will can be known only because we know our will, so these forms of will demand personal and immediate knowledge. Hatred of evil means feeling of evil, and you can not be brought to feel what is not within you. Moral perception must rest on moral experience. (Bradley, 298)

However much we tried to be good, however determined we were to make our will one with the good will, yet we never succeeded. There was always something left in us which was in contradiction with the good. And this we saw was even necessary, because morality meant and implied this contradiction . . . . There remains a perpetual contradiction in myself, no less than in the world, between the 'is to be' and the 'is', a contradiction that can not be got rid of without getting rid of morality; for . . . it is inherent in morality. (Bradley, 175-176)

The ideal . . . for morals is not visibly universal nor fully actual. It is not visibly and in the world seen to be an harmonious system, but in the world and in us realizes, it would seem, itself against itself. And in us it is not a system; our self is not a harmony, our desires are not fully identified with the ideal, and the ideal does not always bring peace in its train. In our heart it clashes with itself, and desires we can not exterminate clash with our good will, and, however much we improve (if we do improve), we are never perfect, we never are a harmony, a system, as our true idea is, and as it calls upon us to be.

The self, which, as the good will, is identified with our type, has to work against the crude material of the natural wants, affections, and impulses, which though not evil in themselves, stand in the way of the good, and must be disciplined, repressed, and encouraged.

A moral will must be finite, and hence have a natural basis; and it must to a certain extent . . . be evil, because a being which does not know characters of good and evil can be known only one against the other, and furthermore can not be apprehended by the mere intellect, but only by inner experience. Morality, in short, implies a knowledge of what the 'ought' means, and the 'ought' implies contradiction and moral contradiction.

So we see morality is negative; the non-moral and the immoral must exist as a condition of it, since the moral is what it is only in asserting itself against its opposite. (Bradley, 232-233)

Of course, morality hides from the dilemma by seeking to divide itself into the good self and the bad. But it cannot have escaped our attention that each human being is one self, not two, and therefore within that good self lurks the bad, which it creates, while within the bad self lies the good, waiting to be rescued.

We have in Shakespeare many foretastes of the ambiguous relation between good and evil, well before its express treatment in *Measure for Measure*. For his realism achieves its effect by making each noteworthy character a blend of mutually implicative moral and immoral qualities. Thus, *e.g.*, the consuming resentment which makes of Aaron in *Titus Andronicus* such an absolute fiend impels him to cradle his dark son with remarkable tenderness. (IV, ii, 72; 106-110; 119-120; 174-179; V,i, 49; 54-55; 59-68; 73-85;) And does not King Harry speak thus? "There is some soul of goodness in things evil, /Would men observingly distil it out. . . ."? (*King Henry V*, IV, i, 4-5)

In *Measure for Measure*, Shakespeare is at pains to illustrate this contradiction through the character of Angelo, who thinks of himself as 'good' while constantly conjuring up the unruly forces of the bad against which to struggle. He therefore is forced to project the bad outwards on others, taking on the role of enforcer of the good. Thus, after he has abandoned Mariana, to whom he was obliged by contract to marry, he chooses to prosecute Claudio for consummating the union he had with Juliet under an identical contract. Executing Claudio is a symbolic way to banish that aspect of himself which he has projected on Claudio. When confronted with Isabella, who is struggling against her own thinly veiled eroticism, he recognizes her as good, yet it is a goodness which inflames his passion for lust and desecration.

Thus *Measure for Measure* is a comedy, not only because of the foibles of Elbow, Pompey, Mistress Overdone, Lucio, Barnadine and other clowns of the lower order, and not just because its tensions are resolved (as we may suppose) by marriage, but just as much because it reveals the folly of human self deception, whose merest visibility is for us its risibility.

2. Law

As morality is schizoid, a weak humanity takes refuge in the "bosom" of the law. There it hopes to overcome the inner discrepancies suffered by morality by means of authority and force. What the naked will cannot accomplish, the terrors of the law will bring about. But the corruption of legal officers and magistrates is notorious because law attracts those in flight from the contradictions and failures of morality. The sheriff or district attorney is therefore so often the criminal who dons a badge. And one can hardly open a newspaper or watch a news broadcast without finding fresh illustration and confirmation of this truth. Isabella, in flight from the heartache of a domestic drama, the details of which we are not given but whose contours are more than hinted at by Shakespeare, hopes to find in the convent a Rule powerful enough to keep out the libidinous objects which beckon from her own loins and her own heart. Meanwhile, Angelo, a fellow who slenderly knows himself, if at all, chooses to make the law all his study in the hopes that he may overcome the unruly urges tugging incessantly at him. It is a bootless strategy. The stronger his self condemnation, the greater becomes the allure of the forbidden Isabella. When Angelo and Escalus become impatient with Elbow, the Duke's constable, they mock him, never seeing that he is but a coarser version of themselves. Elbow arrests Master Froth and Pompey because Elbow's own wife was cavorting in a brothel, no small reflection on the constable. Shakespeare illustrates throughout *Measure for Measure* that the fundamental contradiction with the law is that, on the one hand, to have the force of right, it must be wholly transcendent, and simply recognized by wayward humanity. In other words, Law is morality carved into stony tablets by the Deity Himself. But, on the other hand, at the same time, law is always fashioned, administered and executed by human beings. We would have a government of law but inevitably are compromised by a government of men. And thus the contradictions of morality are only perpetuated, and because of force, aggravated, in the legal apparatus with all its hocus pocus and pompous gravity.

3. Love

From the time of Christ, the regime of law was sought to be supplanted by the regime of love, but this project, which should have yielded by now a paradise on earth, has conferred no benefit. The concept of love is hopelessly ambiguous, an ambiguity for which there is no space to argue here, but which the reader can confirm by consulting his own experience. The essential contradiction of love, neatly captured in Jean-Paul Sartre's maxim that "Love is the desire to be loved," is the fault upon which most amatory affairs founder. And presuming to locate the subtle line dividing love from lust is a classic exercise in futility and rationalization. Not only in *Measure for Measure*, but in *Romeo and Juliet* and many of his other plays, Shakespeare demonstrates the opacities of an emotion whose hold on us far exceeds our ability to comprehend its significance. Consider Lord Angelo. This is the magistrate who threatens to torture and kill Isabella's brother unless she has sex with him. And yet he can say to her, "Plainly conceive, I love you." (II, iv, 141) Strangely, it may be true. Her rare plea for mercy has touched an unfamiliar chord deep within him, and what he asks of her is not simple physical gratification, but her "love." (II, iv, 144) We may take him at his word. He tells us so. (II, iv, 148-149) And yet this poor deluded man has little idea what love is, and less how it might be obtained. Mariana offered it to him, and he walked away, only to have her love thrust upon him at his trial as a penalty. Love, in short, is never in Shakespeare the solution to life's problems, but, to the contrary, it is itself the problem, a problem to which there appears no solution. Duke Vincentio offers his hand to Isabella in apparent proposal of marriage. Does he "love" her? We can never know. If they marry, can we expect the course of this true love to run smoothly? The vice Isabella "abhors" is the very thing she would excuse. (II, ii, 29-33) And when we hear that "I something do excuse the thing I hate, For his advantage that I dearly love," (II, iv, 120-121), we are not totally surprised at the volley of violent rage she expectorates at the brother she professes to love. (III, i, 139-155)

Angelo closes the brothels of Vienna in the name of virtue, but is it within the realm of possibility that some found love there? Angelo feels love not for a professional prostitute but for the woman he is harassing sexually. And given his own sexless and loveless existence, he is well designed to be a loyal brothel patron himself, which, for all we know, he is. After all, does not Lysimachus, governor of Mytilene, find love with Marina in her brothel in *Pericles, Prince of Tyre*?

4. Religion

Return now to the story of David and Bathsheba we touched on earlier and consider its plain symbolism. (II Samuel 11-12) As God is king over the earth, so David is king over Israel. David on his rooftop sees a beautiful woman bathing and, despite her marriage to one of his infantrymen, he seduces her, getting her with child. God is so smitten with his idea of the World that he calls it into existence as Creation. David's seduction of Bathsheba soon leads him to require the death of her husband, Uriah. God's creation of the world entails the death of every creature in it. Of course, through the world God seeks to make amends via his son the Christ, just as from the union of David and Bathsheba is born Solomon and all his wisdom. Who, then, is the bigger sinner? Looked at more closely, the accusations of Nathan may have metaphysical significance.

Philosophy has long demonstrated not so much the non-existence of God as the incoherence and inconsistency of the idea. The best theoretical expositions are found in the dialectical writings of F. H. Bradley and Jean-Paul Sartre. God, the in itself / for itself, would be all in all, yet distinguished from the world, its supreme controller yet the dispenser of its freedom. We for our part would merge with the supreme being yet somehow would maintain our discrete identity. This is not the place to explain contradictions which by now are perhaps familiar to most educated people. What is important for our purposes is that religion in *Measure for Measure* is just as problematic as morality, law and love. It would be difficult indeed to overlook the way in which Shakespeare uses the Duke as a symbol of an ambivalent Deity, who "loves the people," but does not like to "stage himself" to their eyes. (I, i, 69-70) The Duke craves the people's love, but his duplicity and secrecy are not reasonably calculated to win the approbation he seeks. Indeed, Duke Vincentio's love of the people of Vienna is a tad reminiscent of Angelo's love of Isabella.

In his own relation to Isabella, Duke Vincentio recapitulates the vexed relation of God to the human soul. Unlike the so-called "pagan" gods who entered directly into mortal affairs, the God of Christianity is canny and secretive. Duke Vincentio prefers not to exercise power directly but delegate ecclesiastically to his Deputy, Lord Angelo. Isabella, fixated on her father, is forced to take a leave of absence from the religious order, leaving a double void in her life, that caused by the death of her father, and the abortive attempt at replacing her missing father with the invisible God to whom are married the Sisters of Saint Clare. It is in this condition that she meets the Duke disguised as a friar. Though she be ever so sinful, he pities her and works up a plan to save her, as Christianity's God offers salvation to human souls. Just as King David can survey the entire city from his rooftop condominium, and so spies Bathsheba whom he desires, just as God in his heaven descries the world in its potential being and craves the worship and glory it will shed on Him through mortal souls, so Duke Vincentio (who, according to Lucio has a history as a womanizer) recognizes in Isabella a woman in a serious predicament whom he can save and so receive her redeeming love. And like the Christian God we never see, Duke Vincentio cultivates for Isabella a most oblique and guarded affection, filtered through the trappings of the church (Friar Lodowick). At some point, of course, we may wish to ask why it is that Shakespeare gives to the heroine a name which is a variation on the name "Elizabeth," suggesting that Isabella's ambivalences in relation to love, law, morality and religion may reflect Shakespeare's most intellectual comment on the internal conflicts within the last Tudor monarch. That fact alone points away from a Jacobean treatment and calls for a reconsideration of the historical context of this "problem play."

What is the prognosis for their nuptial union? Does the refugee from the convent love the former friar with sufficient dedication and passion to sustain a marriage, or will the ghost of that missing father haunt her still and render the match unsustainable? Was there a fatherly ghost haunting Elizabeth herself? This is but one of the questions which confront us at the play's end, just as Plato's dialogues end not with doctrinaire solutions but with the door to inquiry thrown open. The key to this supremely artful play is how we approach it as readers. If we come with hands on hips to judge this "very odd play," (Planinc, 144) our reward will be a sad parade of follies. But if we proceed with care, submitting ourselves to the text as to a benign riddle, we may find our measure taken and our pains rewarded.

WORKS CITED

Aristotle, *The Nichomachean Ethics*, Oxford: Clarendon Press, 1951

F. H. Bradley, *Appearance and Reality*, Oxford: Clarendon Press, 1935

F. H. Bradley, *Ethical Studies*, Oxford University Press, 1962, as cited in: David Paul Gontar, *Criticism and Speculation in the Philosophy of F. H. Bradley*, 1976, doctoral dissertation, unpub.

Edward Hubler, "The Economy of the Closed Heart," first published in *The Sense of Shakespeare's Sonnets*, Princeton University Press, 1952, reprinted in *Shakespeare: Modern Essays in Criticism*, Oxford University Press, 1961

Zdravko Planinc, "Shakespeare's Critique of Machiavellian Force, Fraud, Spectacle in Measure for Measure," *Humanitas*, Vol. XXIII, 144-168, Nos. 1 and 2, 2010

Plato, *The Collected Dialogues*, E. Hamilton and H. Cairns, eds., The Bollingen Series LXXI, Princeton University Press, 1989

Jean-Paul Sartre, *Being and Nothingness*, Hazel E. Barnes, trans., Washington Square Press, 1992

William Shakespeare, *Measure for Measure*, N. W. Bawcutt, ed., Oxford University Press, 1991 (Cited as 'Bawcutt')

William Shakespeare: The Complete Works, S. Wells and G. Taylor, eds., Oxford: Clarendon Press, 2005 (cited as 'Taylor & Wells')

William Shakespeare, *The Yale Shakespeare: The Complete Works*, W.L. Cross and T. Brooke, eds., Barnes and Noble Books, 1993, reprinted from the Yale University Press edition (cited as 'Yale')

17
An Islamic Reading of *King Henry IV*

> Therefore, my Harry, be it thy course to busy
> giddy minds with foreign quarrels, that action
> hence borne out may waste the memory of the
> former days.
>
> *- Bolingbroke*

I. Martin Lings (Abu Bakr Sinraj Ad-Din)

*P*erhaps the most amusing aspect of contemporary Shakespeare studies is the insouciant ease with which partisan exegetes commend pet paradigms and models to an unsuspecting public. In the welter of contending voices few there are who habitually test their own premises. Whence cometh such sanguine assurance? It is quite impossible, says the Renaissance specialist, to conceive that Shakespeare was not an artist steeped in the amiable cynicism and benign worldliness of Montaigne, Chaucer, Boccaccio, Castiglione, Marguerite of Navarre, et al. On the other hand, it is equally apparent to champions of medievalism that Shakespeare was a heroic reactionary, who served as a staunch "continuer and the summer-up of the past, *the last outpost* of a quickly vanishing age." (Lings, 9, emphasis added) For Martin Lings, an Islamic mystic and antiquarian, it is plain that Shakespeare is about the "perfecting" of the human soul in relation to the "Spirit." It is "obvious" that "his plays far transcend the idea of salvation in its more limited sense," (Lings, 10) aiming at some grand desideratum he terms "sanctification." (Lings, 11) "*There can no longer be any doubt,*" he intones, "that Shakespeare was a skilled adept in the occult, bearing the sacred influences of "many tributaries, Pythagorean, Platonic, Cabalistic, Hermetic, Illuminist, Rosicrucian, [and] Alchemical." (Lings, 4, emphasis added) In skilled hands, *ipse dixit* can go a long way. Renaissance idealists, abandon all hope: Shakespeare was most assuredly not a humanist (Lings, 2-3) but a practitioner of "Sacred art" and an admirer of "theocratic civilizations." Precisely which "theocratic civilizations" are meant is not stated.

Martin Lings, otherwise known as Abu Bakr Sinraj Ad-Din, died in 2005 at age 96. The previous year, 2004, the Globe Theatre in London mounted its trendy extravaganza, "Shakespeare and Islam." 2006 then saw the posthumous reappearance of his now infelicitously titled "Shakespeare's Window Into the Soul," originally issued in 1966 under a different name. Republication thus celebrates the book's 40th anniversary, commemorated by no less a personage than H.R.H. Charles, the Prince of Wales, and Heir to the English crown, who donated a brief Foreword. As we know, Charles has been and remains an avid booster of multiculturalism in general and Islam in particular. Most recently, in 2012, for example, he wrote a Foreword to *1001 Inventions: Muslim Heritage in Our World*, brought out by *National Geographic*. The interested reader can drop by the official website maintained by the Prince of Wales to sample his speech of October 27, 1993, "Islam and the West," given at the opening of the Oxford Centre for Islamic Studies. It is a classic compendium of just about every platitudinous rationalization employed by those advocating the wholesale importation of Islam to English society.

Charles' comments are revealing. Here are pages vii-viii of the text, complete with royal emphasis ("some") and autograph.

FOREWORD

BY H.R.H. The Prince of Wales

I am delighted that it has proved possible to publish a new edition of Dr. Martin Lings' remarkable book. It is a book which seeks to interpret to a wider audience the profound wisdom that is contained within the symbolism of certain plays of Shakespeare. As such it is a book which I found hard to put down as it is clearly written from an intimate, personal awareness of the meaning of the symbols that Shakespeare uses to describe the inner drama of the soul contained, as it is, within the outer earthly drama of the plays.

The trouble, of course, with writing anything about Shakespeare is that so many other people have done the same, and will continue to do so for generations. Every conceivable theory about the meaning of his plays, about their authenticity, and about their author seems to have been aired at one time or another. Some are more esoteric than others and, I daresay, that Dr. Lings' book has been, and will be, seen as too esoteric for many people's comfort.

Whatever the case, the author's perceptive insight into that other realm of human experience will assuredly strike harmonious chords in some people's hearts and may open for them a door hidden in a corner of their being of which they may not have been aware. It may also transform their understanding and appreciation of Shakespeare's plays and of his intuitive genius for comprehending that the true significance of our earthly existence lies within the context of the greater inner odyssey which we are called to perform.

This seeming encomium boils down to discreditable sophistry. We hear that Dr. Lings, rather like the deity, enjoys an "intimate, personal awareness" of the significance of the esoterica employed by prophets and poets. What could that mean? Of course, it's assumed that Shakespeare does employ an occult lexicon, and that the solution to its enigmas has been conferred upon the capacious brain of Dr. Lings. But why approve any such hocus pocus? Charles condescendingly admits a spooky Tarot-Card-dealing-Shakespeare isn't everyone's cup of tea, but hopes pointedly (wink-wink) that some of us are sufficiently astute and broad-minded to have our "hearts" touched by Dr. Lings' "insights." As for the others, well, it's likely they are beasts without circulatory systems. Let them barrenly perish. This is the sort of pathetic twaddle that may intimidate "some" folks into permitting Lings to rub their noses in his "esoteric" fare. As for the rest of us, we may with luck steer clear of his basilisk eye.

Just who was Martin Lings? The dust jacket tells us:

MARTIN LINGS (1909-2005) was a renowned British scholar who taught at several European Universities and the University of Cairo. He was the keeper of Oriental manuscripts in the British Museum and the British Library and the author of numerous books on religion and spirituality, including *The Book of Certainty*, *What is Sufism?*, *Ancient Beliefs and Modern Superstitions*, and the internationally acclaimed *Muhammad: His Life Based on the Earliest Sources*.

In other words, he was an obedient hierophant whose mission was the rendering of arcana exhumed from Islamic texts for the edification of western audiences. Though early on a follower of C.S. Lewis, he stood at all times outside English literary theory, and was never a recognized Shakespeare authority.

The editors further explain:

He traveled to Egypt in 1939 to visit a friend and decided to stay. Also at that time, he completed the conversions that he had been undergoing from Protestant to Atheist and finally to Islam. In Egypt, he became an English professor at the University of Cairo, where he had an annual production of a Shakespeare play, which quickly became the highlight of his year. His love of Shakespeare inspired those around him to read and study Shakespeare's work. In 1952, funding was cut for the British University staff in Egypt, and Lings was forced to move back to London. Back in London, Lings received various degrees for his work in Arabic and African studies, leading to his writing of *A Sufi Saint of the Twentieth Century*, published in 1961. He joined the British Museum in 1955, where he was made assistant keeper of oriental printed books and manuscripts. He was promoted to keeper in 1970, and that same year, he also began performing those tasks at the British Library. In 1966, he published *Shakespeare in the Light of Sacred Art*, the first edition of the now titled *Shakespeare's Window Into the Soul*. (Lings, 209-210)

How else could such an individual interpret Shakespeare but as an ecclesiastic zealot and dogmatic seer? It is well to bear in mind that the dramatic arts were for the great majority of Islamic history either unknown or proscribed. According to one anonymous but credible source: "The Arabs never knew theatre in its western form before the nineteenth century." (See, "Theatre and Islam," online) There were simple shadow shows for juveniles and itinerants, and occasional rituals depicting scenes from scripture, but nothing like what we would regard as plays, which would be viewed as the blasphemous fabrication of graven images. Indeed, anything resembling actual stagecraft was expressly outlawed by the Salafist School of Islam. Much later, as more liberal theologians came to consider that a distinction could be drawn between acting and idol worship, a door was opened to some limited types of performances, making Ling's innovations in Egypt prior to 1952 possible. It was thus plainly incumbent upon him to portray the classics of western theatre as vessels bearing in cryptic form a message compatible with the doctrines and purposes of Islam in order that such a thing as Shakespeare might be tolerated.

Consider the Bibliography of sources in Lings' *Shakespeare's Window Into the Soul*. Of 22 assembled books and articles, we do not even find the *Collected Works of Shakespeare*, nor is there any particular play or poem by him, no quartos or folio editions, nothing. There is mentioned one and only one English language work of Shakespeare commentary: Dover Wilson's *The Fortunes of Falstaff*, 1964. The only other pertinent title in Lings' Bibliography is "Esoterisme de Shakespeare," a 1955 article by Paul Arnold, a Frenchman, in *Mercure de France*. The great expositors of Shakespeare, Coleridge, Bradley, Goddard and far too many others to mention, are all completely ignored.

If not British and American literary critics and Shakespeareans, who were the principal influences on Martin Lings? His two mentors were Frthjof Schuon and René Guénon. (Eaton, Martin)

1. Frithjof Schuon, also known as Shaykh 'Isa al-Din Ahmed - Shadhili Darquwi al - 'Alawi al - Maryami, was a disciple of Sufi Shaikh Ahmad Al 'Alawi. Schuon was the author of *Understanding Islam*. According to the Biographical Note on Schuon online:

The essential theme of Schuon's writings as summarized by Martin Lings is this: the sole Ultimate Reality of Absolute Infinite Perfection and the predicament of man, made in the image of that perfection, an image from which he has fallen, and to which he must return on his way to the final reintegration into his Divine Source.

To take the measure of this dubious influence, consider these foundational comments drawn from the concluding paragraph in Lings' chapter on *King Henry IV*.

If it be asked whether we have the right to place any of Shakespeare's plays, even the mature ones, in the category of sacred art, a powerful plea for yes is implicit in the fact that the central theme of these plays is not merely religion, which in itself would be insufficient, but the very essence of religion, namely the Mysteries. Let us add to this a remark from Schuon's masterly chapter on the degrees of art: "The distinction between a sacred and a profane art is inadequate and too precipitate when one wishes to take account of all artistic possibilities; and it is therefore necessary to have recourse to a supplementary distinction, namely that between a liturgical and an extraliturgical art." This has the advantage of safeguarding the already mentioned category of sacred art in the traditional sense, while at the same time not labeling as profane certain extraliturgical manifestations of the Divine Spirit which "bloweth where it listeth." (Lings, 13)

To argue that we can view Shakespeare's *oeuvre* as "sacred art" on the grounds that the "central theme" of "these plays" is "not merely religion" but "the Mysteries" is about as preposterous a *petitio principii* as one could ever find. Needless to say, Mr. Lings cites no evidence that the predominant theme of any Shakespeare play is "religion," and if a vital theme for Shakespeare as a dramatist is "the Mysteries," the central "mystery" may be why "the Mysteries" (whatever they may be) are never mentioned in those plays. The only "mystery" to which overt reference is made in the plays is death by hanging and beheading. (*Measure for Measure*, IV, ii, 26-45) Evidently Lings felt that he was entitled to view Shakespeare's works as "extraliturgical art" on no greater warrant than this concept having been mentioned by Schuon. Such reasoning is indicative of a mind of limited analytic capacity, and circumscribed by an exceedingly narrow range of ideas from which there was evidently neither the ability nor the inclination to escape.

2. René Guénon, also known as Shaykh 'Abd-al-Wahid Uahya, was a French student who fell under the spell of occultism in Paris, and was initiated into Sufism in 1911, becoming an adept in exoteric and esoteric aspects of Islam. He emigrated to Cairo, Egypt in 1930 to study Islamic esoterism and joined the Hamidiya Shadhiliya Sufi order. He married the daughter of Sufi Sheikh Mohammad Ibrahim, and later established a Masonic Lodge in France called La Grande Triade. He is remembered for, among other things, his studies of Islamic symbolism and esoterism.

We may thus apprehend that the "Shakespeare" of Martin Lings is not the familiar English poet and dramatist whose works have been relished by English-speaking readers and audiences the past four centuries, whose brilliance reshaped and reinvigorated our language and forged the modern sensibility, the man Harold Bloom dubbed "the inventor of the human." Rather, Martin Lings' Shakespeare is an Islamic pod, a collocation of gnostic notions which parallel those in kabbalah and esoteric Islam. Ling's book is nothing less than a high-handed attempt by Islam to neutralize the poetic star of England by shanghaiing him to the ethos of the Koran and ancillary Moslem texts.

II. Reading King Henry IV

Of the ten chapters devoted to the plays in *Shakespeare's Window Into the Soul*, we will take the first, on *King Henry IV*, as representative of the whole. The cavalier hermeneutical method remains constant throughout. For Lings, a typical mature Shakespearean protagonist is essentially a marred image of the Absolute fallen from its true splendor to become partial and stunted. Its aim is not happiness or personal development but a state Lings dubs "perfection." In order to achieve this "perfection," the soul must expel "the devil" and achieve identity with "the Spirit," that is, heal the breach with the Almighty conceived as an uncompromising Absolute. To accomplish that it is first necessary that there be an upsurge within the protagonist's own soul of the Adversary. Though this homeopathic taint causes deformation of character and action, and generates disorder and self-conflict, it must be tolerated so that the hero can become conscious of and ultimately resist the alien element within. When that demonic personam bursts forth, it can be identified and purged or extruded, leaving the soul, in Rosalind's terms, "as clean as a sound sheep's heart," without blemish of any kind and stationed at the gate of redemption. This threefold movement from (1) fragmentation to (2) split personality and thence to (3) spiritual cauterization, wholeness and "perfection," tracks a hierarchy of arcane images which it is the task of the reader to decipher as he traipses along what St. Bonaventure called the *itinararium mentis ad deum*. Of course, interpreting metaphor is an essential part of any literary exercise. There is nothing unique about that. But when such interpretation takes place with constant reference to a fixed register of preconceived ideas, the result can be nothing except a reflection of those *a priori* doctrines. And it is that which disqualifies the magus-on-a-mission as literary guide. The putative "window" into the soul soon becomes a blindfold.

The entire first chapter of Lings' text is devoted to *King Henry IV*. As the author acknowledges, that chronicle comprises two separate and distinct dramatic works. (Lings, 14) Together, they relate a single, integrated tale of English history through dramatic verse, constituting a venture substantially longer than *The Tragedy of Hamlet, Prince of Denmark*. Yet Lings manages to dispose of this juggernaut in just five arch pages. By contrast, the distinguished critic Harold C. Goddard dedicates to the same subject fifty-three pages of painstaking exposition. Prof. Marjorie Garber of Harvard gets the job done in a mere forty-four. But, of course, neither Goddard nor Garber had the advantage of a template out of *spiritus mundi* which reduces a panorama of profundity and wit to a mere thimbleful of symbols. Monstrously omitted by Lings is everything else, including the many endearing secondary characters in *King Henry IV*, Hotspur, Northumberland, Pistol, Pointz, Bardolph, Mistress Quickly, Doll Tearsheet, poor forgotten Robert Shallow and others. By concentrating on "perfect" Harry alone, in virtue of his reunion with the patriarchal Bolingbroke, and consigning everyone else to the limbo of the Unmentioned, Lings gives us a version of *King Henry IV* in which the very life of the play is sucked out, leaving a husk of a prince who reveals himself to be the unholy ghost of his father.

Shakespeare's Window Into the Soul commences with an esoteric hagiography in which Prince Hal's youthful debauchery is swapped for King Henry IV's ambitious personality and policies. Though father and son have their faults, the parable of the Prodigal Son is sufficiently strong to carry all else before it. Not only is King Henry V as limned by Shakespeare a national hero, argues Lings, but, perceived through the prism of Islamic theology, he may be understood as a radiant illustration of the transmogrification of the human soul. Reunion with his royal father coupled with the firm rejection of the diabolical Falstaff betokens the soul's bonding with its Creator. Lings lets us in on the great secret:

> *[W]e do not need to examine [Shakespeare's] text over-care-fully* to see that he conceived the newly crowned King Henry V's rejection of Falstaff as representing more than salvation in the ordinary limited sense of the word; for him it is clearly no less than the equivalent of the Red Crosse Knight's victory over the dragon in *The Fairie Queen*; and this victory, what-ever else it may mean, clearly signifies above all the soul's final purification, its final complete triumph over the devil. (Lings, 15, emphasis added)

Let us not be so naïve as to think that this play is merely an imagi-native rendition of English history. Not so. Understood properly it is the actual purgation of the viewer's soul. Rather than furnish evidence for this counterintuitive proposition, Lings heaps hyperbolical logs on the fire.

> No limit can be set to the extent of Prince Hal's reform. His world is very remote indeed from the world we live in, the world of mediocrities and relativities in which the epic is stifled beyond breathing point, while the psychological novel thrives and grows fat. There is an unmistakable ring of the absolute about the last scenes of *Henry IV*, which makes it difficult, from any point of view, to attribute to the new King, anything that falls short of perfection. (Lings, 16)

It is fairly safe to say that no other Shakespearean has ever haz-arded the bizarre thesis that Prince Hal embodies "perfection" or is even remotely associated with such an outlandish idea. But for one who chooses to receive the play through the prism of occult archetypes, such "insights" must seem not merely plausible but fairly compelling.

> The heir's identification of himself with his father is impor-tant because in order to have a full understanding of *Henry IV* it is necessary to understand that "Everyman" or the hu-man soul is represented not merely by the Prince alone and by the King alone, but also, above all, by a synthesis of the Prince and the King. In its static aspect, as a fallen soul that

"smells of mortality" and must die before a new soul can be born, the soul is personified by the King; and the symbolism is strengthened by the fact that the King is a [sic] usurper to [sic] the throne, just as fallen man is a [sic] usurper to the throne of earth, which belongs by rights only to man in his original state, man created in the image of God. On the other hand, in its dynamic aspect, inasmuch as it is capable of being purified, and inasmuch as the foundations of the new soul are being laid there, the soul is personified by the Prince who . . . will not be a [sic] usurper when he becomes King. It is not only the faults of the Prince that die with his father's death, but also the stigma of a crown that had been usurped. The substance of the soul of "Everyman" is also represented by England, which is in a state of discord and which is gradually brought into *a state of peace.* (Lings, 17, emphasis added)

All of this is, of course, as clear as mud, and tendered as a serious account of *King Henry IV* it is a travesty. Islamic neo-Platonism is taken as the only valid textual model, and this is willy nilly attributed to Shakespeare. But what can be expected from one who is candid enough to tell us *ab initio* that in order to grasp this play we need not trouble ourselves with what Shakespeare actually wrote? (Lings, 15) Why strain in laborious lucubrations when the Most High is at hand to deliver the textual Meaning as though it were an esoteric fortune cookie? In just a few epiphanic paragraphs we learn that (1) the betrayal of Falstaff is an act of exalted redemption, that (2) Prince Hal is "perfect," that (3) the faults of Bolingbroke and Hal are wiped out by the mere ascension of this paragon to the English throne, and that (4) the result of Prince Henry's machinations will be "a state of peace." Yet Hal's first political deed as regent is to heed his dying father's sly counsel to "busy giddy minds with foreign quarrels" [*King Henry IV*; II, IV, iii, 342-343] by invading France! That is organized homicide. Young King Harry, fresh from the agonies of Shrewsbury, now sounds the trumpet blast signaling the chronic bloody struggles which will unfold in France, in the War of the Roses and Bosworth Field. Shall we with Orwell's totalitarians proclaim that "war is peace" to make good our esoteric acceptation of Shakespeare? While it may have been titillating for Charles of Windsor, the Prince of Wales, to discover that his famous precursor in that office was, despite his egregious conduct, metaphysically "perfect," we who must strive in the bowels of the text know nothing of this. The reader will recall that "little touch of Harry in the night" in *King Henry V*, when one of the bedraggled English infantrymen lashes out at the senseless violence instigated by the duplicitous monarch.

KING HARRY (in disguise)

I dare say you love him not so ill to wish
him here alone, howsoever you speak this to feel other
men's minds. Methinks I could not die anywhere so
contented as in the King's company, his cause being
just and his quarrel honourable.

WILLIAMS

That's more than we know.

BATES

Ay, or more than we should seek after. For we
know enough if we know we are the King's subjects.
If his cause be wrong, our obedience to the King wipes
the crime of it out of us.

WILLIAMS

But if the cause be not good, the King himself
hath a heavy reckoning to make, when all those legs
and arms and heads chopped off in a battle shall join
together at the latter day, and cry all, 'We died at such
a place' -- some swearing, some crying for a surgeon,
some upon their wives left poor behind them, some
upon the debts they owe, some upon their children
rawly left. I am afeard there are few die well that die
in a battle, for how can they charitably dispose of
anything, when blood is their argument? Now, if these
men do not die well, it will be a black matter for the
King that led them to it -- who to disobey were against
all proportion of subjection.
(*King Henry V*, IV, i, 128-145)

Hal has no rebuttal to these blunt facts except pitiful and uneasy casuistry (IV, i, 146-184) followed by anxious prayers of petition in which he confesses that his reign is founded on the usurpation of Richard's throne and his brutal murder, and that he fully expects his soldiers will pay for his hasty excursion in France with their lives, unless God grant a miracle. (*King Henry V*, IV, i, 227-281; 286-302) Here we are far removed from "perfection." Though Lings' theological reading of the play finds Bolingbroke's usurpation "wiped out" by Hal's reprise of his father's misbegotten reign, the Prince's overwhelming and ineluctable sense of guilt is always in plain sight. In fact, that shame over his father's overreaching is surely what sent Hal scurrying to the dark corners of Eastcheap in the first place. Did the newly minted King Harry suppose he might bury his dubious past by burying his boon companions?

But to worry about such anthropoid detritus would be for Lings a retreat to "the world of mediocrities and relativities" who are foolish enough to take bourgeois morality seriously. As Prince Hal's rapprochement with his debilitated father has rendered him "perfect," it is axiomatic that he can do no wrong. For those who heed the will of the Absolute, every action in the service of the cosmic imperatives is praiseworthy by definition. The heavenly end justifies the most meretricious of means. Of course, the "unmistakable ring of the absolute" may not quite drown out the cries of its victims. No matter. Those shrieks and groans are mere shadows cast by the magnificent sun of jihad. While Hegel taught that the "slaughter bench of history" is mankind's response to "the cunning of Reason," for the esoteric Islam of Martin Lings, the slaughter bench of history is the necessary and acceptable concomitant of Allah's shining path, from which the elect may not deviate one jot on account of anything so trivial as a mere mountain of mortal amputation and incineration.

It is by now widely recognized that Shakespeare's Prince Hal is one of Elizabethan theatre's most contemptible and duplicitous personae. The rollicking bonhomie of the Boarshead Tavern is counterpoised by Hal's patent deceit, a deceit echoed by the Princess of France when she observes in response to his clumsy wooing: "*O bon Dieu! Les langues des hommes sont pleines de tromperies.*" (See, *King Henry V*, V, ii, 116-121) She knows. After relishing the rough and ready egalitarianism of Hal's socializing with Falstaff and his earthy companions (better comprehended for what it really means at *King Henry V*, III, i, 17-34, and IV, iii, 18-67), are we not shocked to hear Hal's chilling and perfidious soliloquy? Here is a heart as black as ink.

I know you all, and will a while uphold
The unyoked humour of your idleness,
Yet herein will I imitate the sun,
Who doth permit the base contagious clouds
To smother up his beauty from the world,
That when he please again to be himself,
Being wanted he may be more wondered at
By breaking through the foul and ugly mists
Of vapours that did seem to strangle him.
If all the year were playing holidays,
To sport would be as tedious as to work;
But when they seldom come, they wished-for come,
And nothing pleaseth but rare accidents.
So when this loose behaviour I throw off
And pay the debt I never promisèd,
By how much better than my word I am,
By so much shall I falsify men's hopes;
And like bright metal on a sullen ground,
My reformation, glitt'ring o'er my fault,
Shall show more goodly and attract more eyes
Than that which hath no foil to set it off.
I'll so offend to make offence a skill,
Redeeming time when men think least I will.
(*King Henry IV*, I, I, ii, 192-214)

Can it really be that Hal's delightful romps and escapades with Falstaff are nothing but the slithering of a political viper on its way to strike? What kind of person is this? The answer is, he is the spitting image of his father, who expresses precisely the same mendacious and hypocritical philosophy.

By being seldom seen, I could not stir
But, like a comet, I was wondered at,
That men would tell their children, 'This is he.'
Others would say 'Where, which is Bolingbroke?'
And then I stole all courtesy from heaven,
And dressed myself in such humility
That I did pluck allegiance from men's hearts,
Loud shouts and salutations from their mouths,
Even in the presence of the crownèd King.

Thus did I keep my person fresh and new,
My presence like a robe pontifical --
Ne'er seen but wondered at -- and so my state,
Seldom but sumptuous, showed like a feast.
(*King Henry IV*, I; III, ii, 46-58)

It is Falstaff who shrewdly observes that Harry is valiant on account of "the cold blood he did naturally inherit of his father." (*King Henry IV*, II; IV, ii, 13-14) Is this "perfect" - or perfectly wretched?

Those inclined to sympathy may attempt to give Hal the benefit of the doubt, or, like good twenty-first century psychologists, look for adventitious traumas to relieve him of some responsibility for his conduct. Strangely, few scholars pose the question of what Hal was doing when his father was ejected from England by King Richard. Did young Hal suffer banishment too? Exactly where was he when Richard confiscated the Lancastrian estates? We don't know (though historians tell us that Richard served as Hal's guardian during at least some of Boligbroke's absence). But as readers of Shakespeare we do know where Hal's story begins, not in *King Henry IV* but rather in *King Richard II*, shortly after the deposition of Richard, when Bolingbroke, in conversation with - of all people - Hotspur, laments his wastrel son's profligacy.

KING HENRY

Can no man tell me of my unthrifty son?
'Tis full three months since I did see him last.
If any plague hang over us, 'tis he.
I would to God, my lords, he might be found.
Enquire at London 'mongst the taverns there,
For there, they say, he daily doth frequent
With unrestrainèd loose companions --
Even such, they say, as stand in narrow lanes
And beat our watch and rob our passengers --
Which he, young wanton and effeminate boy,
Takes on the point of honour to support
So dissolute a crew.

HARRY PERCY

My lord, some two days since, I saw the Prince,

And told him of these triumphs held at Oxford.

KING HENRY

And what said the gallant?

HARRY PERCY

His answer was he would unto the stews,
And from the common'st creature pluck a glove,
And wear it as a favour, and with that
He would unhorse the lustiest challenger.

KING HENRY

As dissolute as desperate. Yet through both
I see some sparks of better hope, which elder days
May happily bring forth.
(V, iii, 1-22)

Though the King's Men might not think so, the pieces of Humpty Dumpty Hal are not hard to put together. Hal was plainly embarrassed by his father's exile, and mortified by the rebellion Bolingbroke fomented, which culminated in the liquidation of King Richard and in his father's wrongful seizure of the Throne. The anguish Hal feels is still oozing out of every pore on the eve of Agincourt. He therefore staged his own little rebellion against Daddy by vanishing into the squalid bohemian alleyways of London. But Hal's "rash, fierce blaze of riot" cannot last, any more than Richard's could, inasmuch as Bolingbroke is Hal's own father, and only by his father's treason does he have his own chance to become King of England. No matter the ethical niceties, Hal is never so "perfect" as to reject that seat of Mars. His father, though bitterly disappointed in Hal's contumacious retort, senses those "sparks of hope" which will eventually catch fire, leading to (1) their reconciliation, (2) Hal's victory over Hotspur at Shrewsbury, (3) Hal's eventual coronation and (4) his rejection of Falstaff.

And who, pray tell, is Falstaff? No, the question is not intended to induce an historical discussion of John Oldcastle and Lollardism. Rather, we follow in the footsteps of the good Mr. Lings who urges us to see the symbolic meaning of things. For Mr. Lings, Falstaff is "the devil." But what does this intend, exactly? That he eats, drinks, drabs and takes purses? This meager one-size-fits-all *curriculum vitae* would hardly capture the man into whose avuncular orbit the peregrine Prince of Wales falls. Reading with eyes shut tight by verities, Mr. Lings cannot see the person he himself exiles in his wooden theology. For banish Jack Falstaff and you banish all the world. (*King Henry IV*, I; II, v, 482-485) That is because Falstaff is *LIFE*. And in order to know what that entails, it is necessary to read these precious plays, read them more than once, with eyes and ears open. You cannot substitute talk about Falstaff for an encounter with him. His picture cannot be found in a *précis*. Falstaff is Dionysus, the god of wine, the sense of whole-hearted enthusiasm and savoring of our little moment in the sun. To adapt Hegelian language, Falstaff is the Bacchanalian whirl of language in which not a member is sober. Despite his lumbering girth, his instincts are light, dexterous and sharp, and his tongue quicker than Hamlet's. With all his chatter about alchemy, Mr. Lings fails to notice Falstaff's alchemical union of wine and speech. (*King Henry IV*, I; IV, ii, 83-121) When Hal stumbles into East-cheap, most likely trailing along confusedly with Pointz, we must imagine his sense of being utterly marooned. He is not expecting to meet a god in the stews. Yet that is precisely what transpires. And this god loves him and takes him in and gives him a home. Can the devil love? The Hal who finds his way to Eastcheap is a lost soul, down on his luck, rescued by Falstsaff and the denizens of the Boarshead Tavern. Falstaff becomes his mentor, his guide, his Beatrice of the underworld. In short, Hal, who misses a father in Bolingbroke, finds one in Falstaff. "Do thou stand for my father," the Prince entreats Falstaff in the saloon, "and examine me upon the particulars of my life." (*King Henry IV*, I; II, v, 379-380)

And all the while he abides with Falstaff, is sheltered by him, suc-cored by him, Hal is plotting and scheming, already forming the express intention of turning his back on him forever. As Mark Antony might ask: does this sound like perfection? It is a treachery so vile it has no precedent in the annals of the world. Yet according to Mr. Lings the audience should find in this behavior an image of its "sanctification."

But there is more that must be said, and it is high time to say it. What is striking about Falstaff, what is most significant about him, is not his girth or appetite, not his wit, not his fears and desires, no, not even his love of Hal. What stands out about him is his vulnerability, his sensitivity to slight and loss, the pain in his bosom on callous rejection. This is his appeal for Doll, Bardolph and the rest. It is this emotional exposure which endears him to us too, allowing him to spring from the page into our own hearts and render us human. Does Falstaff hope that someday he will benefit in practical ways for being a dear friend of the King of England? Of course. But that natural and forgivable expectation cannot obscure the fact that he loves Hal and would suffer a breakdown were he to be abandoned. Could Hal be that cruel?

One afternoon Falstaff is sojourning in the arbor of Master Robert Shallow when Pistol brings the news: Bolingbroke is dead, and their dear young ward is the new King. The ceremony is imminent. Falstaff is thunderstruck.

> Away, Bardolph, saddle my horse! Master Robert
> Shallow, choose whatever office thou wilt in the land; 'tis
> thine. Pistol, I will double charge thee with dignities.

> Master Shallow -- my lord Shallow -- be what thou wilt,
> I am fortune's steward -- get on thy boots; we'll ride
> all night. -- O sweet Pistol! -- Away, Bardolph!
> Come, Pistol, utter no more to me, and withal devise
> something to do thyself good. Boot, boot, Master
> Shallow! I know the young king is sick for me. Let us
> take any man's horses -- the laws of England are at my
> commandment. Blessed are they that have been my
> friend, and woe to my Lord Chief Justice.
> (*King Henry IV*, II; V, iii, 122-137)

Falstaff is like a fellow who has won the lottery, but his tender regard for Hal shines through.

Now picture Falstaff and his ragamuffin cohorts in the London throng, jumping and jostling for a view. He is as eager as a small child straining for the baubles of a carnival parade.

> Come here, Pistol; stand behind me. (To Shallow)
> O, if I had had time to have made new liveries, I would
> have bestowed the thousand pound I borrowed of you!
> But 'tis no matter; this poor show doth better; this
> doth infer the zeal I had to see him.

> It shows my earnestness of affection.

> My devotion --

As it were, to ride day and night, and not to
deliberate, not to remember, not to have patience to
shift me --

But to stand stained with travel and sweating
with desire to see him, thinking of nothing else, putting
all affairs in oblivion, as if there were nothing else to
be done but to see him.

King Harry V appears in the procession.

FALSTAFF

God save thy grace, King Hal, my royal Hal!
God save thee, my sweet boy!

And then is heard a voice as frigid as the ice of Saturn's Rings, distant
and muted, and filled with asphyxiating contempt.

KING HARRY

My Lord Chief Justice, speak to that vain man.

LORD CHIEF JUSTICE

Have you your wits? Know you what 'tis you speak?

FALSTAFF

My King, my Jove, I speak to thee, my heart!

KING HARRY

I know thee not, old man. Fall to thy prayers.
How ill white hairs becomes a fool and jester!
I have long dreamt of such a kind of man,
So surfeit-swelled, so old, and so profane;
But being awake, I do despise my dream.
Make less thy body hence, and more thy grace.
Leave gourmandizing; know the grave doth gape

Thrice wider than for other men.
Reply not to me with a fool-born jest.
Presume not that I am the thing I was,
For God doth know, so shall the world perceive,
That I have turned away my former self;
So will I those that kept me company.
When thou dost hear I am as I have been,
Approach me, and thou shalt be as thou wast,
The tutor and the feeder of my riots.
Till then I banish thee, on pain of death,
As I have done the rest of my misleaders,
Not to come near our person by ten mile.
For competence of life I will allow you,
That lack of means enforce you not to evils,
We will, according to your strengths and qualities,
Give you advancement.
(*King Henry IV*, II; V, v, 47-70 with minor omissions)

Falstaff's greatest fear is realized. The hideous fate he had always dreaded falls upon him like a bird of prey. Prince Hal is a perfidious backstabber, a user who exploited him and the others in the Boarshead Tavern, and then, when they prove inconvenient, he kicks them to the curb, as he had planned to all along. It's not a pretty picture, but it is a fair and accurate one of Shakespeare's Prince of Wales, and is confirmed by other unwholesome deeds too numerous to catalogue here. King Harry's very first actions as King are to (1) forgive the Lord Chief Justice who had arrested him in his wilder days (*King Henry IV*, II; V, ii, 100-144) and to (2) cast out his loyal friend, who had saved him from ruin and taught him the nature of life among those who toil for a living or are unfit to do so. (V, v, 47-70) Not only is Falstaff rudely dumped in public, but so are all the other men of the tavern with whom Hal had caroused. But ironically the banishment cannot be put into effect. True to the compact with his dying father, Hal immediately declares war on France on the flimsiest of pretexts, and for no other purpose than to siphon attention away from the illegitimacy of his reign, which has been inherited from the traitor Bolingbroke. The invasion of France requires a military conscription which attaches the fellows of Eastcheap, who therefore remain Hal's companions abroad, cannon fodder for a gratuitous and savage expedition. In that struggle, Falstaff's servant Bardolph is caught pilfering and, with a nod from good King Harry, is strangled on a rustic gallows. Hal's *obiter dictum* that "when lenity and cruelty play for a kingdom, the gentler gamester is the soonest winner" must have sounded strangely in Bardolph's ears as he dangled from that rope. (*King Henry V*, III, vi, 112-114) In the midst of the decisive battle of Agincourt in which the English army is losing nary a man, King Harry orders that the totality of the French prisoners be executed, contrary to the rules of war. It is then found that the serving boy who worked in the Boarshead Tavern has been killed by the desperate French. As for Falstaff, he never makes it to France, for he dies of a broken heart, the result of Hal's barbaric betrayal.

* * *

As a would-be Shakespeare guru, Martin Lings spurns Falstaff as the Fiend incarnate. He rather prefers to be a fan of the "Christian" King Henry V, (I, ii, 241) judged to be "sanctified" and "perfect." In the opening scene of *King Henry IV*, the father of that "Christian king," Henry IV, is planning a Crusade to the Holy Land to rout the Mamluk Sultans when the outbreak of local insurrections calls for a change of plans. (*King Henry IV*, I; I, i, 18-30; 47-48) Is that symbolically consonant with the triumph of esoteric Islam? Far from condemning Hal's premeditated jettisoning of Falstaff, Lings praises and emulates it, banishing from his book nearly every major expert in the field of English literature and Shakespeare studies, putting in their place a few accommodating French obscurantists and a handful of Islamic mullahs. Not only are the great students, critics and commentators on Shakespeare deleted by Mr. Lings, the lion's share of the content of the plays about which he writes is censored by omission. A vast army of literature's most enduring characters is barred also. But the substance of Shakespeare's characters is their speech; that is the actual loss to us. Such a high-handed treatment of Shakespeare amounts to outright emasculation of text and author. Those who go to Shakespeare as the grand possessors of Truth have no need of him for any other purpose than to use him as a screen on which to project their own smiling faces.

Offended by what they find of their past in the history plays, and congenitally unable to absorb the simple rhythmic cadences of Elizabethan English, French scholarship has never been able to come to terms with Shakespeare; filled with envy and resentment, it is forever spinning polysyllabic theories aimed at dissolving his art in a bath of toxic noise. This neoplastic hyper-intellectualism of the French metastasizes in the hands of Gallic-Islamic acolytes like Schuon and Guénon, yielding an aggressive and spiritually distempered campaign to wipe out western humanism and replace it with legions of murmuring satraps. This can be finally accomplished when the humble empiricism bequeathed by English philosophy is rooted out, and is supplanted by an opaque *Weltanschauung* in which the cosmos is a riddling chimera to which only a cadre of black-gowned magicians holds the answer.

It is no accident, then, that in Falstaff Mr. Lings finds the "Devil." If he had been a bit more candid and skilled in the symbolic interpretation he professed, he might have identified that "Devil" with greater particularity. Let us do so. It was an Englishman, Dr. Samuel Johnson, who observed that when a man is tired of London, he is tired of life. That is telling. For what is Falstaff if not the genius of London? Martin Lings' despising of him is by logical extension, a hatred of London, a hatred of England and America, a hatred of Shakespeare and a hatred of life. Confirmation is readily found in the daily news reports. Fanatical terrorists tweak the noses of trembling westerners by boasting that the Yankees and Europeans, clutching at life, will do almost anything to preserve it, while the warriors of Islam, enamored of death, cast away their lives like pins. In an age in which literature itself is evaporating in the wake of video games and text messaging, there may be a lesson in all this: Shakespeare is important. He is our citadel, the bulwark shielding all that is good and genuinely sane in the west. Those who would destroy us know this by instinct, and busy themselves forging alliances with other agents of disintegration to annihilate Shakespeare once and for all. Our prognosis must therefore be guarded:

> We have seen the best of our time. Machinations,
> hollowness, treachery, and all ruinous disorders follow
> us disquietly to our graves.
> (*The Tragedy of King Lear*, I, ii, 110-112)

WORKS CITED

Gail Eaton, "Martin Lings, Islamic Scholar Concerned with Spiritual Crisis," *The Guardian*, May 26, 2005

Martin Lings, *Shakespeare's Window Into the Soul*, Inner Traditions, 2006

Martin Lings, "Frithjof Schuon: An Autobiographical Approach," *Sophia*, Vol. 4, No. 2, 1998

Martin Lings, "Frithjof Schuon and René Guénon," *Sophia*, Vol. 5, No. 2, 1999

Douglas Martin, "Martin Lings, A Sufi writer on Islamic Ideas, Dies at 96," *The New York Times*, May 29, 2005

William Shakespeare, The Complete Works, 2d Edition, G. Taylor, S. Wells, eds., Clarendon Press, 2005

Online Sources

Biographical Note on Frithjof Schuon
Theatre and Islamic Tradition, no author identified

18

Hamlet Made Simple

He has found the meaning, but I will gloze with him.
- *Antiochus*

Now, gods, stand up for bastards!
- *Edmund*

Introduction

*W*hen we open our copy of *The Tragedy of Hamlet, Prince of Denmark*, begging admittance, the book raises weary eyes to us, yet another visitor, and complains loudly, "Who's there?" (I, i, 1) We are just the latest intruders in a strange place where secrets lie jealously guarded, like the apples Dorothy picks in the suburbs of Oz. Those peevish trees will never tell her she's still asleep in Kansas. It is the same challenge with which an arch Caterpillar confronts a bewildered Alice: "Who Are You?" We are allowed in, of course, but as we don't supply a fitting answer, the pouting text remains suspicious and aloof, abandoning us to our own devices. We have been reminded of our Delphic duty, something we have not so much discharged as avoided by simply living, growing up, and taking on the motley roles we're assigned in life. (*As You Like It*, II, vii, 139-166; *The Tragedy of Macbeth*, V, v, 18-27)

In *Hamlet*, Shakespeare raises the primal question of our childhood once more. It is the riddle of identity. Questing after the Prince of

Denmark is not trivial pursuit, not sport, nor is it a tedious term paper or clinical exercise conducted by smug intellectuals. No. What we are really after is ourselves, and the search is an enterprise of much pith and moment. Our hope is that by following the Prince in his arduous journey we too can grow to find our truest being. We are not here, guests in a curious land, to sit in judgment on the kingdom of words in which we are inscribing ourselves, signing its register with trembling hand. No, we are here to discover, to learn. The play judges us, takes our measure, catches our conscience. Let us be not like Leontes, who sent to the Oracle but did not heed its counsel. (*The Winter's Tale*, III, ii, 139-140) For Apollo's sentence, when it comes, will sound in our own voice.

I. The Friendly Ghost

What do we know about the ghost in *Hamlet*? Not much. Nor does Prince Hamlet know very much about it. Yet this undead ambassador is the prime mover of the play, the enigmatical figure which sets in motion the wheels of tragedy, the darkling character - if we are to put stock in fable - that "Shakespeare" himself chose to enact. To fail to fathom this spectral vagabond is to risk missing the drama as a whole.

A strange interloper appears in Denmark, a refugee from perdition who suborns a gentle prince to regicide. And, despite his patently malign purpose, he is believed, ardently so. Whatever our estimations of Hamlet's moral character, they are based squarely on his responses to this weird senior citizen's deliverances. But his credentials surely are not the best. What if this shady wanderer is a con artist? What then?

Throughout the action "this fellow in the cellarage" is an object of dread and suspicion, not to be trusted, a hazard to mind and body.

> What if it tempt you toward the flood, my lord,
> Or to the dreadful summit of the cliff
> That beetles o'er his base into the sea,
> And there assume some other horrible form
> Which might deprive your sovereignty of reason
> And draw you into madness? Think of it.
> (I, iv, 50-55)

Protesting too much, Hamlet boasts: "It is an honest ghost, that let me tell you." (I, v, 142) He is immediately thrust upon a path of reprisal by dubious and stentorian testimony for which he has no supporting evidence but his own seasick sensibility. If there can be no external corroboration of its integrity, then "it is a damnèd ghost that we have seen, and my imaginations are as foul as Vulcan's stithy." (III, ii, 80-82) Only when he has finally exposed the king as he recoils from "The Murder of Gonzago" does Hamlet come to embrace its ectoplasmic utterances as dependable. (Greenblatt, 239) "O good Horatio, I'll take the Ghost's word for a thousand pound. Didst perceive?" (III, ii, 274-275) Unwary readers re-enact Hamlet, finding in Claudius's discomfiting ample showing of the ghost's honesty. The king's soliloquies strike us as irrefragable confirmation. For example,

> O, 'tis too true!
> How smart a lash that speech doth give my conscience.
> The harlot's cheek, beautied with plast'ring art,
> Is not more ugly to the thing that helps it
> Than is my deed to my most painted word.
> O, heavy burden!
> (III, i, 52-56)

Yes, indeed, we cluck to ourselves, Claudius fatally harmed his brother. Why doesn't our hero just see and follow through? Further along, our confidence is fortified, as we hear again what Hamlet doesn't.

> O, my offence is rank! It smells to heaven.
> It hath the primal eldest curse upon't,
> A brother's murder. Pray can I not.
> Though inclination be as sharp as will,
> My stronger guilt defeats my strong intent,
> And like a man to double business bound
> I stand in pause where I shall first begin,
> And both neglect. What if this cursèd hand
> Were thicker than itself with brother's blood,
> Is there not rain enough in the sweet heavens
> To wash it white as snow? Whereto serves mercy
> But to confront the visage of offence?
> And what's in prayer but this twofold force,
> To be forestallèd ere we come to fall,
> Or pardoned being down? Then I'll look up.
> My fault is past -- but O, what form of prayer

Can serve my turn? 'Forgive me my foul murder'?
That cannot be, since I am still possessed
Of those effects for which I did the murder --
My crown, mine own ambition, and my queen.
May one be pardoned and retain th' offence?
(III, iii, 36-56)

This anguished confession tends to erase any unease as to the ghost's authenticity and truthfulness. We accept that it is deputized to enlist the Prince's services in its quest for vengeance. By concealing Claudius's admissions from Lord Hamlet, while giving us privileged access thereto, Shakespeare reinforces in subtle form our impression that the ghost spake truth. The fact that the Prince does not overhear these words fills us with indignation and pity, making of us unwitting advocates, believers in the damned. But might we not hesitate, as Hamlet hesitates, as Claudius hesitates? To tell one truth is not to say all true. When Hamlet at the finale plunges to his gravest purpose, he dies still in perfect acceptance of the ghost and all its awful news from nowhere. Was that faith well founded? Or has a fragment of fact been used to bait a hook of deception? O, cunning enemy! (*Measure for Measure*, II, ii, 185-186) Well did Prince Hamlet at the outset realize the peril - but dismissed it. What about us?

The spirit that I have seen
May be the devil, and the devil hath power
T'assume a pleasing shape; yea, and perhaps,
Out of my weakness and my melancholy --
As he is very potent with such spirits --
Abuses me to damn me.
(II, ii, 600-605)

The echo in *Macbeth* is striking:

But 'tis strange,
And oftentimes to win us to our harm
The instruments of darkness tell us truths,
Win us with honest trifles to betray's
In deepest consequence.
(I, iii, 120-124)

Brutus, too, is troubled by his own unsettling visitation.

> I think it is the weakness of mine eyes
> That shapes this monstrous apparition.
> It comes upon me. Art thou any thing?
> Art thou some god, some angel, or some devil,
> That mak'st my blood run cold and my hair to stare?
> Speak to me what thou art.
> (*The Tragedy of Julius Caesar*, IV, ii, 327-332)

And though we may suppose we have to do with great Caesar's "ghost," its self-professed identity is "Thy evil spirit, Brutus." (IV, ii, 334)

Shakespeare is at extraordinary pains to impeach the ghost, and those worries are never quite set to rest. No *deus ex machina* descends from the clouds to grant us assurances, our melodramatic bonus in *Cymbeline*. Horatio's "Stay, illusion!" (I, i, 108) reverberates in our minds. The signs of corruption are unmistakable. Even its very deportment bears an aspect of coverture and untrustworthiness.

> And then it started like a guilty thing
> Upon a fearful summons. I have heard
> The cock, that is the trumpet to the morn,
> Doth with his lofty and shrill-sounding throat
> Awake the god of day, and at his warning,
> Whether in sea, or fire, in earth or air,
> Th' extravagant and erring spirit hies
> To his confine; and of the truth herein
> The present object made probation.
> (I, i, 129-137)

But it is when we turn to the ghost's own words that our doubts should coagulate and turn to accusation. Evil stares us in the face. For this foul pilgrim is:

> Doomed for a certain term to walk the night,
> And for the day confined to fast in fires
> Till the foul crimes done in my days of nature
> Are burnt and purged away.
> (I, v, 10-13)

The figure shaped like the late king is bound in flames, then, *not* simply because of King Hamlet's having ended his earthly sojourn with all his "imperfections" on his head, but on account of mortal sins. We are not talking about breaches of politesse or court decorum, but "foul crimes," instances of moral turpitude, which should disqualify anyone for the role of part-time mentor or cosmic tour-guide. In his excitement the troubled prince doesn't mark the signs that should have alerted him. It is the grisly, sensationalistic murder that holds his attention, not his alleged progenitor's disclosure of profound personal venality. Take the ghost at its word. It is being punished for some severe misconduct, and the soul's grievous wounds are not yet cauterized. Is such a one proof against mendacity? Grant that Claudius poisoned Hamlet the Dane. A single accurate statement of the accused can hardly achieve so great a rehabilitation that his entire story should be credited.

Here is the sticking point: we just do not know what this apparition is. Is it a vestige of the king, or something more alien?

> Be thou a spirit of health or goblin damned,
> Bring with thee airs from heaven or blasts from hell,
> Be thy intents wicked or charitable,
> Thou com'st in such a questionable shape
> That I will speak to thee. I'll call thee Hamlet,
> King, father, royal Dane.
> (I, iv, 21-26)

Prince Hamlet will "call" it King Hamlet, father, for lack of a more precise name based on established facts. In his distraught condition, his better judgment deserts him; he forgets that this thing cannot be his father, and is likely a spiritual imposter. In a play whose root metaphor is the theatre, even the "ghost" is acting a part. His revelations sound well rehearsed.

One commentator is refreshingly candid on this point.

> It is important, even crucial, to think of the Ghost not as we think of ghosts generally, but as the men of Shakespeare's time thought of them. We are all familiar with the play . . . and we think of the apparition as "the ghost of Hamlet's father." But it was no such thing to the Elizabethan audience. The Ghost is a spirit that can take on any shape for any purpose. The most that can be said is that it looks like Hamlet's

father, that it has taken the shape of Hamlet's father. What it is, no one can really say.

Shakespeare makes this plain at every step. When it appears to the three men, Bernardo describes it as:

In the same figure like the king that's dead. Then, nudging Horatio, who's staring openmouthed, he says: *Looks 'a not like the king?* Then, when Horatio finally finds his tongue and . . . addresses the Ghost is stately syllables, he says the same thing in more complicated fashion:

> What art thou that usurp'st this time of night,
> together with that fair and warlike form
> in which the majesty of buried Denmark
> did sometimes march?

"Usurp" is to take without right. The Ghost was a supernatural visitation and by ordinary natural law the place and time should have been free of it. In that sense, it usurped the time of night, and, in addition, it usurped the appearance of the dead king. Horatio seems to feel that it is not really the ghost of the dead king but merely a spirit who assumes that appearance for purposes of his own. In fact, Horatio is questioning the spirit as to its real identity.

If we don't understand this clearly, then we don't really understand the play. (Asimov, 81-82; cp. Greenblatt, 220)

It is clear that the authority such an entity should possess as the late king's residuum is missing. The presumption of dishonesty that attaches to such a dubious character is not rebutted, but glossed. He remains *prima facie* unreliable. An intruder from unquenchable fire tempts the Prince to homicide on the seemingly implied and extraordinary supposition that its commission will, *per impossibile*, somehow shorten his torment. It operates on the primitive legal principle of *lex talionis* in its crudest form: direct retribution. But, as Professor Greenblatt insists, in doctrinal terms, the "souls in Purgatory were saved." Thus, such an entity "could not possibly commit new sins." A "call for vengeance" could only come "from the the place in the afterlife where Seneca's ghosts reside: Hell." (Greenblatt, 237) But those condemned there make no escape to work more mischief. Where does that leave them -- and us?

If "the ghost" wanted to prompt action against Claudius, why not speak to everyone to whom he presented himself, to Marcellus, Bernardo, Horatio and, in fact, all the powers of Denmark? We know they can hear him, for the ghost's bellowing for an oath is audited by Marcellus, Horatio and Hamlet together. (I, v, 151-182) Why confer privily with this lonely prince? Is the requested murder morally acceptable? Since the theological context of the play is the Christian faith (consider Ophelia's burial problems), one might find odd - even comical - that vendetta serves the same function as prayers of indulgence. Shall Hamlet cast the first stone? No one seems to object, least of all the young philosopher from Wittenberg. From the cries for mercy and compassion of Portia, Isabella and Prospero we are light years removed.

Take the other horn of the dilemma. Say the ghost seeks revenge not as a poultice for Purgatorial pains, but in spite of them, heedless of consequences. If the sufferers in Purgatory could sin again, the risk is that post-mortem sins would at the very least redouble the penalty, making such tactics senseless. On any account, then, once we transcend the 'once-upon-a-time' level of meaning, the ghost in *Hamlet*, like Macbeth's weird sisters, becomes *unheimliche*, beyond mortal ken. This is no amiable Homeric shade of a departed loved one, but something "*tout autre*," wholly other, beyond our capacities of understanding. As such, its nature and origins must forever remain obscure, as Greenblatt seems to aver. (Greenblatt, 239) The practical consequence is that when Hamlet finally embraces it as benevolent soothsayer, he errs. At no time does it ever achieve general credibility. And the challenge for us is to try to distinguish, as the prince does not, what is true and what is false among its deliverances. It is this challenge which Greenblatt & company gracefully elide.

Unnoticed is the surprising fact that no fatherly care or solicitude for Hamlet is exhibited by this sepulchral personage, obsessed as it is with its own fratricidal campaign. Not a flicker of interest is shown in this young man's career or salvation, and not the slightest hint of the delicate topic of Hamlet's successive rights is uttered. Greater love had the monitory ghost at Philippi for Brutus than this self-absorbed demon has for his professed "son" at Elsinore. By contrast, even Dickens' Ghost of Christmas Future was on an altruistic mission for the sake of Ebenezer Scrooge, not for its own welfare.

Yet, "*I am thy father's spirit*," announces the ghost *con brio*. Plainly this is no morsel of underdone potato. What intellectual capital accrues to our reading of the text if this proposition is seen as a lie?

For all his erudition and insight, Greenblatt goes astray at just the point on which he lays greatest emphasis: the nature of the ghost. Having established its irreducible ambiguity in terms of the theological categories of the 16th century, and obvious associations with the infernal, no attempt is made to winnow its utterances to separate truth from trash. Nor is there any effort made to see beyond the bizarre categories and dogmatic clashes of English Catholics and Protestants, which obviously are in adventitious relation to a narrative descended from Saxo Grammaticus (1150 -1220 A.D.) about figures in Scandinavian legend. Commendably, Greenblatt shows that the ghost in *Hamlet*, like the witches in *Macbeth*, exists in a no-man's-land separating fantasy and reality, a ghastly betwixt-and-between site which savors of the "uncanny." (Greenblatt, 193, ff.) The topos of the ghost is a world in which there is a constant "bleeding of the spectral into the secular and the secular into the spectral." (Greenblatt, 194) As such a stratum is unheard of in Christian topography, the ghost is inevitably assimilated to personal interiority, subjectivity, history and the theatre. Ultimately, then, the ghost is not taken seriously, and the disturbing new topos is quickly put away, as Columbus might forget America.

> Shakespeare does not want his audience to deride and contemn the illusion and knavery of . . . witches or ghosts. He wants . . . to persuade his audience to credit them, but only in the special sense in which an audience playfully credits what it sees in the theatrical space of fictions. (Greenblatt, 196)

This equivocates on the word "play" and neatly begs the critical question. Everything in the play exists either in text or presentation thereof, but the text points to objects and events beyond itself. What might they be? Raising the existence of the uncanny is a momentous business for which a "playful" crediting may be a tad inappropriate. (Before "playfully" throwing in with Mr. Greenblatt, the student might be well advised to make a very careful study of the life of Abraham Lincoln, his relationship with Shakespeare, with particular reference to *Macbeth* and *Julius Caesar*, and John Wilkes Booth and his family. That there are more things in heaven and earth than are dreamt of in our philosophies may still be so.)

Greenblatt's signal omission is the failure to come to terms with the pagan religions of northern Europe, Scandinavia and the British Isles which long antedated the rigid metaphysics of ecclesiastical Christianity. As Albion succumbed to the Romans, zealous Christian proselytizers and to the Norman French in 1066, the native rituals and gods of the Anglo-Saxons were driven underground, far more deeply underground than the recusant Catholicism of Elizabeth's reign. Think, for example of the witch in Smithfield, whom Henry VI burns to ashes. (*King Henry VI*, Part II, II, iii, 7) It was Christianity which turned the divinities of native religion into "heathen" fiends and demons. Elder women became "witches" while men who made only nominal Christian vows but went their own ways were known by derisive monks as "warlocks." (Sandow) Well after the Norman Invasion, the common people of England clung tenaciously to the autochthonous culture and religion of the old days. When those women who practiced the dying arts of healing and prophecy were not being incinerated as "witches," they were still being honored as midwives, natural healers and guardians of dateless wisdom. (*Twelfth Night*, III, iv, 101) The image of the ghost of Hamlet the Dane rising from the tomb and appearing before certain of the people of Denmark is a remnant of the pagan past which still haunted England in the time of the conflict between the Reformed faith and that of Rome. Unlike Christianity, founded as it was on a rationalistic *Logos*, the ancient rituals and nostrums cleaved to the fundamentally arational nature of things, enshrining it in the pervasive and all-important notion of *Wyrd*. It is this to which Macbeth and the "weird sisters" direct us, as does the ghost in *Hamlet*. Magic flourished then, and nature still glowed with numinous vitality. Greenblatt is correct to point out the "uncanny" aspect of Shakespeare's otherworldly characters, but wrong to find no other home for that dimension than the theatrical imagination. Shakespeare does not invent *Wyrd*, but recreates, reinvigorates and reflects it in his drama. His movement, therefore, is not in the direction of subjectivity, but towards an incommensurable super reality of which the modern mind has no ken.

In *Hamlet*, then, an emissary of *Wyrd*, a Nemesis of those who have betrayed and traduced the gods of the north, avers that it "is" Hamlet's father. If this should be a ruse, what follows?

Gather, and surmise.

II. The Lie With Circumstance, or, How many Children had King Hamlet the Dane?

In approaching any work of the imagination one must beware of treating it as a fragment of history. Fictive persons by definition have no past, subtend no living, breathing agendas as do we. But even though *qua* fiction a story does not reprise a factual substratum, the process of dramatic digestion proceeds by implication and inference, so that we comprehend plot and character as if certain things were true. Thus, when Queequeg hurls his lance with preternatural accuracy, we necessarily and spontaneously view his prowess as a sign of natural talent nurtured by vast experience. Attributing a learning curve to Queequeg, regarding him as if he had a long apprenticeship at sea, allows us to appreciate him as a robust, three-dimensional individual about whom we can come to care, and whom we can grasp as much in potency as in act. This is the foundation of our *Verstehen*. Or, when Beatrice scolds Benedick with a harpy's fury, we catch the tones of a woman scorned, though any illustration of her original betrayal by Benedick is omitted and must be felt. Our acceptance of the meaning of purely literary events rests, then, on taking other events as having occurred, forming a temporal *gestalt*. Though accompanying inferences can be brought to light and examined, most often in casual reading such judgments are as automatic and natural as they are common. Thus, if there are assertions in the text that the ghost represents the father of the prince, it is not an exercise in futility or meaninglessness to sift the script to determine if these assertions conflict with other data.

Set the ghost to one side for a moment and consider directly the issue of Hamlet's genealogy.

Yale's Harold Bloom, of all people, lets a big cat out of the bag.

> The first line spoken by Hamlet is, "A little more than kin, and less than kind," while the next concludes punningly, "I am too much in [sic] the sun." Is there anxiety that Hamlet actually may be Claudius's son, since he cannot know for certain exactly when what he regards as adultery and incest began between Claudius and Gertrude? His notorious hesitations at hacking down Claudius stem partly from the sheer magnitude of his consciousness, but they may also indicate a realistic doubt about his paternity. (Bloom, 7-8)

Why doesn't the nice Mr. Ghost mention this?

Unfortunately, Dr. Bloom quickly drops this arresting insight, preferring to serve up a hyperbolical feast of words in honor of the departed prince which obsesses over his Deep Blue IQ. Bloom's inapposite quantifications are not well suited for an elucidation of *Hamlet*. Where sober deliberation is wanted, he gives rhetoric and bombast. The latter end of his critical commonwealth forgets its sapient beginning.

This is nothing new. Criticism often goes astray, missing textual signals. Subtleties and veiled nuances are ignored. What passes for scholarly consensus may turn out to be encrustations of prejudice or the detritus of sheer inertia. Paradoxes and puzzles spring up like kudzu of the brain. Works of abundant merit are misconceived. T.S. Eliot's vivisection of *Hamlet* is a splendid illustration of the baleful consequences of a criticism which relies only on what is grossly present. For this savant and his epigone, Shakespeare's most celebrated work must be judged an artistic "failure." It is "the Mona Lisa of literature," a silly locution by which is intended not praise but censure. Consisting of nine supercilious paragraphs which appear to have been tossed off as a literary parlor trick, *Hamlet and His Problems* reduces an intellectual colossus to a single isolated fault: the prince's excessive rage over his mother's rapid remarriage. Without an "objective correlative" to render that juvenile tantrum appropriate, it sins against aesthetic principle and so spoils the play. Hamlet's conduct is, in Sartre's phrase, "*de trop*," shocking in intensity and brute opacity. With no adequate motive at hand, Shakespeare's most famed character becomes little more than a symptom of a personal animus the writer could not disgorge. "We must simply admit," Eliot condescends, "that here Shakespeare tackled a problem which proved too much for him. Why he attempted it at all is still an insoluble puzzle; under compulsion of what experience he attempted to express the inexpressibly horrible, we cannot ever know. We may need a great many facts in his biography . . . ." Eliot knew, of course, the Stratfordian "biography" has no such matter in it.

We should mention in passing that if *Hamlet* is put down as a flop for omitting an "objective correlative" to account for Hamlet's rage, we must also reject *The Tragedy of King Lear* on identical grounds, for Lear's seismic rant in response to his youngest daughter's verbal modesty is equally incomprehensible. So *Hamlet* and *Lear* would both be literary junk as far as Tom Eliot is concerned.

Eliot's pontifications have the unintended merit of underscoring a fruitful dilemma. Though his harsh judgment won't withstand scrutiny, his discomfort reminds us that the conventional reading does inevitably run afoul of a seemingly incongruous relationship between Hamlet's feelings and his outward circumstances. A thorough *unreading* is called for, but never undertaken. Though we can agree there is no "*objective correlative*," we have a hunch Hamlet is no mere ham. Eliot has not demonstrated that there is zero reason for his exasperation and hysteria, if not pathology, but only that it is not explicitly exposed. It may be implied by the entire concatenation of events we are shown, together with our unnoticed inferences. The dissonance created by Hamlet's excoriation of his mother functions as an aporia whose exploration may lead us, rugged spelunkers, deeper into the bowels of the text. Like a geologist who, in his attempt to fathom earthquakes, discovers beneath the surface opposed tectonic plates, we may find that Hamlet's explosions are at once both gratuitous and inexplicable, yet tethered to unspoken themes whose names we shrink to mention. And there's the rub. The concealment of these subterranean pressures may make the psychic tremors all the more sudden and effective. Might the correlative we seek be *subjective* in nature?

We have already seen that the assumption of the ghost's veracity is untenable. And we have noticed that doubt about its honor may be connected with the issue of Prince Hamlet's paternity. How would doubts about Hamlet's origins bear on Eliot's critique of the Closet Scene?

III. Mommy Dearest

Hamlet's first soliloquy, "O that this too too solid flesh would melt. . . ," (I, ii, 129-159) is launched by a flirtation with self-destruction, a temptation whose undertow far exceeds mere embarrassment over his mother's need for companionship and love, or her choice of mate. Yet no ghost provokes. What irks him so? A widow's hasty remarriage may be a breach of taste, but hardly warrants dreams of death or, later on, a shrill scene in her bedchamber. Deferring the usual Oedipal speculations for the nonce, what solution can we offer? First, it's odd that Eliot doesn't explore whether Hamlet may blame his mother for the king's demise. That alone would provide some basis for his incandescent and indecent blaze of anger. Aren't the following lines in "The Mousetrap" attributable to Prince Hamlet, himself?

A second time *I kill my husband dead*
When second husband kisses me in bed.
(III, ii, 175-176)

Doesn't this suggest Hamlet associates Gertrude directly with the homicide? Why else would he use these words? And what about:

A bloody deed! --- almost as bad, good-mother,
As kill a king, and marry with his brother.
(III, iv, 27-28)

A clue, a palpable clue.

Given these frightful glimpses into Hamlet's psyche, perhaps spousal intrigue *a la* the Macbeths should have been searched through before trumpeting to an unsuspecting world that there is utterly no textual foundation for his scandalous behavior in his mother's chamber. But for the sake of discussion, let's suppose that Hamlet's pique over his mother arises not because of a conviction that she was an accomplice in the assassination of the king, the man he regards as his father, and not on account of his suspicion that her union with Claudius, as is conjectured, deprived her son of his successive rights. Subliminal doubts, unnoticed by Eliot, but plain to Prof. Bloom, remain. Sudden marriage is naturally associated with prior involvement. Not waiting a respectable interval after King Hamlet's demise to stage nuptial rites, the royal couple's conjugal zeal reflects on the age and character of their liaison. The question is not expressly posed by anyone in the play but lingers in the margins of consciousness. Again, though these be fictional personae, the reader, in thinking of them, taking them to heart, endows them with life, re-inscribing the authorial moment, granting them an implied past according to the trajectory of their actions. To do so is to pose the proverbial question, How long has this been going on? The inevitability of the inference is nicely illustrated by Mr. John Updike in his novel *Gertrude and Claudius*, a meticulous mélange of research and fancy which - not surprisingly - foregrounds the couple's extramarital affair. Did His Majesty turn a blind eye - yet see all, like Odin? Where was younger brother Claudius when Hamlet the Dane was busy smiting "the sledded Polacks on the ice": (I,i, 62) back in Elsinore making of Queen Gertrude a greater acquaintance? If King Hamlet played the royal cuckold - or wittol - for a substantial period of time, any child born to his inauspicious lady would carry the taint of illegitimacy and incestuous provenance. This vexing prospect, about which not a syllable is breathed by any of the dramatis personae, hangs over the action like a smog. The ghost's charge that Claudius is an adulterer (I, v, 42) is a corollary insinuation which then gains sense. We can cheerfully acknowledge the absence of anything as coarse as an "objective" correlative in *Hamlet* without conceding artistic breakdown. On the contrary, the triumph of *Hamlet* as drama is that the protagonist's deeds and omissions seem to arise from unstated origins of which the audience has just enough of an inkling to share in his disquietude.

While Prof. Bloom dotes idolatrously (as does Hamlet) on the dissimilarities of "uncle" and "nephew," there are a few delightful congruencies we wouldn't want to pass unnoticed for the next four hundred years. Why do the big soliloquies in the play belong to just these two? Why does Prince Hamlet's "The time is out of joint" trope (I, v, 189) echo Claudius's judgment that "our state . . . be disjoint and out of frame"? (I, ii, 20) Why does Shakespeare have both Claudius ("O, my offence is *rank*, it smells to heaven") (III, iii, 36) and Hamlet ("things *rank* and gross in nature") (I, ii, 136) in their soliloquies employ the adjective "rank" (coincidentally - weirdly - the name of a twentieth-century psychologist, Otto Rank, who wrote so searchingly about Shakespeare's "father complex")? Hamlet's iteration of this unusual term occurs in his declamations in Gertrude's chamber ("but to live in the *rank* sweat of an enseamèd bed,") (III, iv, 83) ("whilst *rank* corruption, mining all within, infects unseen,") (III, iv, 139-140), and ("do not spread the compost o'er the weeds to make them *ranker*"). (III, iv, 142-143)

Again, why, within a single scene in Act III do both Claudius and Hamlet independently employ the metaphor of feminine cosmetics to represent duplicity, using variations on the verb to "paint"? The outburst to Ophelia ("I have heard of your paintings") (III, i, 145) is a chilling reverberation of the King's "my most painted word" aside just a few stanzas earlier. (III, i, 55) In case that weren't enough, Hamlet and Claudius reprise this little refrain in Acts IV and V, when Claudius's "are you like the painting of a sorrow?" (IV, vii, 91) is heard again in Hamlet's "Now get you to my lady's chamber, and tell her, let her paint an inch thick"). (V, i, 188-189)

And is it not telling that Claudius and Hamlet both exhibit a pronounced paralysis of will upon which they comment in private speeches filled with self-loathing? We have already seen Claudius bemoan his fate in these words:

My stronger guilt defeats my strong intent;
And, like a man to double business bound,
I stand in pause where I shall first begin
And both neglect.
(III, iii, 40-43)

While poor Claudius hovers like Buridan's ass between the twin bales of sin and grace, incapable of attaining either forthrightly, Hamlet crouches in the rearward, frozen mimetically between righteous homicide and cowardly retreat. What should we say of this pretty tableau if not, "like father, like son"?

It should be noted that no one in the play acknowledges at any time a physical resemblance between the late King and the Prince. It is rather the ghost who resembles that monarch, as like to him as Marcellus is to himself. (I, i, 58) The age of the King's form adopted by the ghost is not that of the royal seniority, but of his greener days, when he scourged rival clans. (I, i, 59-62) Therefore, if Lord Hamlet had physical similarity to the man supposed to be his father, gazing upon the ghost should have been a bit like peeping in a mirror. But nobody says so. In his mother's closet Hamlet forces her to look at herself through the mirror of his words, (III, iv, 19-20) and then inspect two portraits, that of Hamlet the Dane and that of his supposed "uncle," to recognize their gross differences. (III, iv, 52-78) But there is for Hamlet personally no Cassius to ask him if he can see his own face, to judge if he even faintly resembles the murdered man. The eye sees not itself, says Brutus, and it is notorious that what we behold in the glass is often what we wish were there. We squint and dream. Had Brutus looked more carefully, would he not have found a mask of Caesar in that glass? But from such terrors we recoil. Hamlet and Brutus are two bookmen, lost in the world's debate.

Most importantly, in consenting to extract a bloody revenge, Prince Hamlet decides to murder the murderer. Thus Psychologist Dr. James Kirsch has no difficulty noticing that: "In the course of the play [Hamlet] assumes more and more of the characteristics of Claudius ..." (Kirsch, 42) Another psychoanalyst notes dryly, "Punishing Claudius does not seem to excite Hamlet nearly as much as does a vicarious involvement in his guilt." (Erlich, 45) And Norman Rabkin adds his voice to the chorus when he says that "the passion to which Hamlet succumbs is only another variety of the bestial willfulness, the mindless impulsiveness, which we have loathed in Claudius." (Rabkin, 6)

Now, it is one thing to be dispossessed by an incestuous, adulterous, homicidal brute, but to feel in one's bones that one might be the very product of his illicit concupiscence is to flirt with madness - or at the least to have a very bad day. Here is the true rottenness of Denmark. In this predicament we seem to stumble on the very "tortuously inexpressible something" Eliot and his admirers could never quite locate.

The roster of paternal candidates on this reading is uncomfortably narrow. There are (1) the late King, condemned to torment for "foul crimes," who hasn't a kind word to say to him, and who promotes a barbarous revenge, or (2) some look-alike wraith equally intent on having the Prince do his dirty work, or (3) Claudius, seducer of the Prince's mother, betrayer of Hamlet, Sr., and his eventual assassin. Hamlet's idealization of the late King is a defensive fetish, a thinly veiled effort to attribute a panoply of inherited virtues to himself so as to ward off filial connection with Claudius. Hamlet is truly haunted, then, in the sense that the loathsome ghost puts the constant lie to the catalogue of merits which the prince would find in the dead King and thereby in himself.

Though Gertrude does not admit to Hamlet that his paternity is an alien one, our memory of the parallel revelation to the Bastard in *King John* by Lady Faulconbridge must color our reception of what happens in Gertrude's boudoir. Of course Hamlet is not wroth with his mother because he has proof positive that he is the fruit of her forbidden union with the man who pretends to be his uncle while repeatedly calling him "my son," e.g., I, ii, 64. Of this he has no tangible, discrete or conclusive evidence, no DNA test. But the instant wedding tacked onto the 'patriarchal' wake is like an abyss opening under his feet, a nasty sty of possibility which cannot be sealed up. Through the Danish court slither whispers of unflattering origins. Patronizing smiles surround him. "Creeping murmur and the poring dark" fill the little vessel of his soul. In his friends he detects "a kind of strange confession in [their] looks which [their] modesties have not craft enough to colour." (II, ii, 281-282) As old Northumberland exclaims:

> *See what a ready tongue suspicion hath!*
> *He that but fears the thing he would not know*
> *Hath by instinct knowledge from others' eyes*
> *That what he feared is chanced.*
> (*King Henry IV*, I, i, 84-87)

Hamlet's bastardy peeps out at him in the smirks and nudges of his friends. All his life, he has been taken in, not taken seriously. This is his situation when the curtain rises, well before the ghost begins its nocturnal promenades upon the battlements of Elsinore. He must suffer these nauseating self doubts or go mad. Might he not say with Quintus, "My heart suspects more than mine eye can see," (*Titus Andronicus*, II, iii, 213) or with Imogen that "[D]oubting things go ill often hurts more than to be sure they do"? (*Cymbeline*, I, vi, 96-97) Hamlet's malaise is deep and personal, and can hardly be ascribed to anything as reserved as thumbing the pages of Montaigne's *Essays*, a well-intentioned anachronism of which some are lately fond, mistaking prescription for the disease. Contrary to popular belief, Hamlet's problems arise in the gut, not the airy and capacious regions of the cerebral cortex so transmogrified by Yale's Prof. Bloom. Over at Harvard things are scarcely better. Prof. Greenblatt easily discerns that Hamlet exhibits "nausea," but this is chalked up to his imagining of sexual intimacies between Gertrude and her new spouse. (Greenblatt, 222) The problem here is to figure out why Hamlet's reaction to these embraces should be so severe. Indeed, we soon learn that the prince's "revulsion," "disgust," and "queasiness," (Greenblatt, 242-243) are not limited to reactions to the sexual indulgences of his mother and supposed "uncle," but seem to flow from a kind of theological miasma, a Manichaean disdain for the grossness of all physical reality. For Prof. Greenblatt, Hamlet's alienation from the corporeal world reflects 16th century doctrinal dissensions detected by the spiritual radar of Shakespeare and transmitted thence into the heart of his most famous character. But such hypotheses are sheer guesswork, a trafficking with remoteness, and patent violations of Occam's Razor, the principle of economy of explanation. The far more accessible reason for Hamlet's angst has nothing to do with the strife of religious theories, and everything to do with who and what he is, that is, his identity as a man and social being. Here his spokesperson might be Lord Angelo in *Measure for Measure*, who stumbles on some very unpleasant truths about what he is, about his character. "O, fie, fie, fie! What dost thou, or what art thou, Angelo?" he cries in self accusation. (II, ii, 177-178) Soon thereafter, in the manner of King Claudius, we hear Lord Angelo's strangely familiar lament after a fitful bout with prayer:

When I would pray and think, I think and pray
To several subjects: heaven hath my empty words,
Whilst my invention, hearing not my tongue,
Anchors on Isabel; God in my mouth,

As if I did but chew his name,
And in my heart the strong and swelling evil
Of my conception.
(II, iv, 1-7)

So it is with Claudius, so it is with Hamlet, whose self-overhearing is inseparable from self abomination. Hamlet's despising of himself, which simmered painfully in the first soliloquy, before he realized that the detested Claudius was the late King's murderer, boils over into delirium when he apprehends the full extent of the depravity of the man he has all along feared might be his progenitor. Again and again Shakespeare shows us mortals who, in their failure to rise above their contingency and weakness, collapse back into disgust with humanity and self. This syndrome, made famous by *Prince Hamlet*, reaches its crescendo in *Timon of Athens*, in whom we behold the very apotheosis of cynicism.

IV. As Swift As Meditation

When Hamlet becomes apprised of the murder of the King, he seems to pledge instant redress. But his language is equivocal. He will sweep to revenge "on wings as swift as meditation," (I, v, 29-30) but is meditation the business of a nanosecond? Ask the yogi on his mat. According to Crystal and Crystal, "meditation" means not only "thought," but also "prayer, spiritual contemplation." (Crystal, 279) When Shakespeare wishes to characterize rapidity, he is usually more clear, less open to other constructions. The career of love, for example, is:

> momentany as a sound,
> Swift as a shadow, short as any dream,
> Brief as the lightning in the collied night,
> That, in a spleen, unfolds both heaven and earth,
> And, ere a man hath power to say 'Behold!',
> The jaws of darkness do devour it up.
> (*A Midsummer Night's Dream*, I, i, 142-148)

Shall the wings of Nemesis be more dilatory than those of Cupid?

The choice of the ambiguous trope "meditation" neatly captures the ambivalent attitude. What stands in his way? The Sphinx's riddle for our Age is, Why cannot Hamlet avenge the murder of his father? We dither (like Hamlet) in our seminars and dorm rooms over this, then depart to dull careers and testy marriages, packing away the puzzled prince as a college souvenir. But signals shimmered just below the surface. For what might Hamlet expect if he does destroy Claudius? A medal? The proposed deed is neither rational, noble nor charitable. If Claudius is sent Up Yonder with no public confession, how would Hamlet prove his guilt, and justify, like honorable Brutus, what he, the avenging angel, has done? And even if Claudius could be shown guilty, will Hamlet receive the approbation of the people for seizing a penalty that properly belongs to them? Hamlet is Claudius's presumptive successor. Liquidating him would appear as a coup d'état aimed at putting the frustrated prince on the throne. How would he then be exonerated? By calling the ghost to testify at his trial for high treason? Hamlet is invited to occupy the position of plotters Grey, Cambridge and Scroop in *Henry V*, or perhaps Antonio and Sebastian in *The Tempest*, knaves all. It is hardly surprising that "revengeful, ambitious" Hamlet (III, ii, 127) would temporize just a bit before committing the capital crime of regicide. Bookworms are not hit men, and Hamlet is, after all, being told to dump his master's thesis to perform a bloody *lèse majesté*, no small step for a neurasthenic lover of words.

But with these pebbles we are yet in the foothills. As we near the summit, we try to put our hands on the central emotional obstacle that keeps Hamlet from his declared purpose. Many of these mundane reservations were noted long ago by A.C. Bradley, who pointed to their ultimate insufficiency. But Bradley's own formulation of melancholia directly begs the question. For it is already obvious from the first soliloquy that Hamlet is upset over his mother's remarriage. The question is, Is this enough to topple a young and agile genius into a depression so deep as to prevent the punishment of the very villain who seduced his mother and took the life of the patriarch of the realm? Certainly not. Bradley's discussion is unpersuasive and savors of special pleading. Hamlet is not consistently depressed as, say, Antonio in *The Merchant of Venice* is. Bradley suggests he is too sad to act. But, to the contrary, he exhibits remarkable alacrity and creativity. He co-writes theatrical pieces and directs them. He grapples in graves, he flirts, he jokes, he socializes. He stabs through curtains at nosy eavesdroppers, and sends sycophantic courtiers to dusty death. Indeed, in a fight at sea, he leaps alone upon the deck of a hostile ship to cross swords with pirates. He is an action hero, like Douglas Fairbanks, Jr. Yet wanting to account for the prince's inability to take revenge, Bradley offers a general diagnosis according to which his "state of feeling is inevitably adverse to *any* kind of decided action." (Bradley, 75, emphasis Bradley's) Why was he not, then, wholly paralyzed? That is why we are driven to take a more specific tack, tailored to one basal incapacity: Hamlet cannot dispatch Claudius because a peculiar field of moral force shields him, because somewhere in Hamlet's bosom he divines that the target is really his biological father.

Furthermore, there is all the difference in the world between killing one's murderous uncle at the behest of the victim father and killing one's murderous father at the behest of one's uncle. Having reduced the world's most evocative poem to a psychiatric case study, Bradley is constrained to admit that "the psychological point of view is not equivalent to the tragic." (Bradley, 77) And this confession spells the doom of his position, for (1) as we have seen, melancholy as such cannot help us to understand why Hamlet is barred from the one deed he has sworn to do, and (2) even if it could be defended, a psychological exegesis removes the play from the field of tragedy.

The ghost wants revenge pronto and Hamlet is conscripted for the job. Had he been told the truth by this trespasser, that he is really Claudius's son, the chances of his actually performing this awful patricide would have been slim; hence the logic of the ghost's ploy.

Yet this does not mean that we can read the text esoterically or ideologically, as though a false meaning enshrouded an inner kernel of fact. Literature is not a "cheveril glove" where the wrong side may be just "turn'd outward" to make all odds even. (*Twelfth Night*, III, i, 12) Rather, our play is punctuated by aporia which point, like the Cheshire Cat, in opposite directions. If Gertrude be her "husband's brother's wife," (III, iv, 15) then Hamlet-the-son-of-the-late-King-of-Denmark is none other than Hamlet-the-misbegotten-son-of-Claudius. In making our way through the text, we have depth perception because we have two eyes, not one. When Hamlet becomes simplistic, it is lost and so are we.

Freud, an Oxfordian who hadn't an opportunity to think through the relation of text and authorial biography, almost got it right: there is an unconscious idea at work. From his point of view, Hamlet cannot do away with Claudius because his "uncle" has done the deeds Hamlet himself coveted: eliminate the father and possess the mother. On this reading, Claudius symbolizes Hamlet himself, and therefore if Hamlet kills him he slays in emotional terms both his father and himself. Such is Hamlet's so-called "Oedipus Complex." This is close but wins no cigar. Hamlet cannot kill Claudius because this man is his actual and symbolic father, an insight Freud could not achieve. Psychoanalysis is always more comfortable analyzing fantasy than fact. Recall Freud's rejection of the seduction theory. The reason Hamlet cannot dispose of Claudius is because to do so would be to perform the very act of patricide he is commanded to avenge. That is what stops him in his tracks. In the corner of his mind's eye, Hamlet sees that Claudius is to him a little more than kin, and less than kind, putting Hamlet too much in the "sun." We sense it too, in spite of ourselves, which is why *The Tragedy of Hamlet, Prince of Denmark* is the brilliant and unsurpassable *tour de force* it is.

Let us mention *en passant* that Freud's assimilation of the "family drama" to the ancient Oedipus myth is fundamentally flawed, and has led to legions of difficulties. Oedipus belongs to a set of myths which should be denominated "Promethean." They have nothing to do with ordinary children and parents. If one inspects the set of myths which includes Phaeton, Daedalus and Icarus, Bellerophon, Oedipus, and Prometheus, one can see that all are fundamentally concerned with Greek anxiety over unrestricted rationality, which, as applied to nature by human existence, places such rationality in conflict with the apprehensive gods. Human knowledge leads to hubris, as mortals aspire to be the lords of the earth. When it is predicted that Oedipus will marry his mother and kill his father, Oedipus is a symbol of *humanity*. The "father" of *humanity* is *divinity*, or *the gods*, while our "mother" is nature, *the earth*. Oedipus (rationality) prevails over unruly nature (the Sphinx) and enters into an intimate relation with her (in the form of Jocasta). That is, humanity seeks to dominate its mother, nature, whom it "knows" in the biblical sense of the term. Oedipus kills Laius, his father, representing the destruction of the gods, ironically a project completed by Freud himself in his book, *The Future of an Illusion*. The significance of the Oedipus myth, then, is not a psychology of the family and the emotional conflicts of infancy, but rather the cosmological or metaphysical fate of humanity in relation to the earth (our mother) and the gods (our father). And just as the myth predicted, we now see, too late, the results of our incestuous (toxic) relationship with the earth and the nihilistic conclusion of our deicidal campaign against the gods. In the myth, the gods slay the hubristic hero; but in reality, as the myth implied, Promethean humanity wipes out the gods, as they rightly feared. The arrival of Nemesis will be broadcast on our flat screen televisions and beloved computers.

In the case of Hamlet, a better classical name for his dilemma would be the "Aegisthus Complex." It may be recalled that Atreus and his brother Thyestes feuded bitterly, and Atreus eventually killed Thyestes' sons and had them served up to his brother for dinner. Thyestes, who had already seduced the wife of Atreus, Aerope, heeded the word of the oracle to have a son by his own daughter. When the daughter of Thyestes, Pelopia, gave birth to her father's son, Aegisthus, the boy was sent into the wilderness and cared for by goats. He was then found by Atreus and brought up in his household as his son. Atreus, the actual uncle of Aesgistus, then commanded Aegisthus to murder Thyestes, who was Aegisthus's biological father but regarded as his uncle. Significantly, Aegisthus, confronted by Thyestes in person, *found himself unable to smite*, for, though strangers to one another, they recognized one another as father and son. (cp. II, ii, 474-485) At last, at the behest of Thyestes, his real though incestuous father, Aegisthus then slew Atreus. It is interesting that after four centuries of trying to account for Hamlet's inability to do away with his apparent 'uncle' Claudius, no one has suggested that the explanation lies in the fact that, like Aegisthus, Hamlet, the incestuous bastard, recognizes in Claudius his own illicit father. The Aegisthus/Thyestes and Hamlet/Claudius analogy implies not only the paternal bond as the explanation of Hamlet's notorious inaction, but as langiappe, points once again to Shakespeare's knowledge of Greek, an arcane tongue unavailable to the sheepish lads of Stratford-Upon-Avon.

V. Nothing Succeeds Like Succession

What we have gleaned from our struggles with the other issues in this play provides the solution to the last. Why is Hamlet at the outset of the play not the King of Denmark? Because, although he is the heir "apparent" to the deceased King of Denmark, there is an unstated impediment: he is the bastard son of Claudius. As nephew of the Sovereign, Hamlet's successive rights are primed by the royal brother, Claudius, whose bastard son he is. The skittish, fawning courtiers wink but dare not speak. Their suspicions are like the hiss of background radiation which confirms the Big Bang. Remove that premise and all reverts to the chaos, confusion, trivia and jittery speculation which has reigned since 1623.

Asked by Rosenkrantz the cause of his malaise, Hamlet does not dissemble. "Sir," he complains, "I lack advancement." That is, he lived in hope of the Danish Crown. So far as we are told, he is the King's first born and only son. Why, then, does he not have his prize? His frustration implies the reality of primogeniture. For "Who should succeed the father but the son?" (*Henry VI, Part Three*, II, ii, 94) The son of King Henry V becomes King Henry VI (though a flaw in his father's title could infect and undermine the title of the son). When Hamlet the

Dane dies at the hands of Claudius, the Prince is away at school. When he returns, Claudius is on the throne and either marries or is married to Gertrude. Some rationalize the ascendancy of Claudius on the grounds of an "election," though we are not shown anything of the sort. And the word "election," used frequently throughout the corpus, signifies nothing more than acceptance by the peers, a choice, or in certain circumstances, an approval of successive right indicating no impediment. How, then, could the Prince have been passed over without a hearing unless a firm bar to inheritance existed? It is true that a descendant regarded as illegitimate could inherit if acknowledged and thus elevated. Elizabeth herself had been declared an incestuous bastard yet became Queen. But there is a vast difference. Elizabeth was the daughter of Henry VIII by Anne Boleyn, born during the marriage of Henry to Anne. Her status as incestuous illegitimate devolved from Henry's prior affair with Anne's sister, Mary Boleyn. (Shell, 13) In the case of Hamlet, things are otherwise. Prince Hamlet was never considered as an illegitimate son of King Hamlet by a woman other than Gertrude. That sort of impediment might have been cured by acclamation or special legislation. But if it were generally understood that Hamlet was the bastard son not of the King but the King's brother by the King's wife, his chances of inheriting the throne would be nil. He would be passed over automatically. And that is what we see as the play opens. Nor do we have to worry that some obscurity in ancient Danish law might have allowed Claudius to inherit the Danish crown on no ground other than having married the late King's widow, an incestuous deed in England. For the play is composed for English audiences who knew nothing of archaic Danish laws and customs. In England one does not become King by virtue of marrying a widowed Queen Consort. Further, when the King dies, the state of Denmark, threatened from without, does not delay the transition to a new government to permit the late King's brother to first celebrate by marrying the King's widow, thereby somehow allowing this brother to assume the mantle of "King." Such an idea must be the king of all *non sequiturs*. Claudius becomes King immediately and then, *fait accompli*, marries Gertrude. That's why the funeral baked meats coldly furnish forth the marriage table. Though the act is incest, it's possible because Claudius is King, and can do as he jolly well pleases.

One scholar of the period writes: "The constitution of the state of Denmark in Hamlet is English, not Danish." (Weitz, 116) In the Middle Ages, a daughter could bring to her husband the lands to which she was heiress, in which case the husband sometimes took her father's title "in right of his wife." (Saccio, 241) But Gertrude is not King Hamlet's daughter but his surviving spouse, and any rights of succession of Claudius pass to him directly as sibling. Under primogeniture he is primed by any male filial descendant. Thus, when Hamlet returns to Elsinore, it is no wonder he is sulking and embarrassed. The presence of Claudius on the throne implies the existence of an impediment which is as effective in barring Hamlet's claim as it is humiliating to name. Thus nothing is said. The prince is as usual allowed to maintain the tenuous fantasy he has cultivated since childhood, that he is the son of King Hamlet.

Credit should be given to Prof. Steve Sohmer, who argued in two brilliant essays in 1996 and 2001 based on calendrical, textual and theological grounds that Prince Hamlet was conceived and born prior to the marriage of Old Hamlet and Gertrude, and "only conditionally legitimated by subsequent marriage of his parents." Importantly, Sohmer presciently suggested that we can thus account for Hamlet's failure to succeed Old Hamlet to the Danish throne on the grounds of being illegitimate. Further, Sohmer has the added distinction of having read the "dram of eale" speech in Q2 as implying that the nodal point of Hamlet's dilemma is a dollop of corruptive substance which has made him what he is, tainted his nature, and set a bar to his advancement. (Sohmer, online) All well and good. Unfortunately, Prof. Sohmer fails to see that the dram of eale can only have full significance if it flows from an *alien* source. If we suppose that the only blot on Hamlet's pedigree is that he was conceived by his parents prior to their nuptial ceremony, illegitimacy may be an effective impediment but is so only in virtue of a technicality. The dram of eale analogy, however, connotes actual estrangement. Hamlet behaves not as a bastard by celerity but rather by adultery. The obstacle to his inheritance is thus far stronger than Prof. Sohmer recognizes. Our hero is not who he seems to be. He is not Old Hamlet's offspring and hence has no claim whatever to the Danish crown. What Hamlet senses is that he is not the son of the man he loves but of the one he loathes.

VI. Whodunnit

When Nicolaus Copernicus first set down his cosmological hypothesis in 1512, it received little attention for over two decades until a student at Wittenberg University by the name of George Joachim (Rheticus) printed an account thereof at Wittenberg. (*Encyclopedia of World Biography*, online) This is of interest for two reasons, first, because Wittenberg is also Prince Hamlet's university, and second, because the type of paradigm shift instituted by Copernicus, which offered a substantial simplification of astronomical phenomena, can be performed in the exegesis of *Hamlet*. In Copernicus's case, the paradigm shift was one tremendous idea, the substitution of the heliocentric for the geocentric model. In the case of Shakespeare's *Hamlet*, we can achieve similar conceptual leverage by supplanting Hamlet the Dane by Claudius as the prince's *pere*. This single alteration yields resolution of the major aporia, which, while not dissolving other, more traditional renderings, affords fresh insight into the depth and significance of the play, and builds a dramatic bridge to the biographic narrative of the author. To review, the quartet of central issues, hitherto insusceptible of satisfactory adjustment, are:

1. Why does the ghost deceive?
2. What makes Hamlet so furious with his mother?
3. Having sworn immediate revenge, why does Hamlet tarry
in the assassination of King Claudius?
4. Why is Claudius, not Hamlet, King of Denmark?

We have seen above how our paradigm shift serves hermeneutical purposes.

1. Because Claudius is the actual father, the ghost, to persuade Hamlet to destroy him, must avoid asking Hamlet to incur the stigma of patricide by seeming to confirm the notion that the prince is merely the King's nephew;

2. Hamlet's rage at his mother expresses his unconscious suspicion that he might be, not the offspring of King Hamlet, but, on account of his mother's chronic infidelity, the bastard son of detested Claudius, and genetic inheritor of his faults and flaws;

3. Hamlet struggles to kill the king because he is Hamlet's own father;

4. Hamlet is ignored in the monarchical 'election' because primogeniture does not apply in a case of a mistaken identity in which the heir apparent is actually the illegitimate son of the decedent's brother.

Our final question then must be:

5. Who might have written such a play?

To deal with this ultimate issue, we must consider anew those historical personages who might be represented by the principal characters. Naturally, the one of most importance is the prince himself. Many have realized that this rebel-without-a-seeming-cause must in some way stand for the author. But since Prince Hamlet resembles the man from Stratford as much as up resembles down, it has always been impossible to make sense of our instinctual identification. Another problem is Polonious. It is said he is a caricature of William Cecil, Lord Burghley, the Queen's chief advisor. The difficulty has been to understand how a William of Stratford could give an unflattering portrait of puissant Cecil without losing his head to the axe.

Did Cecil, like Polonious, have a relationship with any brilliant young aristocrat who followed the arts and whose supposed "father" died under mysterious circumstances? Could such an aristocratic youth have made that caricature? Yes. Cecil was the master of the Court of Wards where the first noble youth to occupy his home was Edward de Vere, 17th Earl of Oxford. Just as Hamlet's supposed father, King Hamlet, died under dubious circumstances, so did John de Vere, the 16 Earl of Oxford. It was this event which led to Edward's transfer to Cecil House at age ten. At the time of his death, August 3, 1562, John de Vere had prepared a will the week before and was in excellent health. (Anderson, 40)

As it is asked whether Queen Gertrude had a hand in King Hamlet's murder, it is quite natural to ask the parallel question: did Queen Elizabeth have a hand in the death of the 16th Earl so as to necessitate his "son's" removal to London where she, his royal mother, waited for him? Apparently, it was all part of the plan. Cecil had a daughter, Anne, technically a commoner, who loved Edward de Vere, just as Polonious has a daughter, Ophelia, who loves Prince Hamlet, but who is told, by her avuncular father that he is "a prince out of thy star." (II, ii, 142)

Following this logic, it is not difficult to discern the main contemporaneous allusions.

1. Polonious is William Cecil;
2. Ophelia is his daughter, Anne Cecil;
3. Prince Hamlet is Edward de Vere

Remember that Prince Hamlet is not a mere courtier, but one deeply involved in literature and the theatre. He is fairly *au courant* with events in the various theatrical companies and knows many of the players personally. Further, he is a poet and a writer of plays, as we know from his emendation of the "Murder of Gonzago," many of whose lines he can recite from memory, as he can Virgil's *Aeneid*. If we were inclined, as many are, to view Hamlet as a self-portrait of the author as a young man, then it follows as the night the day that Hamlet is Shakespeare, and Shakespeare is Edward de Vere. Of course to establish these things in any detail would be a task for which the present essay has not sufficient space. All that can be furnished here is an outline which the interested reader can fill in at his leisure.

Certainly these three historical analogues are the most logical choices. Claudius is not as neat a fit. We might suppose that Elizabeth conspired with lover Robert Dudley, a notorious poisoner, to get rid of John de Vere, but Dudley and Elizabeth never publicly married. Dudley did not become King. He and Edward de Vere may have had bad blood between them, but it is awkward to see Claudius as Dudley. To find a figure equal to Claudius we need to skip a generation to, not the husband of Elizabeth, but her father, King Henry VIII.

The most prominent pair of brothers in Tudor England were Prince Arthur Tudor and his younger sibling, Henry, the two sons of King Henry VII. Groomed and polished like a shining jewel for the English Crown, Arthur wed Catherine of Aragon in November of 1501 and a scant five months later sickened and died of the usual unexplained and suspect causes. His successive rights thus devolved upon little Henry, his supremely ambitious and concupiscent brother. Henry not only assumes the throne after the (again suspicious) death of Henry VII, but incestuously takes his brother's widow, Catherine, as his wife and Queen. Sound familiar? He himself dies of symptoms resembling incremental arsenic ingestion - for well we know of "mortal mineral[s], which, being took, should by the minute feed on life, and, ling'ring, by inches waste you." (*Cymbeline*, V, vi, 50-52, see also, the King of France in *All's Well That Ends Well*, with his "fistula.") The realm then comes under the rule of the Lord Protector, Edward Seymour. But Edward Seymour, too, turns out to be elder sibling in relation to the supremely aggressive, lascivious and porcine Lord High Admiral, Thomas Seymour, whose insane, fanatical aim is to displace his brother and command the state. It is humbly submitted that the author of *The Rape of Lucrece* was conceived in the moment of sexual battery of Henry's daughter by Thomas Seymour. Shakespeare's past is prologue.

One thing is clear: any Elizabethan audience seeing a play about two brothers, one a king, the other younger and ambitious, where the elder dies of unexplained reasons, allowing the younger to become King and marry the older brother's wife, would think immediately of Prince Arthur and his understudy, the vicious and unprincipled Henry Tudor who became Henry VIII. This is interesting because it places Elizabeth herself in the position of Hamlet in relation to her father Henry VIII, who, via his faction, probably murdered Arthur and took his wife. Elizabeth, then, is ravished at age 13 by the other notorious younger sibling, Thomas Seymour, and gives birth to the bastard Edward de Vere. She later disposes of the guardian John de Vere through the usual poisoning. Were young Edward of a literary turn of mind, he'd have plenty of material. It is no wonder that many psychologists have ascribed a father complex to Shakespeare, since he had three of them: (1) Thomas Seymour, executed for imposing himself on Elizabeth and plotting to seize the crown, (2) John de Vere, his step-father, who was likely ordered dead by Elizabeth, and (3) William Cecil, Master of the Wards and second step-father, whom he hated.

Who might have written such a play, if not the one man in Tudor England who most resembled its principal character, Hamlet?

VII. *Concluding Unscientific Prescript*

Why do we bother with the authorship question? What answer do we return to those who remind us we have the plays themselves and need not raise a fuss over the hand that wrote them? The short answer is, we want to know who wrote them because we want to know who is reading them, and how to read them - and ourselves - better. We want to understand the interplay of life and letters. With what consistency or intellectual integrity does one rejoice that Johnson had his Boswell, and that Shakespeare, he had none? Shall we enshrine Johnson but scant the author of Falstaff? What is our profit in that? We do not seek to award a "posthumous" prize for literature to the right fellow, pinning a medal on the proper chest. Reading his Heiligenstadt Testament makes a difference in how we hear Beethoven. Learning about Mozart's father and Salieri helps us respond to *The Magic Flute* and the *Requiem*. And proximity to Shakespeare moves us closer to his alter ego, Prince Hamlet. Changing the idea of our author from Stratford to Oxford gives us insight into the purpose and therefore the meaning of the play. This is not to say that its entire significance lies in the biography of its author. To approach art that way is the worst kind of reductionism. But seen as a supplement to the text, it can hardly be denied that the life of the writer bears on his artistic expressions, especially when they become, as *Hamlet* plainly was, a self-portrait. Who studies Hemingway, Tolstoy, Freud or Van Gogh, and not their lives? It is preposterous. Authorship, too, bears directly on the dating of the plays. Substitute Oxford for William of Stratford and we can accept that the *Ur-Hamlet* of the early 1580's was, in fact, an early draft of the play, eliminating the desperate expedient of attributing it to Kyd.

If we know who Shakespeare really was, his hopes, dreams, agonies and ecstasies, we may find that not only do the works change for us as readers, but so also does history - and perhaps the world around us. When we pass from seeing the silencing of Lavinia as an example of crude poetic apprenticeship to a daring presentation of the silencing of Cynthia Herself, we cast aside our toys and grow up, exchanging our poses of sophisticated disdain and arcane technicality for frank insight, candor and - if we are lucky - compassion. What we gain from the authorship question, then, at the very least, is an opportunity to read not just with the head, but with our hearts, which, after all, is what brought us to literature in the first place. There are many who urge us to content ourselves with an empty formalism, the finagling with the "works themselves" stripped of any connection to the fellow that created them. Ironically, though every other artist's life is a fertile annex of illumination, in the case of our most exemplary writer we are asked to reduce him to the status of a mere shade. Of course this is impossible. No one reads like that. Even the most fanatical formalist inevitably falls back on biographical contextualizing, performed instinctively but without benefit of expressly critical considerations. That is to choose to stroll in the dark, where the ghost of William still wanders. No, it is time to turn on the lights. The alternative is to accept in the case of our finest literature a schizoid split between the poet and his song. And this will never do.

Do we know with apodictic certainty that Prince Hamlet "*is*" the son of Claudius? God forbid. Hamlet is a poem, not an Euclidean deduction. As Aristotle taught, it is the mark of an educated person to demand only that rigor of proof suitable for a given context. But once the shadow is exposed, it cannot be swept away. There is nowhere to hide. *Hamlet* can never be the same. In Wittgenstein's picture, when the rabbit turns into a duck, the rabbit does not hop off, stage left, to oblivion. It comes back to haunt us. What about Edward de Vere? Can we rest assured without a trace of doubt that he was the son of Elizabeth by Seymour? Hardly. But with Socrates we must follow the argument whither it tends. History, too, is a form of literature, and the judgments we make of the past are always tentative. The best we can do is try to resist being swept away by platitudes and truisms, by things "everyone knows."

When Prince Hamlet falls into the Question via the ghost, he undergoes a crisis. That crisis is not finally confronted until the graveyard scene, which serves as the "green world" where so many Shakespearean personae escape the artificial, stifling prison of the court and experience transformation, a theme we can trace all the way back to Thomas of Woodstock's retreat from Richard's court to Plashey House. As the play's dynamics are set in motion by a ghost, so they are concluded by a gravedigger and his exhumed skull. He is the alchemical animus whose cynical banter releases Hamlet's lost psyche. We may think of him as the fellow who buried the late king, and through Hamlet's encounter with him we bury the old king's specter. In the face of musty death, any difference between being the son of Hamlet and being the son of Claudius shrinks to the vanishing point. If the dust that was Alexander can stop a bunghole, so can the dust of Xerxes.

Like Lear's hand that smells of mortality, the little cemetery is rich with pungent odor. It is here in this brooding ground that Hamlet is tossed the skull of Yorick, the motley fool who had "borne [him] on his back a thousand times." (V, i, 181-182) Hurtled by the strong tide of olfactory memory to his childhood, Hamlet suddenly collides with his original self. He will never be granted the security of cognizing his actual father, doubt would always exist. But Yorick, whom he loved, is his symbolic and therefore real father, who cared for him, taught him to laugh and delight in the wry conjunctions of things.

Unlike Prince Hal, who betrays his Socratic mentor, Falstaff, to bond with pater, the duplicitous predator, Bolingbroke, Hamlet's primal union is with a comic, as tragedy turns infinite jest. The last act is laughter. Poisoning the father who poisoned his seeming father, Hamlet poisons himself, and is reborn in the self slaughter he had feared. "To be or not to be" turns out to be not idle wordplay or *Weltschmertz*, but a Shakespearean koan complete with punch line. Thus is he permitted at the end to see through the conundrum of life with its terrible disjunct of being and nothingness. Through the "slaughter" we glimpse the "laughter" concealed. At every moment we are born and die. We are and are not. The irony is all.

Epilogue

It is not often noticed that Hegel's philosophy may be viewed in the end as but a vast restatement of Shakespeare. For all the world was a stage for Hegel, too, many stages, in fact. In 1952, Edward Hubler remarked upon the central significance of the parable of the talents, "for there is no idea," he wrote, "to which Shakespeare returns more often." (Hubler, 416) He correctly cites as thematic Duke Vincentio's disquisition on the subject in *Measure for Measure*:

> Thyself and thy belongings
> Are not thine own so proper as to waste
> Thyself upon thy virtues, they on thee.
> Heaven doth with us as we with torches do,
> Not light them for themselves; for if our virtues
> Did not go forth of us, 'twere all alike
> As if we had them not. Spirits are not finely touched
> But to fine issues; nor nature never lends
> The smallest scruple of her excellence
> But, like a thrifty goddess, she determines
> Herself the glory of a creditor,
> Both thanks and use.
> (I, i, 29-40)

From that most philosophical of all plays we learn:

> [No] man is lord of any thing,
> Though in and of him there be much consisting,
> Till he communicate his parts to others . . . .
> (*Troilus and Cressida*, III, iii, 110-111)

Closer to home, we recall:

> Sure, he that made us with such large discourse,
> Looking before and after, gave us not
> That capability and god-like reason
> To fust in us unused.
> (Taylor & Wells, p. 717)

We find the echo of this view in Hegel's dictum that "Spirit which does not manifest itself is not Spirit." Hegel's entire phenomenological phantasmagoria may be understood, then, as a mimetic tribute to the power of Shakespeare's foundational unfolding of the spirit. What drives life and history for Hegel is precisely the same struggle for recognition that animates Hamlet and -- if we are right -- Shakespeare himself. But tragically this struggle comes only through painful self-sacrifice. Hubler acknowledges this incisively:

> In Shakespeare's view the open heart must give itself away in order to maintain its existence. It is confronted with a perpetual dilemma: it can know its own being only through self-loss. The alternative is to conserve itself until it has withered away. (Hubler, 419)

It is nothing short of astonishing that the quintessence of Shakespeare's thought, as set forth above, was articulated by none other than Edward de Vere, the 17th Earl of Oxford, in his letter to Thomas Bedingfield concerning the translation of *Cardanus Comfort* (1573). While scholars have noted the significance of the Bedingfield letter, few if any have connected the central theme of this letter with Shakespeare's most fundamental principle. But let the gentle reader peruse in the Shakespeare Authorship Sourcebook online the essay "Proof that Shakespeare's Thought and Imagery Dominate Oxford's Own Statement of Creative Principles: A Discussion of the Early Poet Earl's letter to the translator of 'Hamlet's Book,'" by Charles Wisner Barrell, 1946. Nothing in the authorship discussion comes closer than this to being the "smoking gun" which incontrovertibly establishes Oxford as "Shakespeare." De Vere wrote as follows:

> . . . . and when you examine yourself what doth avail a mass of gold to be continually imprisoned in your bags, and never to be employed to your use? I do not doubt even so you think of your studies and delightful Muses. What do they avail, if you do not participate them to others? Wherefore we have this Latin proverb: *Scire tuum nihil est, nisi te scire hoc sciat alter.*

> What doth avail the tree unless it yield fruit unto another? What doth avail the vine unless another delighteth in the grape?

What doth avail the rose unless another took pleasure in
the smell?
Why should the this tree be accounted better than that tree,
But for the goodness of his fruit?
Why should this vine be better than that vine, unless it
brought forth
A better grape than the other?
Why should this rose be better esteemed than that rose, un-
less
In pleasantness of smell it far surpassed the other rose?
And so it is in all other things as well as in man.
Why should this man be more esteemed than that man,
But for his virtue, through which every man desireth to be
accounted of?

Not only does the content of this passage capture directly the basic
concept of Shakespeare's dramaturgy, its prose style, a series of repetitive
rhetorical questions, all making the same point, matches exactly a well-
known passage in Shakespeare's *King Henry VI*, Part One (II, iv, 11-15).

Scholars have long puzzled over the sudden image of the Pelican
brought forward by the Black Prince in Shakespeare's *King Edward III*,
omitted by Taylor and Wells. When King Edward asks about its meaning, the Prince replies:

A Pelican, my lord,
Wounding her bosom with crooked beak,
That so her nest of young ones might be fed
With drops of blood that issue from her heart,
The motto *Sic et Vos*: 'And so should you'.
(Melchiori, 133)

There seems to be no dramaturgical explanation for these lines
and the invocation of this philosophical Pelican by the Prince. Professor
Giorgio Melchiori in his edition of *King Edward III* reproduces a picture
of this icon published in George Whitney's *A Choice of Emblemes and
Other Deuises* (Leyden, 1586) p. 87 (Melchiori, 44) The picture's motto
is, "*Quod in te, Prome.*" This is translated as, "Give utterance to what is
in you." Prof. Melchiori comments:

The motto '*Sic et Vos*' (And so shall you) echoes one that figures in several heraldric crests, *Sic vos non vobis*: 'So you not for yourselves'. According to C.N. Elvin (*Handbook of Mottoes*, 1860, revised 1971, p. 184), it underlines altruistic feelings, and is taken from lines attributed to Virgil, each beginning with the same words implying that neither birds build nests, nor sheep grow fleece, nor bees make honey, nor oxen draw ploughs for their own use. (Melchiori, 207)

But here we have precisely the same outlook expressed by Edward de Vere, 17th Earl of Oxford in his letter to Master Bedingfield, using this humble imagery. "*Sic et Vos*" and "*Quod in te, Prome*" can hardly be distinguished from Oxford's "*Scire tuum nihil est, nisi te scire hoc sciat alter.*" Further, this is identical to the statement in *Troilus and Cressida* of Ulysses "No man is lord of any thing / Till he communicate his parts to others." This direct correspondence of Oxford's personal credo with that of Shakespeare is surely the "smoking gun" all have sought so assiduously, the holy grail of literature. It further tallies with independent scholarly analysis showing that Oxford was the author of *King Edward III*, given in Edward de Vere Newsletters No. 10 (December 1989, February, 2001 and No. 60 February 1994, February, 2001), available online. Not only have we the "smoking gun," we have the bullet itself resting in our own hand. *QED*.

Shakespeare's most famous character is a dramatic playwright whose most strongly felt wish is to tell his story to us, the "unsatisfied." Prince Hamlet was caught in the pincers of an oppressive family and political regime which (1) muzzled him on the one hand, and (2) furnished him with an indomitable will to self revelation on the other. And all that has been argued here is that the same is true of Hamlet's author. We come to this somewhat belatedly, after four sleepy centuries. But, as Hegel remarks, "The Owl of Minerva takes wing only with the coming of dusk."

When J. Thomas Looney inaugurated the Oxfordian movement by demonstrating Shakespeare's secret identity, his unprecedented accomplishment did not stop there. He diligently quarried the corpus and showed that in his works Shakespeare lavishly displayed himself and his world. Most especially, he argued with surpassing skill and modest eloquence that the author's will-to-self-revelation reached its zenith in the character of Prince Hamlet. Thus, the original Oxfordian thesis in its fullness is that Oxford is Shakespeare and Shakespeare is Hamlet. Should our best reading then disclose the Prince's illegitimacy, sheer logic dictates that "Shakespeare" himself was also so blemished.

Looney's compelling exposition faced one major hurdle: while Hamlet is heir to the throne of Denmark, "Oxford, of course, was not a prince of the royal blood." (Looney, 48) Here the analogy seemed to falter. If the reasoning of this paper is sound, the last piece of the mosaic left to us by Looney now falls into place. As the Queen's son and secret heir, as grandson of King Henry VIII and lineal descendant of the Houses of York and Lancaster, no veins were bluer than Oxford's.

Eliot was right, of course, to look for a correlative to account for our hero's behavior, but he went astray in contending that the problem was situated in the Closet Scene. For by the time we reach that spot in the action Hamlet suspects his mother was an accomplice in the murder of the man he regards as his father. Eliot should more logically have directed his formidable acumen to the first soliloquy, which begins: "O, that this too too solid flesh would melt thaw and resolve itself into a dew, Or that the Everlasting had not fixed his canon 'gainst self-slaughter." Let's get this straight: Hamlet is wishing for death, contemplating suicide, because his mother has remarried, to someone he, the poor Prince, doesn't like. One might be put off by such an action, but . . . suicide? It's a solution without a commensurable problem. It is the inability to successfully address this discrepancy which constitutes the single greatest oversight in the history of literary criticism. The weakness is not in the play, as the callow Eliot submitted, but in us, its readers. Hence the armada of commentators, from Bradley to Greenblatt, who have sought psychological explanations in lieu of any actual trauma. Hamlet suffers from "melancholia," that is, clinical depression. But why? Because his mother breached etiquette by marrying too soon? All of nature appears to him "rank and gross." Why? Because he's developed a dyspepsia? Or because his theological studies have unleashed in him a latent Manichaean disgust with the environment? The poverty of such speculation is breathtaking.

Hamlet is just a bit simpler than that. While this graduate student was away at school in Germany, he received word of his father's death. He learned also that his "uncle," Claudius, had sought and obtained the approval of the peers to be elevated to the Danish throne. And by the time he reaches Elsinore, Claudius and Gertrude are husband and wife. What is significant is that Prince Hamlet, not a child, but a brilliant young adult and heir to the throne, has been rejected as the next King of Denmark, unlike "young Fortinbras," who inherits the crown from his father. This is bad enough, but what makes it intolerable is that it entails the existence of some impediment to Hamlet's successive right, an impediment so substantial and embarrassing that it relieved the deliberative body of any need to wait to include the Prince in their decision making process. It is a fait accompli, and a most disheartening one. For it confirms more eloquently than any words that Hamlet's secret fear, that he is not really the son of Hamlet the Dane, is realized, that the knowledge he derived for years "from others' eyes" for years is now confirmed, that "what he feared is chanced."

Omitting this obvious impasse is what's spawned those interminable, sophomoric debates about whether he is crazy or just pretending. Lear goes mad, Ophelia and the Jailer's Daughter too, but not Hamlet. More lucid than any of us, his blunt denial of insanity must be credited. The antic disposition is a put on. (I, v, 173) "[I] is not madness I have uttered; bring me to the test, and I the matter will re-word, which madness would gambol from." (III, iv, 132-135) Psychologizing the play is lame because what is sacrificed is nothing less than tragedy itself, the confrontation of irresistible force and immovable object typified by Antigone's struggle against Creon. Hamlet is quintessential tragedy, inviolably so, as evidenced by the failure of any psychology, sociology or historicizing to capture him. What could be more absurd than trying to approach "th' observed of all observers" via the clumsy psycho-pharmaceutical apparatus of Psychiatry's *Diagnostic and Statistical Manual*? Do we still imagine the prince of poetry is easier to be played on than a pipe? The real key to this tragedy lies just beyond our horizon: as son of King Hamlet, he must kill Claudius, but as son of Claudius he cannot. Listen to Troilus cry out in his bleak and desperate epiphany, "This is and is not Cressid." (V, ii, 149) So *a fortiori* might Hamlet exclaim of Claudius, "This is not, yet is, my father."

J. Hillis Miller writes:

> On the one hand, the 'obvious or univocal reading' always contains the deconstructive reading as a parasite encrypted within itself as part of itself. On the other hand, the 'deconstructive' reading can by no means free itself from the metaphysical reading it means to contest. (Miller, 22)

This illustrates the fascinating complementary nature of art of which Norman Rabkin speaks. We need not fear our contradictions. Light is both wave and particle, and our world is richer for that insight. Prince Hamlet remains son to both the late King and his villainous brother, just as the author will remain the triple threat, (1) "William Shaksper of Stratford," (2) Edward de Vere, 17th Earl of Oxford, and (3) the bastard son of the Virgin Queen. As Blake says, the fool who persists in his folly will become wise. Perhaps, just perhaps, Shakespeare's tragi-comical vision, his "most humorous sadness," has its roots not in an unearthly ballet of "social energies," but in the madness of poetic inspiration, and in the joyous catastrophes of flesh and blood.

WORKS CITED

Mark Anderson, *Shakespeare by Another Name*, Gotham Books, 2005

Isaac Asimov, *Asimov's Guide to Shakespeare*, Wing Books, 1970

Harold Bloom, *Hamlet: Poem Unlimited*, Riverhead Books, 2003

A. C. Bradley, "Hamlet," in *Hamlet*, Harold Bloom, ed., Chelsea House Publishing, 1990

Ben & David Crystal, *Shakespeare's Words*, Penguin Books, 2002

Thomas Stearns Eliot, *The Sacred Wood: Essays on Poetry and Criticism*, Methune, 1921

Avi Erlich, *Hamlet's Absent Father*, Princeton University Press, 1977

Stephen Greenblatt, *Hamlet in Purgatory*, Princeton University Press, 2002

Edward Hubler, "The Economy of the Closed Heart," in *Shakespeare: Modern Essays in Criticism*, Leonard F. Dean, ed., Oxford University Press, 1961

James Kirsch, *Shakespeare's Royal Self*, G.P. Putnam's Sons, 1966

J. Thomas Looney, *Shakespeare Identified*, Duell, Sloan & Pierce, 1920

Giorgio Melchiori, ed., *King Edward III*, Cambridge University Press, 1998

J. Hillis Miller, *The J. Hillis Miller Reader*, Julian Wolfreys, ed., Edinburgh University Press, 2005

Norman Rabkin, *Shakespeare and the Common Understanding*, The Free Press, 1967

Peter Saccio, *Shakespeare's English Kings*, Oxford University Press, 2000

William Shakespeare: The Complete Works, S. Wells, G. Taylor, eds., Clarendon Press, Oxford, 2005

John Updike, *Gertrude and Claudius*, Alfred A. Knopf, 2000

Morris Weitz, *Hamlet and the Philosophy of Literary Criticism*, University of Chicago Press, 1964

Online Sources

Charles Wisner Barrell, "Proof that Shakespeare's Thought and Imagery Dominate Oxford's Own Statement of Creative Principles: A Discussion of the Early Poet Earl's letter to the translator of 'Hamlet's Book,'" 1946

The Bedingfield Letter

Encyclopedia of World Biography, "Nicolaus Copernicus"

"What is a Warlock?" by Matthew Sandow

Steve Sohmer, "Certain Speculations on Hamlet, the Calendar and Martin Luther," *Early Modern Literary Studies*, April, 1996

_____, "A Note on Hamlet's Illegitimacy Identifying a Source of the 'Dram of Eale' Speech," *Early Modern Literary Studies*, January, 2001

Conclusion
Notes on Cymbeline

The year is 5 A.D. Cymbeline, King of Britain, is meeting with the Roman ambassador, who has just demanded a sizable annual fee for Rome's treasury. The Queen, wife to Cymbeline, addresses her husband in stirring words to urge that nothing be paid.

> Remember, sir, my liege
> The kings your ancestors, together with
> The natural bravery of your isle, which stands
> As Neptune's park, ribbed and paled in
> With banks unscalable and roaring waters,
> With sands that will not bear your enemies' boats,
> But suck them up to th' topmast. A kind of conquest
> Caesar made here, but made not here his brag
> Of 'came and oversaw and overcame'. With shame --
> The first that ever touched him -- he was carried
> From off our coast, twice beaten; and his shipping,
> Poor ignorant baubles, on our terrible seas
> Like eggshells moved upon their surges, cracked
> As easily 'gainst our rocks; for joy whereof
> The famed Cassibelan, who was once at point --
> O giglot fortune! to master Caesar's sword,
> Made Lud's town with rejoicing fires bright,
> And Britons strut with courage.
> (III, i, 16-33)

This spark of ethnic pride and independence is eventually doused by Cymbeline, who, although successful in routing the Roman legions, volunteers to pay the tribute after all. He remains rhetorically bold enough to claim for his small realm parity with the Empire.

> Although the victor, we submit to Caesar
> And to the Roman empire, promising
> To pay our wonted tribute, from the which
> We were dissuaded by our wicked queen . . . .
> Publish we this peace
> To all our subjects. So set we forward, let
> A Roman and a British ensign wave
> Friendly together. So through Lud's town march,
> And in the temple of great Jupiter
> Our peace we'll ratify, seal it with feasts.
> Set on there. Never was a war did cease,
> Ere bloody hands were washed, with such a peace.
> (V, vi, 461-464; 479-486)

Thereafter, troubled relations with the Roman behemoth were to continue historically off and on until the fall of the Western Empire. Much later, an Anglo-Saxon England proudly endured for four and a half centuries, until vanquished by the Norman triumph at Hastings in 1066 A.D., and sequent occupation and pillaging put a dismal end to indigenous English law, language and self-rule.

The historical scaffolding on which Shakespeare erected his dramatic narrative is accurate. Cunobelinus was King of pre-Roman Britain early in the first century A.D. The latter portion of his name is a variation on the pagan Celtic sun god Bel or Belenos. His native tribe, the Catuvellauni, are understood to have led the resistance to the first Imperial assault on the island in 43 A.D.

The ideal of English sovereignty articulated by Shakespeare in *Cymbeline* would later be echoed in a Plantagenet context ("This precious stone set in the silver sea") via the well-known soliloquy of John of Gaunt in *The Tragedy of King Richard the Second*. (II, i, 31-68) In the characters of Cymbeline's sons, Guiderius and Arviragus, we find confirmation that, for Shakespeare, royalty is a product of *physis*, for, even without knowledge of their origins or education in court, these sons of autochthonous stock exhibit all the qualities of nobility. ("How hard it is to hide the sparks of nature!"; III, iii, 79; cp. the Queen's reference to "natural bravery" of the isle, quoted above.) In other words, aristocracy for Shakespeare is most properly an expression of the substance of a people, the flowering of an organic culture. An adventitious patriarchy, on the other hand, such as that imposed by the Norman Franks on the English people in 1066 A.D. was a false and tyrannical dynasty, expressing forces and ideals wholly alien to the Anglo-Saxon inhabitants.

Yet, there is a curious tendency in Shakespeare scholarship to view the author as a reactionary and royalist for whom the cardinal virtue is submission to extant authority on no other grounds than tradition and continuity. This is rationalized by E. M. W. Tillyard in his emphasis on the speech of Ulysses on "degree" in *Troilus and Cressida* (I, iii, 74-135), which makes obedience a cosmological imperative. A Tillyardian analysis overlooks the patently rhetorical nature of Ulysses' speech, something now generally recognized. (See, *e.g.*, "The Unknown Ulysses," Kent F. Thompson, *Shakespeare Quarterly*, Vol. 19, No. 2 , 125-128)

On a Tillyardian rendering, the reign of a King Henry V or Henry VI is technically disqualified on account of the usurpation by Bolingbroke of the throne of Richard II. The difficulty with this standard analysis is that it inevitably leads one to question the entire line of Plantagenet devolution from William the Bastard of Normandy, who crushed Anglo--Saxon England in 1066, down to Elizabeth herself. How would King Edward III or his descendants have any greater right of rule than Henry V or Henry VI if the primal act which initiated this chain of command was the brute seizing of total power by the Bastard and his wolfish brethren? Indeed, it is well known that on his deathbed William admitted that in trampling Albion he had acted as a bloody usurper. The argument against the line descending from Bolingbroke would apply *a fortiori* to that descending from William and Edward III.

Further indications of the significance of the organic element in English sovereignty can be seen in *As You Like It*, in which the banished Duke flees with his loyal supporters to the Forest of Arden, where

> they live like the old Robin Hood of England. They
> say many young gentlemen flock to him every day,
> and fleet the time carelessly, as they did in the golden world.
> (I, i, 110-113)

In the harsh reality of winter, Duke Senior and his followers find the welcoming elements emblematic of authentic virtue, far superior to the painted pomp of court. (II, i, 1-17)

The reference to Robin Hood is telling. Shakespeare earlier adverts to the idyllic world of Robin Hood in *The Two Gentlemen of Verona* (IV, i, 35). Were Shakespeare the kind of knee-jerk authoritarian he was made out to be by Tillyard, approval of the rebel Robin Hood would surely not be found. And no matter how bad Jack Cade and his followers appear in *King Henry VI*, this has more to do with uncouth violence and mendacity than with low social standing. This is not to suggest that for Shakespeare, a product of Tudor England, any form of democracy would have been an acceptable alternative to monarchy, but only that for Shakespeare genuine nobility is a natural development of a genetically coherent people.

We should therefore be suspicious of any attempt to portray Shakespeare as a medievalist or advocate of feudalism. For he was active at the very end of the Renaissance, and stood on the cusp of modernity. In his era the hegemony of the Catholic Church had been shattered, and the English people had won the privilege of reading scripture and other writings. The New World was old hat by then; the globe had been circumnavigated by 1522. Shakespeare's most famous character, Prince Hamlet, was a student at the University in Wittenberg, where Martin Luther taught. The writings of Copernicus became known through publications in that very University in the 1530's. And by 1600 the astronomer Giordano Bruno set the educated world ablaze through his teaching of a limitless cosmos. We can detect echoes of this in Hamlet's successive references to doubts about the motion of the sun (II, ii, 117) and "infinite space." (II, ii, 257) The Chorus's reference in *Henry V* to "the wide vessel of the universe," (IV, 4.0, 3) instead of "cosmos" is a reprise of Lucretius, who had anciently taught the boundless nature of space. The medieval notion of the "great chain of being" was therefore for Shakespeare already discredited intellectually. 1609 saw the publication of his *Sonnets* and the invention of the first telescope capable of inspecting the heavens. *Cadit quaestio.* In the Elizabethan reign the "great chain of being" was becoming an outmoded vehicle to employ to prop up claims of political right. While we might find it still employed in various theological or exhortatory pamphlets of the day celebrating monarchical "divine right," as the cosmological correlative was already evaporating, such tropes were losing persuasive impact.

At the same time that the old world was rapidly falling away in theology, science, literature and empirical learning, it still represented an existential threat to England and its jittery Queen. Europe was continuing to seek the re-absorption of England into the orbit of Rome, where it had languished for two millennia. All came to a head in 1588 when the Spanish Armada was destroyed by Elizabeth's fleet and a spot of bad weather.

In this context, Shakespeare served as the artistic spokesperson for England in its integrity, an integrity which could be traced back to its native heroic past. His plays teem with affirmative references to the "pagan" religions, never entirely smothered by Rome, Christianity or generations of avaricious monarchs. One always senses that for Shakespeare there is something rotten in the state of England, a nation which has toppled from an Edenic glory. Over and over, in *Lear*, *Cymbeline* and other works, we harken back to the organic *Kultur* of Brythonic and Brythonic-Romano England (recall Charles' reference to the "golden world" in *As You Like It*, I, i, 113), implying the significance of the later Anglo-Saxon realm in the process. Rather than present indigenous kings whose leadership is the vanguard of the folk, Shakespeare's histories from *Woodstock* through *King Richard III* depict alien, anxious sovereigns whose relation to the common man is a mix of avuncular concern and undisguised envy. (*King Richard II*, V, v, 1-41; *King Henry IV, Part II*, III, i, 4-31; *King Henry V*, IV, i, 227-281; *King Henry VI*, III, II, v, 1-54) These important and revealing passages resemble closely sentiments expressed by Elizabeth herself in correspondence.

> To be a king and wear a crown is a thing more glorious to them that see it than it is pleasant to them that bear it. The cares and troubles of a crown I cannot more fitly resemble than to the drugs of a learned physician, perfumed with some aromatical savor, or to bitter pills gilded over, by which they are made acceptable or less offensive, which indeed are bitter and unpleasant to take. And for my own part, were it not for conscience' sake to discharge the duty that God hath laid upon me, and to maintain His glory, and keep you in safety, in mine own disposition I should be willing to resign the place I hold to any other, and glad to be freed of the glory with the labours; for it is not my desire to live or reign longer than my life and reign shall be for your good. (Strachey, 280)

Indeed, it may not be too much to claim that Shakespeare's tragic hero is modeled on his study of the conflicted British monarch.

Shakespeare on occasion frankly reveals his distaste for the ambition and bellicosities of the English peers descended from the Normans

("Good God, these nobles should such stomachs bear! I myself fight not once in forty year." (*King Henry VI*, I, iv, 87-88) Similarly, the drunken wastrel Christopher Sly's argument in *The Taming of the Shrew* that he need not compensate the hostess for the damage caused by brawling since his forebears "came in with Richard Conqueror" (I, i, 4) tends to put all such descendants in a bad light. Again, in *King Henry V*, the Constable and Dauphin contrast the purity of the French ranks with the "barbarous" English invaders, descended from the Normans:

> O Dieu vivant! Shall a few sprays of us,
> The emptying of our fathers' luxury,
> Our scions, put in wild and savage stock,
> Spirt up so suddenly into the clouds
> And over-look their grafters?
> Normans, but bastard Normans, Norman bastards!
> (III, v, 5-10)

Though he inherited an English language which had blended the Latinate Norman French and the Germanic Anglo-Saxon, and though he made extraordinary and creative use of both dimensions, close study reveals that the principal thrust of Shakespearean linguistics was the re-emphasis on the Anglo-Saxon mother tongue. The mocking of "euphuism" in *Love's Labour's Lost* is perhaps best seen as an advocacy for the rugged beauty of Anglo-Saxon elements, and it is well known that when he wants to place the greatest stress on a line, Shakespeare so often casts it in Teutonic monosyllables. As Harry Monmouth woos Princess Katherine of France, fumbling with oleaginous Gallicisms, we get the sense that a part of his nobility for Shakespeare is his blunt soldierly English. Coincidentally, didn't Hotspur also "speak thick"? (*King Henry IV*, II, iii, 24)

Although King Harry (aka "Harry Monmouth") was not himself Welsh, he facetiously refers to himself as such (*King Henry V*, IV, vii, 103), as he was born at Monmouth Castle, the Welsh property of Bolingbroke his father, and because he bore the title Prince of Wales. The fact is that this Prince of Wales cut his eye teeth putting down the various uprisings of Welsh insurgents over a decade. In his companionable chat with Welsh Captain Fluellen in the play, King Harry, the leader of an aggregate of Anglo-Saxon, Welsh, Irish and Scotch conscripts, in referring to himself as "Welsh," is merely being conciliatory and extending the 'band of brothers' rhetoric. The campaign in France was being used in part to weld various ethnic clans into a united kingdom. This was perhaps more efficaciously carried out by the defeat of Yorkist King Richard III by Henry Tudor, who not only fused the Houses of York and Lancaster, but was actually descended from Welshman *Owain ap Maredydd ap Tudur.* (Roberts, "The Welshness of the Tudors") English monarchs King Henry VII, King Henry VIII, King Edward VI, Queen Mary, and Queen Elizabeth thus all inherited this Welsh blood by lineal descent. And if the authorial thesis urged in the preceding pages is correct, "William Shakespeare" himself partook also of that very same ancestry. Thus, when Shakespeare is referred to as a "bard," that refers not properly to the hazy Homeric tradition, but to the actual bards of the Celtic, Welsh and Gaelic peoples who preserved and celebrated their forebears and their deeds of folkish valor. Shakespeare is the English bard who sings of the English people who sent the Spanish Armada down beneath the waves, and who looks back to the defeats of the French by Edward III, the Black Prince and King Henry V. Distinguished Professor Giorgio Melchiori, noting the connection between 1588 and the naval battle of Sluys in 1340, concurs.

He writes:

> From the beginning of her reign, Queen Elizabeth had revived, in the splendid Accession day tilts, those rites of chivalry that Edward III had founded, making them an essential part of the Elizabethan myth of Astraea. (Melchiori, 19-20)

Further:

> We know for certain that by 1588 the Queen's men had very successfully presented a play . . . *The Famous Victories of Henry the fifth* . . . . Famous Victories was meant as a tribute to the English fighting spirit at a time when Elizabethan England was under a threat of a Spanish invasion. After the defeat of the Armada, *The Reign of King Edward the third* [now accepted in the canon] was conceived in a similar vein, as a celebration of the achievements of the earlier English conquerer of France. In fact, *The Famous Victories of Henry the fifth* and *The Reign of King Edward the third* present an identical pattern, showing at first the weak sides of their respective heroes, and then their reformation and triumph. (Melchiori, 17-18)

Conclusion: Notes on Cymbeline

George Watson writes:

> [I] suggest that what Shakespeare did with English was to see a new possibility in its Englishness, or rather its Anglo-Saxon-ness. He dared to make the traditionally less dignified of two derivations its supremely dignified form: he turned the less learned, momentarily, into more. It is as if "sheep" and "mutton" or "veal" and "cow" were reversed: a sort of delayed revenge for the Norman Conquest. (George Watson, "Shakespeare and the Norman Conquest: English in the Elizabethan Theatre," *The Virginia Quarterly Review*, Autumn, 1990, pp. 613-628, online.)

And it is hard to avoid noticing that morality and human kindness are far better exemplified in the commoners in *Measure for Measure* than they are in the Duke and his administrators. Such textual phenomena, of course, deserve a full exegesis these pages cannot afford. But they create at least serious doubt about Shakespeare's regard for the ruthless Plantagenets who made such a waste of England. One must conclude at least provisionally that for Shakespeare, as for Queen Elizabeth, the English peerage after 1066 was more of a necessary evil than a good in itself. Though keenly aware of the succession problems created by William the Bastard's lupine invasion of 1066, Shakespeare was content to employ the Tudor reconciliation of Lancaster and York as the sign of Elizabeth's legitimacy; to expressly raise the larger (and insoluble) problem of William's conquest would have subverted far too much, including any claim the 17th Earl of Oxford or Henry Wriothesley had to the throne, either through the de Vere clan or through Elizabeth Tudor. One could not find much support for complaints about the Norman conquest amongst a group of lords who, to a man, all traced their lineage, properties, wealth, power and titles to that fateful event. And there is the rub supreme. The entire aristocracy of the realm descended from a Bastard and his wolfish brethren. What recourse, then, but mass denial? England had been raped. That is the back story, the unseemly tapestry behind the plays. Though Gloucester has sufficient integrity to declare that the whoreson must be acknowledged, it was not always done. Caesar never acknowledges Brutus. Bolingbroke never acknowledges Pointz. Richard the Lionhearted never acknowledges Falconbridge. Claudius never acknowledges his dark prince. And Elizabeth never acknowledges the man who relates these tales in his imperishable verse. And so when Prospero finally does the unthinkable and acknowledges Caliban (*The Tempest*, V, i, 278-279) we smile grimly but hardly believe what we hear.

These are some of the momentous ideas we encounter in any consideration of *Cymbeline*. It brings us directly into a turbulent epoch antedating Plantagenet England and gives insight into Shakespeare's philosophy of the relationship between genotype and genius. The interactions of Posthumous and Imogen recapitulate those of Lucretia and Collatine. Yet we hear from editors Taylor and Wells that "the play as a whole is a fantasy, an experimental exercise in virtuosity." (Taylor and Wells, 1185) Here "virtuosity" is used as a term of reproach, bringing to mind a talented poet just acquiring his craft, as Mozart might have written an immature symphony at age six. Yet the same editors, peering into their crystal ball, give a date of composition of 1610-1611, well at the end of William of Stratford's earthly career and long after the death of the 17th Earl of Oxford, 1604, rather late for juvenile improvisations. The play's "tone" is "courtly," yet it is a "tone" which has "puzzled commentators." Citing a few examples of textual incongruence, including the use of a dreamlike *deus ex machina*, the play is found to stumble through a series of awkward revelations "to its impossibly happy ending." It has been "valued mostly" for its Victorian "ideal of womanhood." Yet many of the plays conclude with long scenes of confession or explanation. *Cymbeline* in that respect is typical. And though it may have been appreciated in the 19th century, the cross-dressing Imogen with her strange marriage to her *de facto* sibling, Posthumous Leonatus, can in no way be seen as exemplifying Victorian ideals. Though mentioning *en passant* "the beauty of the verse in which [Innogen] is mourned," no reasons are given to lead any busy person to bother with this work. (Nor is there any excuse for altering a character's customary name from "Imogen" to the discordant "Innogen;" any rationale for such action belongs in a journal article, so as to build a consensus. Issuing a presumptively standard editon of the collected works in which the traditional names of characters are summarily scrapped is more authoritarian than authorized.) A play about the history of England is put down as a "fantasy."

The editors of *The Yale Shakespeare* are more attentive.

Holinshed is at a loss to know whether to believe 'our histories' or 'the Romane writers,' but he records presently the arrival of an ambassador from Augustus at the court of Cymbeline, who came to bring to the British king the thanks of the emperor 'for that he had kept his allegiance toward the Roman empire.' Later, Guiderius, after his accession, refused to pay a yearly tribute of three thousand crowns. Shakespeare, by attributing this refusal to Cymbeline, hoped to heighten the dramatic and emotional appeal of this singularly mild and uneventful portion of Holinshed's Chronicle. (Yale, 1323)

It is obvious that what is at stake here is the perilous relationship of England to Catholic Europe. Whether Albion might preserve its integrity and autonomy or collapse back into the maw of European predominance and control was a matter of more than passing interest at the time *Cymbeline* was penned. The nuanced transition from bold refusal of tribute to its concession after military victory is a symbol of strategy and compromise which seeks to bolster English pride while acknowledging the brute actualities of realpolitik. Such delicate posturing renders *Cymbeline* anything but "fantasy." The oneiric *deus ex machina* (a conventional dramatic device) hardly succeeds in making it the inexplicable lark conjured by Taylor and Wells. Their repetition of the term "tone" is ironic in light of the fact that what should be at issue is not Shakespeare's tone but theirs, which fairly drips with condescension, if not outright disdain. Any play by Shakespeare deserves better than this.

Completely overlooked is the duty of criticism to achieve balance by bringing forward the merits of what it examines. The only positive note in Taylor and Wells' Introduction, a mention of "the beauty of the verse in which [Imogen] is mourned," is sandwiched in a series of pejorative phrases which overshadow the feeble acknowledgement of this wonderful passage. For Harold Bloom, who quotes the entire elegy, this one poem redeems all faults. It is "the finest of all the songs in Shakespeare's plays." (Bloom, 629) He goes so far as to quote one of his students, who remarked that *Cymbeline* "existed for the sake of this lyric." (Bloom, 630) And there, indeed, is the crux of the matter. Instead of an even-handed treatment which brings to the attention of students a poetic miracle, giving them reason to linger and enjoy, Taylor and Wells kill the text and with it its shining moment. Such is the fate of art in the chill hands of morticians.

In considering the metaphysical materialists of his era, Arthur Schopenhauer likened them to the sort of simpletons who would seek to comprehend dramatic art by making precise measurements of theatre seats, stage and proscenium arch rather than attend to the performances. Teachers and scholars of Shakespeare should have as their mission not the mastery of mechanics and trivia, but the revival and transmission of that sense of astonishment and cultural pride of language that accompany first exposure to this sublime artist.

The principal purpose of review of any sort is to facilitate the just and appropriate appreciation of literature. While this must entail the application of principles allowing the distinction between good and bad writing, the censure of negative features is but a portion of a task which should include condign praise.

The craft of editing was not always such a mean enterprise. In 1961, not all that long ago, Edith Hamilton and Huntington Cairns brought out the definitive assembled translations of *The Collected Dialogues of Plato*. It was then still permissible to treat text and reader with a modicum of humanity and geniality. Feeling had not yet become an embarrassment. Considering the influence of Plato on Shakespeare, the closing paragraphs of Hamilton and Cairns' Introduction to *Symposium* (which might have been set down cynically as "fantasy") may be recalled.

> Like Paul in First Corinthians, Agathon speaks of human love. Socrates in his speech passes from the human to the divine, much as does John. (if we love one another God dwelleth in us.) We begin, Socrates says, by loving beauty in people and go on to loving not the beauty we see, but that which is unseen, the beautiful soul. From there we go on to love beautiful thoughts and ideas, ever ascending under the influence of true love. So we draw nearer to the vast sea of beauty until at last we perceive beauty itself, not existing in any being, but beauty alone, absolute, simple, and everlasting. Thither looking we become the friends of God. To that consummation we are led by love.

> From this height Plato leads us down rapidly by way of Alcibiades, who never occupied any height whatsoever and who, moreover, when he breaks in upon the supper party declares that he is very drunk. And yet he pays a hardly surpassed tribute to Socrates, who alone, he says, has made him ashamed of the poor, trivial life he is living, so ashamed that he has sometimes felt it unendurable. For greatness and goodness, he concludes, Socrates stands alone among all the men there have ever been. To all of this the reader sees Socrates listen-

ing with a smile, kindly and amused. (Hamilton and Cairns, 526-527)

In this context, of course, we are put in mind of Shakespeare's tribute to his own Socrates, Falstaff, who also suffered betrayal, but who, unlike Socrates, accepted banishment instead of death. Such was the encomiastic style of Hamilton and Cairns, forthright and without guile, not likely to come again. For as Gloucester says, we have seen the best of our time.

Prof. Harold Bloom astutely observes that in the elegy for Imogen we can detect "Shakespeare's own stance toward dying, and regard it as the *locus classicus* of Shakespeare upon death." (Bloom, 630-631) It is fitting, then, that his be our last words.

> Fear no more the heat o' th' sun,
> Nor the furious winter's rages,
> Thou thy worldly task hast done,
> Home art gone, and ta'en thy wages.
> Golden lads and girls all must,
> As chimney-sweepers, come to dust.
>
> Fear no more the frown o' th' great,
> Thou art past the tyrant's stroke,
> Care no more to clothe and eat,
> To thee the reed is as the oak:
> The sceptre, learning, physic, must
> All follow this and come to dust.
>
> Fear no more the lightning-flash.
> Nor th' all-dreaded thunder-stone.
> Fear not slander, censure rash.
> Thou hast finished joy and moan.
> All lovers young, all lovers must
> Consign to thee, and come to dust.
>
> No exorciser harm thee!
> Nor no witchcraft charm thee!
> Ghost unlaid forbear thee!
> Nothing ill come near thee!
> Quiet consummation have,

And renownèd be thy grave!

WORKS CITED

Harold Bloom, *Shakespeare: The Invention of the Human*, Riverhead Books, 1998

Plato, *The Collected Dialogues*, Edith Hamilton and Huntington Cairns, eds., Bollingen Series, Princeton University Press, 1961, 1989

Peter R. Roberts, "The Welshness of the Tudors," *History Today*, Vol. 36, Issue 1.

William Shakespeare, *The Yale Shakespeare*, Wilbur L. Cross and Tucker Brooke, eds., Barnes and Noble Books, 1993

William Shakespeare: The Complete Works, S. Wells and G. Taylor, eds., Oxford, Clarendon Press, 2005

Lytton Strachey, *Elizabeth and Essex: A Tragic History*, Harcourt Brace & Co., 1928

Kent F. Thompson, "The Unknown Ulysses," *Shakespeare Quarterly*, Vol. 19, No. 2 (Spring, 125-128)

E.M.W. Tillyard, *The Elizabethan World Picture*, Vintage, 1959.

CPSIA information can be obtained at www.ICGtesting.com
Printed in the USA
LVOW11s0959020914

401845LV00001B/3/P